EU Regional Policy

EU Regional Policy

Dr Andrew Evans
Reader in European Studies, Queen's University, Belfast

RICHMOND

Published by:
Richmond Law & Tax Ltd
12-14 Hill Rise
Richmond TW10 6UA
United Kingdom
Tel. +44 (0) 20 8614 7650
Fax +44 (0) 20 8614 7651
info@richmondlawtax.com
www.richmondlawtax.com

ISBN 1-904501-44-3

British Library Cataloguing in Publication Data
A catalogue record for this publication is available from the British Library

Cover design by Bill Anderson Associates
Printed and bound by Antony Rowe Ltd

Table of Contents

Table of Cases

Table of Legislation and Preparatory Acts

Communications

Decisions

1
INTRODUCTION

The European Union pursues its regional policy through the Structural Funds and other financial instruments (that is, the 'Union funds'[1]). Each fund has its own characteristics, which will be systematically examined. What all the funds have in common, however, is that they provide financial assistance[2] designed to support the attainment of objectives favoured by the Union. The provision of such assistance is said, in fact, to seek modification of the existing economic structure, in order to direct market forces towards an improved configuration.[3] In other words, promotion of what the EC Treaty calls 'economic and social cohesion' is sought.[4]

Article 158 EC deals with the relationship between regional policy and cohesion. It provides: 'In order to promote its overall harmonious development, the Community shall develop and pursue its actions leading to the strengthening of its economic and social cohesion. In particular, the Community shall aim at reducing disparities between the levels of development of the various regions and the backwardness of the least favoured regions or islands, including rural areas.'

A. THE STRUCTURAL FUNDS

The Structural Funds comprise: the European Regional Development Fund (ERDF), the European Social Fund (ESF), the Guidance Section of the European Agricultural Guidance and Guarantee Fund (EAGGF), and the Financial Instrument for Fisheries Guidance (FIFG).[5]

These Funds, which each contribute according to the specific provisions governing their operations to the strengthening of cohesion,[6] are the subject of the first part of this section. In particular, Chapter 2 examines the European

1 This expression is used throughout the book to denote the Structural Funds and other financial instruments generally.
2 Assistance: means the forms of assistance provided by the Structural Funds, ie: (a) operational programmes or single programming documents; (b) Community initiative programmes; and (c) support for technical assistance and innovative measures (Art 9(e) of Reg 1260/1999 ([1999] OJ L161/1) laying down general provisions on the Structural Funds).
3 Cf P Bianchi, 'La Réorientation des politiques structurelles de la CEE' (1991) RMC 599–603, 599.
4 According to Art 159 EC, the Union funds are all to support achievement of such cohesion. Art III-116 of the Draft EU Constitution refers to the strengthening of 'economic, social and territorial cohesion'.
5 Art 2(1) of Reg 1260/1999 ([1999] OJ L161/1). It is now proposed that only the ERDF and ESF will be Structural Funds. See Art 1 of the Proposal of 14 July 2004 for a regulation laying down general provisions on the ERDF, the ESF, and the Cohesion Fund, COM(2004)492.
6 Art 2(2) of Reg 1260/1999 ([1999] OJ L161/1).

Regional Development Fund.[7] According to Regulation 1260/1999,[8] this Fund is responsible for Objectives 1 and 2.[9] Objective 1 is 'promoting the development and structural adjustment of regions whose development is lagging behind'. Objective 2 is 'supporting the economic and social conversion of areas facing structural difficulties'.[10] Chapter 3 turns to the European Social Fund. Its primary responsibility is for Objective 3, which is 'supporting the adaptation and modernization of policies and systems of education, training, and employment'.[11] It also contributes to the other Objectives.[12] Chapter 4 examines the Guidance Section of the European Agricultural Guidance and Guarantee Fund.[13] The Guidance Section is involved in activity relating to Objective 1. Finally, Chapter 5 examines the Financial Instrument for Fisheries Guidance.[14] It contributes to Objective 1 and also assists restructuring in the fisheries sector outside Objective 1 regions.[15] A measure[16] or operation[17] may benefit from a contribution from a Structural Fund under only one of the Objectives 1, 2 and 3 at a time.[18] In pursuing these objectives, the Union shall contribute to the harmonious, balanced and sustainable development of economic activities, the development of employment and human resources, the protection and improvement of the environment, and the elimination of inequalities and the promotion of equality between men and women.[19]

7 See, now, the Proposal of 14 July 2004 for a regulation on the ERDF, COM(2004)495; and the Proposal of 14 July 2004 for a regulation establishing a European grouping of cross-border cooperation, COM(2004)496.

8 [1999] OJ L161/1.

9 Ibid, Art 3(1).

10 Ibid, Art 1.

11 Ibid, Art 1.

12 Ibid, Art 2(2). It is now proposed that the 3 objectives should be: Convergence, Regional competitiveness and employment, and European territorial cooperation. See Art 3(2) of the Proposal of 14 July 2004 for a regulation laying down general provisions on the ERDF, the ESF, and the Cohesion Fund, COM(2004)492.

13 It is proposed that this Section should become the European Agricultural Fund for Rural Development. See Art 2 of the Proposal of 14 July 2004 for a regulation on the financing of the CAP, COM(2004)489; and the Proposal of 14 July 2004 for a regulation on support for rural development by the EAFRD, COM(2004)490.

14 It is now proposed that the FIFG should become the European Fisheries Fund. See the Proposal of 14 July 2004 for a regulation establishing the EFF, COM(2004)497.

15 Art 2(3) of Reg 1260/1999 ([1999] OJ L161/1).

16 A measure denotes the means by which a priority is implemented over several years which enable operations to be financed. Any aid scheme pursuant to Art 87 EC or any aid granted by bodies designated by the Member States, or any group of aid schemes or aid grants of this type or any combination thereof which have the same purpose and are defined as a measure (ibid, Art 9(j)).

17 An operation is any project or action carried out by the final beneficiaries of assistance (ibid, Art 9(k)).

18 Ibid, Art 28(1).

19 Ibid, Art 1.

Council Regulation 1260/1999[20] lays down general provisions on these Funds. More specific provisions are contained in regulations adopted for each Fund. The Commission shall be in charge of the implementation of this Regulation[21] and shall adopt detailed rules of implementation. It shall also, where it appears necessary in unforeseen circumstances, adopt other rules for the implementation of this Regulation[22]

The resources available for commitment from the Structural Funds for the period 2000 to 2006 are €195 billion at 1999 prices.[23] The division of resources between objectives are such as to achieve a significant concentration on Objective 1 regions. Thus 69.7 per cent of the Structural Funds are allocated to Objective 1, including 4.3 per cent for transitional support (ie, a total of €135.9 billion). 11.5 per cent of the Structural Funds are allocated to Objective 2, including 1.4 per cent for transitional support (ie, a total of €22.5 billion). 12.3 per cent of the Structural Funds are allocated to Objective 3 (ie, €24.05 billion).[24] Additional funding has been provided following the latest enlargement of the Union. For the 10 new Member States the resources available for commitment from the Structural Funds from the date of accession to 2006 shall be €14.2 billion.[25] It is proposed that for the period 2007 to 2013 total funding should be €336.1 billion.[26]

B. OTHER FINANCIAL INSTRUMENTS

The 'other financial instruments' of the Union are the subject of the second part of this section. Union legislation[27] has expressly treated as instruments of

20 Art 1 of Reg 1260/1999 ([1999] OJ L161/1).

21 Ibid, Art 53(1).

22 Ibid, Art 53(2).

23 Art 7(1) of Reg 1260/1999 ([1999] OJ L161/1). The annual breakdown of those resources is shown in the Annex.

24 Ibid, Art 7(2). The figures stated for Objectives 1, 2 and 3 do not include assistance to Community initiatives or innovative measures and technical assistance or FIFG financing outside Objective 1.

25 The annual breakdown of those resources is shown in Annex II to Reg 1260/1999 (ibid), as amended by Reg 1447/2001 ([2001] OJ L198/1). For the 10 new Member states the breakdown of resources between objectives shall be as follows: 93.49% of the Structural Funds will be allocated to Objective 1 (ie, a total of €13.2 billion); 0.86% of the Structural Funds will be allocated to Objective 2 (ie, a total of €0.12 billion); 0.79% of the Structural Funds will be allocated to Objective 3 (ie, a total of 0.11 billion) (Art 7(2) of Reg 1260/1999, as amended by the Accession Act ([2003] OJ L236/1)).

26 Art 15 of the Proposal of 14 July 2004 for a regulation laying down general provisions on the ERDF, the ESF, and the Cohesion Fund, COM(2004)492.

27 Art 3(1) of Reg 2082/93 ([1993] OJ L193/20) amending Reg 4253/88 laying down provisions for implementing Reg 2052/88 as regards coordination of the activities of the different Structural Funds between themselves and with the operations of the EIB and the other existing financial instruments. Cf Art 2(5) and (6) of Reg 1260/1999 ([1999] OJ L161/1).

this kind: the Cohesion Fund;[28] European Investment Bank (EIB) loans and guarantees;[29] Euratom loans and guarantees; structural assistance from the Guarantee Section of the European Agricultural Guidance and Guarantee Fund; Framework Programmes for research and technological development; trans-European networks; Phare;[30] and other Budgetary resources (particularly 'other actions for structural purposes'). In addition, there are the Financial Instrument for the Environment (LIFE)[31] and the EEA Financial Mechanism.[32] These seem classifiable as 'other financial instruments', since they are concerned with the structural development of the Union.

Instruments of this kind may be contrasted with the Guarantee Section of the European Agricultural Guidance and Guarantee Fund, when it provides price support in agricultural markets,[33] and with the administrative expenditure of the Union institutions.[34]

Under the Cohesion Fund a total of €18 billion will be available for Greece, Spain, Portugal and Ireland in the period 2000 to 2006.[35] Total resources available for the 10 new Member States from the date of accession to 2006 will be €7.6 billion.[36]

Total annual receipts in any Member State from the Structural Funds – in combination with assistance provided under the Cohesion Fund – are limited by reference to national absorption capacity. This limit has been set at 4 per cent of national GDP.[37]

No operation may benefit simultaneously from a contribution from a Structural Fund under Objective 1, 2 or 3 and under the EAGGF Guarantee Section. No operation may benefit simultaneously from a contribution from a

---

28 See, now, the Proposal of 14 July 2004 for a regulation establishing a Cohesion Fund, COM(2004)494.

29 According to Art 2(6) of Reg 1260/1999 ([1999] OJ L161/1), the EIB shall contribute to achieving the 3 objectives.

30 See also 38th recital in the preamble (ibid).

31 Reg 1655/2000 ([2000] OJ L192/1) concerning the Financial Instrument for the Environment.

32 Protocol 38a to the EEA Agreement.

33 It also contributes to the achievement of Objective 2. See Reg 1260/1999 ([1999] OJ L161/1), Art 2(3). It is now proposed that this Section should become the European Agricultural Guarantee Fund and that it should only assist market measures. See Art 2 of the Proposal of 14 July 2004 for a regulation on the financing of the CAP, COM(2004) 489.

34 Cf the distinction between 'an operating budget' and 'a financial policy instrument' in Opinion 1/94 Competence of the Community to Conclude International Agreements concerning Services and Protection of Intellectual Property [1994] ECR I-5267, I-5395.

35 Reg 1164/94 establishing a Cohesion Fund ([1994] OJ L130/1), as amended by Reg 1264/1999 ([1999] OJ L161/57) and Reg 1265/1999 ([1999] OJ L161/62), Art 4(3).

36 Art 4(4) of Reg 1260/1999, as amended by the Accession Act ([2003] OJ L236/1).

37 Art 7(8) of Reg 1260/1999 ([1999] OJ L161/1) and Art 5 of Reg 1164/94 ([1994] OJ L130/1), as amended by Reg 1264/1999 ([1999] OJ L161/57).

Structural Fund under a Community initiative and under the EAGGF Guarantee Section.[38]

C. COORDINATION

Coordination between the various funds shall be carried out in particular through development plans, Community Support Frameworks, operational programmes and Single Programming Documents, including the frame of reference where relevant, the monitoring and evaluation of assistance, and Commission guidelines.[39]

Coordination is the responsibility of the Commission and each Member State. They shall, in a manner consistent with the partnership principle, ensure coordination of assistance from the different Structural Funds and between such assistance and assistance from the European Investment Bank and other existing financial instruments. In order to maximize the stimulus provided by the resources deployed, making use of appropriate financial instruments, Union assistance provided in the form of grants may be combined in an appropriate way with loans and guarantees. This combination may be determined in conjunction with the European Investment Bank when the Community Support Framework or Single Programming Document is being drawn up. It may take account of the balance in the proposed financing plan, the contribution from the funds, and the development goals pursued.[40]

D. COMPATIBILITY WITH UNION LAW AND POLICY

Operations assisted by the Union funds shall be in conformity with the provisions of the EC Treaty, with instruments adopted under it and with Union policies and actions, including the rules on competition, on the award of public contracts, on environmental protection and improvement and on the elimination of inequalities and the promotion of equality between men and women.[41]

Accordingly, the Commission and the Member States shall ensure that the operations of the funds are consistent with other Union policies and operations, in particular in the areas of employment, equality between men and women, social policy and vocational training, the common agricultural policy, the common fisheries policy, transport, energy and the trans-European networks, and the incorporation of the requirements of environmental

---

38 Art 28(1) of Reg 1260/1999 ([1999] OJ L161/1).
39 Art 10(1) of Reg 1260/1999 ([1999] OJ L161/1).
40 Art 10(2) of Reg 1260/1999 ([1999] OJ L161/1).
41 Art 12 of Reg 1260/1999 ([1999] OJ L161/1).

protection into the definition and implementation of the operations of the funds.[42]

E. COMPLEMENTARITY AND ADDITIONALITY

The operations of the Union funds may be subjected by the terms of Union legislation to the principles of 'complementarity' and 'additionality'. According to the former principle, the provision of Union assistance presupposes complementary national assistance. According to the additionality principle, Union assistance should not lead Member States to reduce their own cohesion efforts, but should be additional to these efforts.[43]

Hence, Union actions shall complement or contribute to corresponding national operations. In order to achieve a genuine economic impact, Union assistance may not replace public or other equivalent structural expenditure by the Member State.[44] For this purpose, the Commission and the Member State concerned shall determine the level of such expenditure that the Member State is to maintain in the sum of its regions covered by Objective 1 during the programming period.[45] For Objectives 2 and 3 taken together, the Commission and the Member State concerned shall determine the level of expenditure on active labour-market policy and, where justified, other actions designed to make it possible to achieve the goals of those two Objectives which the Member State is to maintain during the programming period. Such expenditure shall be determined by the Member State and the Commission in advance of the Commission decision approving any Community Support Framework or Single Programming Document relating to the Member State concerned and shall be integrated into these. As a general rule, the level of expenditure shall be at least equal to the amount of average annual expenditure in real terms during the previous programming period and shall be determined in the light of the general macroeconomic circumstances in which the funding takes place. Account should be taken of certain specific economic situations, namely privatizations, an exceptional level of public structural effort or equivalent effort on the part of the Member State during the previous programming period, and national economic trends. Account shall also be taken of any reduction in Structural Fund expenditure when compared to the period 1994 to 1999.[46]

---

42 Art 2(5) of Reg 1260/1999 ([1999] OJ L161/1).
43 See, generally, JA Winter, 'The ERDF and the Principle of Additionality' in In Orde, Liber Amicorum Pieter Verloren van Themaat (Kluwer, Deventer, 1982), 365-80.
44 Reg 1260/1999 ([1999] OJ L161/1), Art 11(1).
45 Programming: means the organizing, decision-making and financing process carried out in a number of stages to implement on a multiannual basis the joint action of the Union and the Member States to attain the Objectives of the Structural Funds (ibid, Art 9(a)).
46 Ibid, Art 11(2).

Additionality shall be verified at three points during the programming period: an *ex-ante* verification, to provide a frame of reference for the whole programming period; a mid-term verification no later than three years after approval of the Community Support Framework or the Single Programming Document, following which the Commission and the Member State may agree to revise the level of structural expenditure to be attained if the economic situation has resulted in developments in public revenue or employment in the Member State concerned significantly different from those expected at the time of the *ex-ante* verification; and a verification before 31 December 2005.

To these ends, the Member State shall provide the Commission with appropriate information at the time when the plans are submitted and when the mid-term verification and the verification before 31 December 2005 are made. Independently of these verifications, the Member State shall inform the Commission at any point during the programming period of developments likely to call into question its ability to maintain the required level of expenditure.[47]

These principles imply for the Union institutions what the Commission describes as 'leverage'.[48] It derives from the tendency of national governments and financial institutions to favour interventions of a kind which qualify for Union assistance, because the burden and risk of financing the interventions will not fall exclusively on their own resources. As a result, national policies may be significantly affected by the availability of Union assistance. For example, the conditions which the Union attaches to the grant of assistance from the European Regional Development Fund are said to have a significant influence on the shape of the regional policies of the Member States, though the influence would be even greater if the additionality principle were fully implemented.[49] In other words, harmonization of national policies or even of the conduct of undertakings which benefit from Union assistance may take place.[50] Indeed, the Commission describes the regional policies of Member States as 'the Union's primary instruments for achieving cohesion'.[51] A less sanguine view is that the operations of the Union funds may have the effect of 'crowding out ... plausible, alternative social policy solutions to the Union's regional problem'.[52]

---

47 Art 11(3) of Reg 1260/1999 ([1999] OJ L161/1).

48 First cohesion report, COM(96)542, 114.

49 Committee on Regional Policy and Regional Planning, Report on the tenth annual report on the activities of the ERDF, EP Doc A2-76/86, 6.

50 The Commission implicitly admits that, by providing finance, it influences the investment decisions of undertakings. See Commission Reply by Mr Millan to WQ 251/91 ([1991] OJ C227/15) by Mrs Cristiana Muacandini.

51 First cohesion report, COM(96)542, 6.

52 JJ Anderson, 'Structural Funds and the Social Dimension of EU Policy: Springboard or Stumbling Block?' in S Leibfried and P Pierson (eds), European Social Policy (Brookings Institute, Washington, 1995), 123-58, 124.

F. OPERATIONAL FRAMEWORK

The limitations of language,[53] social demands, and their status as elements in the framework established by the Treaties[54] imply that the meaning of provisions governing the Union funds may not necessarily depend simply on their terms.[55] Their meaning may also depend on conclusions which the Union institutions draw from this framework. In other words, the operations of Union funds may be affected by 'fundamental' principles of the Treaties.[56]

The multiplicity of objectives embodied in the Treaties and the consequent necessity of evaluation entail that, in referring to the framework established by the Treaties, the Union institutions may enjoy wide discretion.[57] The discretion entailed may be so broad that, for example, the Commission may picture the requirements of the law differently from the Council of the Union.[58] Insofar as such differences occur, the highly selective nature of the law's 'internal models of social reality'[59] may be demonstrated.[60]

Even so, in referring to the framework provided by the Treaties, the Union institutions may seek to use their discretion to achieve a consistency in decision making which would otherwise be precluded by the numerous variables involved in the application of individual Union law provisions. However, propelled as it is by social demands, the framework is evolutionary

---

53 It may be asserted that 'the tasks performed by rules are tasks for which the primary tool is the specific linguistic formulation of a rule' (F Schauer, 'Formalism' (1988) 97 Yale LJ 509-48, 510). However, it may also be admitted that 'legal terms possess a core of settled meaning and a penumbra of debatable meaning' (ibid, 514) and that the choice of meaning may be determined by 'external factors' (ibid, 516).

54 Cf Opinion 1/91 Draft Agreement with the EFTA Countries relating to the Creation of the EEA [1991] ECR I-6079, I-6103.

55 AG Roemer in Joined Cases 10 & 18/68 Società 'Eridania' Zuccherifici Nazionali v EC Commission [1969] ECR 459, 496.

56 Cf, regarding ECSC assistance, Case 8/57 Groupement des Hauts Fourneaux et Aciéries Belges v ECSC High Authority [1957-58] ECR 245, 253; and Case 13/57 Wirtschaftsvereinigung Eisen- und Stahlindustrie, Gußstahlwerk Carl Bönnhoff, Gußstahlwerk Wilten, Ruhrstahl, and Eisenwerk Annahütte Alfred Zeller [1957-8] ECR 265, 278.

57 AG Roemer in Joined Cases 63-69/72 Wilhelm Wehrhahn Hansamühle v EC Council [1973] ECR 1229, 1261.

58 Cf, in connection with Art 33(1) EC, AG Cosmas in Case C-122/94 EC Commission v EU Council: aid to wine producers [1996] ECR I-881, I-907.

59 G Teubner, 'Autopoiesis in Law and Society: A Rejoinder to Blankenburg' (1984) 18 Law and Society Rev 291-301.

60 Cf, regarding 'policy choices', Joined Cases T-480 & 483/93 Antillean Rice Mills NV v EU Council and EC Commission [1995] ECR II-2305, II-2340-2.

---

rather than static. It is for this reason that changes in the operations of the Union funds may reflect changes to the Union itself.[61]

For the purposes of the section, evolution of the operational framework for the Union funds is seen as being associated with establishment of the common market, development of the common market, and the search for cohesion. In the agricultural sector, establishment and development of the common market has been subsumed by, or perhaps transformed into, establishment and development of common organizations of the agricultural markets.

1. Establishment of the common market

Establishment of the common market sought the elimination of barriers to economic activity between Member States during a transitional period of 12 years.[62] According to the EEC Treaty, the process was to be facilitated by the provision of assistance to farmers from what came to be called the Guidance Section of the European Agricultural Guidance and Guarantee Fund. During the transitional period for establishment of the common market, it was to support action furthering the objectives set out in Article 39(1)(a) EEC, including structural changes necessitated by the establishment of this market.[63] Express provision was also made for assistance to workers from the European Social Fund and for assistance to undertakings from the European Investment Bank. The former assistance was to facilitate establishment of the common market through assisting the adjustment of labour to its establishment.[64] Equally, the Bank owed its creation to a concern that companies should not be denied opportunities to participate in the common market by their lack of access to investment capital.[65] No specific reference was made to a European Regional Development Fund. However, an early proposal for the creation of such a fund was submitted by the Commission to the Council under Article 235 EEC.[66] According to this provision, the Council, acting unanimously, might adopt acts which were necessary in the operation of the common market for the attainment of Treaty objectives and could not be based on any other Treaty provision. This proposal was not adopted by the Council.

---

61 P Cheshire, R Camagni, J-P de Gaudemaar, and JR Cuadrado Roura, '1957 to 1992: Moving Toward a Europe of Regions and Regional Policy' in L Rodwin and H Sazanami (eds), Industrial Change and Regional Economic Transformation: The Experience of Western Europe (Harper Collins Academic, London, 1991), 268-300, 268.
62 Art 8 EEC.
63 Art 3(1)(d) of Reg 25 ([1962] JO 991) on the financing of the CAP.
64 Comité Intergouvernemental Créé par la Conférence de Messine, Rapport des Chefs de Délégation aux Ministres des Affaires Etrangères (Brussels, 1956), 58.
65 M Keating, 'Europeanism and Regionalism' in B Jones and M Keating (eds), The European Union and the Regions (Clarendon Press, Oxford, 1995), 1-22, 17.
66 Now Art 308 EC.

2. Development of the common market

Progress in the elimination of barriers to economic activity between Member States exposed problems which, it was felt, could not be addressed simply through the application of provisions prohibiting such barriers. This feeling was reinforced by realization that establishment of the common market did not in itself offer a solution to economic problems faced by Member States. In particular, it did not offer a solution to problems arising from changes in international economic conditions, such as the 1973–74 'oil shock' and its aftermath.[67] Hence, Community efforts to fashion economic policies were associated with development of the common market.[68] A more policy-oriented role for Community assistance was implied.[69] This implication might be critical for the work of the European Regional Development Fund, which was finally established by Regulation 724/75.[70]

Competition policy: According to Article 92(1) EEC,[71] save as otherwise provided in this Treaty, any aid granted by a Member State or through State resources in any form whatsoever which distorted or threatened to distort competition by favouring certain undertakings or the production of certain goods should, insofar as it affected trade between Member States, be incompatible with the common market.[72] However, the principles of complementarity and additionality meant that assistance from the European Regional Development Fund might not simply encourage what might be characterized, from the perspective of Article 92(1), as financial interventions distorting competition. The same principles meant that, in granting assistance, the Fund might also increase the scale or scope of the kind of interventions with which this provision was concerned.[73]

Resolution of such contradictions in Community practice might be seen as dependent on adaptation of Fund operations to competition policy requirements. Certainly, it was noted that in the application of Article 92 the Commission coordinated regional aid granted by Member States. Such coordination was selective, in that account was taken of the differing intensity

---

67 Eleventh EC General Report (1978), 137-8. Cf the explanatory memorandum to the proposal for a regulation amending Reg 724/75, COM(81)589.

68 According to Art 2 EEC, Community objectives were to be achieved not only through establishment of the common market but also through the approximation of national economic policies.

69 Cf the arguments concerning the 'programming' of Community legislative activity by policy in Case 13/83 European Parliament v EC Council: transport policy [1985] ECR 1513.

70 Establishing an ERDF ([1975] OJ L73/1). See, generally, L Van Depoele, 'Het Europees Fonds voor Regionale Ontwikkeling' (1975) SEW 387-94.

71 Now Art 87(1) EC.

72 Cf, regarding Art 81 EC and the allocation of Union assistance, T-369/94 & 85/95 DIR International Film Srl v EC Commission [1998] ECR II-357.

73 A Evans, EC Law of State Aid (Oxford Series in EC Law, Clarendon Press, Oxford 1997), 201–5. See also COA annual report for 1996 ([1997] OJ C348/1), para 6.66.

---

of the problems facing different regions.[74] The Community would have been inconsistent, it was argued, if the same selectivity was not shown in the operations of the Fund.[75]

This argument might lead to claims that the Community itself was bound by Article 92, when it granted 'pecuniary advantages' to individual undertakings.[76] Certainly, Article 19(1) of Regulation 1787/84[77] seemed consistent with Commission objections under Article 92 EEC to State aid which merely kept inefficient undertakings in operation.[78] It required that investment projects in industry or the craft or service sector which might be assisted by the Fund were to relate to economically sound activities intended to help create or maintain permanent jobs. Moreover, this Regulation did 'not prejudice the application of Articles 92 to 94 EEC, particularly as regards establishing and modifying the areas aided by national regional aid schemes'.[79]

In practice, the result might be a preference for assisting infrastructure and training, because such assistance was regarded as less likely to distort competition than other kinds of assistance.[80] However, such assistance might not necessarily be the most appropriate for regional development purposes.[81]

Sectoral policies: The *Guidelines for Community Regional Policy* envisaged 'regional impact assessment.'[82] In all the major policy fields the Commission would take account of the regional effects which its proposals might have, especially as regards employment. Where necessary, it would propose appropriate additional measures to permit the achievement of the policy aims concerned and the correction of any unfavourable effects on the regions. In particular, assistance from the Fund would be used to facilitate application of the relevant policy or to correct any effects likely to jeopardize the 'proper functioning of the Community'.[83] Equally, Recommendation 79/535[84] stated that the regional aspects of sectoral policies had to be taken into account in regional development programmes, which were to be drawn

---

74 First Resolution of 20 October 1971 ([1971] JO C111/1) of the representatives of the Governments of the Member States, meeting within the Council, on general systems of regional aid, Annex, para 7.

75 ESC Opinion of 29 April 1982 ([1982] OJ C178/38) on the proposal for a regulation amending Reg 724/75, para 8.4.

76 AG Verloren van Themaat in Joined Cases 213-215/81 Norddeutsches Vieh- und Fleischkontor Herbert Will, Trawako, Transit-Warenhandels-Kontor GmbH & Co, and Gedelfi Grosseinkauf GmbH & Co v Bundesanstalt für Landwirtschaftliche Marktordnung [1982] ECR 3583, 3617.

77 On the ERDF ([1984] OJ L169/1).

78 A Evans, para [27], n 3 above.

79 [1984] OJ L169/1, Art 44.

80 A Evans, para [27], n 3 above.

81 A Cutler, C Haslam, J Williams, and K Williams, 1992 – the Struggle for Europe (Berg, New York, 1989), 79.

82 Bull EC, Supp 2/77, 9.

83 Ibid, 12.

84 On the regional development programmes ([1979] OJ L143/9), para 4.

up by Member States and on which the grant of assistance from the Fund was to be planned.

In practice, attention focused on policies for 'crisis' sectors. Thus research was undertaken into the regional impact of Community policies for textiles, steel, and shipbuilding.[85] It was observed, for example, that the problems of the shipbuilding industry were particularly serious because of the current high levels of unemployment and because the shipyards were generally to be found at coastal locations where there were few alternative job opportunities.[86] Accordingly, a special assessment was made of the regions likely to be most severely affected by the restructuring of this industry.[87]

Regulation 214/79,[88] which amended Regulation 724/75,[89] reflected such practice. It enabled the Fund to intervene where the Communities had become responsible as a result of a decision in one of their areas of competence, such as external relations, agricultural policy, or industrial policy, which had regional consequences.[90] Accordingly, the Commission began to perform analyses designed to make it possible to determine which regions would be affected by such policies and to propose intervention by the Fund.[91]

The assistance might be presented as compensating Member States in accordance with the outcomes of intergovernmental bargaining. For example, the creation of the European Regional Development Fund might be presented as compensating the United Kingdom for the costs of implementing a common agricultural policy ill adapted to the structure of its agricultural industry.[92] Its creation might also be presented as compensating Italy for the costs of implementing a policy ill adapted to the composition of its agricultural production.[93] In reality, however, the funds might assist Member States in facilitating the economic restructuring which was in any case demanded by international economic conditions.

---

85 EC Eleventh General Report (1978), 140.

86 Seventh Report on Competition Policy (1978), 140. Cf the Council Resolution of 19 September 1978 ([1978] OJ C229/1) on the reorganization of the shipbuilding industry, paras 1 and 4.2.

87 EC Thirteenth General Report (1980), 127.

88 Amending Reg 724/75 ([1979] OJ L35/1), Art 2.

89 [1975] OJ L73/1.

90 Proposals of 15 October 1979 for regulations instituting specific Community regional development projects, COM(79)540, 2.

91 Report of the Committee on Regional Policy and Regional Planning on action taken on the European Parliament's resolutions in the field of regional policy since 1979, EP Doc A 2-65/86, 11.

92 Cf Reg 1888/84 ([1984] OJ L177/1) introducing special measures of Community interest in the field of employment; Reg 1889/84 ([1984] OJ L177/4) introducing special measures of Community interest relating to transport infrastructure; and Reg 1890/84 ([1984] OJ L177/7) introducing special measures of Community interest relating to energy strategy. All three measures involved the grant of Community assistance to the UK, though the last two also benefitted Germany.

93 C André, J-F Drevet, and E Landaburu, 'Regional Consequences of the Internal Market' (1989) Contemporary European Affairs 205-14; and P Cheshire, R Camagni, J-P de Gaudemaar, and JR Cuadrado Roura, para [23], n 1 above, 279.

Possible conflict between interpretation of the relevant provisions according to the outcomes of such intergovernmental bargaining and the interpretation of the same provisions adopted by Union institutions tended to be obscured by policy orientation. On the one hand, Commission competition policy might be seen not only as making assistance to regional development more effective but also as ensuring that the assistance was not diverted from less-favoured regions contrary to the outcomes of intergovernmental bargaining. On the other hand, the influence of sectoral policies pursued by the Union institutions meant that the assistance might be consistent with 'fair return' bargains reached by Member States in sectoral contexts.

3. Cohesion

The concept of cohesion was formally introduced into the EEC Treaty by the Single European Act.[94] Its introduction reflected doubts whether existing arrangements for Community assistance would be adequate to counteract the regional effects of completion of the internal market,[95] which the Commission admitted were likely to be 'uneven'.[96] In particular, it was feared that increased competition would tend to favour the more developed, central regions of the Community at the expense of less developed, peripheral regions.[97] This tendency might, it was also feared, be reinforced by the deregulation of transport[98] and by the implementation of accompanying policies, such as social or environmental policy, which would prevent 'social dumping'[99] by such regions. Hence, the less developed Member States demanded compensation for the social costs likely to result from completion of the internal market.[100]

Accordingly, seemingly important amendments to the EEC Treaty were introduced by the Single European Act.[101] Thus Article 130a EEC now provided that, to promote its overall harmonious development, the Community was to develop and pursue its actions leading to the strengthening of its economic and social cohesion. In particular, the operations of the funds were to aim at reducing disparities between[102] the various regions and the

94 [1987] OJ L169/1.
95 The 'internal market' is defined in Art 14(2) EC.
96 Completing the internal market, COM(85)310, 8. See, generally, I Begg, 'The Regional Dimension of the "1992" Proposals' (1989) Regional Studies 368-76.
97 G Tichy, 'Theoretical and Empirical Considerations on the Dimension of an Optimum Integration Area in Europe' (1992) Aussenwirtschaft 107-37.
98 P Cheshire et al, para [23], n 1 above, 287.
99 Such dumping is said to occur where producers in a Member State with low standards of social or environmental protection are able to undercut producers in Member States with higher standards.
100 P Bianchi, para [1], n 3 above, 600.
101 [1987] OJ L169/1.
102 The Maastricht Treaty later inserted 'levels of development of'.

backwardness of the least favoured regions.[103] It was thus underlined that Union assistance was no longer to be limited to establishment and development of the common market. Rather, it was to meet cohesion requirements.

In fact, this provision meant that cohesion became an 'implicit objective' of the Treaty[104] rather than merely a consequence of policies pursued under the Treaty. It thereby created the need to transform the organization of Community assistance.[105]

The Treaty on European Union went further. Article 2 TEU[106] expressly established that the strengthening of cohesion as well as the common market were both means of achieving the economic and social progress sought by the Union.[107] The EC Treaty was also amended, so as to establish the promotion of cohesion as part of the 'task' of the European Community[108] and the strengthening of cohesion as one of its 'activities'.[109] Further amendments to the EC Treaty confirmed the fundamental character of cohesion, in the sense that cohesion requirements had to be respected in action under this Treaty generally.[110] Hence, cohesion is said to have been 'constitutionalized'.[111]

At the same time, these amendments and, more particularly, the creation of the Cohesion Fund[112] reflected demands from the less developed Member States for assistance in coping with the disciplines to be associated with establishment of monetary union and introduction of a single currency. From this perspective, the introduction of Treaty provisions on cohesion may be seen as giving legal legitimacy to financial transfers between Member States. However, Member States may have limited interest in giving content to

---

103 The Maastricht Treaty later added 'including rural areas', and the Amsterdam Treaty inserted 'or islands'.

104 Cf, regarding the concept of 'solidarity', the argument of the Commission in Joined Cases T-551/93 & 231-234/94 Industrias Pesqueras Campos SA v EC Commission [1996] ECR II-247, II-313.

105 C Mestre and Y Petit, 'La Cohesion économique et sociale après le Traité sur l'Union européenne' (1995) RTDE 207-43.

106 Moreover, according to the 7th recital in the preamble to the TEU, the Member States are determined to promote economic and social progress for their peoples within the context of the accomplishment of the internal market and of reinforced cohesion and environmental protection.

107 However, even if policy objectives are reconciled in accordance with this provision, conflicts between means may remain. Cf, regarding 'conflict of method', T Frazer, 'The New Structural Funds, State Aids, and Interventions on the Single Market' (1995) ELR 3-19, 10.

108 Art 2 EC.

109 Art 3(k) EC.

110 Art 159 EC.

111 A Valle Galvez, 'La Cohesion economica y social como objetivo de la Union europea: analisis e perspectivas' (1994) Revista de Instituciones Europeas 341-78, 352. Cf, regarding the constitutionalization of 'social rights', E Szyszczak, 'Future Directions in European Union Social Policy Law' (1995) ILJ 19-32, 31.

112 Reg 1164/94 ([1994] OJ L130/1).

---

cohesion requirements, because interference with their pursuit of national policies may be entailed.

The practical significance of these legal developments for the operations of the Union funds is uncertain. In part, this uncertainty may reflect lack of definition of the 'social meaning' of cohesion. In part, it may reflect problems in the relationship between particular provisions on cohesion and the more general framework of the Treaties.

The concept of cohesion may be regarded as designed to allow all regions to compete in the internal market. To these ends, the Commission has argued that the Union funds should seek to promote equality between levels of development and employment in the various regions through 'lending impetus to the most backward areas' potential for internally generated development'.[113]

Such action may not necessarily be sufficient for the 'political functions' attributed to cohesion. The attribution of such functions implies that the work of the Union funds should be designed to demonstrate the value of Union membership to weaker regions. Thus Article 158 EC may be regarded as requiring the reduction of regional disparities to a level which is considered politically acceptable rather than economically efficient.[114]

Such thinking implies that EU regional policy has a function going beyond any purely economic rationale. Thus, for example, it may be seen as concerning 'the quality of life'[115] or, according to the Commission, 'the quality of European citizenship'.[116]

Attempts may be made in Union practice to present such thinking as being reconcilable with the requirements of the competitiveness sought through the common market. It may be said, for example, that competitive Union industry can contribute to cohesion and that cohesion can provide industry with the benefits of a wider commercial and geographical base.[117] Again, assistance to research and technological development, including assistance to promote the full use of the capabilities of less-favoured regions, is regarded as encouraging European industry to become more competitive.[118]

A formal basis for such reconciliation is apparently provided by the EC Treaty. According to Article 159 EC,[119] the formulation and implementation of Union policies, presumably including competition policy, shall take into

113 Social dimension of the internal market, SEC(88)1148, 18.
114 ESC Opinion on economic and social cohesion ([1992] OJ C98/50), para 12.1.1.
115 J Scott, Development Dilemmas in European Community Law (Open University Press, Buckingham, 1995).
116 First Cohesion Report, COM(96)542, 13-14.
117 Dec 96/413 ([1996] OJ L167/55) on the implementation of a Community programme to strengthen the competitiveness of European industry, para 9.
118 Evaluation of the Effects of the EC Framework Programme for Research and Technological Development on Economic and Social Cohesion in the Community (EC Commission, Brussels, 1991), 13.
119 Formerly, Art 130b EEC.

account cohesion objectives and contribute to their achievement,[120] as shall Union actions and the implementation of the internal market.

However, the potential for conflict is implicitly admitted in the Treaty. Article 157(3) EC provides that action to promote the competitiveness of European industry 'shall not provide a basis for the introduction by the Community of any measure which could lead to a distortion of competition'.

Conflict between cohesion and other Union concerns may be most acute in the context of economic and monetary union.[121] In particular, the convergence criteria,[122] to be met by Member States adopting the Euro, require public expenditure to be limited. On the other hand, the principles of complementarity and additionality mean that Union assistance encourages such expenditure. The relationship between the cohesion sought by Union assistance and convergence is only partly reconciled by the Cohesion Fund.[123] This Fund seeks to assist certain Member States with a programme for meeting the convergence criteria to tackle their cohesion problems. The legislation governing this Fund withholds application of the additionality principle, 'in the light of the undertaking by the Member States not to decrease their investment efforts in the fields of environmental protection and transport infrastructure', though it maintains the complementarity principle.[124]

The Commission considers that more radical efforts at reconciliation are required. According to the Commission, overall reductions in public expenditure necessary to meet the convergence criteria should be accompanied by a restructuring of expenditure, to improve the competitiveness of the weaker regions. Through Union assistance to improve their competitiveness, it is claimed, 'nominal convergence' (that is, compliance with the convergence criteria) and 'real convergence' (that is, cohesion) can be rendered mutually compatible objectives.[125]

Such claims exemplify the heavy demands implied for Union law by the evolution of the role expected of the Union funds. This evolution means that the operations of the funds are no longer governed by the terms of provisions concerning the establishment of the common market or by the requirements of Union policies. Rather, their operations are supposed to be determined by

120 Cf Art 6 EC, which requires that environmental protection requirements must be integrated into the definition and implementation of other Union policies. In contrast, Art 178 EC merely requires that the Union 'shall take account' of development cooperation objectives in the policies it implements that are likely to affect developing countries.
121 See the link made with cohesion in Dec 90/141 ([1990] OJ L78/23) on the attainment of progressive convergence of economic policies and convergence during stage one of EMU, 1st recital in the preamble.
122 Art 121(1) EC and the Protocol on the convergence criteria.
123 Reg 1164/94 ([1994] OJ L130/1).
124 Ibid, 19th recital in the preamble and Art 7.
125 Fifth periodic report on the social and economic situation and development of the regions of the Community, COM(94)322, 14.

reference to the contribution which each fund may make to cohesion. As a result, the law needs, in regulating these operations, to absorb the various conceptions of cohesion and economic reasoning as to the most effective means of achieving it. This need is evident not only in Commission reports on the work of the funds. It is also evident in the criticisms of such work regularly made by the European Parliament, the Economic and Social Committee, and the Court of Auditors, as well as national bodies, such as the House of Lords Select Committee on the European Communities.[126] At the same time, the law may have need of information about the impact of the operations of the Union funds on cohesion.[127]

G. PROCESSES

Given the variety of definitions of cohesion and the complications in the relationship of cohesion with various Union policies, the decision making involved in the pursuit of cohesion may be said to be of the 'multicriteria' kind.[128] Traditional approaches to designing appropriate processes for such decision making are said to swing between two extremes. Either the decision maker should be given complete freedom, or restrictive assumptions should be introduced which allow decisions to be taken using the classical, single-criterion approach.[129] Such approaches may be unable to take account of the complexities involved, of which policy conflicts are particular manifestations rather than the essence. These complexities mean that the content of a policy cannot be separated from the decision-making processes.[130]

The inference may often be drawn that only 'political' processes can give content to cohesion and to the action necessary to promote it.[131] However, the possibility may not be excluded of cohesion contributing to these processes as an 'interpretative principle' in Union law.[132] This possibility is considered in Chapter 7, which concerns decision-making processes related to the operations of the Union funds.

---

126 References to the criticisms will be made, as appropriate, in the following chapters.
127 An analogy might be drawn with the effect given to the express requirement in Art 187 EC that association with the OCT be implemented on the basis of the principles set out in this Treaty and of the experience acquired in Joined Cases T-480 & 483/93 Antillean Rice Mills NV v EC Council and EC Commission [1995] ECR II-2305, II-2340-1.
128 M Paruccini, Decision Support Systems for Environmental Management (EC Commission, Brussels, 1992).
129 J Spronk (ed), Multiple Criteria Decision Methods and Applications (Springer, Berlin, 1985).
130 M Paruccini, n 1 above, 27.
131 AValle Galvez, para [39], n 6 above, 361.
132 Ibid, 376.

2
EUROPEAN REGIONAL DEVELOPMENT FUND

A. INTRODUCTION

The European Regional Development Fund only acquired an express legal basis in the Treaties as a result of the Single European Act.[133] However, in terms of the amount of resources used,[134] it has now become the most important of the Structural Funds.

B. ESTABLISHMENT OF THE COMMON MARKET

According to Article 2 EEC, a harmonious development of economic activities, a continuous and balanced expansion, an increase in stability, an accelerated raising of the standard of living, and closer relations between Member States were to be promoted. This provision could be read together with the fifth recital in the preamble to the Treaty, according to which the Member States were anxious to strengthen the unity of their economies. They were also anxious to ensure their harmonious development by reducing the differences existing between the various regions and the backwardness of the less-favoured regions.[135] Therefore, the Treaty expressed a commitment to balanced development of the Community as a whole, but also emphasized the need to develop 'backward' regions. However, the apparent concern was with regional difficulties rather than regional development.[136]

No specific role was envisaged for Community assistance in tackling such difficulties, and the adoption of a regional policy was not expressly required. This was partly because equity in the distribution of benefits from integration was expected to result from a 'package agreement'[137] embodied in the Treaty.

---

133 [1987] OJ L169/1.
134 See the conclusions of the European Council meeting in December 1992 (Bull EC 12-1992, I.55).
135 According to H Smit and P Herzog, The Law of the European Economic Community: a Commentary on the EEC Treaty (Matthew Bender, New York, 1990), i, 37, Art 2 EEC and the preamble required that economic 'growth ... occur in an orderly fashion and ... lead neither to overdevelopment of already developed regions nor to greater poverty in the areas already suffering from underdevelopment, but instead ... equalize development throughout the Community'.
136 F Massart-Pierard, 'La Dialectique européanisation-régionalisation' in L'Europe et ses régions (Faculté de Droit de Liège, The Hague, 1975), 289-310, 294.
137 L Tsoukalis, The New European Economy: the Politics and Economics of Integration (Oxford University Press, 1991), 234-5.

Any problems of adjustment to establishment of the common market were to be tackled through assistance from the European Social Fund, the European Agricultural Guidance and Guarantee Fund, and the European Investment Bank.[138] Basically, however, it was anticipated that growth associated with establishment of the common market would resolve regional problems.[139]

In reality, the establishment of the common market deprived Member States of protectionist instruments, such as tariffs and quotas. These instruments had been used to further national growth and, insofar as protected industries were regionally concentrated, regional growth. If they could no longer be used, it might be feared that the 'deglomeration effect of national agglomeration' would be weakened and that 'inter-European agglomeration' would be reinforced.[140] Such fears may explain why Member States increasingly resorted to State aid and sought to outbid one another with escalating offers to attract mobile investment.[141]

The very divergence of the approaches adopted by Member States to their regional problems might be damaging to the undistorted competition sought through establishment of the common market.[142] The Commission drew the conclusion that the provision of Community assistance to such regions was necessary, if overall economic growth was not to be endangered.[143] Community assistance specifically for regional development thus came to be seen as necessary to correct distortions of competition arising from differences in national regional policies.[144]

Hence, the Commission proposed the creation of a European Regional Development Fund in 1969.[145] According to the Commission, such a Fund was needed to assist the reduction of regional disparities in a manner consistent with establishment of the common market. Specifically, by coordinating national action, the operations of the Fund could protect Member States from feeling compelled to bid against each other for mobile investment through the grant of State aid.[146] In other words, the thrust of the Commission proposal

138 Cf Memorandum on Regional Policy in the Community, Bull EC, Supp 12/69, 15.
139 PSRF Mathijsen, 'The Role of Regional Policy in the European Economic Integration Process' in S Bates, W Finnie, JA Usher, and H Wildberg (eds), In Memoriam JDB Mitchell (Sweet and Maxwell, London, 1983), 171-83. See also JJ Anderson, para [20], n 5 above, 135.
140 H Giersch, 'Economic Union between Nations and the Location of Industries' (1949-50) 16 Review of Economic Studies 87–97.
141 J Jordan, 'The Compatibility of Regional Aid Systems with the Common Market' (1976) ELR 236–42.
142 Proposal of 17 October 1969 ([1969] JO C152/6) on the organization of Community means of action in the regional policy field.
143 Memorandum on Regional Policy in the Community, Bull EC, Supp 12/69, 34.
144 Cf D Bureau and P Champsaur, 'Fiscal Federalism and European Economic Unification' (1992) 82 American Economic Review 88-108.
145 Proposal of 17 October 1969 ([1969] JO C152/6).
146 Commissioner Thompson (EP Debs No 158, 41, 13 February 1973).

was to secure greater consistency between the regional development efforts of Member States and the requirements of establishing the common market.

Article 1(1) of the proposal[147] envisaged that Member States would draw up regional development plans. These plans were to take account of the implications of the common market, and their implementation was to be assisted by the Community. Thus the objective of such assistance was to ensure that regional development measures taken by Member States were organized consistently with the requirements of establishment of the common market.[148]

According to the European Parliament in 1960, Community assistance should concentrate on regions of a frontier or peripheral character.[149] However, broader conceptions of regional problems were not precluded, and in 1964 three reports were drawn up favouring action to enable all regions to contribute efficiently to establishment of the common market.[150] The thinking which underlay these reports seems to have been influential. For example, in 1966 the European Parliament maintained that certain regions should have priority for assistance. The regions concerned were: peripheral regions, 'regions in difficulty', regions near to frontiers between Member States, and regions situated on the eastern borders of Germany and Italy. Nevertheless, the Parliament insisted that assistance should concern all the regions of the Community.[151]

According to the Commission proposal itself, the need for assistance was urgent in the case of four kinds of regions. They were: regions which were undeveloped, above all because of the predominance of agriculture; regions in decline, because of the evolution of the predominant economic activities; regions suffering from structural unemployment; and border regions, where cooperation between Member States was particularly necessary.[152] Extension of assistance to other regions was implicitly left open as a future possibility.

Assistance was to concern: the coordination of national measures, particularly for frontier regions; infrastructure; agricultural restructuring; industrial policy and the need to avoid uneconomic activity; and vocational training and guidance.[153]

The assistance was to be limited to interest rebates and guarantees on loans from the European Investment Bank.[154]

---

147 [1969] JO C152/6.
148 Ibid, 6th recital in the preamble.
149 Resolution of 17 May 1960 ([1960] JO 827) on conjunctural, regional, and structural aspects of the long-term economic policy of the Community.
150 Rapports de groupes d'experts sur la politique régionale dans la CEE (EEC Commission, Brussels, 1964).
151 Resolution of 27 June 1966 ([1966] JO 2427) on regional policy in the EEC.
152 Art 1(1) of the proposal of 17 October 1969 ([1969] JO C152/6).
153 Art 5 of the proposal of 17 October 1969 ([1969] JO C152/6).
154 Arts 6 and 7 of the proposal of 17 October 1969 ([1969] JO C152/6).

However, the 1969 proposal was not adopted by the Council. Apparently, the latter was content to leave regional problems to individual Member States.

C. DEVELOPMENT OF THE COMMON MARKET

Regional problems became more pressing along with efforts to develop the common market. Indeed, the Commission maintained in the *EC Sixth General Report*[155] that Community assistance should be the vehicle for an overall economic policy aiming to guide the development of economic structures. Emphasis was placed on promoting the best use by regions of their own resources. Realization of all growth opportunities within the Community might thus be facilitated, and the stability and competitiveness of the Community might be ensured.

Such concerns contributed to the background against which Regulation 724/75[156] established the European Regional Development Fund. The rationale for creation of the Fund, as expressed by the Commission, had evolved. According to the Commission, it was an illusion to hope for the convergence of Member States' economies as long as regional problems continued to weigh so heavily on certain economies. Hence, the development of Community regional policy was considered to be one of the conditions of continuing economic integration.[157]

1. Objectives of assistance

According to the *Report on the Regional Problems in the Enlarged Community* ('the Thomson Report'), the objective of Community assistance should be to give areas suffering from regional imbalances the means to correct them and to enable them to put themselves on a footing of more equal competitiveness. It would then be possible for the various factors of production in the Community to be more fully utilized. In particular, it would be possible for the idle human resources and underused social capital and infrastructure to be more fully employed.[158]

Failure to achieve this objective would, it was argued, be 'undesirable for the Community as a whole. For example, according to the European Parliament, uncontrolled congestion and migration were more costly than measures to encourage the balanced development of the regions.[159] To entrepreneurs, expansion in an already crowded region might appear attractive, given the availability there of a network of suppliers and access to a

---

155 EC Commission, Brussels, 1973, 115–16.
156 Establishing an ERDF ([1975] OJ L73/1).
157 Community Regional Policy _ New Guidelines, Bull EC, Supp 2/77, 6.
158 Bull EC, Supp 8/73, 8.
159 Resolution of 21 April 1977 ([1977] OJ C118/51) on aspects of the Community's regional policy to be developed in the future, part (a).

mass market. However, such expansion could lead to the very congestion which the Parliament considered undesirable.[160]

The undesirable consequences were recognized as likely to go beyond the integration process in a purely economic sense. For example, the then President of the Commission told the European Parliament in May 1968 that an effective regional policy had become a *sine qua non* of integration in a broader sense. In his view, this policy should be in the Community 'as the heart is in the human body'.[161] According to the Thomson Report, no Community could maintain itself or have a meaning for the peoples which belonged to it, so long as some had very different standards of living and had cause to doubt the common will of all to help each Member State to improve the conditions of its people. Therefore, unless the Community's economic resources were moved where human resources were, thus sustaining living local communities, there was bound to be disenchantment over the idea of European unity.[162]

Such thinking was only partly reflected in Regulation 724/75.[163] Article 1 of this Regulation provided that the Fund was intended to correct the principal regional imbalances within the Community resulting in particular from agricultural preponderance, industrial change, and structural underemployment. Article 6(1) added that the imbalances to be corrected were those likely to prejudice the attainment of economic and monetary union.

This reference to economic and monetary union reflected the conception of the Fund adopted by some at least of the Member States. They conceived of the Fund as a means of 'compensating' weaker Member States for the costs of their participation in such a union.[164]

However, from the 'regional policy' perspective of the Commission, the formulation of Fund objectives might be found too narrow. Certainly, a broader approach was favoured in Commission guidelines of 1977. According to these guidelines, the Fund should not only seek to reduce existing regional problems, which appeared both in the traditionally less developed regions and in regions undergoing industrial or agricultural reconversion. The Fund should also seek to prevent new regional imbalances arising from structural changes in the world economy or from policy measures adopted by the Community.[165]

These guidelines reflected a feeling that the economic and social context within which the Fund operated had changed fundamentally since its conception. The economic crisis had not only aggravated existing regional inequalities. It had also created additional problems of adaptation and

160 Ibid.
161 PE Débs No 103, 126, 15 May 1968.
162 Report on the Regional Problems in the Enlarged Community, Bull EC, Supp 8/73, 7.
163 Establishing an ERDF ([1975] OJ L73/1).
164 S George, Politics and Policy in the European Union, 3rd edn (Oxford University Press, 1996), 233.
165 Community Regional Policy – New Guidelines, Bull EC, Supp 2/77, 7.

development, which contained the seeds of new regional imbalances. Therefore, according to the Commission, the Fund had to be reviewed, and its objectives redefined.[166]

However, the existing formulation of the objectives of the Fund was essentially retained in Regulation 214/79,[167] Article 6 of Regulation 724/75[168] only being slightly modified. In its modified version it provided that the regional imbalances to be corrected were those which might prejudice the proper functioning of the common market and the convergence of the Member States' economies, with a view, in particular, to the attainment of economic and monetary union.

In Regulation 1787/84,[169] which replaced the earlier legislation on the Fund, the implication was not drawn that any radical reformulation of Fund objectives was needed. Article 3 of this Regulation defined the objective of the Fund as being to contribute to the correction of the principal regional imbalances within the Community. In pursuit of this objective, the Fund was to participate in the development and structural adjustment of regions whose development was lagging behind and in the conversion of declining industrial regions.[170]

2. Eligibility for assistance

The *Report on the Regional Problems in the Enlarged Community*[171] distinguished between 'agricultural problem areas' and 'areas suffering from industrial change'.[172]

'Agricultural problem areas' were defined in the Report as those which had a greater share of the workforce in agriculture than the Community average and a relatively low *per capita* income. They tended to be situated on the periphery of the Community, and over recent years they had experienced a sharp decline in the proportion of employment devoted to agriculture. They usually suffered from severe structural underemployment and often from high long-term unemployment.[173]

'Areas suffering from industrial change' were defined in the Report as those with at least 20 per cent of employment in declining industries, such as

---

166 Eleventh EC General Report (1978), 137-8. Cf, later, the explanatory memorandum to the proposal for a regulation amending Reg 724/75, COM(81)589.
167 Amending Reg 724/75 ([1979] OJ L35/1).
168 [1975] OJ L73/1.
169 On the ERDF ([1984] OJ L169/1). See, generally, B De Witte, 'The Reform of the European Regional Development Fund' (1986) 25 CML Rev 419-40; J Elizade, 'La Reforma del FEDER: principios de una autentica politica regional comunitaria' (1985) Revista de Instituciones Europeas 93-107. See also J Curral, 'Le Fonds européen de développement régional des originés jusqu'à l'acte unique européen' (1988) CDE 39-102.
170 Art 18(2) of Reg 1787/84 ([1984] OJ L169/1) followed Art 6 of Reg 214/79 ([1979] OJ L35/1).
171 Bull EC, Supp 8/73.
172 Ibid, 9.
173 Bull EC, Supp 8/73.

coal and textiles, persistently high unemployment (over 3.5 per cent or more than 20 per cent above the national average), or annual emigration exceeding 1 per cent over a long period. Such regions were usually those where there had been a high dependence for employment on ageing industries. Their problems of economic transformation were often underlined by a constantly slow rate of growth and by high levels of unemployment stretching over many years.[174]

Such thinking about definition of regions eligible for assistance was reflected in the 1973 proposal for creation of the ERDF.[175] Article 3(1) of this proposal envisaged that the Council, on the basis of a Commission proposal, would adopt a list of regions eligible for Fund assistance. According to Article 3(2), these regions would be chosen from those which benefitted from a national system of regional aids and where the *per capita* gross domestic product (GDP) was below the Community average. They were to include those with regional imbalances resulting from the preponderance of agriculture, industrial change, or structural unemployment. Account would be taken of heavy dependence on agricultural employment, heavy dependence on employment in declining industrial activities, and persistently high unemployment[176] or net emigration.

These criteria were elaborated in a further proposal, drawn up to implement Article 3. According to this proposal, regions with a preponderance of agriculture were those with a percentage of the working population engaged in agriculture above the Community average[177] and a percentage engaged in industry lower than the Community average. Regions undergoing industrial change included those with at least 20 per cent of the working population employed in the coal or textiles industry, those where unemployment had averaged at least 2 per cent over several years, and those where there had been net emigration over a long period. In the case of the last two categories of such regions, the number of persons employed in the coal or textiles industry had to have been at least 5,000. Regions with structural underemployment were those where unemployment was at least 20 per cent above the national average, representing at least 3.5 per cent of the working population, and where there had been net outward migration at an average annual rate of at least 1 per cent of the population over a long period. In addition, a region would qualify for

174 Bull EC, Supp 8/73.
175 Proposal of 31 July 1973 ([1973] OJ C86/7) for a regulation establishing a Regional Development Fund.
176 High unemployment and low per capita GDP tended to be closely linked. See the Second periodic report on the social and economic situation and development of the regions of the Community, COM(84)40, 2.4–4.
177 Areas within ineligible regions would qualify where more than 11.3% were engaged in agriculture.

assistance where its *per capita* GDP was less than 50 per cent of the Community average.[178]

These proposals were criticized for failing adequately to require concentration of assistance on the most needy regions. The net result could even be to increase rather than decrease regional disparities, because Member States in the greatest economic difficulties had the fewest resources for carrying out the necessary restructuring.[179] Thus a more systematic classification of all regions according to the relative seriousness of the imbalances found in relation to the Community average was advocated.[180]

Such criticism had no apparent impact on the terms of Regulation 724/75.[181] According to Article 3 of the Regulation, to be assisted by the Fund, regions simply had to be amongst those established by Member States in applying their own systems of regional aid.

The Commission itself subsequently sought more precise definition of eligible regions. It proposed the following indicators for assessment of the relative intensity of regional imbalances: the trend of unemployment rates during the preceding five years; the proportion of the active population occupied in agriculture; the proportion of the active population occupied in declining industrial sectors; the migration balance during the preceding five years; and the development and level of GDP.[182] However, the Council did not favour the use of these indicators, and so they were not included in Regulation 214/79.[183]

Instead, Article 3 of Regulation 214/79[184] merely introduced provision for the Fund to grant certain assistance to regions other than those covered by national regional aid systems, if the Member State had granted aid or did so at the same time. The former regions were to be selected by the Council[185] in legislation adopting specific Community regional development measures.

---

178 Proposal of 11 October 1973 ([1973] OJ C106/26) for a regulation on the list of regions and areas referred to in the regulation establishing an ERDF; Bull EC 10-1973, 1303.

179 Report of the Committee on Economic and Monetary Affairs on the fourth report on competition policy, EP Doc 164/75, 24.

180 Resolution of 13 December 1973 ([1974] OJ C2/49) on the proposals for a regulation on the list of priority agricultural regions and areas referred to in the regulation on finance from the Guidance Section of the EAGGF for projects falling within development programmes in priority agricultural regions; and a regulation on the list of regions and areas referred to in the Regulation establishing an ERDF, para 7. See also the Resolution 13 March 1974 ([1974] OJ C40/26) on Community regional policy, para 4.

181 [1975] OJ L73/1.

182 Art 2(2)(b) of the proposal of 3 June 1977 ([1977] OJ C161/11) for a regulation amending Reg 724/75.

183 [1979] OJ L35/1.

184 [1979] OJ L35/1.

185 Ibid, Art 12(3)(b).

186 [1984] OJ L169/1.

Similarly, Regulation 1787/84[186] provided that the only regions which could benefit from assistance to projects[187] or national programmes of Community interest[188] were those established by Member States in applying their systems of regional aid. Community programmes could cover other regions, where such coverage was appropriate for the solution of problems forming the subject of Community action, the Member State concerned gave its consent, and that Member State had also granted aid or did so at the same time.[189]

In other words, the legislation continued to rely essentially on national designations for determining eligibility.

3. Allocation of assistance

Assistance was to be allocated according to criteria laid down in Community legislation. However, application of these criteria was affected by national quotas and, later, 'ranges'.

Criteria: According to the 1973 proposal for the creation of an ERDF,[190] assistance was to be allocated to regions for projects approved by the Commission with reference to the relative severity of the economic imbalance of the region.[191]

Such thinking was reflected in the preamble to Regulation 724/75.[192] According to the preamble, assistance was to be allocated on the basis of the relative severity of regional imbalances. Account was also to be taken of other factors affecting the importance of projects from the perspectives of the region concerned and the Community.[193]

According to the operative provisions of the legislation, assistance was to be allocated in the light of the relative severity of the economic imbalance in the region concerned and the direct and indirect effect of the project on employment.[194] Priority was to be given to projects in national priority areas,[195] taking account of the Community principles for the coordination of regional aid granted by Member States.[196] Special account was to be taken of the following: the consistency of the project with the regional development programmes to be drawn up by each Member State; the contribution of the

---

186 [1984] OJ L169/1.
187 Ibid, Art 17(3).
188 Ibid, Art 11(3).
189 Ibid, Art 9(3).
190 [1973] OJ C86/7.
191 Ibid, Art 13.
192 [1975] OJ L73/1.
193 Ibid, 10th recital in the preamble.
194 Art 5(1) of Reg 724/75 ([1975] OJ L73/1).
195 Ibid, Art 3.
196 First Resolution of 20 October 1971 of the Representatives of the Governments of the Member States, meeting within the Council, on general systems of regional aid ([1971] JO C111/1).

---

project to the economic development of the region; the consistency of the project with the programmes or objectives of the Community; the situation of the economic sector concerned and the profitability of the project; whether the project fell within a frontier area within adjacent regions of separate Member States;[197] other contributions made by Community institutions or by the European Investment Bank, either to the same project or to other activities within the same region; and the effect of the project on the environment, particularly as regards living and working conditions.

Regulation 1787/84[198] added two new criteria for allocating assistance to projects. These additional criteria were: specific problems due to the island, landlocked, or peripheral character of the area in which the project was located; and the effects of the project on the region's natural resources.[199]

In allocating assistance to national programmes of Community interest, the Commission was to take account of similar criteria. It was also to take account of the mobilization of the indigenous potential of the regions concerned; and the integrated use in appropriate cases of any other Community structural financial instruments.[200]

Quotas: Article 2(1) of Regulation 724/75[201] provided for assistance from the Fund to be allocated by national quotas. Concessions are said to have been made to the wish not to divide the Community into 'givers' and 'takers'. Hence, the quotas were calculated so that Member States with fewer regional difficulties would receive some – though limited – assistance from the Fund.[202] The implication drawn from the allocation of a quota to each Member State was that Community assistance should be used according to the regional policy pursued by the Member State concerned.

Certainly, by submitting a number of projects whose combined Fund financing requirements approximated to the national quota, governments could effectively eliminate any scope for real Commission discretion. In 1980, for example, only 143 out of 3,252 applications for assistance were rejected by the Commission on 'substantive grounds', such as grounds related to sectoral or competition policy considerations.[203] Hence, the criteria for allocation of assistance laid down in the legislation might only be of formal significance.

---

197 The Commission considered that frontier regions 'generally [felt] the effects of integration most acutely and so problems of development or conversion often [arose]'. See Community Regional Policy – New Guidelines, Bull EC, Supp 2/77, 12.
198 [1984] OJ L169/1.
199 Ibid, Art 21(1).
200 Art 11(2) of Reg 1787/84 ([1984] OJ L169/1).
201 [1975] OJ L73/1.
202 Report of the Committee on Regional Policy and Transport on regional policy as regards the regions at the Community's internal frontiers (EP Doc 467/75), 13.
203 ERDF Sixth Annual Report (1981), 21.

The Commission had stressed the need for reform in the 1977 regional policy guidelines.[204] In the case of underdeveloped regions and declining regions, remedial action should be taken by and through national governments. In the case of 'regional impact areas' and frontier areas, their situation inherently called for Community rather than national action. Fund resources should make separate provision for the first two categories on the one hand – complementing and not displacing national action – and for the second two categories on the other hand. Accordingly, the resources should be divided between a 'quota section', which would finance projects in the first two categories, and a 'non-quota section', which would be reserved for the second two categories.

Such thinking was reflected in Regulation 214/79.[205] Article 2(3) of this Regulation distinguished between 'quota measures' in support of regional policy measures taken by Member States (paragraph (a)) and 'non-quota measures' in the form of specific Community regional development measures (paragraph (b)). Allocation of assistance to the latter measures was not subject to the national quotas. However, according to Article 3, only 5 per cent[206] at most of Fund resources could be devoted to such measures.

Ranges: Increasing regional disparities as well as concern that the existing rules entailed a very limited power for the Commission to coordinate national regional policy measures[207] led the Commission to propose replacement of national quotas with regional quotas.[208] However, since this proposal was not acceptable to the Council, the Commission amended its proposal, so that Fund resources would be allocated according to ranges.[209]

Accordingly, Regulation 1787/84[210] provided for national quotas to be replaced by upper and lower limits for national allocations. For each Member State the lower limit constituted the minimum amount of Fund assistance it was guaranteed, if it submitted an adequate volume of applications for assistance which satisfied the conditions set out in the Regulation. The upper limits were calculated so that, except for Denmark, each Member State was theoretically able to obtain a larger share than under the quota system.

---

204 Community Regional Policy – New Guidelines, Bull EC, Supp 2/77, 6.

205 [1979] OJ L35/1.

206 The Commission had proposed in its preliminary draft budget for 1978 that 13% of ERDF finance should be available for 'non-quota measures'. The European Parliament objected that the figure adopted by the Council was too low and was not commensurate with the objectives of such measures. See the Resolution of 19 June 1981 ([1981] OJ C172/117) on the fifth annual report on the ERDF, para 9.

207 Report and proposals on ways of increasing the effectiveness of the Community's Structural Funds, COM(83)501, Annex, 8.

208 Proposal of 29 October 1981 ([1981] OJ C336/60) for a regulation amending Reg 724/75, Art 4(3).

209 Proposal of 18 November 1983 ([1983] OJ C360/1) for a regulation amending Reg 724/75, Art 4(3).

210 [1984] OJ L169/1.

Obviously, however, they could not all do so. In the case of that portion of the Fund resources falling between the lower and upper limits, allocations were to depend on the implementation of the priorities and criteria laid down in the Regulation.[211] In effect, it would be put up for competitive tender amongst Member States.

The Commission hoped that the increased competition for assistance would encourage Member States to submit a larger number of applications in order to improve their chances of obtaining the maximum possible allocation.[212] However, the total of the lower limits for each Member State, which had been 83.16 per cent of Fund resources in the amended Commission proposal,[213] amounted to 88.63 per cent in the Regulation itself. Only 11.37 per cent remained, therefore, to be allocated at the discretion of the Commission.[214]

4. Scope of assistance

Assistance from the Fund might relate to productive investment, infrastructure investment, and 'endogenous development'.

Productive investment: Article 4(1)(a) of Regulation 724/75[215] envisaged Fund support for investments in industry, handicraft, or service activities which were economically sound and benefitted from State regional aid. At least 10^{216} new jobs had to be created or existing jobs maintained.[217] In the latter case the investments had to fall within the framework of a conversion or restructuring plan to ensure that the undertaking concerned became competitive. The only service activities which could be supported were those having a direct impact on the development of the region and the level of employment.

However, it proved difficult to ensure that Fund assistance to productive investments was optimal.[218] Indeed, by reducing the cost of capital for new investments, such assistance could artificially boost their capital intensity, thus

211 Ibid, Art 4(5).
212 Eleventh report on the ERDF, COM(86)545.
213 [1983] OJ C360/1.
214 The Committee on Regional Policy and Regional Planning sought greater concentration through establishment of quotas for the weaker regions. See the Report on second-generation regional development programmes for 1981–85, EP Doc 2-63/85, 10.
215 [1975] OJ L73/1.
216 The Commission proposal ([1973] OJ C86/7) had required in Art 4(1) that investments had to exceed ua 50,000 and to involve the creation or maintenance of jobs (no figure was stipulated).
217 This requirement was difficult for SMEs to meet (COA special report on job creation or maintenance in the granting of aid to regional investments ([1982] OJ C345/1), para 2.3) and was dropped in Reg 1787/84 ([1984] OJ L169/1). According to Art 17(1) (ibid), the investment had to cost more than ECU 50,000 and, according to Art 19(1) (ibid), be intended to help create or maintain jobs.
218 ESC Opinion of 29 September 1977 ([1977] OJ C292/5) on the guidelines for Community regional policy, para 4.6.

substituting capital for labour.[219] This distortion of factor costs could lead to a misallocation of resources generating, for example, a capital-intensive pattern of development in regions with an abundance of labour.[220] Even when employment was increased in the unit of a company receiving assistance, the effect might be closure of a related unit or that an unassisted company elsewhere might be rendered uncompetitive.[221]

Infrastructure investment: The *Medium-Term Economic Policy Programme (1966-70)*[222] stressed problems of deficiencies in inter-regional infrastructures, especially in relation to transport. The Commission guidelines for regional policy of 1977[223] and 1981[224] maintained, more generally, that underdeveloped regions needed an economic and social infrastructure amenable to sustained growth.

However, Article 4(1)(b) of Regulation 724/75[225] only provided for the Fund to support investments in infrastructures directly linked with the activities covered by Article 4(1)(a).[226] According to the former provision, as subsequently amended by Regulation 214/79,[227] no more than 70 per cent of Fund resources were to be available to infrastructure investments, unless the Council decided otherwise. In practice, this limit was never respected,[228] and it was formally relaxed in 1983.[229] Regulation 1787/84[230] itself merely provided that the Member States and the Commission were to endeavour to ensure that an appropriate proportion (if possible, 30 per cent) of Fund resources was available for investments in industry, crafts, and services.[231]

219 COA special report on job creation or maintenance in the granting of aid to regional investments ([1982] OJ C345/1), para 4.1.
220 RP Camagni, 'Development Scenarios and Policy Guidelines for the Lagging Regions in the 1990s' (1992) Regional Studies 361-74.
221 Report of the Committee on Regional Policy and Regional Planning on the contribution of the ERDF to the creation of jobs in the Community, EP Doc A2-120/86, 11.
222 [1967] JO 1513, 1564.
223 Community Regional Policy – New Guidelines, Bull EC, Supp 2/77, 12.
224 New regional policy guidelines and priorities, COM(81)152.
225 [1975] OJ L73/1.
226 Art 4(2)(c) (ibid) imposed no similar restriction on infrastructure assistance in regions covered by Dir 75/268 (see paras [416] ff below). Art 4(b) of the Commission proposal ([1973] OJ C86/7) had envisaged assistance for infrastructure required for the development of industrial or service activities.
227 [1979] OJ L35/1.
228 Between 1975 and 1984 assistance to industrial investment represented only 18% of total ERDF resources.
229 Dec 83/595 ([1983] OJ L340/24) enabling the ERDF to exceed the 70% limit for infrastructure investment projects for the period 1981–83.
230 [1984] OJ L169/1.
231 Ibid, Art 35.

This emphasis on infrastructure investments was controversial.[232] On the one hand, it was argued that infrastructural projects very often created the preconditions for industrial investment, particularly in weaker regions. By acting as a magnet for the attraction of further investments, such projects also promoted the long-term development of such regions.[233] On the other hand, emphasis on infrastructure might lead to neglect of production weaknesses[234] and the particular needs of business at the local level.[235] Moreover, industrial investments costing less than 10 million European units of account had created the largest number of jobs relative to the size of investments and the amount of the assistance from the Fund.[236] Hence, the European Parliament recommended that assistance be directed to smaller industrial investments, which created more employment, rather than to infrastructure investments. In reality, there might be a 'chicken and the egg' problem. Without adequate infrastructure there was little hope or purpose in investing in industry; without industry there was little use in providing supporting infrastructures.[237]

In practice, infrastructure projects might generate employment during their construction phase but little, if any – at least directly – after completion. Moreover, assistance to such projects might merely help to finance investments which would have been made anyway.[238] The Fund might thus make a contribution to general national budgets rather than stimulating additional regional development.[239]

These disadvantages of infrastructure assistance were exacerbated by the narrow view of infrastructure needs adopted in the legislation. In fact, the European Parliament had proposed that infrastructure investments 'in the broad sense, required for the development of a region within the framework of

232 See, regarding doubts about the effectiveness of infrastructure expenditure in the promotion of regional development, AM Comfort, 'Alternatives to Infrastructure? Possible Ways Forward for the ERDF: a View from Luxembourg' (1988) Regional Studies 542–51. Cf the objection that ERDF financing of infrastructure work might amount to operating aid in the COA annual report for 1986 ([1987] OJ C336/1), para 9.11.

233 ESC Opinion of 22 February 1979 ([1979] OJ C133/27) on the ERDF third annual report, para 2.

234 R Hall and D van der Wee, 'Community Regional Policies for the 1990s' (1992) Regional Studies 399–404.

235 Second periodic report on the social and economic situation and development of the regions of the Community, COM(84)40, III.

236 Report of the Committee on Regional policy and Regional Planning on the eighth annual report and the ninth annual report on the ERDF, EP Doc A2-5/85, 7.

237 Report of the Committee on Regional Policy, Regional Planning, and Transport on the second annual report on the ERDF, EP Doc 452/77, 10.

238 See, regarding the emphasis on road projects, the Report of the Committee on Regional Policy and Regional Planning on the tenth annual report on the ERDF, EP Doc A2-76/86, 6.

239 Report of the Committee on Regional Policy and Regional Planning on the eighth annual report and the ninth annual report on the ERDF, EP Doc A2-5/85, 13.

a regional development programme' should be covered.[240] Thus the Parliament, like the Economic and Social Committee,[241] considered that the Fund should go beyond assisting investments in physical infrastructure. According to the Parliament, infrastructure needs were more general and related, above all, to education and occupational training. The ability of firms to invest in the regions was considered to depend, first, on the availability of local people with the right skills or on the willingness of local people to acquire the right skills. Secondly, it was considered to depend on the availability of an efficient infrastructure.[242]

Article 4(4) of Regulation 214/79[243] went some way to meet such concerns, by extending the range of infrastructure investments that could be assisted by the Fund. Provided that the investment was justified by a regional development programme, support could be extended to an investment in any infrastructure contributing to the development of the region in which it was situated. This broadening of the definition of infrastructure investments eligible for assistance was, according to the preamble to the Regulation,[244] necessitated by the diversity of regional situations in the Community.

Similarly, Article 18(1) of Regulation 1787/84[245] provided that assistance could be granted to infrastructure projects which contributed to the development of the region. The Annex listed those categories of infrastructure which the Fund could not assist.

Endogenous development: The 'endogenous growth' approach to regional development seeks to develop the 'economic vocation' of each region.[246] This approach holds that labour and capital subsidies are ineffective,[247] particularly in the face of increased exposure to international competition.[248]

---

240 [1973] OJ C108/51, (amendment to Art 4(1)(b) of the Commission proposal).

241 Opinion of 29 April 1982 ([1982] OJ C178/38) on the proposal for a regulation amending Reg 724/75, para 4.1.

242 Report of the Committee on Regional Policy and Regional Planning on the eighth and ninth annual reports on the ERDF, EP Doc A2-5/85, 11.

243 [1979] OJ L35/1.

244 Ibid, 11th recital in the preamble.

245 [1984] OJ L169/1.

246 Report of the Committee on Regional Policy and Transport on the proposals for a decision on the creation of a Committee for Regional Policy; a financial regulation relating to special provisions to be applied to the ERDF; and a regulation establishing the ERDF, EP Doc 178/73, 21.

247 See, eg, A Whiting (ed), The Economics of Industrial Subsidies (HMSO, London, 1976).

248 The influence of external effects was advancing at the national level, but it was far more severe at the regional level, especially after the elimination of national regulations that used to take a core set of social and constitutional conditions out of inter-regional competition. See W Streeck and PC Schmitter, 'From National Corporatism to Transnational Pluralism: Organised Interests in the Single European Market' (1991) Politics and Society 133-64. Moreover, 'institutional competition' might entail increased power for large corporations. See M Dunford and G Benko, 'Neo-Fordism or Post-Fordism? Some Conclusions' in G Benko and M Dunford (eds), Industrial Change and Regional Development (Belhaven Press, London, 1991), 286-305.

In accordance with such thinking, the Commission proposal of 1981 concerning reform of the Fund favoured a broadening of the definition of infrastructure investment which could be supported. According to the Commission, the task was above all to use the local potential available, particularly by developing the latent capacities of undertakings. To this end, the Fund should provide information, research, and technical assistance.[249]

Articles 15 and 16 of Regulation 1787/84[250] duly provided for measures to exploit the potential for internally generated development of regions. In particular, Article 15(1) provided that, for the purposes of greater exploitation of such potential, the Fund might contribute to the financing of consistent sets of measures for existing undertakings, primarily small and medium-sized undertakings, in industry, crafts, and tourism. Such assistance should seek to provide these undertakings with facilities enabling them to expand their activities and to obtain access to new technology. It should also seek to facilitate their access to the capital market.

The assistance might still be regarded as too limited. According to the Committee on Regional Policy and Transport, individuals had to be prepared (through cultural and educational infrastructures) to take part in regional development. They also had to be trained (through vocational training infrastructures) for such participation.[251]

Such thinking might imply the need for intervention going beyond the terms of the legislation governing the Fund. For example, Regulation 815/84[252] provided for 'exceptional Community financial support'[253] from the General Budget,[254] to assist Greece in the construction of vocational training centres. It also provided for assistance to the construction of centres for the rehabilitation of the mentally and physically ill and handicapped, with a view to helping them return to gainful employment.[255] This measure was a 'derogation from Fund rules'.[256]

---

249 Explanatory memorandum to the proposal for a regulation amending Reg 724/75, COM(81)589, 4.
250 [1984] OJ L169/1.
251 Report on the proposals for a decision on the creation of a Committee for Regional Policy; a financial regulation for special provisions to be applied to the ERDF; and a regulation establishing a Regional Development Fund, EP Doc 178/73, 14.
252 On exceptional financial support in favour of Greece in the social field ([1984] OJ L88/1).
253 Ibid, Art 1.
254 See, eg, Art 542 of the Budget for 1984 ([1984] OJ L12/1).
255 See, eg, Dec 85/703 ([1985] OJ L30/31) on applications for assistance from the EC concerning exceptional financial support for Greece in the social field (1984).
256 COA special report 5/90 ([1990] OJ C331/1) on the implementation of Reg 815/84, para 1.3.

5. Forms of assistance

Assistance from the Fund might take the form of interest rebates on loans from the European Investment Bank[257] and the part-financing of projects. It might also take the form of specific Community regional development measures, national programmes of Community interest, Community programmes, and studies. Coordination of assistance from the ERDF with operations of other Union funds might be sought through Integrated Development Operations and Integrated Mediterranean Programmes.

Projects: The legislature sought gradually to subject project support to programming, which was supposed to increase Community influence over use of the assistance provided. According to the Commission, the financing of individual projects should be phased out in favour of a programme approach in which coherent groups of related projects would receive assistance over a period of years.[258]

In practice, support for individual projects remained the dominant form of assistance. Article 6 of Regulation 1787/84[259] provided that assistance for programme financing should 'as far as possible' be gradually increased to reach at least 20 per cent of total assistance within three years.[260] In the event, programmes received only 5.5 per cent of total Fund resources in 1985 and 7.7 per cent in 1986.

Specific Community regional development measures: According to the Commission proposal for what became Regulation 214/79,[261] in view of the economic and social trends in the Community and particularly the economic crisis resulting from the increased cost of primary products, Fund assistance had to be diversified. The diversification should enable it to support not only regional policy measures taken by the Member States but also specific Community regional development measures in favour of regions experiencing problems of restructuring and of conversion.[262] The latter measures were to comprise, in particular: measures related to other Community policies or complementary thereto, intended to reinforce or to complement the convergent efforts of Community policies to correct structural imbalances in

257 Art 4(2)(b) of Reg 724/75 ([1975] OJ L73/1). Cf, earlier, the proposal of 28 May 1971 ([1971] JO C90/23) concerning a European fund for interest rebates on regional development loans. Cf, later, the proposal of 3 June 1977 ([1977] OJ C161/17) for a regulation establishing an interest rebate scheme within the ERDF, which envisaged that the ERDF should be empowered to provide interest rebates on loans from the Community or from the EIB.
258 New regional policy guidelines and priorities, COM(81)152; and the explanatory memorandum to the proposals for a regulation amending Reg 724/75, COM(83)649.
259 [1984] OJ L169/1.
260 The additional target of 40% after four years, contained in the proposal of 18 November 1983 ([1983] OJ C360/1), was not accepted by the Council.
261 Of 3 June 1977 ([1977] OJ C161/11) for a regulation amending Reg 724/75.
262 Ibid, 7th recital in the preamble.

the regions, particularly in those covered by Directive 75/268;[263] measures made necessary by the regional consequences of other Community policies; measures to accelerate the creation of jobs in the Community's less developed regions or in conversion regions, particularly by facilitating the access of investors to the capital market and the location in the regions of investments originating outside them; development measures in frontier regions; and emergency measures to meet unforeseeable regional situations.[264]

Regulation 214/79[265] itself, which provided in Article 2(3)(b) for specific Community regional development measures to be adopted, was more limited. According to Article 13(1), the measures should be linked with Community policies and with measures adopted by the Community, in order to take better account of their regional dimension or to reduce their regional consequences. In exceptional cases, they should be intended to meet the structural consequences of particularly serious occurrences in certain regions with a view to replacing jobs lost and creating the necessary infrastructures for this purpose.

When adopting this Regulation, the Council declared its readiness to consider any request for assistance concerning frontier problems in the least favoured regions of the Community, submitted jointly by two or more Member States concerned.[266] Accordingly, Regulation 2619/80[267] provided for a measure to assist the border regions of Ireland and Northern Ireland.

Again, Regulation 2615/80[268] sought to assist certain French and Italian regions in the context of Community enlargement, and Regulation 215/84[269] concerned Greek regions affected by enlargement. Other measures concerned declining sectors. The emphasis was on assisting 'regions liable to be affected by the consequences of decisions and measures taken under other Community policies, especially outlying regions facing special problems to do with their remoteness'.[270] In other words, the measures were designed to assist regions

---

263 See paras [409] ff below.

264 Art 13 of the proposal of 3 June 1977 ([1977] OJ C161/11).

265 [1979] OJ L35/1.

266 Proposals of 15 October 1979 for Council regulations instituting specific Community regional development projects under Art 13 of the ERDF Regulation, COM(79)540, 3.

267 Instituting a specific Community regional development measure contributing to the improvement of the economic and social situation of the border areas of Ireland and Northern Ireland ([1980] OJ L271/28).

268 Instituting a specific Community regional development measure contributing to the development of certain French and Italian regions in the context of Community enlargement ([1980] OJ L271/1).

269 Instituting a specific Community measure contributing to the development of certain regions of Greece in the context of Community enlargement ([1984] OJ L27/5).

270 Ninth report on the ERDF, COM(84)522, 45.

where other Community policies caused or might cause major imbalances, so that the adverse regional consequences of these policies could be countered.[271]

In particular, Regulation 2616/80[272] concerned regions adversely affected by restructuring of the steel industry. Regulation 2617/80[273] concerned United Kingdom regions[274] adversely affected by the restructuring of the shipbuilding industry.[275] It was extended to similar German regions by Regulation 217/84.[276] Regulation 219/84[277] concerned regions adversely affected by restructuring of the textile and clothing industry. Similarly, Regulation 3638/85[278] concerned regions adversely affected by the implementation of the common fisheries policy.

Regulation 2618/80[279] was somewhat different. It sought to assist reduction of dependence on imported petroleum and to promote regional development in the Mezzogiorno, particularly its mountain areas. Regulation 218/84[280] extended the measure to the Greek islands, except for Salamina, which was not covered by a national aid scheme.[281]

Particular attention was paid to the need to encourage entrepreneurship in the framework of such measures. For example, Article 3 of Regulation 3638/85[282] provided for the improvement of the physical environment, development of small and medium-sized enterprises and craft activities, stimulation of economic activity in general, and promotion of tourism.

National programmes of Community interest: Regulation 1787/84[283] provided for the Fund to assist national programmes of Community interest.

271 ESC Opinion of 13 December 1979 ([1980] OJ C83/4) on the proposal for regulations instituting specific Community regional development projects, para 3.1.
272 Instituting a specific Community regional development measure contributing to overcoming constraints on the development of new economic activities in certain zones adversely affected by the restructuring of the steel industry ([1980] OJ L271/9).
273 Instituting a specific Community regional development measure contributing to overcoming constraints on the development of new economic activities in certain zones adversely affected by restructuring of the shipbuilding industry ([1980] OJ L271/16).
274 Ibid, Art 2.
275 The ERDF had already been involved in efforts to tackle the problems of shipbuilding regions. See Community Regional Policy New Guidelines, Bull EC, Supp 7/77, 5.
276 [1984] OJ L27/15, Art 2.
277 Instituting a specific Community regional development measure contributing to overcoming constraints on the development of new economic activities in certain zones adversely affected by restructuring of the textile and clothing industry ([1984] OJ L27/22).
278 Instituting a specific Community regional development measure contributing to the development of new economic activities in certain zones affected by implementation of the common fisheries policy ([1985] OJ L350/17).
279 Instituting a specific regional development measure contributing to improving security of energy supply in certain Community regions by way of improved use of new techniques for hydro-electrical power and alternative energy sources ([1980] OJ L271/23).
280 Amending Reg 2618/80 ([1984] OJ L27/15).
281 Ibid, Art 2.
282 [1985] OJ L350/17.
283 [1984] OJ L169/1.

According to Article 10(1) of the Regulation, such a programme was to be defined at national level. It was to consist of a series of multiannual measures corresponding to national objectives and serving Community objectives and policies. In particular, it was to assist the convergence of Member States' economies through the reduction of regional disparities and thus to translate into operational commitments the indications contained in regional development programmes.[284]

Community programmes: Regulation 1787/84[285] provided that the Fund could assist Community programmes and that they should have priority in Fund operations.[286] Such a programme was defined as a series of consistent, multiannual measures directly serving Community objectives and the implementation of Community policies.[287] In practice, these programmes generally sought to counteract the regional impact of other Community policies.

The Resider programme was established for steel regions by Regulation 328/88.[288] This programme sought to improve the infrastructure and the physical and social environment in the regions concerned. It also sought to promote the establishment of new activities, the growth of small and medium-sized enterprises, and innovation.[289]

Similarly, the Renaval programme was established for shipbuilding regions by Regulation 2506/88.[290] The programme was to contribute, in the regions concerned, to the removal of obstacles to the development of new, job-creating activities. To this end, the programme was to aim at improving the infrastructure and the physical and social environment in these regions. It was also to promote the establishment of new activities, the growth of small and medium-sized undertakings, and innovation. A better link was thereby sought between Community objectives for the conversion of regions and the objectives of Community policy on shipbuilding.[291]

The Star programme, established by Regulation 3300/86,[292] was different. According to Article 2 of the Regulation, the objectives of this programme were to contribute to strengthening the economic base in the regions

---

284 See paras [698] ff below, regarding such programmes (now known as regional development plans).

285 [1984] OJ L169/1.

286 Ibid, Art 7(6). The Commission had originally proposed that 20% of ERDF resources should be devoted to them (proposal of 29 October 1981 ([1981] OJ C336/60) for a regulation amending Reg 724/75).

287 Art 7(1) of Reg 1787/84 ([1984] OJ L169/1).

288 Instituting a Community programme to assist the conversion of steel areas ([1988] OJ L33/1).

289 Ibid, Art 2.

290 Instituting a Community programme to assist the conversion of shipbuilding areas ([1988] OJ L225/24).

291 Ibid, Art 2.

292 Instituting a Community programme for the development of certain less-favoured regions of the Community by improving access to advanced telecommunications services ([1986] OJ L305/1).

concerned, to foster job creation, and to help raise technological standards in those regions. It was to seek these objectives through improving the supply of advanced telecommunications services and by integrating these regions into large telecommunications networks. The programme was thereby to provide a better link between the Community's objectives for the structural development of regions and the objectives of Community telecommunications policy. Eligible regions were those which satisfied four criteria simultaneously. The criteria were: a particularly difficult economic situation compared with the Community as a whole; peripheral or insular geographical location; inadequate supply of telecommunications services, notably advanced services for the productive sector; and, as a general rule, eligibility under a national regional aid scheme.[293]

Finally, the Valoren programme was established by Regulation 3301/86.[294] This programme concerned regions facing serious energy problems affecting their socio-economic situation. The regions also had to be located in Member States which, because of their structural economic difficulties, found it difficult to meet the energy objectives laid down in the Council Resolution of 16 September 1986.[295] The programme sought to contribute to strengthening the economic base in the regions concerned. It sought to do so by improving local energy supply conditions on satisfactory economic terms, while respecting the objectives of the Community environmental policy, fostering job creation, and raising technological standards in those regions. The programme was thereby to provide a better link between the Community's objectives for the structural development of regions and its energy policy objectives.[296]

Studies: Article 1(1) of the 1973 proposal[297] envisaged that studies undertaken on the initiative of the Commission could be assisted. However, Article 10 of Regulation 724/75[298] stipulated that assisted studies had to be 'closely related to the operations of the Fund and undertaken at the request of a Member State'.[299] The requirement that they be requested by a Member State was removed by Regulation 1787/84.[300]

---

293 Ibid, Art 3(1).
294 Instituting a Community programme for the development of certain less-favoured regions of the Community by exploiting endogenous energy potential ([1986] OJ L305/6).
295 Concerning new Community energy policy objectives for 1995 and convergence of the policies of the Member States ([1986] OJ C241/1).
296 Art 2 of Reg 3301/86 ([1986] OJ L305/6).
297 [1973] OJ C86/7.
298 [1975] OJ L73/1.
299 Art 14 of Reg 214/79 ([1979] OJ L35/1) removed the ceiling of 50% on Commission contributions to the financing of studies.
300 Art 24 of Reg 1787/84 ([1984] OJ L169/1) provided that studies could be funded up to a maximum of 0.5% of the annual ERDF endowment.

Integrated development operations: Integrated development operations[301] were first advocated by the Commission in 1978. They were designed to increase the impact of Community interventions, particularly in regions affected by serious problems.[302] At the same time, they might be seen as countering undesirable compartmentalization between assistance for infrastructure and assistance to productive activities.[303] To these ends, assistance from the Structural Funds and other Community financial instruments for structural purposes was to be combined.[304]

Such operations may be thought to have been essential for the effectiveness of the ERDF, given the link between regional problems and problems with which the other funds were concerned. They might, however, be less attractive to at least some Member States if arrangements for allocation of assistance established by legislation governing the individual funds were undermined. Such legislation, though ostensibly favourable to integrated operations, was careful to avoid prejudicing the 'individuality' of the various funds.

The operations could take the form of development programmes, assisted by the Guidance Section of the European Agricultural Guidance and Guarantee Fund under Article 6(1) of Regulation 729/70.[305] Indeed, Regulation 355/77[306] introduced priority for projects which fell within such programmes and formed part of an integrated approach.[307]

Moreover, in 1981 the Commission introduced priority treatment for operations jointly financed by two or more funds in the Guidelines for the Management of the European Social Fund.[308]

More particularly, in the management of the ERDF, investments and measures which were part of an integrated development approach, for example, in the form of integrated operations or programmes,[309] might,

301 G Bernardini, 'Les Operations integrées de développement communautaire' (1982) RMC 265-71.
302 Procedures and content for the implementation of an integrated approach, COM(86)401.
303 ESC Opinion of 12 July 1989 ([1989] OJ C221/3) on the ERDF thirteenth annual report, para 3.5.
304 Fifth Annual Report on the ERDF (1980), 27; Eighth Annual Report on the ERDF (1983), 79. 4 Preparatory studies were initiated in 1982 (ibid, 80).
305 On the financing of the CAP ([1970] JO L94/13).
306 On common measures to improve the conditions under which agricultural products were processed and marketed ([1977] OJ L51/1).
307 Art 3(1)(f) (ibid) required information regarding the relationship of the programme to any other measures to encourage the harmonious development of the overall economy of the region in question.
308 Para 1.1.2 of the Guidelines for 1981–82 ([1981] OJ C110/2).
309 The concept of 'integrated programmes' did not appear in the Commission proposal of 18 November 1983 ([1983] OJ C360/1) for a regulation amending Reg 724/75. In mentioning this concept, the Council may have been thinking of the IMPs, which were discussed at the time and were subsequently established.

according to Article 34(1) of Regulation 1787/84,[310] have priority for assistance. Article 34(2) of the Regulation defined an integrated development operation as:

> a coherent set of public and private measures and investments which [had] the following characteristics: (a) they relate[d] to a limited geographical area affected by particularly serious problems involving, in particular, delayed development or industrial or urban decline and likely to affect the development of the region in question; (b) the Community, through the joint use of various structural financial instruments, and the national and local authorities in Member States contribute[d] in a closely coordinated manner to their implementation.

The Member State concerned was to ensure concerted use of Community and national financial resources and close coordination between the various public authorities involved in the execution of the operation.[311] The Commission was, likewise, to ensure concerted use of the Structural Funds and other financial instruments of the Community.[312]

Integrated Mediterranean Programmes: In the case of the Integrated Mediterranean Programmes, unified arrangements for the three Structural Funds were embodied in legislation. Such programmes were introduced by Regulation 2088/85.[313] This measure was enacted pursuant to three different EEC Treaty provisions: Article 235 (the original legal basis for the ERDF), Article 43 (agricultural policy), and Article 127 (operations of the European Social Fund).[314]

According to Article 1 of the Regulation, the object of the programmes was to improve the socio-economic structures of the Mediterranean regions,[315] particularly those of Greece. The programmes were thereby to facilitate the adjustment of these regions to the new conditions created by Community enlargement in the best possible conditions. They should comprise multiannual operations which were consistent with one another and with Community policies. According to Article 2(2), the operations had to relate, in particular, to investments in the productive sector, the creation of infrastructures, and better use of human resources.

Finance for the programmes might be drawn from the ERDF, the European Social Fund, the Guidance Section of the European Agricultural Guidance and Guarantee Fund, European Investment Bank loans, New Community

---

310 [1984] OJ L169/1.
311 Art 34(3) of Reg 1787/84 ([1984] OJ L169/1).
312 Ibid, Art 34(4).
313 Concerning the IMPs ([1985] OJ L197/1).
314 See, eg, Dec 86/477 ([1986] OJ L282/21) approving an IMP for Crete.
315 The geographical scope of the IMPs was defined by Annex I to Reg 2088/85 ([1985] OJ L197/1).

Instrument loans, and from additional resources.[316] In particular, Article 551 of the General Budget[317] could be used to provide assistance above the thresholds laid down by the provisions governing the Structural Funds. It could also be used for providing assistance outside the geographical scope of the Funds.[318]

These arrangements were said to constitute a 'qualitative leap forward' from the integrated development operations. They established as a precondition for assistance a programme,[319] the purpose of which was to direct the bulk of available resources towards specific objectives in given regions.[320]

On the other hand, Article 12 of the Regulation provided that loans from the European Investment Bank should be granted according to the specific criteria and procedures applicable to such loans. This provision laid the foundations for a separation of the preparation and management of the programmes from the contribution provided by the Bank.[321] Thus financing by a combination of grants and loans was accepted as a general principle but not put into effect.[322] Even in the case of grants, coordination problems arose.[323] Assistance from the ERDF and assistance under Article 551 of the General Budget were managed globally by annual installments in respect of which advance payments were made. In contrast, assistance from the European Social Fund and assistance to the fisheries sector under Regulation 4028/86[324] were provided on the basis of specific projects.[325]

D. COHESION

The ERDF is now treated as the principal instrument for achieving cohesion. Article 160 EC provides that the purpose of the Fund is to help to redress the main regional imbalances[326] in the Union. It is to do so through participation in the development and structural adjustment of regions whose development is lagging behind and in the conversion of declining industrial regions.

316 Art 3 of Reg 2088/85 ([1985] OJ L197/1).
317 General Budget for 1985 ([1985] OJ L206/3).
318 [1985] OJ L197/1, Art 4.
319 Art 5 of Reg 2088/85 ([1985] OJ L197/1).
320 Report of the Committee on Budgetary Affairs on the IMPs, EP Doc A3-0340/91, 7.
321 See, regarding a general lack of EIB interest in the programmes, the European Parliament Resolution of 17 December 1993 ([1994] OJ C20/515) on the Commission's fifth progress report on IMPs, para 11.
322 Report of the Committee on Budgetary Affairs on the IMPs, EP Doc A3-0340/91, 12.
323 COA special report 4/90 ([1990] OJ C298/1) on the IMPs. Cf COA special report 2/88 ([1988] OJ C188/1) on the integrated approach to Community financing of structural measures.
324 On Community measures to improve and adapt structures in the fisheries and aquaculture sector ([1986] OJ L376/7).
325 IMPs 1988 progress report, SEC(89)1665, 25.
326 This provision originally referred to the 'principal' regional imbalances.

Accordingly, the Fund acquired the 'essential task' of supporting Objectives 1 and 2. It was also to participate in Objective 5b operations[327] and contribute to Objective 6 operations.[328]

1. Original Objectives 1, 2 and 5b

Objective 1 was promoting the development and structural adjustment of regions whose development was lagging behind.[329] It was Objective 1 regions to which the bulk of Union assistance was directed.[330] For the four Member States eligible for assistance under the Cohesion Fund, resources available under this Fund and Objective 1 were to be doubled in real terms between 1992 and 1999.[331]

Objective 2 was converting the regions, frontier regions, or parts of regions (including employment areas and urban communities) seriously affected by industrial decline.[332] According to the preamble to the original version of Regulation 2052/88,[333] action in favour of Objective 2 regions could cover up to 15 per cent of the Community population living outside Objective 1 regions.[334] As amended by Regulation 2081/93,[335] the preamble referred simply to 15 per cent of the Union population.[336]

Objective 5b was, according to Article 1 of the original version of Regulation 2052/88,[337] concerned with promoting rural development by facilitating the structural adjustment of rural areas. As amended by Regulation 2081/93,[338] this provision stated that Objective 5b was concerned with

327 Art 3(1) of Reg 2081/93 ([1993] OJ L193/5) amending Reg 2052/88 on the tasks of the Structural Funds and their effectiveness and on the coordination of their activities between themselves and with the operations of the EIB and the other existing financial instruments.
328 Protocol 6 to the Accession Agreement with Austria, Finland, and Sweden, as amended by Dec 95/1 ([1995] OJ L1/1) adjusting the instruments concerning the accession of new Member States to the EU, Art 1.
329 Art 1.1 of Reg 2081/93 ([1993] OJ L193/5).
330 Ibid, Art 12(2).
331 Ibid, Art 12(4). This provision accorded with the conclusion of the European Council meeting in December 1992 (Bull EC 12-1992, I.55), that Objective 5a commitments outside Objectives 1 and 5b regions were not to increase in real terms. See, regarding the problems involved, COA annual report 1995 ([1996] OJ C340/1), para 5.25.
332 Art 1.2 of Reg 20981/93 ([1993] OJ L193/5).
333 On the tasks of the Structural Funds and their effectiveness and on the coordination of their activities between themselves and with the operations of the EIB and the other existing financial instruments ([1988] OJ L185/9).
334 Ibid, 22nd recital in the preamble.
335 [1993] OJ L193/5.
336 Ibid, 22nd recital in the preamble.
337 [1988] OJ L185/9.
338 [1993] OJ L193/5.

promoting rural development by facilitating the development and structural adjustment of rural areas.[339]

Eligibility for assistance: *Objective 1:* The Commission originally envisaged that account would be taken of the situation of each Member State in determining whether any of its regions qualified for assistance under Objective 1. Hence, a Commission Statement was contained in Annex 2 to the March 1988 version of the proposal for what became Regulation 2052/88.[340] According to this statement, *per capita* GDP of the Member State would be taken into account together with the *per capita* GDP of the region in designating Objective 1 regions.[341]

Regulation 2052/88,[342] as adopted by the Council and subsequently amended by Regulation 2081/93,[343] made no reference to the *per capita* GDP of Member States. Article 8(1) provided that the regions concerned by Objective 1 should be regions at NUTS[344] Level II. Their *per capita* GDP in purchasing power parities,[345] on the basis of the figures for the last three years,[346] must be less than 75 per cent of the Union average.[347] Northern Ireland, the five new German *Länder*, East Berlin,[348] the French overseas departments, the Azores, the Canary Islands, and Madeira should be covered.

339 Establishment of Objective 5ba, which would have been concerned with conservation of the environment and the continuation of farming in certain mountain and less-favoured regions, was advocated by the European Parliament in its Resolution of 20 May 1988 ([1988] OJ C167/443) on the amended Commission proposal for what became Reg 2052/88.

340 COM(88)144.

341 It was also specified that Ireland would be included in those regions.

342 [1988] OJ L185/9.

343 [1993] OJ L193/5.

344 Nomenclature of Territorial Units for Statistical Purposes. NUTS regions basically reflect national administrative classifications. Eg, Länder in Germany are Level I regions; counties in the UK, regions in France and Italy, and provinces in Belgium and the Netherlands are Level II; and nomoi in Greece, Kreise in Germany, and Maakunat in Finland are Level III. According to the ECJ, the whole of the territory of a Member State may be regarded as a single region, provided that such treatment is not manifestly unsuited to the structures of the Member State in question. See Case C-375/96 Galileo Zaninotto v Ispettorato Centrale Repressione Frodi – Ufficio di Conegliano – Ministero delle Risorse Agricole, Alimentari and Forestali [1998] ECR I-6629. Cf the definition of 'region' in Art 1 of Dir 79/109 ([1979] OJ L29/20) amending Dec 64/432 as regards brucellosis. See, now, Reg 1059/2003 ([2003] OJ L154/1) on the establishment of a common classification of territorial units for statistics.

345 21st recital in the preamble to Reg 2052/88 ([1988] OJ L185/9).

346 The European Parliament complained about the lack of a transitional period for regions whose per capita GDP rose slightly above this figure. See the Resolution of 22 January 1993 ([1993] OJ C42/211) on Community structural policies: assessment and outlook ('mid-term review'), para 53. The Council decided in Art 8(1) of Reg 2081/93 ([1993] OJ L193/5) that Abruzzi, where the GDP figure had risen to 89%, would be eligible from 1 January 1994 to 31 December 1995.

347 The figures for the new Länder and Eastern Berlin were not included in the calculation of this average.

348 Its inclusion accorded with the conclusions of the European Council in December 1992 (Bull EC 12-1992, I.55).

Other regions whose *per capita* GDP was close to that of the regions mentioned might be covered by Objective 1 for 'special reasons'. Moreover, in view of their unique adjacent position to Hainaut in Belgium and their regional GDP, at NUTS III, the Council agreed that the *arrondissements* of Avesnes, Douai, and Valenciennes[349] should 'exceptionally' be covered. The Council also agreed that Argyll and Bute, Arran, the Cambrae, and western Moray should be covered.

A list of eligible regions was given in Annex I to the Regulation.[350] This list included regions which were neither specifically mentioned in Article 8(1) nor, in principle, met the GDP criterion laid down therein. In particular, it included Hainaut in Belgium, with a *per capita* GDP of 77 per cent. It also included Merseyside and the Highlands and Islands of Scotland in the United Kingdom, both with a figure of 79 per cent.[351]

Inclusion of Flevoland in the Netherlands, which had a *per capita* GDP of 62 per cent of the Union average, was not proposed by the Commission. According to the Commission, there was 'a lot of anomalies' in the position of this region.[352] Its low GDP figure was largely a consequence of a disassociation between the place of work and the place of residence of the active population. Moreover, except for one city, this region was not eligible under the Dutch regional aid scheme.[353] Nevertheless, its inclusion in the list was agreed by the Council.[354] The impression given is that Council negotiations, which preceded enactment of the legislation, were affected by concern to maximize the number of Member States which could benefit under Objective 1.

Even so, eligible regions were those which were underdeveloped by reference to the average GDP *per capita* for the Union as a whole. However, it was not universally accepted that GDP figures alone were adequate to identify Union regions with the most serious problems. It might be objected, for example, that GDP was only one of a number of relevant indicators, such as employment, emigration, and poverty.[355] The principal indicators of regional

---

349 No GDP figures were available for these regions. See Commission Reply by Mr de Silguy to WQ E-4196/97 ([1998] OJ C323/17) by José García-Margallo y Marfil.

350 A new list might be established by the Council, on a Commission proposal and after consulting the European Parliament, from 2000 (Art 8(3) of Reg 2081/93 ([1993] OJ L193/5)).

351 COA annual report 1995 ([1996] OJ C340/1), Table 5.3. The idea that Molise in Italy and the French island of Corsica, where the figure was also 79%, should be removed from the list (European Report 1831 (30 January 1993)) was not pursued. These regions were peripheral and rural and were originally included in the list because of specific reasons of a technical and political nature. See Structural Funds: amendment of Regs 2052/88 and 4253/88, SEC(93)651, 3.

352 European Report 1831 (30 January 1993).

353 Structural Funds: amendment of Regs 2052/88 and 4253/88, SEC(93)651, 3.

354 The inclusion of Cantabria, where the per capita GDP was of 73% of the Community average (COA annual report 1995 ([1996] OJ C340/1), Table 5.3), was also agreed by the Council.

355 ESC Opinion of 25 May 1992 ([1992] OJ C106/20) on the annual report on the implementation of the reform of the Structural Funds, para 2.2.5.

problems were not the disparities in *per capita* GDP but the disequilibria in the utilization of regional resources.[356]

The only response to such objections seems to have been flexible application of the 75 per cent threshold and acceptance of the eligibility of regions smaller than NUTS Level II.[357] This response did little to address the underlying methodological problems in determination of regional eligibility.

Objective 2: Article 9(2), first paragraph, of Regulation 2052/88[358] provided that regions might be found by the Commission to be eligible for assistance if they represented or belonged to a NUTS Level III region and satisfied three criteria. First, the average rate of unemployment recorded over the last three years must have been above the Union average. Secondly, the percentage share of industrial employment in total employment must have equalled or exceeded the Union average in any reference year from 1975 onwards. Thirdly, there must have been an observable fall in industrial employment compared with that reference year. However, the unemployment rates calculated by Eurostat were thought to give an inaccurate and incomplete picture of the situation in individual regions.[359]

The second paragraph of Article 9(2) of Regulation 2052/88[360] originally provided that assistance might also be granted to:

(a) adjacent areas meeting the same criteria;

(b) urban communities with an unemployment rate at least 50 per cent above the Community average which had recorded a substantial fall in industrial employment; and

(c) other areas which had recorded substantial job losses over the last three years or were experiencing or threatened with such losses in industrial sectors which were vital to their economic development, with a consequent serious worsening of unemployment in those areas.[361]

---

356 R Camagni and R Cappellin, 'Policies for Full employment and More Efficient Utilization of Resources and New Trends in European Regional Development' (1981) Lo Spettatore Internazionale 99-135, 120.

357 The Commission considered that the stronger concentration of Structural Fund operations on Objective 1 (around 70% of total allocations in 1997) should be accompanied by increased flexibility in terms of both the rate of assistance and the eligibility criteria. See Community finances between now and 1997, COM(92)2001, 24. According to Commissioner Millan, 'political considerations' should come into play in the application of the criterion (Europe 5927, 25 February 1993).

358 [1988] OJ L185/9.

359 COR Opinion of 17 September 1998 ([1998] OJ C373/1) on the proposal for a regulation laying down general provisions on the Structural Funds, para 2.1.1.6.

360 [1988] OJ L185/9.

361 These criteria were less 'objective' than those employed for determination of eligibility for state aid under Art 87(3)(c) EC. See A Evans, EC Law of State Aid (Clarendon Press, Oxford, 1997), Chapter 4.

At the same time, Article 9(4) provided that assistance should be genuinely concentrated on the regions most seriously affected, at the most appropriate geographical level, taking into account the particular situation of the regions concerned.

More particularly, according to the March 1988 version of the Commission proposal for what became Regulation 2058/88,[362] the sectors concerned by the second paragraph of Article 9(2) were to be coal, steel, textiles and clothing, and shipbuilding. Other sectors might be considered for assistance where the Commission so decided, having regard to the general developments in those sectors in the Community. The Council, however, was opposed to listing relevant sectors, and so this part of the proposal was not approved by the Council.

While the Council was apparently unwilling to limit Objective 2 to regions with problems in given sectors, it was willing in Article 9(2) to limit this Objective to regions having industrial problems of some kind. Consequently, regions having a share of industrial employment[363] in total employment below the Community average fell outside Objective 2, even if unemployment there was far above the Community average.[364] For example, depressed coastal resorts fell outside, because tourism was not considered industrial.[365] Moreover, certain urban zones fell outside, because their economic and social problems could not be attributed to industrial decline.

The original list of regions falling within Objective 2 was adopted by the Commission in Decision 89/288.[366] For the future, the Commission envisaged that the list of eligible regions would continue to be compiled on the basis of unemployment and industrial employment statistics. However, it was not possible to identify, on the basis of Community statistics, all the regions currently affected by industrial decline.[367] Nor was it possible to allow for the anticipation of the consequences of new industrial change. The Commission sought, therefore, a measure of discretion, to be used in consultation with the Member States concerned, but with no easing of the geographical

---

362 Art 9(3), 2nd para of the amended proposal of 23 March 1988 ([1988] OJ C151/4).

363 Industrial employment was treated as referring to mining and quarrying and utilities, manufacturing, and building and civil engineering. Service industries were not taken into account. See Commission Reply by Mr Millan to WQ 2955/90 ([1991] OJ C195/21) by Lord Inglewood.

364 Commission Reply by Mr Millan to WQ 1445/92 ([1992] OJ C345/19) by Mr Max Simeoni.

365 EEC regional development policy, House of Lords Select Committee on the European Communities, HL(1991–92)20, 16.

366 Establishing an initial list of declining industrial areas concerned by Objective 2 ([1989] OJ L112/19).

367 See, regarding some parts of Western Germany, the European Parliament Resolution of 22 January 1993 ([1993] OJ C42/228) on the regional and social redevelopment plan and the CSF for the areas of Germany included in Objective 2, para 10.

concentration. Otherwise, strict interpretation of the statistics would make it impossible to assist the regions most in need of help.[368]

Accordingly, the third indent of the second paragraph of Article 9(2) was amended by Regulation 2081/93.[369] It now included a reference to job losses caused by industrial changes and changes in production systems, with a consequent serious worsening of unemployment in the areas concerned.[370] The aim was to introduce greater flexibility, allowing areas to be submitted for consideration which a Member State considers to be vulnerable to industrial decline.[371]

Moreover, two new indents were added to the second paragraph of Article 9(2). The first new indent referred to areas, especially urban areas,[372] with severe problems linked to the rehabilitation of large numbers of derelict industrial sites. The second new indent referred to other industrial or urban areas where the socio-economic impact of restructuring of the fisheries sector, assessed on the basis of objective criteria, justified assistance.

In applying this paragraph, the Commission was to take account of how the national situations with respect to unemployment, industrialization and industrial decline compared with the Union average.

These changes to eligibility criteria were accompanied by procedural reforms. Originally, a list of eligible regions was to be established by the Commission after consulting an advisory committee of representatives of the Member States.[373] The procedure for determining regional eligibility was revised in Article 9(3) of Regulation 2081/93.[374] According to this provision, Member States, taking into account the concentration principle in Article 9(4),[375] proposed to the Commission regions to be treated as covered by Objective 2. The Commission decided on the basis of their proposals. It did so after consulting an advisory committee composed of representatives of the Member States. It also took account of national priorities and situations in close consultation with the Member State concerned. The role of the

---

368 From the Single Act to Maastricht and beyond: the means to match our ambitions, COM(92)2000; and Community structural policies: assessment and outlook, COM(92)84, 38.
369 [1993] OJ L193/5.
370 In addition, Art 9(5) (ibid) provided that West Berlin should continue to be eligible for 3 years. This provision reflected the inclusion of the new Länder and East Berlin in Objective 1 and the concern of the Commission to secure coherence in the development efforts for Berlin and Brandenburg as a whole (Community Structural Fund operations 1994–99, COM(93)67, 13).
371 Ibid, 10. The Commission proposal that a reasoned request from the Member State concerned should be necessary (Proposal of 10 March 1993 ([1993] OJ C118/21)) was not accepted by the Council.
372 Eg, an area of Madrid with a population of 5,000 persons was now covered by Objective 2. See Dec 96/472 ([1996] OJ L193/54) establishing the list of declining industrial areas concerned by Objective 2 for the programming period 1997–99.
373 Art 9(3) of Reg 2052/88 ([1988] OJ L185/9).
374 [1993] OJ L193/5.
375 This provision followed Article 9(4) of Reg 2052/88 ([1988] OJ L185/9).

Commission in drawing up the list of eligible regions for Objective 2 was thus reduced. In practice, the Member States proposed the regions and negotiated with the Commission. The outcome of the negotiations, which might be lengthy,[376] was an increased geographical spread of regions found to be eligible.[377]

The negotiations were, presumably, complicated by the fact that many data relevant to the application of the second paragraph of Article 9(2) were not comparable at Union level. Hence, the data only enabled comparisons to be made within each Member State. Therefore, it was not possible to say whether the principle in Article 9(4) was respected.[378]

Objective 5b: Article 11(2) of Regulation 2052/88[379] provided that Objective 5b regions were to be selected by the Commission after consultation of a management committee. The Commission was to take into account, in particular: the degree to which they were rural in character; the number of persons occupied in agriculture; their level of economic and agricultural development; their degree of peripherality; and their sensitivity to changes in the agricultural sector, especially in the context of reform of the common agricultural policy. They did not have to be NUTS Level III regions.

More details were provided in Regulation 4253/88.[380] According to Article 4(1), the regions that might receive assistance under Objective 5b had to satisfy each of three criteria. First, there had to be a high share of agricultural employment in total employment. Secondly, there had to be a low level of agricultural income, notably as expressed in terms of value added by agricultural work unit. Thirdly, there had to be a low level of socio-economic development assessed on the basis of GDP per inhabitant. Moreover, account had to be taken of socio-economic parameters which indicated the seriousness of the general situation in the regions concerned and how it was developing.

It was also provided in Article 4(2) of the same Regulation that, on receipt of a reasoned request from a Member State, assistance might be extended to other rural regions with a low level of socio-economic development on the basis of one or more of the following criteria:

(a) low population density and/or a significant depopulation trend;

(b) peripherality in relation to major centres of economic and commercial activity in the Community;

376 New regional programmes 1997-9 under Objective 2, COM(97)524, 4.
377 Commission Reply by Mrs Wulf-Matthies to WQ E-0303/97 ([1997] OJ C367/11) by Amedeo Amadeo. See also COA annual report 1995 ([1996] OJ C340/1), para 5.27.
378 COA annual report 1995 ([1996] OJ C340/1), para 5.29.
379 [1988] OJ L185/9.
380 Laying down provisions for implementing Reg 2052/88 as regards coordination of the activities of the different Structural Funds between themselves and with the operations of the EIB and the other existing financial instruments ([1988] OJ L374/1).

(c) sensitivity to developments in agriculture, especially in the context of reform of the common agricultural policy, assessed on the basis of the trend in agricultural incomes and the size of the agricultural labour force;

(d) pressures exerted on the environment and on the countryside; and

(e) status as mountain or less-favoured regions classified pursuant to Directive 75/268.[381]

In applying these criteria, the Commission was required by Article 4(4) of the Regulation to ensure that assistance was effectively concentrated on regions suffering from the most serious problems of rural development.[382] Subject to this general requirement, it seems that rural problems other than that of the low *per capita* GDP traditionally associated with the peripheral regions could be tackled.

Certainly, the Commission considered that *per capita* GDP was 'neither a sufficient measure of the gravity of the situation of the regions concerned nor a suitable instrument for determining the allocation of assistance among the various regions'.[383] 'Very qualitative' assessments, which left the authorities broad discretion and favoured political compromises, might be preferred.[384]

In the event, the regions originally selected, and listed by the Commission in Decision 89/426,[385] were in Belgium, Denmark, France, Germany, Italy, Luxembourg, the Netherlands, Spain, and the United Kingdom. These regions were smaller than those of NUTS Level III. Moreover, the Commission sought to reduce overlaps between Objective 2 and Objective 5b regions, while limiting the coverage of Objective 2 regions to 15 per cent of the Community population. A result was fragmentation of the regions found to be eligible under Objective 5b.[386]

Intervention in such regions needed, according to the Commission, to be 'boosted'. While assistance should be directed towards all rural regions of the Community, it should be concentrated where the needs were greatest and the capacity to contribute at the national level was weakest.[387] To this end, the criteria for what constituted an eligible region should be applied more flexibly

---

381 See paras [409] ff below. The ESC favoured establishment of an ERDF programme for upland areas in its Opinion of 28 April 1988 ([1988] OJ C175/47) on a policy for upland areas, para 6.4.4.
382 Concentration was to take place within the context of reform of the CAP, but this requirement was removed in Art 11a(4) of Reg 2081/93 ([1993] OJ L193/5).
383 COA annual report for 1991, [1992] OJ C330/1, para 7.18 (Commission reply).
384 D Gadbin, 'Le Droit communautaire des structures agricoles: organisation ou dilution?' (1991) RMC 218–30, 224.
385 Selecting rural areas eligible to receive Community assistance under Objective 5b ([1989] OJ L198/1).
386 COA annual report for 1991 ([1992] OJ C330/1), para 5.2.1.
387 Commission Reply by Mr MacSharry to WQ 2860/91 ([1992] OJ C168/24) by Mr John Cushnahan.

and the range of measures broadened.[388] Particular attention should be paid to problems of rural exodus.[389] Accordingly, studies were carried out regarding definition of Objective 5b regions.[390]

However, the problems raised might not be simply those of such definition. In particular, Highlands and Islands Enterprise, the body responsible for development of the Highlands and Islands, argued that this was a region of extreme peripherality and sparsity of population. Hence, Objective 5b, under which it was originally classified, did not suit its needs.[391] Such considerations seem subsequently to have been recognized by the Council, in that this region came to be included within Objective 1.

On the other hand, only limited changes to the definition of Objective 5b regions were made by Regulation 2081/93.[392] The regions that might now receive assistance under Objective 5b were those which had a low level of socio-economic development assessed on the basis of GDP per inhabitant and satisfied at least two of the following criteria:

(a) high share of agricultural employment in total employment;

(b) low level of agricultural income, notably as expressed in terms of agricultural value added by agricultural work unit; and

(c) low population density and/or a significant depopulation trend.[393]

Other regions with a low level of socio-economic development might receive Objective 5b assistance,[394] if they were affected by one or more of six listed criteria. These criteria were the same as those in Article 4(2) of Regulation 4253/88,[395] except that the depopulation criterion was now moved to the first paragraph, and two new criteria were added. The new criteria were the structure of agricultural holdings and the age structure of the gainfully employed agricultural labour force, and the socio-economic impact on the region, as measured by objective criteria, of the restructuring of the fisheries sector.[396]

These changes to eligibility criteria were accompanied by procedural reforms. According to Article 11a(3) of Regulation 2081/93,[397] Member States proposed to the Commission the regions which, in their view, met these criteria and provided the Commission with all useful information to this end. On the basis of this information and its overall assessment of the proposals

---

388 Community finances between now and 1997, COM(92)2001, 24.

389 Europe 5927 (25 February 1993).

390 Commission Reply by Mr MacSharry to WQ 1039/91 ([1991] OJ C315/26) by Mr Verbeek.

391 EEC regional development policy, House of Lords Select Committee on the European Communities, HL(1991–92)20, 17–18.

392 [1993] OJ L193/5.

393 Ibid, Art 11a(1).

394 A reasoned request from a Member State was no longer required.

395 [1988] OJ L374/1.

396 Art 11a(2) of Reg 2081/93 ([1993] OJ L193/5).

397 [1993] OJ L193/5.

submitted, the Commission established the list of eligible areas.[398] It must take into account national priorities and situations, act in close consultation with the Member State concerned, and consult a management committee.

Allocation of assistance: *Objective 1:* Article 12(6) of Regulation 2052/88[399] provided that, to facilitate the planning of assistance in the regions concerned, the Commission should, for a period of five years and as a guide, establish allocations by Member State of 85 per cent of Fund resources. These allocations were to be based on the socio-economic criteria determining the eligibility of regions for Fund assistance under Objectives 1, 2, and 5b. The Commission was also to ensure that there was a substantial increase in assistance in Objective 1 regions, particularly the least prosperous.

The allocations were originally established by Decision 89/250.[400] They might not be entirely uncontroversial. For example, the Northern Ireland authorities were disappointed that their allocation did not reflect the doubling of the Structural Funds. They complained that Northern Ireland had been granted Objective 1 status for non-economic reasons, but the Commission based the allocation largely on economic criteria. According to the Commission, the allocation could not be increased, because Northern Ireland was the most prosperous of the Objective 1 regions.[401]

Article 12(4) of Regulation 2081/93[402] provided that the Commission should, using transparent procedures, make indicative allocations by Member State for each of Objectives 1 to 4 and 5b of Structural Fund assistance. Full account, 'as previously', was to be taken of national prosperity; regional prosperity; population of the regions and the relative severity of structural problems, including the level of unemployment; and, as appropriate, the needs of rural development. These criteria were to be 'appropriately' weighted in the allocation of assistance.

In practice, the allocations, as established by Decision 93/589,[403] were apparently distorted by 'non-transparent factors'. For example, the allocations to Greece and Portugal were identical. However, there were considerable disparities between these two Member States, as regards population, GDP, rate of unemployment, and rate of industrial activity.[404]

---

398 Dec 94/197 ([1994] OJ L96/1) establishing, for 1994–99, the list of rural areas under Objective 5b.

399 [1988] OJ L185/9.

400 Fixing an indicative allocation between Member States of 85% of the commitment appropriations of the ERDF under Objective 1 ([1989] OJ L101/41).

401 EEC regional development policy, House of Lords Select Committee on the European Communities, HL(1991–92)20, 19.

402 [1993] OJ L193/5.

403 Fixing an indicative allocation between Member States of the commitment appropriations of the Structural Funds and FIFG under Objective 1 ([1993] OJ L280/30).

404 COA annual report 1995 ([1996] OJ C340/1), Table 5.3, n (e).

More fundamentally, Council definition of each Objective and, more particularly, its determination of regions covered by Objective 1 might limit the scope of effective Commission discretion in application of the criteria for establishing the allocations. In fact, Member States apparently insisted on firm guarantees regarding their allocations before adopting any Commission proposals in the Council.[405] To this extent, the real distinction between indicative allocations and the earlier quotas should not, perhaps, be exaggerated.

Objective 2: According to Commission Decision 89/289,[406] most Objective 2 assistance was allocated to the United Kingdom, Spain, and France. However, all the more developed Member States received some assistance.

There was no direct proportionality between the allocations and the seriousness of unemployment in the regions concerned.[407] In the case of Luxembourg, the national unemployment rate had been around 1.6 per cent since 1983. However, the employment situation in the two eligible regions could not be measured directly and was 'masked' by the national figure. In the period from 1986 to 1989 alone, over 2,700 jobs had been lost, and new reductions (of about 2,000 jobs) had been announced by the steel industry for 1990 to 1992. Moreover, the economic situation in the South of the country had implications for the industrial areas just across the border, especially in view of the close links with the Longwy area. On these grounds, the allocation of assistance was considered justified.[408]

The Commission based its subsequent allocation of Objective 2 assistance[409] on the population in each Member State's eligible regions compared with the total Union population eligible for such assistance. It then combined these figures with the unemployment rate of each region as a proportion of the average unemployment rate across all the Objective 2 areas.[410]

Objective 5b: Most assistance under Objective 5b was allocated to France and Germany.[411] However, the allocations were criticized on the ground that the amount of assistance was calculated on a *per capita* basis.[412] In fact, it was calculated by reference to the total population of each region covered, adjusted

---

405 European Report 1872 (3 July 1993).

406 Fixing an indicative allocation between Member States of 85% of the commitment operations of the ERDF under Objective 2 ([1989] OJ L113/29).

407 COA annual report for 1991 ([1992] OJ C330/1), 122.

408 CSF 1989-91 for Converting the Regions Affected by Industrial Decline, Luxembourg (1990), 11.

409 Dec 94/176 ([1994] OJ L82/35) fixing an indicative allocation by Member State of Structural Fund commitment appropriations under Objective 2.

410 European Report 1921 (29 January 1994).

411 Dec 89/379 ([1989] OJ L180/54) fixing an indicative allocation between Member States of 85% of the commitment appropriations of the ERDF under Objective 5b.

412 The future of rural society, House of Lords Select Committee on the European Communities, HL(1989-90)80-I, 33.

to take account of the impact of the reform of the common agricultural policy on employment in the respective agricultural sectors. Hence, the amount of assistance allocated to underpopulated regions would be less than that allocated to more densely populated regions.[413]

A more particular problem for rural regions in more developed Member States might result from Article 13 of Regulation 2081/93.[414] According to this provision, assistance was to be differentiated taking into account, *inter alia*, the financial capacity of the Member State concerned. Such capacity was to be assessed in the light of, in particular, the relative prosperity of that Member State.

Scope of assistance: The scope of the assistance which the ERDF might provide was outlined in Article 1 of Regulation 2083/93.[415]

Productive investment: The Fund might assist productive investment, to enable permanent jobs to be created or maintained.[416] However, the regional development impact of such investment might be limited, because the proportion of supplies bought within the assisted regions might not be significant. Hence, a substantial part of the income multiplier effect of assistance to these regions might effectively benefit advanced regions.[417] Even where purchases within the former regions were reasonably important in quantitative terms, the products bought might be mainly raw materials or products which had only been slightly processed with little exploitation of existing industrial capabilities being entailed. Therefore, the assistance might do little to secure the self-sustained growth of these regions.[418] The assistance might even adversely affect local labour markets, jeopardizing the small, local industrial activities already in existence.

Infrastructure investment: The Fund might assist the creation or modernization of infrastructure which contributed to the development or conversion of the regions concerned.[419] A broader range of investments might be supported in Objective 1 regions than in Objective 2 or 5b regions.

In Objective 1 regions, infrastructure investments contributing to increasing the economic potential, development and structural adjustment of these regions might be supported. Where appropriate, investments

---

413 This criterion meant that the Highlands and Islands region was effectively penalized by its sparsity of population. See EEC regional development policy, House of Lords Select Committee on the European Communities, HL(1991–92)20, 17.

414 [1993] OJ L193/5.

415 Amending Reg 4254/88 laying down provisions for implementing Reg 2052/88 as regards the ERDF ([1993] OJ L193/34).

416 Regulation 2083/93, Art 1(a).

417 RP Camagni, 'Development Scenarios and Policy Guidelines for the Lagging Regions in the 1990s' (1992) Regional Studies 361–74.

418 Cf, regarding lack of lasting effects of Union assistance, COA special report 15/98 ([1998] OJ C347/1) on the assessment of Structural Fund intervention for the 1989–93 and 1994–99 periods, para 7.3.

419 Art 1(b) of Reg 2083/93 ([1993] OJ L193/34).

contributing to the establishment and development of trans-European networks in the areas of transport,[420] telecommunications and energy infrastructures might be included. Where the need was demonstrated, financing might also be provided for investments in education and health which contribute to structural adjustment.[421]

In Objective 2 regions the Fund might assist infrastructure investments relating to the regeneration of regions suffering from industrial decline, including inner cities. It might also assist infrastructure investments which provided the basis for the creation or development of economic activity in such regions. In Objective 5b regions the Fund might assist infrastructure investments directly linked to economic activity which created jobs other than in agriculture, including communications infrastructure on which the development of such activity depended.

'*Endogenous development*': The Fund might assist measures to exploit the potential for internally generated development of the regions concerned. Such measures were those which encouraged and supported local development initiatives and the activities of small and medium-sized enterprises. They might include: assistance towards services for firms, particularly in the fields of management, study and research of markets, and services common to several firms; financing the transfer of technology, particularly the collection and dissemination of information and the introduction of innovations in firms; improvement of access for firms to the capital market, particularly by the provision of guarantees and equity participation; direct assistance to investment; and the provision of small-scale infrastructure.[422]

At least in the context of assistance to Objective 2 regions, the Fund was criticized for paying insufficient attention to development of the endogenous potential of such regions.[423] According to this criticism, in periods of stagnation traditional infrastructure projects were unlikely to attract new industry to an assisted region and, in any case, other regions also had the necessary infrastructure.[424]

Other assistance: The Fund might assist the financing of two further kinds of investment. It might assist investment contributing to regional development

420 See also Trans-European networks 1997 annual report, COM(1998)391, 16.

421 Art 1(d) of Reg 2083/93 ([1993] OJ L193/34). See also Art 3(1)(d) of Reg 2081/93 ([1993] OJ L193/5).

422 Reg 2081/93 ([1993] OJ L193/5), Art 3(1)(c).

423 M Quévit, J Houard, S Bodson, and A Dangoisse, Impact régional 1992: les régions de tradition industrielle (De Boeck, Brussels, 1991), 338. Cf, regarding the concentration of ECSC assistance on restructuring, ibid, 341, and regarding the concentration of EIB loans on physical infrastructure projects, ibid, 344. See, generally, regarding the assistance which used to be provided under the ECSC Treaty, A Evans, The EU Structural Funds (Oxford University Press, 1999), 185–93.

424 Insofar as such assistance went to the productive sector, it related to restructuring rather than conversion. See the COA annual report for 1986 ([1987] OJ C336/1), para 9.11.

in the field of research and technology.[425] It might also assist productive investment and investment in infrastructure aimed at environmental protection, according to the principles of sustainable development, where such investment was linked with regional development.[426]

Forms of assistance: Assistance from the Fund was to be provided in a variety of forms, including non-repayable direct assistance, repayable assistance, interest-rate subsidies, guarantees, equity holdings, and venture-capital holdings, that reflected the nature of the operations concerned.[427] By a qualified majority and on a proposal from the Commission the Council might introduce other forms of assistance of the same type.[428]

Projects: The Fund might contribute to the financing of projects. The projects might concern productive investments, to enable permanent jobs to be created or maintained,[429] or investments in infrastructure.[430]

Regional aid schemes: Fund assistance to regional aid schemes of Member States should constitute one of the main forms of incentive to investment in firms.[431] To decide the financial participation of the Fund, the Commission examined, with the competent authorities designated by the Member State, the characteristics of the aid scheme concerned. Account was to be taken of: the relationship between the rate of aid and the socio-economic situation of the regions concerned and the consequent locational disadvantages for firms; the relationship between operating procedures and the types of assistance, including rates, and the needs to be met; the priority given to small and medium-sized enterprises and to the encouragement of services supplied to them, such as management advice and market surveys; the economic repercussions of the aid scheme; and the characteristics and impact of any other regional aid scheme in the same region.[432]

Regional operational programmes: The Fund might contribute to the financing of regional operational programmes.[433] Such a programme meant the document approved by the Commission to implement a Community Support Framework. It must be composed of a consistent set of priorities and comprise multiannual measures. It might be implemented through recourse to one or more of the Structural Funds, one or more of the other financial

---

425 Art 1(e) of Reg 2083/93 ([1993] OJ L193/34). The original Commission proposal of 12 March 1993 (COM(93)67) had envisaged an express reference to the contribution of such measures to the implementation of the Framework Programmes for R & D.
426 Art 1(f) of Reg 2083/93 ([1993] OJ L193/34).
427 Art 5(1) of Reg 2081/93 ([1993] OJ L193/5).
428 Ibid, Art 5(2).
429 Art 1(a) of Reg 2083/93 ([1993] OJ L193/34).
430 Ibid, Art 1(b).
431 Art 4(1) of Reg 2083/93 ([1993] OJ L193/34).
432 Ibid, Art 4(2).
433 Art 3 of Reg 2083/93 ([1993] OJ L193/34).

instruments, and the European Investment Bank.[434] Where recourse was had to a Union fund additional to the ERDF, an integrated approach might be employed.[435]

Global grants: On the initiative of the Member State or the Commission in agreement with the Member State concerned,[436] the Fund might finance global grants.[437] Their management was entrusted to appropriate intermediaries, including regional development bodies designated by the Member State in agreement with the Commission. These grants should be used primarily to assist local development initiatives. The intermediaries must be present or represented in the regions concerned, operate in the public interest, and associate adequately the socio-economic interests directly concerned by the implementation measures planned.[438]

Studies and pilot schemes: The Fund might, using up to 1 per cent of its annual budget, contribute to the financing of studies and pilot schemes.[439] According to Article 10(1)(a) of Regulation 2083/93,[440] such studies should be undertaken on the initiative of the Commission. They should aim to identify the spatial consequences of measures planned by the national authorities, particularly major infrastructures, when their effects went beyond national boundaries; measures aiming to correct specific problems of the border regions within and outside the Union; and the elements necessary to establish a prospective outline of the utilization of Union territory.

Pilot schemes should, according to Article 10(1)(b) of the same Regulation, constitute incentives to the creation of infrastructure, investment in firms, and other specific measures having a marked Union interest,[441] particularly in border regions within and outside the Union. They should also encourage the

---

434 Art 5(5) of Reg 2081/93 ([1993] OJ C193/5).
435 Art 13(1) of Reg 2082/93 ([1993] OJ L193/20).
436 See para [260] below, regarding global grants introduced on the initiative of the Commission.
437 Art 6(3) of Reg 2083/93 ([1993] OJ L193/34).
438 Ibid, Art 6(1).
439 The regions concerned need not fall within the geographical scope of Objective 1, 2 or 5b. A list of studies and pilot projects financed under Art 10 of Reg 4254/88 ([1988] OJ L374/15) was provided in the Commission Reply to WQ 1866/90 ([1991] OJ C90/24) by Mr JG Urizza.
440 [1993] OJ L193/34.
441 See, eg, Call for proposals for pilot actions aiming at integrating the concept of the information society into regional development policies of less-favoured regions ([1996] OJ C253/27).

pooling of experience and development cooperation between different Union regions[442] and innovative measures.[443]

For example, the Recite (Regions and cities of Europe) programme concerned cooperation networks for the realization of joint economic projects.[444] The selected projects were those designed to involve, as far as possible, networks representing partners from strong and weak regions. Again, the Ecos-Ouverture (Cooperation network with Central and Eastern European countries) programme[445] was designed to encourage regions, particularly the less developed regions of the Union, to establish links and to cooperate with counterparts in Eastern Europe. Under this programme the Fund, along with Phare, supported the establishment of various cooperation networks.

Technical assistance: The Fund might finance, up to a limit of 0.5 per cent of its annual budget, preparatory, accompanying, and assessment measures necessary for implementation of Regulation 2083/93.[446] The measures might be carried out by the Commission or by outside experts.[447] They should include studies, among them general studies concerning Union regional action, and technical assistance or information measures, including measures to provide information for local and regional development agents.[448] They might be embodied within sub-programmes of regional operational programmes or added to Community Support Frameworks.[449]

Community initiatives: Community initiatives might be adopted by the Commission under Article 11(1) of Regulation 2082/93[450] and Article 3(2) of Regulation 2083/93.[451] The former provision stated that the Commission might, on its own initiative, propose to the Member States that they apply for assistance in respect of measures of significant interest to the Union which

442 See, eg, Call for proposals from networks of regional and local authorities wishing to implement joint pilot inter-regional cooperation projects for economic development in the cultural field ([1996] OJ C253/26); and Networks of local regional authorities to carry out innovative and/or demonstrative pilot projects on spatial planning in specific areas ([1996] OJ C119/9).

443 See, eg, Innovative measures: new sources of employment, particularly local employment initiatives – call for proposals ([1996] OJ C253/29).

444 Call for network proposals from regional and local authorities wishing to carry out joint economic projects ([1991] OJ C198/8); and Recite II Call for proposals ([1996] OJ C326/9).

445 European Report 1728 (11 December 1991); and Ecos-Ouverture 1997–99 ([1997] OJ C125/5) and Ecos-Ouverture 1998–2001 ([1998] OJ C183/26). Cf the Med-Urbs programme ([1993] OJ C140/8), which supported cooperation between local authorities in the Union and those of Mediterranean non-Member States through networks.

446 [1993] OJ L193/34.

447 Ibid, Art 7(1).

448 Ibid.

449 COA annual report for 1993 ([1994] OJ C327/1), para 7.68.

450 Amending Reg 4253/88 laying down provisions for implementing Reg 2052/88 as regards coordination of the activities of the different Structural Funds between themselves and with the operations of the EIB and the other existing financial instruments ([1993] OJ L193/20).

451 [1993] OJ L193/34.

were not covered by regional development plans. Up to 1.9 per cent of Structural Fund resources might be devoted to such initiatives.[452]

For a limited part of the resources available, Community initiatives might apply to regions other than those eligible for assistance under Objectives 1, 2 and 5b.[453] In the view of the Commission, the flexibility entailed assisted it in responding to new economic and social problems as they arose, including unforeseen industrial problems, which might not necessarily occur in eligible regions.[454] In other words, effective pursuit of cohesion might be found to demand exceptions from basic Union criteria for eligibility for assistance. However, this feature of Community initiatives, given the limited resources available for their implementation, might be more an indication of, than a solution to, underlying problems in the legislation governing the operations of the Fund.

The initiatives were designed to help resolve problems common to certain categories of region; to help resolve serious problems directly associated with the implementation of other Union policies and affecting the socio-economic situation of one or more regions; or to promote the application of Union policies at regional level.[455]

Four initiatives were designed to help resolve problems common to certain categories of region. The Regis initiative[456] concerned Guadeloupe, French Guyana, Martinique, Réunion, the Canary Islands, the Azores, and Madeira. These regions were selected because of their great distance from the rest of the Union; their economic dependence, in most cases, on tropical agriculture; and their proximity to third countries which were party to preferential trade agreements with the Union. The initiative was designed to speed up adaptation of the economies of the regions, so that they might be better integrated into the internal market.

The Leader (Links between actions for the development of the rural economy) initiative[457] concerned rural regions more generally. It sought to encourage integrated rural development at local level, through the allocation of global grants to local rural development action groups. The grants were to be used to assist the organization of rural development and the provision of information on all Union measures and finance likely to encourage rural development in the regions covered by the group; vocational training and

---

452 Art 12(5) of Reg 2081/93 ([1993] OJ L193/5).

453 Art 11(2) of Reg 2082/93 ([1993] OJ L193/20).

454 Difficulties met in the implementation of the Interreg initiative (see para [209] below), where crossborder cooperation between eligible and non-eligible areas was involved, might also be removed. See Community Structural Funds 1994–99, COM(93)67, 22.

455 Art 3(2) of Reg 2083/93 ([1993] OJ L193/34).

456 Notice laying down guidelines for operational programmes in the framework of a Community initiative concerning the most remote regions ([1990] OJ C196/15).

457 Notice laying down guidelines for integrated global grants in the framework of a Community initiative for rural development ([1991] OJ C73/33).

employment measures; rural tourism; small firms, craft enterprises and local services; and exploitation and marketing of local agricultural products.

In contrast, the Urban initiative[458] was directed towards regions that were densely populated, with a minimum size of population, a high level of unemployment, a decayed urban fabric, bad housing conditions, and a lack of social amenities.

Finally, the Interreg initiative[459] concerned cooperation between regions. It aimed to assist both internal and external border regions of the Union in overcoming the special development problems arising from their relative isolation within national economies and within the Union as a whole, in the interests of the local population and in a manner compatible with the protection of the environment; to promote the creation and development of networks of cooperation across internal borders and, where relevant, the linking of these networks to wider Union networks, in the context of the completion of the internal market; to assist the adjustment of external border regions to their new role as border regions of a single integrated market; and to respond to new opportunities for cooperation with third countries in external border regions of the Union.[460]

Five further initiatives were designed to help resolve serious problems directly associated with the implementation of other Union policies and affecting the socio-economic situation of one or more regions. Resider II[461] sought to assist the conversion of steel regions. Eligible regions must be covered by Objective 1, 2, or 5b[462] and be steel production regions as defined under the ECSC Treaty.[463] Assistance might cover environmental improvement; renovation and modernization of social and economic infrastructure; promotion of alternative economic activities; construction of new, advanced factory units and workshop premises; promotion of tourist activities, especially those based on industrial heritage; promotion of economic conversion bodies and regional development teams; and vocational training and employment measures.

458 Notice laying down guidelines for operational programmes in the framework of a Community initiative concerning urban areas ([1994] OJ C180/6), para II.10. The European Parliament had inserted Item B2-1405 in the Budget for 1994 ([1994] OJ L34/3), entitled 'urban policy' within the Chapter on Community initiatives.
459 Notice laying down guidelines for operational programmes in the framework of a Community initiative concerning border areas ([1990] OJ C215/4).
460 See, in connection with Andorra, the Commission Reply by Mrs Wulf-Matthies to WQ ([1996] OJ C280/65) by Joan Vallre.
461 Notice laying down guidelines for operational programmes or global grants in the framework of a Community initiative concerning the economic conversion of steel areas ([1994] OJ C180/22).
462 Ibid, para II.5.
463 Ibid, para II.6.

Similarly, the Rechar II initiative[464] sought to assist the conversion of coal-mining regions. It was adopted because many such regions were amongst those which had been or were likely to be hardest hit by problems of industrial restructuring. They also had special difficulties in adjusting rapidly to changing economic circumstances.[465] Eligible regions must be included in a list of eligible regions drawn up by the Commission and, in principle, must fall within Objective 1, 2 or 5b.[466]

The adoption of this initiative affected the operation of the Structural Funds even to the extent of requiring a redesignation of Objective 2 regions. This redesignation concerned certain parts of coal-mining regions in Germany, France and the United Kingdom.[467] It highlighted the possibility that in some cases at least assistance from the ERDF was employed to solve what were really sectoral problems. Such assistance was said to exacerbate regional inequality, since the poorest regions of the Union might have no eligible industries.[468]

The Retex initiative[469] concerned regions heavily dependent on the textiles and clothing industry. However, unlike Resider II and Rechar II, it was not limited to assisting conversion. It might also assist modernization of the textile industry.

The Pesca initiative[470] concerned the restructuring of the fishing industry. It recognized that changes in this sector were necessitated by a structural crisis of unprecedented seriousness.[471] It aimed to enable these changes to be effected successfully, to help the sector to cope with the attendant social and economic consequences, and to contribute to the diversification of the regions concerned by developing job-creating activities.[472]

Finally, the Konver initiative[473] sought to assist the diversification of economic activities in regions heavily dependent on the defence industry and

---

464 Notice laying down guidelines for operational programmes in the framework of a Community initiative concerning the economic conversion of coal-mining areas ([1994] OJ C180/26).

465 Ibid, para 3.

466 Ibid, para II.5.

467 Dec 90/400 ([1990] OJ L206/26) amending Dec 89/288 establishing an initial list of declining industrial areas concerned by Objective 2.

468 The Regional Impact of Community Policies (Regional Policy and Transport Series No 17, European Parliament, Luxembourg, 1991), 11.

469 Notice laying down guidelines for operational programmes within the framework of a Community initiative for regions heavily dependent on the textiles and clothing sector ([1992] OJ C142/5).

470 Notice laying down guidelines for global grants or integrated operational programmes within the framework of a Community initiative concerning the restructuring of the fisheries sector ([1994] OJ C180/1).

471 Ibid, para I.4.

472 Ibid, para I.6.

473 Notice laying down guidelines for operational programmes or global grants in the framework of a Community initiative concerning defence conversion ([1994] OJ C180/18).

to encourage the adjustment of commercially viable businesses in all industrial sectors. A maximum of 50 per cent of the total Union assistance under this initiative might be granted to regions not eligible under Objective 1, 2 or 5b.[474]

Three initiatives were designed to promote the application of Union policies at regional level. The Télématique initiative[475] concerned the accessibility of advanced telecommunications services. It was designed to promote the use of such services in Objective 1 regions, including improved access to advanced services located elsewhere in the Union. Again, the Stride initiative[476] sought to strengthen the research, technological, and innovatory capacity of Objective 1 regions. This initiative was to be coordinated with other Union actions in favour of research and development,[477] especially those within Community Support Frameworks, the Framework Programme for research and development, and the Sprint programme.[478] The Prisma initiative[479] sought, in turn, to assist enterprises in Objective 1 regions to adapt to the completion of the internal market, so that they could benefit fully from the opportunities which arose.

The SME initiative, for small and medium-sized enterprises, was designed to take over the tasks of Télématique, Stride and Prisma. It aimed to stimulate such enterprises, particularly in the less-developed regions, to adapt to the single market and to became internationally competitive.[480]

Finally, the Envireg initiative[481] acknowledged the link between regional development and the resolution of environmental problems. It aimed to help the least-favoured regions to tackle their environmental problems and thereby put their economic and social development on a firmer footing.[482]

Integrated development operations: At the initiative of a Member State or of the Commission in agreement with the Member State concerned, assistance might be implemented as an integrated approach. Three conditions must be met for adoption of such an approach. First, financing by more than one

474 Ibid, para III.8.

475 Notice laying down guidelines for operational programmes in the framework of a Community initiative for regional development concerning services and networks related to data communication ([1991] OJ C33/7).

476 Notice C(90)1562/2 ([1990] OJ C196/18) laying down guidelines for operational programmes in the framework of a Community initiative concerning regional capacities for research, technology, and innovation.

477 Ibid, para 3.

478 See paras [588] ff below.

479 Notice laying down guidelines for operational programmes in the framework of a Community initiative concerning the preparation of enterprises for the single market ([1991] OJ C33/9).

480 Notice laying down guidelines for operational programmes or global grants in the framework of a Community initiative concerning the adaptation of SMEs to the single market ([1994] OJ C180/10).

481 Notice laying down guidelines for operational programmes within the framework of a Community initiative concerning the environment ([1990] OJ C115/3).

482 Ibid, para 4.

Structural Fund or at least one Structural Fund and one financial instrument other than a loan instrument must be involved.[483] Secondly, the measures to be financed must be mutually reinforcing, and significant benefits must be likely to accrue from close coordination between all the parties involved. Thirdly, appropriate administrative structures must be provided at national, regional and local level in the interests of integrated implementation of these measures.

The desirability of adopting an integrated approach should be considered when a Community Support Framework was established or revised.[484] In the implementation of such an approach, the Commission should ensure that Union assistance was provided in the most effective manner, taking into account the special coordination effort required.[485] However, the Commission was criticized for tending to rely more on 'multifund operational plans', made up of sub-programmes, each managed by one fund.[486]

2. Objective 6

The northern parts of Finland and Sweden exhibited problems of low population density, unfavourable climate, and peripherality. However, they might fail to qualify as Objective 1 or even Objective 5b regions by reference to *per capita* GDP.[487] They might also benefit little from Objective 2 assistance, because there was limited industry to decline and unemployment problems might not be serious by Union standards.

To cater for these regional problems, Objective 6[488] was created. This Objective covered regions of Finland[489] and Sweden[490] with a population density of no more than 8 persons per square kilometre.[491] Objective 1 rules applied to regions covered by Objective 6.[492]

---

483 Art 13(1) of Reg 2082/93 ([1993] OJ L193/20). Eg, the IDO for Merseyside brought together the ERDF and the ESF to co-finance a programme for 1989–91. See the Commission Reply by Mr Millan to WQ 1776/91 ([1992] OJ C78/24) by Mr Kenneth Stewart.

484 Art 13(2) of Reg 2082/93 ([1993] OJ L193/20).

485 Ibid, Art 13(3).

486 Report of the Committee on Budgetary Control on the management of the budget of the Structural Funds within the framework of the reform: assessment and outlook, EP Doc A-0191/92, 12.

487 Note the GDP figures for Swedish regions published in Norrbotten inför EG-förhandlingen (Lanstyrelsen Norrbottens län, Luleå, 1992).

488 European Report 1928 (23 February 1993).

489 Dec 95/360 ([1995] OJ L208/13) on the approval of the SPD for Community structural assistance in the regions concerned by Objective 6 in Finland.

490 Dec 96/116 ([1996] OJ L33/1) on the approval of the SPD for Community structural assistance in the regions concerned by Objective 6 in Sweden.

491 Protocol 6 to the Accession Agreement, as amended by Dec 95/1 ([1995] OJ L1/1) adjusting the instruments concerning the accession of new Member States to the EU.

492 Ibid, Art 4.

3. New Objectives 1 and 2

Objective 1 is now promoting the development and structural adjustment of regions whose development is lagging behind. Objective 2 is supporting the economic and social conversion of areas facing structural difficulties. Assistance under Objective 5b is replaced by assistance under the new Objective 2.[493] Objective 6 regions will be assisted under Objective 1.[494] This reduction in the number of 'priority objectives' is designed to 'increase the concentration and simplify the operation of the Structural Funds'.[495]

Eligibility for assistance: *Objective 1:* The regions covered by Objective 1 shall be NUTS Level II regions whose *per capita* GDP, measured in purchasing power parities and calculated on the basis of Union figures for the last three years available on 26 March 1999, is less than 75 per cent of the Union average. The outermost regions (the French overseas departments, the Azores, the Canary Islands and Madeira), which are all below the 75 per cent threshold, are also covered,[496] though only on 'an *ad hoc* basis'.[497] The Commission (rather than the Council) shall draw up the list of regions covered by Objective 1 strictly in accordance with these requirements. This list, which shall be valid for seven years from 1 January 2000,[498] is annexed to Commission Decision 1999/502.[499]

The Commission seeks through strict application of the 75 per cent criterion to reduce the percentage of the Union population covered by Objective 1 from 25 per cent to 20 per cent.[500] The aim, 'in the interests of efficient programming', is to limit the coverage of Objective 1 to regions where State aid may be authorized under Article 87(3)(a) EC.[501] Even so, Objective 6 regions are to be brought within Objective 1,[502] by virtue of 'special arrangements'.[503] In addition, transitional assistance will be available in favour

---

493 Reg 1260/1999 ([1999] OJ L161/1), Art 4(1).

494 Ibid, Art 3(1).

495 Ibid, cl 4 in the preamble.

496 Reg 1260/1999 ([1999] OJ L161/1).

497 Agenda 2000, Bull EC, Supp 5/97, 22.

498 Reg 1260/1999 ([1999] OJ L161/1), Art 3(2). This coverage reflects Art 299(2) EC (Agenda 2000, Bull EC, Supp 5/97, 22).

499 Drawing up the list of regions covered by Objective 1 of the Structural Funds for the period 2000 to 2006 ([1999] OJ L194/53).

500 Explanatory memorandum to the Proposal of 19 March 1998 for a regulation laying down provisions on the Structural Funds, COM(98)131, 18.

501 Agenda 2000, Bull EC, Supp 5/97, 22. See, regarding this provision, A Evans, EC Law of State Aid (Clarendon Press, Oxford, 1997), Chapter 4.

502 Reg 1260/1999 ([1999] OJ L161/1), 12th recital in the preamble and Art 3(1). Cf the ambiguous approach envisaged in the Explanatory memorandum to this Proposal, COM(98)131, 14.

503 Agenda 2000, Bull EC, Supp 5/97, 22.

of regions previously covered by Objective 1 which are found no longer to be eligible.[504]

The regions covered by Objective 1 in 1999 pursuant to the legislation then in force[505] which are not now covered by Objective 1 shall continue to receive support from the Funds under Objective 1 on a transitional basis from 1 January 2000. Those which meet the eligibility criteria for Objective 2 may receive transitional assistance until 31 December 2006. Those which do not meet these criteria will only receive such assistance until 31 December 2005. At the time of adoption of the list of Objective 1 regions, the Commission shall draw up the list of the NUTS Level III areas belonging to those regions which are to receive support from the Funds under Objective 1 on a transitional basis in 2006.[506]

More particularly, a PEACE programme in support of the peace process in Northern Ireland shall be established under Objective 1 for the years 2000 to 2004 for the benefit of Northern Ireland and the border areas of Ireland.[507] A special programme of assistance for the period 2000 to 2006 shall also be established under Objective 1 for the Swedish NUTS Level II regions which are not covered by the list of Objective 1 regions and which meet the criterion of low population density laid down in Article 2 of Protocol 6 to the Act of Accession for Austria, Sweden and Finland.[508]

For the 10 new Member States the regions covered by Objective 1 shall be regions corresponding to NUTS Level II, whose *per capita* GDP, measured in purchasing power parities and calculated on the basis of Union figures for 1997-99, was less than 75 per cent of the Union average at the time of conclusion of the accession negotiations.[509] The Commission shall draw up the list of regions covered by Objective 1. All regions of the CEECs are eligible except Prague and Bratislava. This list shall be valid from the date of accession until 31 December 2006.[510]

Objective 2: Objective 2 regions must face structural problems of socio-economic conversion, and their population or territory must be sufficiently substantial. They shall include, in particular: areas undergoing socio-economic change in the industrial and service sectors; declining rural areas; urban areas in difficulty; and depressed areas dependent on fisheries.[511] The Commission and the Member States shall seek to ensure that assistance is

---

504 Reg 1260/1999 ([1999] OJ L161/1), Art 6(1).
505 Reg 2052/88 ([1988] OJ L185/9), as amended by Regulation 2081/93 ([1993] OJ L193/5).
506 Ibid, Art 6(1).
507 Special programme for peace and reconciliation in Northern Ireland and the border areas of Ireland (Item B2-1041 of the General Budget for 2003, [2003] OJ L54/1).
508 Art 7(4) of Reg 1260/1999 ([1999] OJ L161/1).
509 Reg 1260/1999 ([1999] OJ L161/1), as amended by Reg 1447/2001 ([2001] OJ L198/1), Art 3(1).
510 Ibid, Art 3(2).
511 Reg 1260/1999 ([1999] OJ L161/1), Art 4(1).

genuinely concentrated on the areas most seriously affected and at the most appropriate geographical level.

Areas undergoing socio-economic change in the industrial and service sectors ('industrial areas') shall represent or belong to a NUTS Level III territorial unit which satisfies three criteria: an average rate of unemployment over the last three years above the Union average; a percentage share of industrial employment in total employment equal to or greater than the Union average in any reference year from 1985 onwards; and an observable fall in industrial employment compared with that reference year.[512]

Rural areas must represent or belong to a NUTS Level III territorial unit which satisfies two criteria: either a population density of less than 100 people per square km or a percentage share of agricultural employment in total employment which is equal to, or higher than, twice the Union average in any reference year from 1985; and either an average unemployment rate over the last three years above the Union average or a decline in population since 1985.[513]

These two categories of areas must contain at least 50 per cent of the population covered by Objective 2 in each Member State, except where duly justified by objective circumstances.[514]

Urban areas shall mean densely populated areas which also meet at least one of the following criteria: a rate of long-term unemployment higher than the Union average; a high level of poverty, including precarious housing conditions; a particularly damaged environment; a high crime and delinquency rate; a low level of education among the population.[515]

Areas dependent on fisheries are those where two criteria are met. First, the number of jobs in fishing as a percentage of total employment must be significant. Secondly, there must be structural, socio-economic problems relating to restructuring of the fishing industry which result in a significant reduction in the number of jobs in that sector.[516]

Assistance may extend to other areas whose population or area is significant which fall into one of three categories: areas undergoing socio-economic change which are adjacent to an industrial area, rural areas which are adjacent to a rural area, areas undergoing socio-economic change or rural areas which are adjacent to a region covered by Objective 1; rural areas with socio-economic problems arising either from the ageing or decline of the agricultural working population; or areas facing or threatened by serious structural problems on account of relevant, verifiable characteristics, or a high

---

512 Reg 1260/1999 ([1999] OJ L161/1), Art 4(5).
513 Reg 1260/1999 ([1999] OJ L161/1), Art 4(6).
514 Reg 1260/1999 ([1999] OJ L161/1), Art 4(4).
515 Reg 1260/1999 ([1999] OJ L161/1), Art 4(7).
516 Reg 1260/1999 ([1999] OJ L161/1), Art 4(8).

level of unemployment arising from an ongoing or planned restructuring of one or more activities in the agricultural, industrial or service sector.[517]

Member States propose eligible regions to the Commission.[518] On the basis of the information provided, the Commission, in close concertation with the Member State concerned, will draw up a list of Objective 2 regions, with due regard to national priorities.[519] The list is to be valid for seven years.[520]

The Commission considers that the percentage of the Union population covered by Objectives 1 and 2 together should be reduced from 51 per cent to between 35 and 40 per cent.[521] The population of the areas covered by Objective 2 may not exceed 18 per cent of the total population of the Union.[522] More particularly, industrial areas should cover no more than around 10 per cent of the Union population, rural areas 5 per cent, urban areas 2 per cent, and fisheries areas 1 per cent.[523]

To ensure that the limit to population coverage for Objective 2 is respected, the Commission will draw up a population ceiling for each Member State. The ceilings are to be drawn up on the basis of three factors: the total population in the NUTS Level III areas of each Member State which are eligible under Objective 2; the severity of the structural problems at national level in each Member State as compared with the other Member States concerned;[524] and the need to ensure that each Member State makes a fair contribution to the overall concentration effort. The maximum reduction in the population covered by Objective 2 shall not exceed one-third compared to the population covered by Objectives 2 and 5b.[525]

Commission Decision 1999/503[526] duly establishes a population ceiling for each Member State. For the CEECs, the population ceiling for Objective 2 support shall be 31% of the population of all NUTS Level II regions covered by Objective 2 in each of these countries.[527] The Commission shall draw up the

---

517 Reg 1260/1999 ([1999] OJ L161/1), Art 4(9).
518 Reg 1260/1999 ([1999] OJ L161/1), Art 4(3).
519 Ibid, Art 4(4).
520 Ibid, Art 4(11). It may be amended by the Commission, where 'there is a serious crisis in a region' (ibid).
521 Communication on the links between regional and competition policy – reinforcing concentration and mutual consistency ([1998] OJ C90/3), para 3.2.
522 Reg 1260/1999 ([1999] OJ L161/1), 15th recital in the preamble and Art 4(2) (ibid).
523 Ibid, 14th recital in the preamble.
524 Such severity shall be assessed on the basis of total unemployment and long-term unemployment outside the regions eligible under Objective 1.
525 Reg 1260/1999 ([1999] OJ L161/1), 15th recital in the preamble. The aim is 'to ensure that each Member State contributes to the overall effort towards concentration' of resources (ibid).
526 Establishing a population ceiling for each Member State under Objective 2 of the Structural Funds for the period 2000 to 2006 ([1999] OJ L194/58).
527 Reg 1260/1999 ([1999] OJ L161/1), as amended by Reg 1447/2001 ([2001] OJ L198/1), Art 4(2).

list of regions covered by Objective 2. The list of areas shall be valid from the date of accession until 31 December 2006.[528]

The Commission preference is to bring eligibility into line with rules regarding the permissible coverage of State aid. Thus, in principle, the Commission will not accept a region under Objective 2, unless it qualifies for regional aid granted by the Member State concerned under Article 87(3)(c) EC.[529] For this provision to be the *de facto* determinant of eligibility may be controversial.[530] Exceptions may only be made where two conditions are met. First, no more than 2 per cent of the population not covered by Objective 1 may benefit. Secondly, there must be consistency with the general aim of concentration. In other words, the 35 to 40 per cent limit to the population coverage of Objectives 1 and 2 together[531] must be respected.

The regions covered by Objectives 2 and 5b in 1999 pursuant to previous legislation[532] which are not on the list of Objective 2 regions shall receive support from the ERDF, from 1 January 2000 to 31 December 2005, under Objective 2, on a transitional basis. Such areas shall receive support from 1 January 2000 to 31 December 2006 from the ESF under Objective 3 on the same basis as Objective 3 areas, the EAGGF Guarantee Section under its support to rural development, and from the FIFG under its structural measures in the fisheries sector outside Objective 1.[533]

Any one area may be eligible for assistance under only one of Objectives 1 or 2.[534]

Allocation of assistance: Indicative breakdowns by Member State of assistance for Objectives 1 and 2 are made on the basis of the following criteria: eligible population, regional prosperity, national prosperity and the relative severity of the structural problems, especially the level of unemployment. The breakdowns shall distinguish allocations of appropriations to regions and areas benefitting from transitional support. The annual breakdown of appropriations for transitional support shall be degressive from 1 January 2000 and shall be lower in 2000 than in 1999. The profile of transitional support may be tailored to the specific needs of

---

528 Ibid, Art 4(11).

529 Communication on the links between regional and competition policy – reinforcing concentration and mutual consistency ([1998] OJ C90/3). According to cl 16 of Reg 1260/1999 ([1999] OJ L161/1), Objective 2 regions 'should correspond to a large extent to the areas assisted by the Member States pursuant to Art 87(3) EC'.

530 COR Opinion of 17 September 1998 ([1998] OJ C373/1) on the proposal for a regulation laying down general provisions on the Structural Funds, para 2.1.1.7.

531 42.7% of the Union population are to be eligible for national aid under Art 87(3)(a) or (c) EC (Communication on the links between regional and competition policy – reinforcing concentration and mutual consistency ([1998] OJ C90/3)).

532 Reg 2052/88 ([1988] OJ L185/9), as amended by Reg 2081/93 ([1993] OJ L193/5).

533 Art 6(2) of Reg 1260/1999 ([1999] OJ L161/1).

534 Art 4(10) of Reg 1260/1999 ([1999] OJ L161/1).

individual regions, in agreement with the Commission, provided the financial allocation for each region is respected.[535]

An allocation by Member State for Objective 1 assistance is contained in Commission Decision 1999/501.[536] An allocation by Member State for Objective 2 assistance is contained in Commission Decision 1999/505.[537]

Four per cent of the allocations are allocated by the Commission at the mid-term point. This is the 'performance reserve'.[538] It is allocated to the operational programmes or Single Programming Documents whose performance the Commission, on the basis of proposals from the Member State, considers successful. Each Member State, in close consultation with the Commission, shall assess under each Objective the performance of each of their operational programmes or Single Programming Documents on the basis of monitoring indicators reflecting effectiveness, management and financial implementation and measuring the mid-term results in relation to their specific initial targets. These indicators shall be decided by the Member State in close consultation with the Commission, taking account of all or part of an indicative list of indicators proposed by the Commission, and shall be quantified in the existing different annual implementation reports as well as the mid-term evaluation report. The Member States shall be responsible for their application.[539]

The Commission shall allocate the reserve in close consultation with the Member States concerned and on the basis of proposals from each Member State, taking account of its specific institutional features and their corresponding programming. The allocation entails the commitment of appropriations to the operational programmes or Single Programming Documents or their priorities which are considered to be successful.[540]

These procedures should ensure that allocation of the reserve is based on objective, simple and transparent criteria which reflect efficiency and the quality of management and financial execution.[541]

Scope of assistance: The scope of the assistance which the ERDF may provide is outlined in Article 2 of Regulation 1783/1999[542] on the ERDF.

---

535 Art 7(3) of Reg 1260/1999 ([1999] OJ L161/1).
536 Decision fixing an indicative allocation by Member State of the commitment appropriations for Objective 1 of the Structural Funds for the period 2000 to 2006 ([1999] OJ L194/49).
537 Decision fixing an indicative allocation by Member State of the commitment appropriations for Objective 2 of the Structural Funds for the period 2000 to 2006 ([1999] OJ L194/60).
538 Art 7(5) of Reg 1260/1999 ([1999] OJ L161/1). The Commission had proposed that 10% should be allocated in this way (Proposal of 19 March 1998 ([1998] OJ C176/1), Art 7(3)).
539 Art 44(1) of Reg 1260/1999 ([1999] OJ L161/1).
540 Art 44(2) of Reg 1260/1999 ([1999] OJ L161/1).
541 55th recital in the preamble to Reg 1260/1999 ([1999] OJ L161/1).
542 Reg 1783/1999 ([1999] OJ L213/1).

Productive investment: The Fund may assist productive investment, to create and safeguard sustainable jobs.[543]

Infrastructure investment: The Fund may assist investment in infrastructure which contributes to the development or conversion of the regions concerned. In Objective 1 regions, infrastructure investments contributing to increasing the economic potential, development, and structural adjustment and creation or maintenance of sustainable jobs in those regions may be supported. The investment may include that contributing to the establishment and development of trans-European networks in the areas of transport, telecommunications and energy infrastructures, taking account of the need to link the central regions of the Union with regions suffering from a structural handicap because of their insular, landlocked, or peripheral status. Where the need is demonstrated, financing may also be provided for investments in education and health which contribute to structural adjustment.

In regions covered by Objective 1 or 2 or by a Community initiative, the Fund may assist infrastructure investments relating to the diversification of economic sites and industrial areas suffering from decline, the renewal of depressed urban areas and the revitalization of, and improved access to, rural areas and areas dependent on fisheries; instruments in infrastructure where modernization or regeneration is a prerequisite for the creation or development of job-creating economic activities, including infrastructure links on which the development of such activities depends.[544]

'Endogenous development': The Fund may assist measures to exploit the potential for internally generated development of the regions concerned. Such measures are those which encourage and support local development and employment initiatives and the activities of small and medium-sized enterprises. They may include: assistance towards services for enterprises, particularly in the fields of management, market studies and research, and services common to several enterprises; financing the transfer of technology, particularly the collection and dissemination of information, common organization between enterprises and research establishments and financing the implementation of innovations in firms; improvement of access for firms to finance and loans, particularly by the provision of guarantees and equity participation; direct assistance to investment, where no aid scheme exists; the provision of infrastructure on a scale appropriate to local and employment development; aid for structures providing neighbourhood services to create new jobs but excluding measures financed by the ESF; and technical assistance measures.[545]

---

543 Art 2(1)(a) of Reg 1783/1999 ([1999] OJ L213/1).
544 Art 2(1)(b) of Reg 1783/1999 ([1999] OJ L213/1).
545 Art 2(1)(c) of Reg 1783/1999 ([1999] OJ L213/1).

Accordingly, the ERDF shall support, *inter alia*: the productive environment, in particular to increase competitiveness and sustainable investment by firms, especially the small and medium-sized enterprises, and to make regions more attractive, particularly by improving the standard of their infrastructure; research and technological development with a view to promoting the introduction of new technologies and innovation and the strengthening of research and technological development capacities contributing to regional development; the development of the information society; the development of tourism and cultural investment, including the protection of cultural and natural heritage, provided that they are creating sustainable jobs; the protection and improvement of the environment, in particular taking account of the principles of precaution and preventative action in support of economic development, the clean and efficient utilization of energy and the development of renewable energy sources; equality between women and men in the field of employment, principally through the establishment of firms and through infrastructure or services enabling the reconciliation of family and working life; and transnational, cross-border and inter-regional cooperation on sustainable regional and local development.[546]

Forms of assistance: Assistance from the Fund shall principally take the form of non-repayable direct assistance as well as other forms, such as repayable assistance, an interest-rate subsidy, a guarantee, an equity holding, a venture-capital holding or another form of finance.[547]

'Venture capital and loans' are investment vehicles established specifically to provide equity or other forms of risk capital, including loans, to small and medium-sized enterprises. 'Venture capital holding funds' means funds set up to invest in several venture capital and loan funds. ERDF participation may be accompanied by co-investments or guarantees from other Union financing instruments.[548]

'Guarantees' are financing instruments that guarantee venture capital and loan funds and other risk-financing schemes (including loans) against losses arising from their investments in small and medium-sized enterprises. The funds may be publicly-supported mutual funds subscribed by such enterprises, commercially-run funds with private-sector partners, or wholly publicly-financed funds. ERDF participation may be accompanied by part-guarantees provided by other Community financing instruments.[549]

Major projects: As part of any assistance, the ERDF may finance expenditure in respect of major projects. These are projects which comprise an economically indivisible series of works fulfilling a precise technical function

546 Art 2(2) of Reg 1783/1999 ([1999] OJ L213/1).
547 Art 28(3) of Reg 1260/1999 ([1999] OJ L161/1).
548 Rule 8 in the Annex to Reg 1685/2000 ([2000] OJ L193/39) laying down detailed rules for the implementation of Reg 1260/1999 as regards eligibility of expenditure of operations co-financed by the Structural Funds.
549 Rule 9 in the Annex to Reg 1685/2000 ([2000] OJ L193/39).

and which have clearly identified aims; and whose total cost taken into account in determining the contribution of the Fund exceeds €50 million.[550] Investments in infrastructure and in production facilities may be assisted.[551]

Regional operational programmes: A regional operational programme is a document approved by the Commission to implement a Community Support Framework and comprising a consistent set of priorities with multiannual measures and which may be implemented through recourse to one or more Structural Funds, to one or more of the other existing financial instruments and to the EIB. An integrated operational programme is an operational programme financed by more than one fund.[552]

Each operational programme shall contain: the priorities of the programme, their consistency with the relevant Community Support Framework, their specific targets, quantified where they lend themselves to quantification, and an evaluation of the impact expected; and a summary description of the measures planned to implement the priorities, including the information needed to check compliance with aid schemes pursuant to Article 87 EC, and, where appropriate, the nature of the measures required to prepare, monitor and evaluate the operational programme. There must also be an indicative financing plan specifying for each priority and each year the financial allocation envisaged for the contribution of each Fund, the EIB where appropriate, and the other financial instruments – including, for information, the total amount from the EAGGF Guarantee Section for assistance to the adaptation and development of rural areas – insofar as they contribute directly to the financing plan, as well as the total amount of eligible public and estimated private funding relating to the contribution of each Fund. This financing plan shall distinguish in the total contribution of the various Funds the funding planned for the regions receiving transitional support. The total contribution of the Funds planned for each year shall be compatible with the relevant financial perspective, taking account of degressivity requirements.[553] Finally, the provisions for implementing an operational programme must be contained in the programme. The provisions shall include: designation by the Member State of a managing authority responsible for managing the operational programme; a description of the arrangements for managing the operational programme; a description of the systems for monitoring and evaluation, including the role of the monitoring committee; a definition of the procedures concerning the mobilization and circulation of financial flows to

---

550 Art 25 of Reg 1260/1999 ([1999] OJ L161/1).
551 Ibid, Art 26(1).
552 Art 9(f) of Reg 1260/1999 ([1999] OJ L161/1). Assistance covered by a CSF shall as a general rule be provided in the form of an integrated operational programme by region (ibid, Art 18(1)).
553 3rd subparagraph of Art 7(3) of Reg 1260/1999 ([1999] OJ L161/1).

ensure their transparency; and a description of the specific arrangements and procedures for checking on the operational programme.[554]

Global grants: Global grants concern assistance the implementation and management of which may be entrusted to one or more approved intermediaries, including local authorities, regional development bodies, or non-governmental organizations, and used preferably to assist local development initiatives. The decision to employ a global grant shall be taken in agreement with the Commission by the Member State or, in agreement with the Member State, by the managing authority. In the case of Community initiatives and innovative measures, the Commission may decide to employ a global grant for all or part of the assistance. In the case of Community initiatives, this decision may only be taken with the prior agreement of the Member States concerned.[555]

The procedures for the use of global grants shall be the subject of an agreement between the Member State or managing authority and the intermediary body concerned. In the case of Community initiatives and innovative measures, the procedures for the use of global grants shall be the subject of an agreement between the Commission and the intermediary body concerned. In the case of Community initiatives, these procedures must also be agreed with the Member States concerned.[556]

The procedures for the use of the global grant shall detail in particular: the measures to be implemented; the criteria for choosing beneficiaries; the conditions and rates of assistance from the Funds, including the use of any interest accruing; the arrangements for monitoring, evaluating and ensuring the financial control of the global grant; and where applicable, any use of a bank guarantee, in which case the Commission must be informed.[557]

Innovative actions and technical assistance: 0.65 per cent of the appropriations shall be devoted to funding innovative actions and technical assistance.[558]

At the initiative of the Commission and subject to a ceiling of 0.40 per cent of their respective annual funding, the Funds may finance innovative actions at Union level. These shall include studies, pilot projects, and exchanges of experience. Such innovative actions shall contribute to the preparation of innovative methods and practices designed to improve the quality of assistance under Objectives 1, 2 and 3. They shall be implemented in a simple,

---

554 Ibid, Art 18(2).
555 Art 9(i) of Reg 1260/1999 ([1999] OJ L161/1).
556 Art 27(2) of Reg 1260/1999 ([1999] OJ L161/1).
557 Art 27(3) of Reg 1260/1999 ([1999] OJ L161/1).
558 Art 7(6) of Reg 1260/1999 ([1999] OJ L161/1). See also, regarding eligible actions, Rule 11 in the Annex to Reg 1685/2000 ([2000] OJ L193/39) laying down detailed rules for the implementation of Reg 1260/1999 as regards eligibility of expenditure of operations co-financed by the Structural Funds.

transparent fashion and in accordance with the principles of sound financial management.[559]

There are three 'strands' to innovative actions: part-financing of regional programmes of innovative actions and of the pilot projects deriving from them; accompanying measures – support for exchange of experiences and the creation of interregional networks; and organization of competitions aimed at identifying and developing best practice.[560]

Each field of action for pilot projects shall be financed by one Fund only. The decision on the contribution of a Fund may amplify the scope of each Fund as defined in the Regulations specific to each Fund, but without broadening it, to include all measures required to implement the pilot project concerned.[561]

Eligible regions are those listed in Annex A to the Guidelines for Innovative Actions under the ERDF in 2000–06. They must be eligible in whole or in part under Objective 1 or 2 or receive transitional support under one of these Objectives. The entire region, including those not covered by Objective 1 or 2, is considered eligible under the regional programmes of innovative actions.[562]

At the initiative or on behalf of the Commission and subject to a ceiling of 0.25 per cent of their respective annual allocation, the Funds may also finance the preparatory, monitoring, evaluation and checking measures necessary for implementing Regulation 1260/1999.[563] These shall include: studies, including studies of a general nature, concerning the operations of the Funds; measures of technical assistance, the exchange of experience and information aimed at the partners, the final beneficiaries of assistance from the Funds[564] and the general public; the installation, operation and interconnection of computerised systems for management, monitoring and evaluation; and improvements in evaluation methods and exchange of information on practices in this field.[565]

Community initiatives: 5.35 per cent of the commitment appropriations for the Structural Funds shall be devoted to funding the Community initiatives. Community initiatives shall cover four fields:[566] cross-border, transnational and interregional cooperation intended to encourage the harmonious, balanced and sustainable development of the whole of the Community area

559 Art 22(1) of Reg 1260/1999 ([1999] OJ L161/1).
560 Guidelines for Innovative Actions under the ERDF in 2000-06, Commission Communication of 31 January 2001, para 20.
561 Art 22(2) of Reg 1260/1999 ([1999] OJ L161/1).
562 Commission Communication of 31 January 2001, para 21.
563 [1999] OJ L161/1.
564 Final beneficiaries are the bodies and public or private firms responsible for commissioning operations. In the case of aid schemes pursuant to Art 87 EC and in the case of aid granted by bodies designated by the Member States, the final beneficiaries are the bodies which grant the aid (ibid, Art 9(l)).
565 Ibid, Art 23.
566 Reg 1260/1999 ([1999] OJ L161/1), Art 20(1).

('Interreg');[567] economic and social regeneration of cities and of urban neighbourhoods in crisis with a view to promoting a sustainable urban development ('URBAN');[568] rural development ('Leader');[569] and transnational cooperation to promote new means of combating all forms of discrimination and inequalities in connection with the labour market ('EQUAL').[570] At least 2.5 per cent of the Structural Funds commitment appropriations shall be allocated to Interreg, under which due attention should be given to cross-border activities, in particular in the perspective of enlargement, and for Member States which have extensive frontiers with the applicant countries,[571] as well as to improved coordination with Phare. Due attention shall also be given to cooperation with the outermost regions and to the social and vocational integration of asylum seekers in the framework of EQUAL.[572] Programmes approved within the framework of the Community initiatives may cover areas other than those covered by Objective 1 or 2.[573]

Each of the three fields shall be financed by a single Fund: Interreg and URBAN by the ERDF, Leader by the EAGGF Guidance Section, and EQUAL by the ESF. The decision on the contribution of a Fund may amplify the scope of each Fund as defined in the Regulations specific to each Fund, but without broadening it, to include all measures required to implement the Community initiative concerned.[574] In other words, the scope of assistance of a single Fund may be extended to include that of the other Funds, where this is necessary for implementation of an initiative.[575] On the basis of proposals drawn up in accordance with the guidelines and with *ex-ante* evaluation requirements and submitted by the Member State(s), the Commission shall decide on Community initiatives.[576] The Community initiatives shall be re-examined following a mid-term evaluation and amended where required on application by the Member State(s) concerned or by the Commission by agreement with

---

567 Commission Communication laying down guidelines for a Community initiative concerning trans-European cooperation intended to encourage harmonious and balanced development of the European territory – Interreg III ([2000] OJ C143/6).

568 Commission Communication laying down guidelines for a Community initiative concerning economic and social regeneration of cities and of neighbourhoods in crisis in order to promote sustainable urban development (Urban II) ([2000] OJ C141/8).

569 Commission Notice laying down guidelines for the Community initiative for rural development (Leader+) ([2000] OJ C139/5).

570 Commission Communication establishing the guidelines for the Community initiative Equal concerning transnational cooperation to promote new means of combatting all forms of discrimination and inequalities in connection with the labour market ([2000] OJ C127/2).

571 B2-1411 of the Union Budget ([2003] OJ L53/1) was headed 'Support for regions bordering candidate countries'.

572 Art 20(2) of Reg 1260/1999 ([1999] OJ L161/1).

573 Ibid, Art 20(3).

574 Art 21(2) of Reg 1260/1999 ([1999] OJ L161/1).

575 Explanatory memorandum to the Proposal of 19 March 1998 for a regulation laying down provisions on the Structural Funds, COM(98)131, 17.

576 Art 21(3) of Reg 1260/1999 ([1999] OJ L161/1).

the Member State(s).[577] The Community initiatives shall cover a period of seven years, beginning on 1 January 2000.[578]

E. CONCLUSION

Practice regarding the ERDF focusses more on questions of the distribution of assistance as between Member States than on ensuring that these resources are effectively used to promote cohesion. The basic criterion for eligibility for assistance from the Fund and, more particularly, for selection of Objective 1 regions is *per capita* GDP relative to the Union average. In principle, to qualify for Objective 1 assistance, regions must have a *per capita* GDP which is less than 75 per cent of this average.

Application of this criterion has the advantage of apparent objectivity.[579] Certainly, in determining eligibility for assistance from the Fund, the Council and Commission have been concerned to use figures which are available throughout the Union on as nearly as possible a comparable basis. Figures are available, unreliable as they are admitted to be,[580] for GDP.[581]

The criterion may also be claimed to secure the concentration necessary to ensure that limited resources are not so thinly spread as to lack real impact.[582] More particularly, it enables the assistance to be concentrated on regions in Member States which have sought 'side-payments' for acceptance of the deepening of integration envisaged in the Single European Act[583] and the Treaty on European Union. In this connection, it is notable that Ireland, Greece, Portugal and Spain, as well as Italy, favour a strict application of the 75 per cent criterion for determining eligibility under Objective 1.[584]

The disadvantage of the criterion of *per capita* GDP is that it does not enable account to be taken of the diverse and changing regional conditions within the Union. Community initiatives alone are unlikely to be sufficient to permit reconciliation of the need for concentration of funding emphasized by the above Member States with the need for flexibility to take account of such conditions.[585] From the start, therefore, the application of the criterion had to be relaxed in the case of Northern Ireland. Northern Ireland had a *per capita*

---

577 Ibid, Art 21(4).

578 Ibid, Art 21(5).

579 Note the objections of the French Government that Hainaut in Belgium was classified as an Objective 1 region, whereas neighbouring Hainaut-Cambresis in France, which was little better off, was to remain an Objective 2 region (European Report 1842 (10 March 1993)).

580 See also COA annual report 1995 ([1996] OJ C340/1), para 5.21.

581 EEC regional development policy, House of Lords Select Committee on the European Communities, HL(1991–92)20, Evidence, 7.

582 Cf First cohesion report, COM(96)542, 117.

583 [1987] OJ L169/1.

584 Europe 6006 (23 June 1993).

585 Cf Future of Community initiatives under the Structural Funds, COM(93)282.

GDP of around 80 per cent of the Community average in 1986,[586] and the 'special reasons' for its original classification as an Objective 1 region essentially concerned its recent history of civil unrest.[587] The 1993 reforms entailed further relaxation in relation to Hainaut, Merseyside and the Highlands and Islands of Scotland. These three regions were 'not areas of lagging development in the traditional sense but regions where the decline from relative prosperity based on industrial activity ha[d] been particularly acute. East Berlin and the new *Lander* ... also represent[ed] a new type of problem – one of transition from a centrally planned to a market economy'.[588] Viewed against this background, introduction of Objective 6 seems to have been more a recognition of a symptom of the underlying difficulties rather than a solution to these difficulties. The inference may be drawn that relaxation of criteria based on *per capita* GDP may be necessary for the development of a Fund which genuinely addresses the diversity of cohesion problems within the Union.[589]

At the same time, adoption of more sophisticated criteria may be necessary, to curb the intergovernmental haggling over the designation of Objective 1 regions and over the eligibility criteria for Objective 2. Such haggling underscores how Union assistance can be abused by the Member States.[590] As the Commission admits, the distribution of such assistance reflects 'political compromises'.[591]

The Commission response to these problems is to seek to limit eligible regions to those where the Commission authorizes Member States to grant regional aid under Article 87(3) EC.[592] Thus eligibility is ultimately to be determined by reference to competition policy requirements,[593] rather than by

---

586 However, its unemployment rate was 1.7 times the Community average.

587 EEC regional development policy, House of Lords Select Committee on the European Communities, HL(1991–92)20, 19.

588 Fifth periodic report on the situation and socio-economic development of the regions of the Community, COM(94)322, 130.

589 See, eg, Community Structural Fund operations, COM(93)67, 4.

590 J Bachtler, 'Policy Agenda for the Decade' in S Hardy, M Hart, L Albrechts, and A Katos, An Enlarged Europe (Jessica Kingsley, London, 1995), 313–24, 317.

591 First cohesion report, COM(96)542, 6.

592 See, regarding inconsistencies between regions covered by this provision and regions covered by Objectives 1, 2 and 5b, Commission Reply by Mr Van Miert to WQ E-0473/98 ([1998] OJ C304/113) by Richard Howitt.

593 Cf the concern that there might be 'an excessive reduction in areas' covered by Objective 2 in the ESC Opinion of 27 May 1998 ([1998] OJ C235/38) on the new regional programmes 1997-9 under Objective 2, para 4.3.4. Cf, more generally, F Wishlade, 'Competition Policy or Cohesion Policy by the Back Door: the Commission Guidelines on National Regional Aid' (1998) ECLR 343-57.

reference to cohesion requirements.[594] At the same time, 'political compromises' apparently remain influential, in that old Objective 6 regions are to be treated as 'special cases'.[595]

Less attention is paid to ensuring that assistance, once it has been allocated to a Member State, is used effectively to promote cohesion. For example, much assistance concerns physical infrastructure, even though such assistance may not be the most appropriate for regional development. Equally, assistance to productive investment may not necessarily be an effective means of reducing disparities between regions. Comparatively limited resources are devoted to 'endogenous growth' measures, which may be more successful in reducing such disparities.[596]

594 Cf the call for improved allocation of assistance, with particular attention being paid to the outermost regions, the ESC Opinion of 19 March 1997 ([1997] OJ C158/5) on the annual report of the Cohesion Fund 1995, para 4.1.
595 Communication on the links between regional and competition policy – reinforcing concentration and mutual consistency ([1998] OJ C90/3), para 3.2.
596 Cf A Cutler, C Haslam, J Williams and K Williams, 1992 – the Struggle for Europe (New York, 1989), 79.

3
EUROPEAN SOCIAL FUND

A. INTRODUCTION

In Article 117 EEC Member States agreed upon the need to promote improved working conditions and an improved standard of living for workers. They believed that such improvements would ensue not only from the functioning of the common market but also from the procedures provided for in the Treaty. Presumably, these procedures were to include the provision of assistance by the European Social Fund (ESF).

Articles 123 to 127 EEC provided for the creation of this Fund. According to Article 123, the Fund was to improve employment opportunities for workers in the common market and to contribute thereby to raising the standard of living. To these ends, the Fund was to render the employment of workers easier and to increase their geographical and occupational mobility within the Community.[597]

More particularly, Article 49(3)(d) EEC required the establishment of machinery to facilitate the achievement of a balance between supply and demand in the employment market. This was to be done in such a way as to avoid serious threats to the standard of living and level of employment in the various regions and industries. It led to the establishment of a system known as SEDOC,[598] which was designed to prevent new regional problems in countries of immigration.[599]

The apparent emphasis in these provisions was on increasing the mobility of workers rather than assisting the economic development of regions of high unemployment. This emphasis may go some way towards explaining the need felt by Italy to secure the adoption of a Protocol to the Treaty. The Protocol on Italy[600] envisaged use of the Fund and the European Investment Bank to assist implementation of an Italian regional development programme.

---

597 Art 128 EEC also required the Council to 'lay down general principles for implementing a common vocational training policy capable of contributing to the harmonious development both of the national economies and the common market'. In Dec 63/266 ([1963] JO 1338) determining general principles for the implementation of a common policy for vocational training the 'fourth principle' emphasized the aim of promoting the geographical and professional mobility of workers. Note also the reference to Art 128 EEC in Art 1 of Reg 9/60 ([1960] JO 1189) on the ESF.
598 Système européen de diffusion des offres et des demandes d'emploi enregistrés en compensation internationale.
599 Art 15(2) of Reg 1612/68 ([1968] JO L257/2) on freedom of movement for workers within the Community. This system has now been replaced. See Dec 93/569 ([1993] OJ L274/32) on the implementing of Reg 1612/68 as regards, in particular, a network entitled Eures (European Employment Services).
600 Protocols annexed to the Treaty by common accord of the Member States were an integral part of the Treaty. See Art 239 EEC.

B. ESTABLISHMENT OF THE COMMON MARKET

The ESF originally had the function of facilitating establishment of the common market. According to Article 123 EEC, the Fund was to act 'to improve employment opportunities for workers in the common market'. By providing assistance to migration it would contribute to realizing the potential of the common market to reduce unemployment in the less developed regions and to improve the welfare of individual workers and the general economy. In other words, it would counter distortions of competition associated with the 'imperfect mobility of labour as a factor of production'.[601]

In particular, Article 125 EEC provided for the grant of assistance for training, resettlement, and conversion. This provision was narrower in scope than Article 123 EEC, and only concerned the 'immediate task' of the ESF.[602] Such assistance was to be provided under Article 125 during the transitional period for establishment of the common market and could be abolished by the Council at the end of this period.[603] To implement this provision, the Council adopted Regulation 9/60.[604]

1. Objectives of assistance

Apparently, the Fund was originally intended to alleviate the social costs of establishing the common market[605] and was thus viewed as essential for its establishment.[606] This view certainly seems to have adopted in the Spaak Report, on the basis of which the EEC Treaty was negotiated. According to this Report, the Fund was to help workers adjust to the industrial restructuring which would be demanded by the establishment of the common market. Since the restructuring would lead to increased efficiency and thereby benefit the Community as a whole, it was considered justified for the social costs to be

---

601 See, regarding this 'market imperfection', 'State Aid Control in the Context of Other Community Policies' (1994) 4 European Economy, Supp A, 4.

602 6th recital in the preamble to Reg 9/60 ([1960] JO 1189). The enactment of this Regulation did not prejudice other ESF tasks under the Treaty (ibid, 8th recital in the preamble).

603 During the negotiation of the EEC Treaty there had been some support, particularly from France and Germany, for limiting ESF operations to this period. See S Neri and H Sperl, Traité instituant la Communauté économique européenne (Court of Justice of the European Communities, Luxembourg, 1960), 307.

604 On the ESF ([1960] JO 1189). It was 'technically' amended by Reg 47/63 ([1963] JO 1605) and Reg 37/67 ([1967] JO 526).

605 D Collins, The Operation of the European Social Fund (Croom Helm, London, 1983); and P Hatt, 'Thirty Years of ESF Assistance', Social Europe 2/91, 78–91.

606 R Quadri, R Monaco, and A Trabucchi, Trattato istitutivo della Comunità economica europea: commentario (Giuffré, Milan, 1965), ii, 961.

shared.[607] However, the impossibility of accurately determining when unemployment could be attributed to the establishment of the common market was acknowledged.[608]

At the same time, it was recognized that surplus labour exerted downward pressure on pay and working conditions. Establishment of the common market meant that this pressure would be exerted throughout the Community.[609] Hence, for the Fund to intervene where the retraining or re-employment of workers became necessary would be of general benefit.[610]

In setting these limited objectives for the Fund, the Treaty authors may be said to have held an overly sanguine view of the self-regulating powers of the common market. In a context of overall economic growth, they reasoned, backward regions, assisted by decentralized, loosely coordinated measures that focused primarily on the labour market, would catch up with the more prosperous regions.[611]

2. Eligibility for assistance

Assistance was available in respect of three categories of persons. They were: unemployed persons[612] receiving vocational training; unemployed persons changing their place of residence for employment purposes; and workers who required retraining because their company was undergoing conversion. In particular, assistance for vocational training was available in the case of workers who completed at least six months of productive employment in the occupation for which they had been retrained. Moreover, assistance for resettlement was available in the case of workers who completed at least six months of productive employment in their new place of residence. Finally, assistance for conversion was available in the case of workers who completed at least six months of full employment in the converted undertaking.[613]

---

607 Comité Intergouvernemental Crée par la Conference de Messine, Rapport des Chefs de Délégation aux Ministres des Affaires Etrangères (Secretariat of the Committee, Brussels, 1956), 83. At the Messina Conference it had been recognized that the establishment of a common market would require the creation of a 'readaptation fund'.

608 S Neri and H Sperl, para [283], n 2 above, 308 and 313.

609 J Tessier, 'Le Fonds social européen' (1960) RMC 325–37, 334.

610 Ibid, 325.

611 JJ Anderson, 'Structural Funds and the Social Dimension of EU Policy: Springboard or Stumbling Block?' in S Leibfried and P Pierson (eds), European Social Policy (Brookings Institute, Washington, 1995), 123–58, 135.

612 Persons clearly underemployed for a prolonged period were assimilated to the unemployed. See Art 2(3)(a) of Reg 9/60 ([1960] JO 1189). See also Reg 12/64 ([1964] JO 537) fixing the conditions of clear and prolonged underemployment within the meaning of Art 2(3)(a) of Reg 9/60.

613 Art 125(2) EEC; and Arts 1 and 2 of Reg 9/60 ([1960] JO 1189).

3. Allocation of assistance

The Protocol on Italy was referred to in the preamble to Regulation 9/60.[614] It was interpreted as meaning that the Fund should be used to assist the Italian Government in its efforts to reduce unemployment.[615] No reference to the particular needs of Italy was made in the operative provisions of the Regulation, though in practice many Italians benefitted from Fund assistance during the first decade of its existence. In the period 1961 to 1972 the re-employment of more than 1.1 million jobless, including 850,000 Italians, and the resettlement of about 800,000 job applicants, half of whom were Italian, were assisted.[616]

4. Scope of assistance

Article 125 EEC provided for the ESF to assist two kinds of State measures. First, it was to meet 50 per cent of the cost of State measures to ensure productive re-employment of workers by means of vocational training or resettlement allowances. Secondly, the Fund was to assist State measures in favour of workers whose employment was reduced or temporarily suspended, in whole or in part, as a result of the conversion of an undertaking to other production. Such measures, it was envisaged, would enable the workers to retain the same wage level pending their full re-employment. According to Regulation 9/60,[617] the conversion envisaged was that involving a change in the production programme of an enterprise. The change had to be designed to lead to the production of new goods differentiated from their predecessors by more than mere improvements or additions.[618] The first kind of measures was 'active' in character, and the second kind 'passive'.[619]

The Commission considered that the scope of assistance from the Fund should be wider. According to the Commission, the creation of a 'real' common market required that, along with a customs union, an economic union be established. To this end, a social policy should be implemented,[620] so as to enable undertakings to adapt and to maintain a high level of employment. In

---

614 [1960] JO 1189.

615 Ibid, 7th recital in the preamble.

616 P Hatt, para [284], n 1 above, 80. Though the proportion of Fund assistance received by Italy was lower than these figures might have led one to expect (Annex to the Commission Opinion of 10 June 1969 ([1969] JO C131/4) on reform of the ESF). See also A Gallizioli, I Fondi strutturali delle Comunite europee (CEDAM, Padova, 1992), 79.

617 [1960] JO 1189.

618 Ibid, Art 9. During the negotiation of the Treaty, Germany had suggested that assistance should be conditional on its being shown that the conversion would promote establishment of the common market. See S Neri and H Sperl, para [283], n 2 above, 318.

619 W Steinle, 'Labour Markets and Social Policies' in W Molle and R Cappellin (eds), Regional Impact of Community Policies in Europe (Avebury, Aldershot, 1988), 111–26, 115–16.

620 The European Parliament also called for reform of the ESF, so that it could make a greater contribution to regional development. See the Resolution of 27 June 1966 ([1966] JO 2427) on regional policy in the EEC, para 13.

---

particular, the actions of the Fund in favour of labour mobility should be intensified.[621] Hence, in 1965 the Commission proposed new legislation under Article 235[622] rather than Article 125 EEC.[623] According to the proposal, the Fund would have been able to provide assistance to retrain persons in employment;[624] to maintain incomes of workers affected by conversion by way of the substitution of enterprises;[625] to construct, enlarge and equip retraining centres;[626] and to construct housing.[627] This proposal was supported by the European Parliament[628] and the Economic and Social Committee,[629] but it was not adopted by the Council. Apparently, the Council considered that labour-market policy should be left essentially to individual Member States.

5. Forms of assistance

Every year, Member States were to present to the Commission estimates of their needs for Fund assistance for the following year.[630] These estimates were aggregated, and the contributions required of each Member State to finance the aggregate amount of estimated Fund expenditure[631] were calculated according to the scale laid down in Article 200(2) EEC.[632] The percentage contributions required of Italy and the Netherlands under this provision were lower than the percentage contributions which they were required to make to the General Budget under Article 200(1). This disparity was justified by reference to the economic and social situation of the two countries at the time of adoption of the Treaty.[633] Each Member State was subsequently to claim from the Fund reimbursement of expenditure which it had actually incurred.

621 Preamble to the draft decision of 11 November 1964 (Bull EEC, Supp 1/65, 6) on certain aspects of social policy.
622 According to this provision, if action by the Community proved necessary to attain, in the course of the operation of the common market, one of the objectives of the Community and the Treaty had not provided the necessary powers, the Council should, acting unanimously on a proposal from the Commission and after consulting the European Parliament, take the appropriate measures.
623 Draft supplementary regulation on the ESF of 27 January 1965 (Bull EEC, Supp 3/65, 13).
624 Ibid, Arts 2–5.
625 Ibid, Arts 6–13.
626 Ibid, Arts 14–18.
627 Ibid, Arts 19–20.
628 Resolution of 16 June 1965 ([1965] JO 2006) on the Commission proposals for regulations to increase the effectiveness of ESF interventions. See also the Resolution of 1 December 1967 ([1967] JO 307/24) on the evolution of the social situation in the Community in 1966, para 6(a).
629 Opinion of 26 May 1965 ([1965] JO 2244) on the Commission proposals for regulations to increase the effectiveness of ESF interventions.
630 Art 16 of Reg 9/60 ([1960] JO 1189).
631 More details of Art 125 EEC expenditure were provided in Arts 15–24 of the Financial Regulation of 31 January 1961 ([1961] JO 509).
632 This expenditure was only included in the General Budget from 1971 ([1971] JO L62/1), Arts 451 and 452.
633 Annex to the Commission Opinion of 10 June 1969 ([1969] JO C131/4).

Therefore, the Fund did not take initiatives.[634] Rather, its assistance took the form of a 'clearing system'[635] or an intergovernmental compensation system for social risks entailed by the establishment of the common market.[636]

C. DEVELOPMENT OF THE COMMON MARKET

Despite the operations of the ESF, structural unemployment persisted in certain regions and industrial sectors. Its persistence was considered attributable not simply to the relocation of job opportunities resulting from establishment of the common market. More fundamentally, its persistence was considered attributable to the fact that much of the workforce lacked the qualifications and skills needed in an increasingly competitive world economy.[637] At the same time, migration for economic necessity came to be regarded as undesirable in terms of integration goals.[638] Greater emphasis, it was felt, should be placed on enabling workers to find employment in their own region.[639] In these circumstances, the targeting of assistance was considered necessary.

However, the Fund was only empowered under Article 125 EEC to assist State measures. The implication was that Member States could control the use of Fund assistance. As a result, such assistance tended to be used to tackle the most pressing, short-term problems of the Member States,[640] rather than being designed systematically to tackle what from the Community point of view were the long-term, structural problems. To overcome this tendency, the Commission sought transformation of the Fund into 'an instrument of economic policy'.[641] According to Commission plans, the Fund should stimulate and guide national employment policies. In doing so, the work of the

---

634 R Quadri, R Monaco, and A Trabucchi, para [284], n 2 above, ii, 968.

635 See the German argument in Case 2/71 Germany v EC Commission: ESF aid [1971] ECR 669, 674. See, similarly, R Quadri, R Monaco, and A Trabucchi, para [284], n 2 above, ii, 982.

636 J Tessier, para [285], n 1 above, 325.

637 Commission Opinion of 10 June 1969 ([1969] JO C131/4). See also A Gruber, 'Le Fonds social européen à la veille d'un bilan' (1982) RTDE 251–87, 255.

638 The Communiqué issued by the Heads of State or Government on 20 October 1972 (Bull EC 10-1972, 14–23), para 3 stressed that economic expansion was not an end in itself but should result in an improvement of the quality of life as well as of the standard of living.

639 Council Resolution of 21 January 1974 ([1974] OJ C13/1) concerning a social action programme aimed at achieving a policy of full and better employment in the Community as a whole and in the regions.

640 Cf Dec 66/740 ([1966] JO 4168) on the grant of a Community contribution to Italy to enable it to grant certain aids to sulphur miners affected by redundancy and a certain number of scholarships to their children, which was adopted under Art 235 EEC.

641 Opinion of 10 June 1969 ([1969] JO C131/4), preface.

Fund would prevent Member States from protecting jobs through measures which would undermine the working of the common market.[642]

A legal basis for reform of the Fund was provided by Article 126 EEC. According to this provision, after the end of the transitional period, the Council, acting unanimously on a Commission opinion, could replace the original tasks of the Fund with new tasks within the framework of Article 123.[643] Following the call at the Hague Summit of December 1969 for reform of the Fund within the framework of 'a closely concerted social policy',[644] this replacement was effected by Decision 71/66.[645]

1. Objectives of assistance

Decision 71/66[646] stressed the interdependence of social and economic policies,[647] and aimed to assist restructuring associated with the development of the common market and Community policies.[648] According to the preamble to this Decision, account was to be taken of the demands of social progress in the face of technical development.[649] Hence, not only should efforts to remedy the structural unemployment and underemployment still existing in various Community regions continue;[650] action should also be taken to prevent unemployment from arising in the first place.[651] At the same time, the Fund should seek more positively to secure for all workers employment that best corresponded to their abilities and to ensure continuity of employment and income for them.[652]

Decision 83/516[653] subsequently modified these objectives, with a view to making the Fund a more active instrument to promote employment policies.[654] Accordingly, the Fund was now to concentrate on assisting the implementation of policies designed to equip the workforce with the skills required for stable employment and to generate employment opportunities.[655] It was, in particular, to assist the socio-vocational insertion and integration of young people and disadvantaged workers, the adaptation of the workforce to

642 Ibid, para 5.
643 Thus the original tasks were 'provisional'. See R Quadri, R Monaco, and A Trabucchi, para [284], n 2 above, ii, 977.
644 Communiqué (Bull EC 1-1970, 11), para 12.
645 On the reform of the ESF ([1971] JO L28/15).
646 [1971] JO L28/15.
647 Ibid, 3rd recital in the preamble.
648 A Gruber, para [293], n 1 above, 260.
649 2nd recital in the preamble to Dec 71/66 ([1971] JO L28/15).
650 Ibid, 4th recital.
651 Ibid, 6th recital.
652 Ibid, 17th recital.
653 On the tasks of the ESF ([1983] OJ L289/38).
654 Ibid, 7th recital in the preamble.
655 See also AG Da Cruz Vilaça in Case 84/85 UK v EC Commission: assistance for part-time employment [1987] ECR 3765, 3777.

labour-market developments and to technological change, and the reduction of regional imbalance in the labour market.[656]

2. Eligibility for assistance

According to Regulation 2396/71,[657] five categories of persons were eligible for assistance. They were: the unemployed; those who would become unemployed after a specific period; those who were underemployed; those who had had to cease work in a self-employed capacity;[658] and those whose qualifications had to be adapted to permit them to pursue occupations requiring high qualifications.[659] Moreover, subject to the approval of the employment services of the Member State or Member States concerned, assistance could also be granted in respect of three further categories of persons. Thus it could be granted in respect of workers who were difficult to place in employment again on account of their age. It could also be granted in respect of women over 35 years who wished to pursue a professional or trade activity for the first time or whose qualifications were no longer in demand. Finally, it could be granted in respect of young people under 25 years who were unemployed through lack of qualifications or whose qualifications were no longer those in demand.[660] In addition, assistance might be granted generally for operations in favour of handicapped persons who might be able to pursue a professional or trade activity after medical rehabilitation, vocational training or vocational retraining.[661]

The Fund might contribute to financing assistance to those within the above categories where they were to pursue activities as employed persons.[662] In special cases, to be determined by the Council, assistance could also be granted where they were to pursue activities as self-employed persons.[663] Since agriculture and textiles were treated as such cases by the Council, those who were to pursue self-employed activities in these sectors became eligible for assistance.[664] The distinction between persons who were to pursue employed activities and those who were to pursue self-employed activities was subsequently removed in 1977.[665]

---

656 Art 1(1) of Dec 83/516 ([1983] OJ L289/38).
657 Reg 2396/71 ([1971] JO 249/54) implementing Dec 71/66.
658 Ibid, Art 1(2)(a).
659 Ibid, Art 1(2)(b).
660 Ibid, Art 1(2)(c).
661 Ibid, Art 1(3).
662 Art 3(1) of Dec 71/66 ([1971] JO L28/15).
663 Ibid, Art 3(2).
664 Art 1(2) of Dec 72/428 ([1972] JO L291/158) on assistance from the ESF for persons leaving agriculture to pursue non-agricultural activities; and Art 1(2) of Dec 72/429 ([1972] JO L291/160) on intervention by the ESF in favour of persons occupied in the textile industry.
665 Art 1(2) of Dir 77/801 ([1977] OJ L337/8) amending Dec 71/66. Assistance was made available to the self-employed by Reg 3824/85 ([1985] OJ L370/25) amending, with a view to its extension to cover self-employed persons, Reg 2950/83.

Age acquired more central importance as a criterion of eligibility in Decision 83/516.[666] It was felt that, to respond effectively to the requirements of the labour market, vocational guidance systems should be made more widely available to young people and job-seekers. As a precaution, they should also be available to those whose employment was threatened.[667] Accordingly, assistance could be granted generally in favour of persons under 25 years.[668] Those over 25 years were only eligible if they were: unemployed or threatened with unemployment or underemployment; women wishing to return to work; handicapped persons capable of working in the open labour market; migrants; or persons employed, particularly those in small and medium-sized enterprises, who required retraining in new technology or improved management techniques.[669]

3. Allocation of assistance

According to Regulation 2396/71,[670] in the allocation of assistance, priority was to be given to eliminating long-term structural unemployment in regions which were either less developed or dependent on declining industries.[671] Hence, 60 per cent of the resources of the Fund not devoted to 'specific' operations under Article 4 of Decision 71/66[672] were to be directed each year to operations in such regions.

Regulation 2893/77[673] reinforced the regional bias in allocations. The 60 per cent figure now became a minimum figure for the priority regions.[674] Moreover, Fund assistance was ordinarily limited to 50 per cent of eligible costs. However, regions might be designated as having especially serious and prolonged unemployment problems. Such designation was to be based, in particular, on the lower level of the economic and social development of such regions, their peripheral location in the Community, and their significance for their respective national economies.[675] In their case, the limit to Fund assistance was raised to 55 per cent[676] They originally comprised: Greenland, the French overseas departments, Ireland, Northern Ireland, and the Mezzogiorno.[677]

---

666 [1983] OJ L289/38.
667 Council Resolution of 27 June 1980 ([1980] OJ C168/1) on guidelines for a Community labour market policy, para II.2.
668 [1983] OJ L289/38, Art 4(1).
669 Ibid, Art 4(2).
670 [1971] JO L249/54.
671 Ibid, Art 2.
672 [1971] JO L28/15.
673 Amending Reg 2396/71 ([1977] OJ L337/1).
674 Ibid, Art 1.2.
675 5th and 6th recitals in the preamble to Reg 2895/77 ([1977] OJ L337/7).
676 Art 1.6 of Dec 77/801 ([1977] OJ L337/8).
677 Reg 2895/77 ([1977] OJ L337/7).

Operations located in these regions were accorded 'first-level priority' by the 1977 Guidelines of the Commission for management of the Fund, which meant that assistance was 'virtually guaranteed'.[678] 'Second-level priority' was accorded to operations in other regions qualifying for assistance from the ERDF.[679] These were operations which might not be carried out without assistance from the ESF and were proposed for approval without delay.[680]

Decision 83/516[681] added an age bias in the allocation of assistance. Operations for young people were to receive at least 75 per cent of the assistance from the Fund.[682] At least 40 per cent of the assistance for these operations were to be directed towards regions qualifying for the higher rate of assistance,[683] which now included Greece.[684] The remainder was to support operations in respect of employment in other regions of high and long-term unemployment[685] and/or industrial restructuring.[686]

New Commission Guidelines[687] envisaged that Fund assistance would be concentrated on operations to further employment in regions qualifying for the higher rate of assistance and in two other categories of regions. The first category concerned regions of industrial and sectoral restructuring[688] assisted or proposed by the Commission to be assisted from the non-quota section of the ERDF or assisted under Article 56 ECSC. The second category concerned

---

678 [1977] OJ C141/2, para III.A.1.

679 The Commission, however, considered that the distinction between these priority regions should be abolished (ibid, para B.2).

680 Ibid, para I.D.3.

681 [1983] OJ L289/38.

682 Ibid, Art 7(1).

683 Ibid, Art 7(3).

684 Reg 1989/81 ([1981] OJ L194/4) concerning operations qualifying for a higher rate of intervention by the ESF. Dec 85/568 ([1985] OJ L370/40) amending, on account of the accession of Spain and Portugal, Dec 83/516 added these two countries to the priority regions. It also raised the percentage of Fund resources reserved for such regions to 44.5%.

685 In a Statement ad Art 6 of Dec 83/516 ([1983] OJ L289/38) the Council and Commission declared that special attention should be given to projects to promote employment in regions where the unemployment rate was exceptionally high compared with the national average.

686 In a Statement ad Art 7 (ibid) the Council requested the Commission to prepare proposals regarding 'reliable statistical machinery, taking account, inter alia, of the criterion of GDP per capita'.

687 Guidelines for the management of the ESF for 1984–86 ([1984] OJ C5/2), para I; and Dec 85/261 ([1985] OJ L133/26) on the Guidelines for the management of the ESF for 1986–88, para 1.1.

688 Para 4.3 (ibid) introduced priority for operations outside the priority regions where the restructuring was of an exceptional scale and was located in an area of particularly high unemployment or where the public authorities had introduced exceptional measures to support vocational training and job creation.

regions of high and long-term unemployment. They were drawn up by reference to unemployment rates and *per capita* GDP.[689]

However, there was a permanent disproportion between the applications for financing submitted and the resources available to the Fund. Consequently, allocations of assistance had to be reduced in line with priorities adopted in the legislation and the management guidelines.[690] Thus reductions applied to operations classified at the lowest level of priority for which appropriations were still available.[691] The reduction for each Member State might be weighted to take account of its unemployment rate and *per capita* GDP.[692] However, for 1986 to 1988, where appropriations were insufficient to cover priority operations, a linear reduction was applied. It was calculated in proportion to the financial volume of remaining applications by each Member State.[693]

In practice, the bulk of the assistance from the Fund went to regions with the highest unemployment and lowest *per capita* GDP[694] within the Community and to restructuring regions eligible under the non-quota section of the ERDF.[695] Hence, the geographical allocation of the assistance from the ESF was largely determined by the requirements of regional policy pursued under the EEC Treaty and sectoral policies pursued under the ECSC Treaty.

In fact, the Community legislature had sought to develop the objectives of the Fund so as to make it a more active instrument to promote employment policies. However, increased unemployment produced patterns of assistance allocation which suggested that the Fund still operated more as an equalization or compensatory mechanism.[696] In other words, there were contradictions between 'legislative dynamism' and practical constraints.[697]

---

689 See, later, Dec 87/329 ([1987] OJ L167/56) on the Guidelines for the management of the ESF for 1988–90, para 1.1.

690 AG Da Cruz Vilaça in Case 84/85 UK v EC Commission: assistance for part-time employment [1987] ECR 3765, 3779. See also the Sixteenth Report on the ESF (1989), 5.

691 Guidelines for the management of the ESF for 1979–81 and transitional guidelines for 1978 ([1978] OJ C116/2), para D.1.

692 Para. I.D.2(c) of the Guidelines for the management of the ESF for 1980–82 ([1979] OJ C159/2); for 1981–83 ([1980] OJ C119/3), para 1.4; and for 1982–84 ([1981] OJ C110/3), para 1.3.

693 Dec 85/261 ([1985] OJ L133/26) on the Guidelines for the management of the ESF for 1986–88, para 1.7. In the Guidelines for 1984–86 ([1984] OJ C5/2) a linear reduction method had already been applied in relation to assistance to the priority regions (para 6.3). See, generally, COA special report 1/88 ([1988] OJ C126/1) on national and Community systems and procedures relating to the management of the ESF.

694 Thus, eg, because of its high per capita GNP Groningen was not a priority area for ESF assistance. See Commission Reply to WQ 1380/86 ([1987] OJ C82/25) by Mr Bran van der Lek.

695 Commission Reply to WQ 2304/86 ([1988] OJ C140/2) by Mr Heinz Schreiber.

696 P Hatt, para [284], n 1 above, 90. Cf COA special report 1/88 ([1988] OJ C126/1) on national and Community systems and procedures relating to the management of the ESF, para 5.2.

697 A Gruber, para [293], n 1 above.

4. Scope of assistance

Decision 71/66[698] provided for the Fund to assist 'specific' and 'general' operations.[699] Specific operations were envisaged by the Commission in its opinion,[700] on which the Decision was based. The provision for general operations was added by the Council.[701]

General operations were those which, according to Article 5(2) of the Decision, were to be undertaken pursuant to Regulation 2396/71.[702] Specific operations were those which, according to Article 4 of the Decision, required the enactment of specific Council measures authorizing them.

In the case of either kind of operation, the private sector[703] as well as the public sector could now receive assistance. Employment assistance to businesses, provided that there was no conflict with Community competition policy, could thus be provided.[704]

General operations: General operations were to be 'essentially of a remedial nature'.[705] According to Article 5 of Decision 71/66,[706] they concerned difficulties resulting indirectly from the working of the common market or impeding the harmonious development of the Community. In the case of such difficulties, assistance could be granted without the need for a specific Council decision. It could be granted: to eliminate long-term structural unemployment and underemployment; to train a labour force with the skills needed; and to assist the absorption and reabsorption into active employment of the disabled, older workers, women, and young workers.[707] Such operations were to receive not less than 50 per cent of total Fund resources. In the longer term, however, the greater part of the resources was to be reserved for specific operations.[708]

698 [1971] JO L28/15.
699 See also Notice concerning the presentation of requests for assistance from the ESF ([1972] JO C96/1); and Communication concerning the procedures laid down by the Member States for the submission of applications for assistance from the ESF and their transmission to the Commission ([1982] OJ C6/4).
700 [1969] JO C131/4.
701 J Mégret, JV Louis, D Vignes, M Waelbroeck, JL Dewost, P Brueckner and A Sacchettini, Le Droit de la Communauté économique européenne (University of Brussels, 1973), vii, 57–8.
702 [1971] JO 249/54.
703 Art 8(2) of Dec 71/66 ([1971] JO L28/15). See also the Communication concerning those public authorities which were empowered by Member States to provide financial assistance for operations by entities governed by private law, and which guaranteed the completion of such operations ([1982] OJ C6/2). The distribution as between public and private bodies between 1984 and 1988 was indicated in the Commission Reply by Mr Marin to WQ 676/88 ([1989] OJ C95/11) by Geoffrey Hoon.
704 Commission Reply by Mr Richard to WQ 1304/82 ([1982] OJ C333/26) by Mrs Fuillet.
705 8th recital in the preamble to Dec 71/66 ([1971] JO L28/15).
706 Ibid.
707 Ibid, Art 1(2) and (3).
708 Ibid, Art 9(2).

According to Article 1(1) of Regulation 2396/71,[709] the general operations were to:

(a) aim at solving the problems which arose in a region which, because it was less developed or there was a decline in the main activities, suffered a serious and prolonged imbalance in employment;

(b) aim at facilitating adaptation to the requirements of technical progress of those branches of economic activity in which such progress gave rise to substantial changes in manpower and professional knowledge or skill; or

(c) be undertaken because of substantial changes in conditions of production or disposal of products in groups of undertakings with similar or connected activities which were thus forced to cease, reduce, or transform their activities permanently.

In the context of these operations, assistance could be provided for training programmes, resettlement expenses, tideover allowances, counselling, removal of barriers to employment for disadvantaged (handicapped or elderly) groups of workers, and the improvement of working conditions in less developed regions.[710]

The scope of such assistance might be more closely defined in Commission guidelines. Thus 'adaptation operations'[711] under Article 1(1)(b) were accorded first-level priority in the guidelines where they were carried out in sectors which manifested a reduction in the labour force, notably for reasons of technological changes in production; concerned small and medium-sized enterprises; or envisaged the introduction, in a given sector, of the first applications of a new technology.[712]

In the case of assistance to groups of undertakings facing changed conditions under Article 1(1)(c), first-level priority was accorded to operations which fell within sectors manifesting large-scale structural change of a long-term nature, particularly for reasons of product outlets, and were developed in line with guidelines for assistance to particular sectors. The same priority was accorded to operations carried out by groups of small and medium-sized enterprises, especially those which had a subcontracting or similar activity and were regarded as the most vulnerable.[713]

However, prospects of limited growth, demographic trends and structural adjustment problems, particularly those resulting from the energy crisis, the introduction of new technologies and changes in the international economy

709 [1971] JO 249/54.
710 Art 3(2) of Reg 2396/71 ([1971] JO 249/54).
711 Other Community policies, notably competition policy, meant that operations not opened up to the whole economic sector could not be assisted (para V.B of the 1977 Guidelines, [1977] OJ C141/2).
712 Ibid, para V.B(a).
713 Para V.B(b) of the 1977 Guidelines, [1977] OJ C141/2.

implied the need for reform.[714] Without reform, the resources of the Fund would be too thinly spread, and its work rendered 'defensive' by economic conditions.

Accordingly, under Decision 83/516,[715] general operations were to be carried out within the framework of the labour-market policies of the Member States.[716] Thus the 'Fund [was to] intervene in policy actions to promote employment adopted by the Member States'.[717] The operations were to include those intended to improve employment opportunities for young people, notably by means of vocational training measures after completion of full-time compulsory schooling.[718] Under Article 7(2) of the Decision at least 95 per cent of Fund resources were to be used for such operations.

The operations were now to concern: vocational training and guidance; recruitment and wage subsidies; resettlement and socio-vocational integration in connection with geographical mobility; and services and technical advice concerned with job creation.[719]

Specific operations: Specific operations were to be concerned with improving the employment situation and preventing employment problems; adapting employment to structural developments in the industry concerned;[720] and adding to the effectiveness of Council decisions by alleviating social obstacles to their implementation.[721] According to Article 4 of Decision 71/66,[722] the Council could provide for the Fund to assist such operations. The Council could do so when the employment situation was affected or in danger of being affected either by special measures adopted by the Council in the framework of Community policies or by 'jointly agreed operations' to further Community objectives. The Council could also provide for the Fund to assist such operations when the employment situation called for 'specific joint action' to improve the balance between the supply of, and the demand for, manpower within the Community. The assistance was thus intended to meet situations arising from Community decisions or requiring action at Community level and to meet situations arising indirectly from the

---

714 1st recital in the preamble to the Council Resolution of 27 June 1980 ([1980] OJ C168/1) on guidelines for a Community labour market policy.
715 [1983] OJ L289/38.
716 Ibid, Art 3(1).
717 AG Darmon in Case C-157/90 Infortec Projectos & Consultadoria, Lda v EC Commission [1992] ECR I-3525, I-3532.
718 Art 3(1) of Dec 83/516 ([1983] OJ L289/38).
719 Art 1(2) of Dec 83/516 ([1983] OJ L289/38).
720 See also the Report of the Committee on Social Affairs and Employment on the proposal for a decision on assistance from the ESF to persons employed in the shipbuilding industry, EP Doc 86/74, 14.
721 See also A Gruber, para [293], n 1 above, 262.
722 [1971] JO L28/15.

---

functioning of the common market or impeding the harmonious development of the Community.[723]

Accordingly, assistance was introduced to facilitate implementation of 'jointly agreed operations' for workers leaving the agricultural,[724] textile[725] and clothing industries.[726] At the same time, assistance by way of 'specific joint actions' was made available in respect of the handicapped,[727] migrant workers,[728] young people[729] and women.[730]

Article 4 of Decision 75/459[731] sought to give the former category of specific operations a more systematic basis. It provided that by 30 November 1975 the Council would deliberate on a Commission proposal for persons who were or had been employed in sectors particularly affected by employment imbalances resulting from recession. Due regard was to be had to the regions most affected by employment difficulties.

The resulting proposal[732] envisaged assistance relating to sectors with an unemployment increase since the beginning of 1974 considerably above the Community average. Assistance was also envisaged in regions with an unemployment increase since the beginning of the same year considerably above the national average or in which unemployment in one of the above sectors affected a substantial part of the active population. Due account was to be taken of the absolute level of unemployment in the region concerned.[733]

More particularly, the Commission proposed that the Fund should assist persons affected by the restructuring of the shipbuilding industry.[734] Assistance was envisaged for operations designed to facilitate the employment

---

723 Ibid, 11th recital in the preamble.

724 Dec 72/428 ([1972] JO L291/158).

725 Dec 72/429 ([1972] JO L291/160). For a critical analysis of such assistance, see MJ Macmillen and JS Chard, 'European Social Fund Aid to Textile Workers: the Early Experience' (1978) European Economic Review 269–90.

726 Dec 76/206 ([1976] OJ L39/39) on intervention by the ESF in favour of persons occupied in the textile and clothing industries.

727 Dec 74/328 ([1974] OJ L185/22) on action by the ESF for handicapped persons.

728 Assistance towards courses of specialized teaching for children of migrant workers was provided for by Reg 1761/74 ([1974] OJ L185/1) amending Reg 2397/71. See, later, Dec 77/803 ([1977] OJ L337/12) on action by the ESF for migrant workers.

729 Dec 75/459 ([1975] OJ L199/36) on action by the ESF for persons affected by employment difficulties. See, later, Reg 3039/78 ([1978] [1978] OJ L361/3) on the creation of two new types of aid for young people from the ESF.

730 Dec 77/804 ([1977] OJ L337/14) on action by the ESF for women.

731 On action by the ESF for persons affected by employment difficulties ([1975] OJ L199/36). The 1st recital in the preamble referred to para 26 of the December 1974 Summit Communiqué (Bull EC 12-1974, 1104).

732 Of 14 October 1975 ([1975] OJ C258/5) for a decision on intervention by the ESF in favour of vocational training adjustment measures.

733 Ibid, Art 1.

734 Proposal of 11 January 1974 ([1974] OJ C13/6) for a decision on assistance from the ESF to persons employed in the shipbuilding industry.

and increase the geographical and occupational mobility of such persons,[735] where their jobs were, or risked being, directly affected by the restructuring of this industry.[736] Such assistance was to take the form of a specific programme designed to contribute towards the long-term improvement of the competitiveness of undertakings, so that they could compete on a worldwide basis.

However, these proposals were not accepted by the Council. Consequently, the assistance to implementation of 'jointly agreed operations' remained limited to agriculture and textiles. These were sectors which had already been selected in Council enactments. Yet the problems of other sectors and the need for Fund intervention therein might have been just as great.

Even in relation to agriculture and textiles, legislative arrangements for assistance from the Fund might be inadequate. Thus the Commission sought closer targeting of Fund assistance to agriculture than was required by the Council legislation through its guidelines for the management of the Fund. According to the Guidelines for 1977,[737] first-level priority was accorded to operations which related to the consequences for agriculture of the implementation of the Directives of 17 April 1972;[738] included the same objectives; were carried out in Directive 75/268 regions[739] and concerned those leaving agriculture with a view to vocational retraining in the same regions; or were aimed at certain farm home-helps such as young persons, who had been unemployed or underemployed since leaving school, and wives of farmers seeking employment outside agriculture, even if their husbands remained in that sector.[740] Other operations in this sector might receive second-level priority.[741]

The Guidelines for 1978 to 1981[742] were more restrictive. Priority was accorded only to two kinds of operations. The first kind concerned operations on behalf of persons (farmers, hired agricultural workers or family workers) who left farming – or had left more than two years previously – to take up employment in another sector. The second kind concerned operations on behalf of persons who wished to pursue an activity additional to farming, particularly tourism and craft activities. Both kinds of operations had to be

---

735 The European Parliament considered that the action envisaged should form part of a reorganization and investment policy coordinated at the Community level, due regard being given to regional policy. More particularly, workers in industries related to shipbuilding should be eligible for assistance. See the Resolution of 13 June 1974 ([1974] OJ C76/42) on the proposal for a decision on assistance from the ESF to persons employed in the shipbuilding industry, para 10.
736 Art 1 of the 1974 proposal ([1974] OJ C13/6).
737 [1977] OJ C141/2.
738 See paras [409] ff below.
739 Ibid.
740 Para III.A.1 of the Guidelines for the management of the ESF for 1977 ([1977] OJ C141/2).
741 Ibid, para III.A.2.
742 Guidelines for the management of the ESF for 1979–81 and transitional guidelines for 1978 ([1978] OJ C116/2).

carried out in Directive 75/268 regions or in regions with agricultural income below the Community average.[743] The Guidelines for 1982 to 1984 added priority for operations coming within the framework of specialized measures for the agricultural sector or for the rural environment.[744] Other operations were not accorded priority, which meant that they would be held over until the end of the year and their approval would be subject to finance being available.[745]

In the case of assistance to textiles and clothing, first level priority was accorded by the 1977 Guidelines[746] to two categories of operations. First, it was accorded to operations in favour of persons having to leave the textile and clothing sectors in order to pursue activities in another sector of economic activity. Such operations had to show clearly the scope of the employment problems to be resolved and the strategy to be implemented. Secondly, such priority was accorded to persons who, as a result of structural adjustment measures, left one job in this sector for another in a branch of the same sector showing prospects in due course of viability at Community level.[747]

The Guidelines for 1979 to 1981[748] added the requirement that the first category of operations was to be carried out in textile-producing regions with a particularly high rate of unemployment. They also introduced a proviso regarding operations of the second category. This proviso concerned training operations which led directly to employment in producing goods considered particularly sensitive because of a high-level of market penetration by cheap imports or because of a recognized crisis in the Community market. They could only be assisted, insofar as the products involved were capable of reaching a satisfactory level of competitiveness, particularly in terms of average costs.[749] In other words, training was not to concern production which offered poor prospects of future employment.[750]

The Guidelines for 1982 to 1984[751] were more demanding and required that operations within the second category had to take place within the framework of a conversion or restructuring programme. Second-level priority was accorded to other operations, either for persons remaining in the sector or for those leaving it, when training corresponded to the requirements of jobs assured in advance by employers.[752] No priority was accorded to operations concerning products which were either in a critical situation with regard to

---

743 Ibid, para II.A.
744 Para 2.1.1.1 of the Guidelines for the management of the ESF for 1982–84 ([1981] OJ C110/2).
745 [1977] OJ C141/2, para I.D.3.
746 1977 Guidelines, [1977] OJ C141/2.
747 Ibid, para III.B.1.
748 [1978] OJ C116/2.
749 Ibid, para B.1.
750 Ibid, para 1.A(d).
751 [1981] OJ C110/2.
752 Ibid, para 2.2.1.2.

intra-Community trade (synthetic fibres, tights and stockings, worsted yarn, and pullovers) or were identical to those supplied at low prices by certain 'third world' countries, when such operations were linked to increased productive capacity liable to create new employment problems.[753]

5. Forms of assistance

Decision 71/66[754] envisaged that Member States would propose 'sets of specific measures' for assistance.[755] Accordingly, Regulation 2396/71[756] provided that, save in exceptional circumstances, Fund assistance had to contribute towards the implementation of a specific programme directed at remedying the causes of imbalance affecting employment. Such programmes were to be established for the region, sector, group of undertakings or category of persons concerned. They were to indicate clearly the economic interrelationship of the operations being planned and were to state the objectives and methods for attaining them.[757]

Assistance could also take the form of preparatory studies and pilot schemes. These were to be designed to give guidance to the Council and Commission in the choice of interventions by the Fund. They were also to enable the Member States and those in charge of operations to choose the most effective assistance and to organize the implementation thereof to best effect.[758]

Decision 83/516[759] envisaged assistance from the Fund to operations,[760] including innovatory projects. Assistance to innovatory projects generally had to fall within a Council action programme.[761] Studies and exchange of experience might also be assisted.[762]

D. COHESION

The search for cohesion has imposed new demands on the ESF. However, definition of these demands has not been without problems.

---

753 Ibid, para 1.1.3.2.
754 [1971] JO L28/15.
755 Ibid, Art 6.
756 [1971] JO L245/54.
757 Ibid, Art 1(4).
758 Art 7 of Regulation 2396/71 ([1971] JO L245/54).
759 [1983] OJ L289/38.
760 Ibid, Art 1(2).
761 See also Dec 88/319 ([1988] OJ L143/45) on the Guidelines for the management of the ESF for 1989–91, Annex, para 5.1
762 [1983] OJ L289/38, Art 3(2).

1. Original Objectives 3 and 4

The Single European Act[763] sought to develop the role of the Fund by making it an instrument of cohesion. A closer definition of Fund objectives was considered necessary to prevent the shortage of resources, combined with an excessive number of priorities, leading to use of the linear reduction method in the allocation of assistance.

Objectives 3 and 4 were originally established for the Fund by Regulation 2052/88.[764] The former Objective was 'combating long-term unemployment',[765] and the latter Objective was 'facilitating the occupational integration of young people'.[766] Both Objectives were to be pursued throughout the Community.

Eligibility for assistance: In principle, only assistance to persons unemployed for over 12 months could originally be supported under Objective 3, though this period could be reduced in specific cases to be decided upon by the Commission.[767] Assistance to persons under 25 years of age, however long or short the period during which they had been seeking employment, could be supported under Objective 4.[768]

Moreover, in Objective 1, 2, or 5b regions assistance could be granted in respect of four further categories of persons. They were: unemployed persons generally; persons threatened with unemployment; persons employed in a small or medium-sized enterprise; and working persons involved in an operation which was essential to the achievement of the development and conversion objectives of an integrated programme.[769] In Objective 1 regions apprentices and vocational trainees at secondary school were also eligible.[770]

Allocation of assistance: The Commission, when allocating assistance, should take into account 'the requirements of the labour market and the priorities laid down in employment policies within the Community'.[771] In practice, most assistance was allocated to the United Kingdom, followed by Italy, Germany and France.[772]

---

763 [1987] OJ L169/1.
764 On the tasks of the Structural Funds and their effectiveness and on coordination of their activities between themselves and with the operations of the EIB and the other financial instruments ([1988] OJ L185/9).
765 Ibid, Art 1(3).
766 Ibid, Art 1(4).
767 Art 2(a) of Reg 4255/88 ([1988] OJ L374/21) laying down provisions for implementing Reg 2052/88 as regards the ESF. The Commission responded positively to a request from the Member States for it to make use of this possibility. See Promoting economic recovery in Europe (the Edinburgh growth initiative), COM(93)164, 8–9.
768 Art 2(a) of Reg 4255/88 ([1988] OJ L374/21).
769 Reg 4255/88 ([1988] OJ L374/21), Art 2(b).
770 Ibid, Art 2(c).
771 Reg 2052/88 ([1988] OJ L185/9), Art 3(2).
772 Twenty-Third EC General Report (1990), 191.

Scope of assistance: Regulation 4255/88[773] provided that the Fund could contribute to financing vocational training, recruitment into newly stable jobs, and the creation of self-employed activities.[774] Accordingly, throughout the Community the Fund could support training measures aimed at providing the skills necessary to carry out specific types of employment, except for apprenticeship schemes. Equally, it could support training with the relevant technology content required by technological change and developments in the labour market.[775]

In Objective 1, 2, or 5b regions any vocational training and further training required for the use of new production and/or management techniques in small and medium-sized enterprises could also be supported.[776] More particularly, in Objective 1 regions support could extend to the theoretical portion of apprenticeship training given outside the firm. Again, in specific cases, to be defined according to the particular needs of the Member States and regions concerned, support could extend to that part of the national secondary (or corresponding) education system specifically devoted to vocational training following compulsory full-time schooling. It was stipulated that that part had to meet the challenges posed by economic and technological changes.[777] Finally, training under apprenticeship contracts and training under national secondary vocational education systems could be assisted.[778]

Moreover, in Objective 1, 2, or 5b regions assistance could be granted to measures to encourage job stability and to develop new employment possibilities for persons who were unemployed, threatened with unemployment, particularly within the context of restructuring requiring technological modernization or substantial changes in the production or management system, or employed in small and medium-sized enterprises. Assistance could also be granted to measures to facilitate vocational training for any working person involved in an operation essential to the achievement of the development and conversion objectives of an integrated programme.[779]

The scope of Fund assistance was thus to be somewhat broader in such regions than elsewhere in the Community. However, the 'horizontal' nature of Objectives 3 and 4 was felt generally to preclude *a priori* the selection of

773 Laying down provisions for implementing Reg 2052/88 as regards the ESF ([1988] OJ L374/21).
774 Ibid, Art 1(1).
775 Ibid, Art 1(3).
776 Art 1(4) of Reg 4255/88 ([1988] OJ L374/21).
777 Ibid, Art 1(5). In the same regions, and for three years after the entry into force of the Regulation, recruitment assistance could, according to Art 1(6) (ibid), be extended to non-productive projects which fulfilled a public need involving the creation of additional jobs of at least 6 months' duration for the long-term unemployed aged over 25.
778 Ibid, Art 2(c). Persons employed within the framework of the operations referred to in Art 1(6) (ibid) might also be assisted.
779 Art 2(b) of Reg 4255/88 ([1988] OJ L374/21).

measures to be financed on the basis of the regionalization of intervention.[780] Rather, the need to increase the impact of assistance implied rigorous selection, based essentially on qualitative factors, particularly the requirements and prospects of the labour market.[781]

Accordingly, Commission Guidelines[782] stated that assistance would be allocated preferentially to operations in Objective 1, 2, or 5b regions which were not directly linked to regional or rural development or industrial restructuring. The operations had to demonstrate a special effort to take account of the needs and prospects of the labour market; be of transnational character; concern training in advanced technology; be of innovatory character; concern training and recruitment in the interests of modernization; concern improved and more efficient training structures; or concern operations for persons encountering special difficulties on the labour market.[783]

Forms of assistance: Operational programmes and global grants constituted the main forms of assistance.[784] The Fund could also participate, with up to 5 per cent of its resources, in financing innovatory measures; transfer of knowledge between undertakings; guidance and advice for the reintegration of the long-term unemployed; and measures of preparation, accompaniment and management necessary for implementation of Regulation 4255/88.[785] In addition, pilot projects might be assisted.[786]

More particularly, the Fund was involved in implementation of three Community initiatives.[787] The Euroform initiative was concerned with new skills and new employment opportunities induced by the completion of the internal market and technological change.[788] The Now initiative was concerned with promoting equal opportunities for women in employment and

---

780 Guidelines concerning ESF intervention in respect of action against long-term unemployment and occupational integration of young people ([1989] OJ C45/6), para III.3.
781 Ibid.
782 Guidelines concerning ESF intervention in respect of action against long-term unemployment and occupational integration of young people ([1989] OJ C45/6), para III. 4.
783 Ibid, para V.
784 Art 5 of Reg 2052/88 ([1988] OJ L185/9); and Art 6(1) of Reg 4255/88 ([1988] OJ L374/21).
785 Ibid, Art 1(2).
786 See, eg, Call for proposals for the implementation of the 'Local Social Capital' pilot project – Art 6 of the ESF Regulation ([1998] OJ C228/15).
787 Cf Dec 90/267 ([1990] OJ L156/1) establishing an action programme for the development of continuing vocational training in the EC, which was designed to improve the quality and availability of continuous vocational training in the Community and, in particular, to improve the competitiveness of firms by improving the skills of their employees. It was adopted under Art 128 EEC and was financed under Items B3-1023 and B8-3123 of the General Budget for 1991 ([1991] OJ L30/3).
788 Notice laying down guidelines for operational programmes/global grants in the framework of a Community initiative concerning new qualifications, new skills, and new employment opportunities ([1990] OJ C327/3).

vocational training.[789] The Horizon initiative was concerned with handicapped persons and certain other disadvantaged groups.[790] In addition, there was Youthstart, which concerned the labour-market integration of young people.[791]

2. Revised Objectives 3 and 4

Experience of pursuing the original Objectives 3 and 4 indicated a need for reform. According to the Commission, the legislation allowed for assistance applications to be presented with little justification other than that technically they met the eligibility criteria. In other words, the Fund passively assisted the financing of national policies.[792]

Arrangements of a 'more policy-driven' kind were favoured by the Commission.[793] Such arrangements would take into account economic developments, particularly the effects of further industrial changes on human resource needs.[794] At the same time, account had to be taken of the amendment to Article 123 EEC[795] and the Protocol on Economic and Social Cohesion. The Treaty amendment added 'adaptation [of workers] to industrial changes and to changes in production systems, in particular through vocational training and retraining' to the tasks of the Fund.[796] Moreover, the Protocol established the integration of persons excluded from the labour market as a 'Community policy'.[797] Accordingly, Regulation 2052/88[798] was amended by Regulation 2081/93,[799] and Regulation 4255/88[800] was amended by Regulation 2084/93.[801]

As a result of these amendments, Objective 3 concerned combating long-term unemployment and facilitating integration into working life of

789 Notice laying down guidelines for operational programmes/global grants within the framework of a Community initiative to promote equal opportunities for women in the field of employment and vocational training ([1990] OJ C327/5).

790 Notice laying down guidelines for operational programmes/global grants in the framework of a Community initiative concerning handicapped persons and certain other disadvantaged groups ([1990] OJ C327/9).

791 Community initiative for the occupational integration of young people (Item B2-1423 of the Budget for 1998 ([1998] OJ L44/3)).

792 Operation of the Community Structural Funds, COM(93)124, 11.

793 Operation of the Community Structural Funds, COM(93)124.

794 Community Structural Fund operations 1994–99, COM(93)67, 4.

795 See, now, Art 146 EC.

796 From the Single Act to Maastricht and beyond: the means to match our ambitions, COM(92)2000.

797 Report of the Committee on Social Affairs, Employment, and the Working Environment on the European Parliament's approach to the revision of the ESF, EP Doc A3-57/93, 4.

798 [1988] OJ L185/9.

799 [1993] OJ L193/5.

800 [1988] OJ L374/21.

801 [1993] OJ L193/39.

young people and of persons exposed to exclusion from the labour market.[802] According to the Commission, Objective 3 supported and strengthened policies which were already well established in Member States.[803]

Objective 4 concerned facilitating the adaptation of workers of either sex to industrial changes and to changes in production systems.[804] It sought to forestall the effects of the relevant changes on unemployment.[805] Pursuant to this Objective, it was envisaged that the Fund would address the underlying causes of problems relating to industrial adaptation and not deal with short-term, market-related symptoms. At the same time, it should meet the general needs of workers resulting from changes in production systems identified or predicted and not be designed to benefit a single firm or a particular industry.[806] According to the Commission, Objective 4 'represent[ed] a specific approach to the employment, training, and competitiveness problem'.[807]

Eligibility for assistance: Under Objective 3 the following persons were eligible for assistance: unemployed persons exposed to long-term unemployment;[808] young people[809] in search of employment; persons exposed to exclusion from the labour market; and women not possessing vocational qualifications or returning to the labour market after a period of absence.[810]

Under Objective 4 persons of either sex needing to adapt to changed conditions were eligible. In particular, persons threatened with unemployment or faced with industrial changes and changes in production systems were eligible.[811]

Allocation of assistance: At least 80 per cent of the total resources for Objectives 3 and 4 must be allocated to Objective 3, 'in view of the seriousness of the unemployment problem'.[812] In other words, most of the resources of the Fund were to be used to assist national employment policies. In practice, 35 per cent of spending under Objective 3 was targeted on promoting the

---

802 See, eg, the Call for proposals for pilot actions aiming at integrating the concept of the information society into regional development policies of less-favoured regions ([1995] OJ C253/27).
803 ESF – the new Objective 4, COM(94)510, 3–4.
804 Art 1(3) and (4) of Reg 2081/93 ([1993] OJ L193/5). See, eg, the Call for proposals for pilot projects and demonstration projects concerning innovative schemes for women in agricultural and in rural areas ([1996] OJ C284/21).
805 ESC Opinion of 30 April 1992 (CES(92)501) on the Commission document 'From the Single Act to Maastricht and beyond: the means to match our ambitions', 7. See, more particularly, the Council Resolution of 16 May 1994 ([1994] OJ C149/1) on the automobile industry, para I.9.
806 Operation of the Community Structural Funds, COM(93)124, 15.
807 ESF – the new Objective 4, COM(94)510, 3–4.
808 Rather than 'persons unemployed for more than 12 months'.
809 There is no longer any express age limit.
810 Art 1(1) of Reg 2084/93 ([1993] OJ L193/39).
811 Art 1(2) of Reg 2084/93 ([1993] OJ L193/39).
812 Statement regarding Objective 3 in the Minutes of the meeting between the European Parliament, the Council, and the Commission of 12 July 1993 ([1993] OJ C255/17).

occupational integration of young people.[813] Most assistance was allocated to the United Kingdom and France.[814]

Scope of assistance: In pursuit of Objective 3, the Fund was to assist vocational training; temporary employment; and the development of appropriate training, employment and support structures.[815] In pursuit of Objective 4, assistance was to cover anticipation of labour market trends and vocational qualification requirements; vocational training and retraining, guidance and counselling; and the improvement and development of appropriate training systems.[816]

Further measures were envisaged in regions covered by Objective 1, 2, or 5b. In these regions the Fund was to support employment growth and stability, particularly through continuing training and vocational guidance, and was to boost human potential in research, science and technology.[817] More particularly, in Objective 1 regions it was also to strengthen and improve education and training systems and to contribute to development through the training of public officials.[818]

The Fund might contribute towards expenditure to cover the income and related costs as well as subsistence and travel costs of people participating in the above actions. It might also assist the preparation, management and evaluation of operations in the Member States[819] and provide technical assistance.[820]

Forms of assistance: The forms which assistance might take under Objectives 3 and 4 were the same as in the case of the original Objectives.[821] However, two new initiatives – the Adapt initiative and the initiative on Employment and Development of Human Resources – were adopted.

The Adapt initiative[822] sought to accelerate the adaptation of the workforce to industrial change; to increase the competitiveness of industry, services and commerce; to prevent unemployment by developing the workforce through improving the qualifications of workers and their 'internal and external flexibility' and ensuring greater occupational mobility; and to anticipate and accelerate the development of new jobs and new activities, particularly

813 Commission Reply by Mrs Cresson to WQ 0766/96 ([1996] OJ C297/25) by Thomas Megahy.
814 EU General Report 1994 (1995), 155.
815 Art 1(1) of Reg 2084/93 ([1993] OJ L193/39).
816 Ibid, Art 1(2).
817 Art 1(3) of Reg 2084/93 ([1993] OJ L193/39).
818 Ibid, Art 1(4).
819 Art 2(1) of Reg 2084/93 ([1993] OJ L193/39).
820 Ibid, Art 2(2).
821 See, eg, Call for proposals for innovatory measures under the ESF in the field of new job sources ([1996] OJ C323/13).
822 Communication laying down guidelines for operational programmes or global grants within the framework of the Community initiative, Adaptation of the Workforce to Industrial Change, aimed at promoting employment and the adaptation of the workforce to industrial change ([1994] OJ C180/30).

labour-intensive ones, including exploitation of the potential of small and medium-sized enterprises. Attention was to be given to actions aimed at promoting equal opportunities for women.[823] The initiative was applicable throughout the Union, but particular emphasis was to be placed on the needs of the 'less-favoured regions'.[824]

A further 'priority' within this initiative – Adapt-bis – (building the information society) was adopted.[825] It was to facilitate the transition to the information society and minimize the social exclusion which can result from it.[826]

The initiative on Employment and Development of Human Resources[827] aimed, in turn, to contribute to the development of human resources and to improve the working of the labour market. It was applicable throughout the Union, but particular emphasis was to be given to the needs of less-favoured regions.[828] The allocation of assistance among Member States was based on the relative severity of structural problems, particularly unemployment levels, as well as the quality of proposals submitted.[829]

This initiative absorbed Now, Horizon and Youthstart, and a further 'strand' – Integra – was added. This strand was designed to promote measures to improve the access to the labour market and the employability of vulnerable groups who were excluded or risked being excluded from it.[830]

3. New, sole Objective 3

Objectives 3 and 4 have now been merged to form a sole Objective 3. It is supporting the adaptation and modernization of policies and systems of education, training and employment.[831] This Objective shall provide financial assistance outside the regions covered by Objective 1 and provide a policy frame of reference for all measures to promote human resources in a national territory without prejudice to the specific features of each region.[832] The policy frame of reference is a document which sets the context for assistance concerning employment and human-resource development throughout the

823 Ibid, para 6.
824 Ibid, para 8.
825 Communication laying down amended guidelines for the Adapt initiative ([1996] OJ C200/7).
826 Ibid, para 4.
827 Communication laying down guidelines for operational programmes or global grants within the framework of the Community initiative on Employment and the Development of Human Resources aimed at promoting employment growth mainly through the development of human resources ([1994] OJ C180/36).
828 Ibid, para III.7.
829 Ibid, para VI.17.
830 Communication laying down guidelines for operational programmes or global grants within the framework of the Community initiative on Employment and the Development of Human Resources aimed at promoting employment growth mainly through the development of human resources ([1996] OJ C200/13).
831 Art 1 of Reg 1260/1999 ([1999] OJ L161/1).
832 Ibid, 17th recital in the preamble.

territory of each Member State, and which identifies the relationship with the priorities set out in the National Action Plan for Employment.[833]

The Fund shall support measures to prevent and combat unemployment and to develop human resources and social integration into the labour market in order to promote a high level of employment, equality between men and women, sustainable development, and economic and social cohesion. In particular, the Fund shall contribute to the actions undertaken in pursuance of the European Employment Strategy and the Annual Guidelines on Employment.[834]

Eligibility for assistance: The areas eligible for financing under Objective 3 shall be those not covered by Objective 1.[835]

The financial support of the Fund shall be devoted to the following activities to develop human resources: education and vocational training, including vocational training equivalent to compulsory schooling, apprenticeships, pre-training, in particular the provision and upgrading of basic skills, rehabilitation in employment, measures to promote employability on the labour market, guidance, counselling and continuing training; employment aids and aids for self-employment; in the fields of research, science and technology development, post-graduate training and the training of managers and technicians at research establishments and in enterprises; and development of new sources of employment, including in the social economy.[836]

In order to increase the effectiveness of the above activities, assistance may also be given to structures and systems and accompanying measures. The former concern development and improvement of training, education and skills acquisition, including the training of teachers, trainers and staff, and improving the access of workers to training and qualifications; modernization and improved efficiency of employment services; development of links between the worlds of work and education, training and research establishments; and development, as far as possible, of systems for anticipating changes in employment and in qualification needs, particularly in relation to new patterns of work and new forms of work organization, taking into account the need for reconciliation of family and working life and for enabling older workers to have a fulfilling occupation until retirement. This shall not, however, include the financing of early-retirement schemes. Accompanying measures concern: assistance in the provision of services to beneficiaries, including the provision of care services and facilities for dependants; promoting socio-educational development to facilitate the

833 Ibid, Art 9(c).
834 Art 1 of Reg 1784/1999 ([1999] OJ L213/5) on the ESF.
835 Arts 1 and 5 of Reg 1260/1999 ([1999] OJ L161/1).
836 Art 3(1) of of Reg 2084/93 ([1993] OJ L193/39)

pathway approach to labour market integration; and awareness-raising, information and publicity.[837]

Allocation of assistance: The allocation of assistance is based principally on the eligible population, the employment situation, and the severity of the problems, such as social exclusion, education and training levels, and participation of women in the labour market.[838] Particular emphasis will be given to improving systems for anticipating and facilitating economic and social change as well as improving the participation of women in the labour market. In practice, there will be an indicative allocation of 15 per cent of Fund resources for each of these two policy fields.[839] An allocation by Member State is contained in Commission Decision 1999/505.[840]

With due regard to national priorities as laid down in particular in the national action plans for employment as well as to the *ex-ante* evaluation, a strategy shall be set out taking account of all relevant policy fields and paying particular attention to training and equal opportunities for women. In order to maximize the efficiency of Fund support, its interventions within this strategy shall be concentrated on a limited number of areas or themes and be directed towards the most important needs and the most effective operations. In allocating appropriations to each intervention by the Fund, a joint selection shall be made of the policy fields to be given priority.[841]

The programming of Fund interventions shall provide that a reasonable amount of the Fund appropriations shall be available in the form of small grants, with special arrangements for access by non-governmental organizations and local partnerships.[842]

Scope of assistance: The Fund shall support and complement the activities of Member States directed towards developing the labour market and human resources in the following policy fields, in particular in the context of their multiannual national action plans for employment: developing and promoting active labour market policies to combat and prevent unemployment, to prevent both women and men from moving into long-term unemployment, to facilitate the reintegration of the long-term unemployed into the labour market, and to support the occupational integration of young people and of persons returning to the labour market after a period of absence; promoting equal opportunities for all in accessing the labour market, with particular emphasis on those exposed to social exclusion; promoting and improving training, education, counselling as part of lifelong learning policy to

837 Art 3(2) of Reg 2084/93 ([1993] OJ L193/39).
838 Art 7(3) of Reg 1260/1999 ([1999] OJ L161/1).
839 Explanatory memorandum to the Proposal of 19 March 1998 for a regulation laying down provisions on the Structural Funds, COM(98)131, 31.
840 Decision fixing an indicative allocation by Member State of the commitment appropriations for Objective 3 of the Structural Funds for the period 2000 to 2006 ([1999] OJ L194/63).
841 Art 4(1) of Reg 1784/1999 ([1999] OJ L213/5).
842 Art 4(2) of Reg 1784/1999 ([1999] OJ L213/5).

facilitate and improve access to, and integration into, the labour market, improve and maintain employability, and promote job mobility; promoting a skilled, trained and adaptable workforce, innovation and adaptability in work organization, developing entrepreneurship and conditions facilitating job creation, and enhancing skills and boosting human potential in research, science and technology; and specific measures to improve women's access to and participation in the labour market, including their career development, their access to new job opportunities and to starting up of businesses, and to reduce vertical and horizontal segregation on the basis of sex in the labour market.[843]

In providing such assistance, the Fund shall take account of support for local initiatives concerning employment, in particular initiatives to support local employment and territorial employment pacts; the social and labour market dimensions of the information society, notably by developing policy and programmes designed to harness the employment potential of the information society and by ensuring equal access to its facilities and benefits; and equal opportunities for women and men.[844]

This broad definition of the scope of assistance is designed to facilitate effective dovetailing between the assistance provided and the national action plans for employment. It is also designed to ensure that the assistance is appropriate to the national and regional priorities and policies of each Member State.[845]

Forms of assistance: The Fund will assist operations of an innovatory nature and pilot projects; studies, technical assistance and exchange of experience; technical assistance for the preparation, monitoring, evaluation and control of Fund operations; operations regarding the transfer of special knowledge concerning areas of intervention by the Fund; and information activities. In addition, the Fund is to be responsible for a Community initiative on new forms of combating all forms of discrimination and/or inequalities in access to the labour market.[846]

Innovative measures and technical assistance: The Commission may finance preparatory, monitoring and evaluation operations in Member States or at Union level which are necessary for the implementation of Objective 3 operations. They may include: operations of an innovatory nature and pilot projects concerning labour markets, employment and vocational training; studies, technical assistance and the exchange of experience having a multiplier effect; technical assistance connected with the preparation, implementation, monitoring and evaluation, as well as control of, operations

---

843 Art 2(1) of Reg 1784/1999 ([1999] OJ L213/5).
844 Art 2(2) of Reg 1784/1999 ([1999] OJ L213/5).
845 Explanatory memorandum to the Proposal of 19 March 1998 for a regulation laying down provisions on the Structural Funds, COM(98)131, 17.
846 Art 20(2) of Reg 1260/1999 ([1999] OJ L161/1).

financed by the Fund; operations directed, within the framework of social dialogue, at staff from enterprises in two or more Member States and concerning the transfer of special knowledge relating to areas of intervention by the Fund; and informing the various partners involved, the final beneficiaries of assistance from the Fund, and the general public.[847]

The scope of the operations shall be extended, by a decision for Fund participation, to measures that may be financed under the legislation on the other Structural Funds, so as to cover all the measures necessary for the implementation of the innovative actions in question.[848]

Community initiative: The Fund shall contribute to the implementation of the Community initiative for combating discrimination and inequalities in connection with the labour market ('EQUAL').[849] Decisions on the contribution of the Fund to this initiative may extend the scope of eligible activities to cover measures which can be funded under legislation on the other Structural Funds so as to permit the implementation of all the measures provided for in the initiative.[850]

E. CONCLUSION

The ESF is said to contribute to strengthening the human resource base of the weaker regions, where the lack of a suitably trained workforce is a serious problem. By assisting with training, the Fund, it is also said, helps such regions to develop their endogenous potential.[851] Substantial lasting effects on these regions are expected to result.[852]

In reality, such assistance may merely lead successful trainees to migrate to more prosperous regions where their acquired skills are in demand. As a result, national rather than regional development may be encouraged.

This problem has implicit recognition in a Treaty amendment. In particular, Article 3(i) EEC provided for the creation of an ESF, to improve employment opportunities for workers and to contribute to the raising of their standard of living. As amended, it now provides for a policy in the social sphere comprising this Fund. The implication is that the role of the Fund is to be broadened.

In practice, however, the operations of the Fund may still have more to do with assisting labour-market interventions by Member States than with

847 Art 6(1) of Reg 1784/1999 ([1999] OJ L213/5).
848 Art 6(2) of Reg 1784/1999 ([1999] OJ L213/5).
849 Art 5(1) of Reg 1784/1999 ([1999] OJ L213/5).
850 Ibid, Art 5(2).
851 M Quévit, J Houard, S Bodson, and A Dangoisse, Impact régional 1992: les régions de tradition industrielle (De Boeck, Brussels, 1991), 347 and 352.
852 R Hall and D van der Wee, 'Community Regional Policies for the 1990s' (1992) Regional Studies 399–404.

promoting the regional equality demanded by cohesion.[853] The continuing emphasis on assisting such interventions, particularly training,[854] means that 'those who regard the EC as a Community rather than as a market ... must be rather disappointed'.[855]

---

853 Cf the contrast drawn between the operations of the Structural Funds and an 'entitlement based social policy' in JJ Anderson, para [20], n 5 above, 149.
854 A Cutler, C Haslam, J Williams, and K Williams, 1992 – the Struggle for Europe (Berg, New York, 1989), 81.
855 J Harrop, The Political Economy of Integration in the European Community (Edward Elgar, Aldershot, 2nd edn, 1992), 167–8.

4
EAGGF, GUIDANCE SECTION

A. INTRODUCTION

Article 39(1)(a) EEC provided that the common agricultural policy should seek to increase agricultural productivity. It should seek to do so by promoting technical progress and by ensuring the rational development of agricultural production and the optimum utilization of factors of production, in particular labour.[856] At the same time, concern was expressed for social aspects of farming. According to Article 39(1)(b), the policy should seek to ensure a fair standard of living for the agricultural community, particularly by increasing the individual earnings of persons engaged in agriculture. Moreover, in the elaboration of this policy and the special methods for its application, Article 39(2)(a) required that account be taken of various factors. These factors included the particular nature of agricultural activity, which resulted from the social structure of agriculture and from structural and natural disparities between the various agricultural regions.

To these ends, common organizations of the markets for the various agricultural products might be established under Article 40(2) EEC. Moreover, according to Article 40(4), one or more agricultural guidance and guarantee funds might be created. The rationale for providing for the creation of such funds was that a common organization might necessitate the grant of assistance to farmers. If the organization was really to be 'common' and there was to be 'equal burden sharing',[857] the grant of the assistance could not be left to individual Member States.[858] Rather, the Union must play a central role in its grant. In particular, according to Article 42 EEC, the Council might authorize assistance:

(a) for the protection of enterprises handicapped by structural or natural conditions; and

(b) within the framework of economic development programmes.

---

856 The agricultural and processed products concerned were defined in Annex II to the EEC Treaty.
857 See, eg, Case C-324/96 Odette Nikon Petridi Anonymos Kapnemporiki v Athanasia Simou [1998] ECR I-1333.
858 R Quadri, R Monaco, and A Trabucchi, Trattato istitutivo della Comunità economica europea: commentario (Giuffré, Milan, 1965), i, 296.
859 Ibid.

Such assistance was sought primarily by Italy.[859] Special arrangements were also made for assistance to Luxembourg.[860]

In addition, Article 41 EEC envisaged coordination of efforts in the spheres of vocational training, research, and dissemination of agricultural knowledge, to achieve the objectives of the common agricultural policy. Joint financing of projects or institutions might be entailed. This provision thus authorized the provision of assistance to training[861] and research in the agricultural sector.[862]

All such assistance must be designed to secure 'permanent reconciliation' of the objectives of the common agricultural policy. However, contradictions between these objectives might arise, and in given cases one objective might have to be accorded the temporary priority demanded by economic circumstances.[863]

At the same time, there might be problems of reconciling assistance with competition policy. As the Commission recognized, many factors affected the competitive position of farmers. The climate, soil types, rainfall and proximity to population centres could be an advantage, or disadvantage, to particular farms or regions. Farmers might also be affected by the price of labour, land, or other inputs into the farming process, which might differ on a regional basis. Some of these differences might justify the provision of assistance. Others would not.[864] Indeed, they might be perceived as fuelling the competitive process and as leading to the benefits that society gains from specialization and trade.[865]

---

859 Ibid.

860 See the Protocol on Luxembourg, annexed to the EEC Treaty. This Protocol was invoked in the 8th recital in the preamble to Reg 541/70 ([1970] JO L68/3) on agriculture in Luxembourg, which provided for the grant of assistance by the Guidance Section to Luxembourg.

861 There were proposals of 3 February 1965 concerning Community grants towards the retraining of farmers wishing to change their occupation within agriculture; and concerning Community grants towards the training of advisers to provide information services for farmers and farmworkers wishing to change their occupation. Assistance from the General Budget (special chapter on the CAP) was to be made available under Art 41 EEC (Bull EEC, Supp 3/65, 23 and 27).

862 See, eg, Dec 73/127 ([1973] OJ L153/13) adopting a research programme for the EEC in the field of teledetection of earth resources, which was based on Arts 41 and 235 EEC. However, Dec 75/460 ([1975] OJ L199/37) adopting common research programmes and programmes for the coordination of research in the field of animal leucoses, livestock effluents, beef production, and plant protein protection referred only to Art 43 EEC. It was financed under Chapter 253 of Annex I to the General Budget (see for 1974, [1974] OJ L115/1).

863 Case C-353/92 Greece v EU Council: aid to cereal producers [1994] ECR I-3411, I-3448-9.

864 Distortions of competition in hothouse agriculture, COM(80)306, 32.

865 State aids to agriculture, House of Lords Select Committee on the European Community, HL(1981–82)90, vi–vii.

B. ESTABLISHMENT OF THE COMMON ORGANIZATIONS

The Guidance Section of the European Agricultural Guidance and Guarantee Fund (EAGGF) was created explicitly as an integral element in the establishment of common organizations of agricultural markets.[866] As was judicially recognized, at their initiation the common organizations might not completely measure up to Treaty objectives for agriculture, as listed in Article 39 EEC. Rather, they might contain gaps capable of endangering market stability in a part of the Community.[867] Thus assistance was originally to be an 'accessory' to the establishment of the common organizations.[868]

In March 1963 the Commission had sought to go further and produced a proposal concerning a Fund for the Improvement of Agricultural Structures.[869] According to the explanatory memorandum to the proposal, establishment of the common organizations produced new problems.[870] It also rendered existing problems more difficult to tackle, because old solutions might be prohibited.[871] Hence, the proposed Fund was needed to stimulate and guide efforts to improve agricultural structures consistently with the requirements of this policy and thus to contribute to ensuring a balanced socio-economic situation.[872] To these ends, the Fund would be empowered to assist projects where the socio-economic situation, particularly in agriculture, suffered from backwardness, threatening the implementation of the common agricultural policy. It would also be empowered to intervene, where the implementation of this policy led or would lead to deterioration in the socio-economic situation.[873] Assisted projects had to be included in a regional development programme.[874] Assistance could take the form of interest rebates and loans,[875] though it was not to substitute aids normally granted by national authorities or lead to their

866 Art 1 of Reg 25/62 ([1962] JO 991) on the financing of the CAP.
867 Case 153/73 Holtz and Willemsen GmbH v EC Council and EC Commission [1974] ECR 675, 695.
868 D Gadbin, 'Le Droit communautaire des structures agricoles: organisation ou dilution?' (1991) RMC 218–30, 218.
869 Bull EEC, Supp 4/63.
870 Cf Reg 742/67 ([1967] JO 258/4) creating special sections I and II of the EAGGF concerning Community compensatory measures in favour of Germany, Italy, and Luxembourg and the grant of ua 4 millions to Luxembourg, which provided 3 Member States with compensation to cover the losses of their cereal farmers following application of a common price in this sector. See also Dec 70/355 ([1970] JO L157/27) on the application by Germany of compensatory measures for cereal producers, which authorized complementary state aid under Art 93(2) EEC.
871 Bull EEC, Supp 4/63, paras 4-5.
872 Ibid, Art 1(2).
873 Ibid, Art 2.
874 Ibid, Art 3(2)(a).
875 Ibid, Art 5.

reduction.[876] However, the Commission had to abandon plans for the creation of this Fund in the face of Council objections.[877]

As a result, Regulation 17/64[878] simply divided the EAGGF into two Sections, the Guidance Section[879] and the Guarantee Section.[880] The Guarantee Section sought to affect market development in the short term through financing price support, while the Guidance Section sought in the long term to affect structural conditions of production and marketing.[881] In other words, it was only the Guidance Section which was constituted as a Structural Fund.

The Guidance Section was, during the transitional period for establishment of the common market, to finance common measures undertaken for attaining the objectives set out in Article 39(1)(a) EEC,[882] including structural changes necessitated by the establishment of the common market.[883] Such measures were considered necessary because agricultural returns were often insufficient to finance the necessary changes.[884] In practice, its work during the transitional period was to be limited to coping with such changes.[885]

In a later Commission proposal for a regulation on the implementation of a Community programme for agricultural restructuring,[886] a rather more elaborate statement of the rationale for financing such measures was given. According to the preamble to this proposal, the rationale was that, in much of the Community, agriculture could not adapt to economic developments because of obstacles connected with land as a factor of production. Hence, it was thought that Community assistance for the rationalization of farms and labour mobility was necessary to secure the restructuring which would lead to competitiveness. This proposal was not accepted by the Council, though it was revealing as to the considerations which underlay the provision of Community assistance to farming.

Similar considerations led to the common organization of the market in fishery products[887] being supplemented by structural assistance for the fishing

---

876 Ibid, Art 6(b).

877 R Quadri, R Monaco, and A Trabucchi, para [284], n 2 above, i, 297.

878 On the conditions for granting aid from the EAGGF ([1964] JO 586).

879 See, generally, 'EAGGF: the European Community's Expenditure on the Common Agricultural Policy' (1986) 42 Green Europe.

880 Art 1 of Reg 17/64 ([1964] JO 586).

881 R Priebe, 'Le Droit communautaire des structures agricoles' (1988) CDE 3-38.

882 Now Art 33(1)(a) EC.

883 Art 3(1)(d) of Reg 25/62 ([1962] JO 991).

884 17th recital in the preamble to Reg 17/64 ([1964] JO 586).

885 AG Capotorti in Joined Cases 117/76 & 16/77 Albert Ruckdeschel & Co and Hansa-Lagerhaus Stroh & Co v Hauptzollamt Hamburg-St Annen [1977] ECR 1753, 1783.

886 Proposal of 19 June 1967 ([1967] JO 254/20).

887 Reg 2142/70 ([1970] JO L236/5) on the common organization of the market in fishery products. It was replaced by Reg 100/76 ([1976] OJ L20/1) and Reg 3796/81 ([1981] OJ L379/1).

industry.[888] The aim was to promote harmonious and balanced development of this industry within the general economy and to encourage rational use of the biological resources of the sea and inland waters.[889] Accordingly, assistance could be granted to promote the rational development of the fishing industry within the framework of economic growth and social progress. Assistance could also be granted to ensure an equitable standard of living for the population which depended on fishing for its livelihood.[890] The Commission considered that such assistance should be directed towards alleviating the social costs of restructuring.[891]

The Guidance Section was originally to receive one-third of the total resources made available to the EAGGF.[892] It was to assist adaptation and improvement of agricultural production and of the marketing of agricultural products. It was also to assist development of outlets for agricultural products.[893] Accordingly, assistance was granted for Italian fruit and vegetable production;[894] for fruit production throughout the Community;[895] and for the 'integration of Luxembourg agriculture into the common market'.[896]

Moreover, assistance could be granted for projects for the adaptation or improvement of agriculture necessitated by the economic consequences of implementing the common agricultural policy. Assistance could also be granted for projects which sought to meet the requirements of that policy and to secure improvements in agricultural structures of lasting economic effect.[897] In addition, the Commission proposed that assistance should be granted to agricultural infrastructure,[898] but this proposal was not adopted by the Council.

---

888 5th recital in the preamble to Reg 2141/70 ([1970] JO L236/1) laying down a common structural policy for the fishing industry.
889 Ibid, Art 1.
890 Ibid, Art 10(1). See, later, Art 9(1) of Reg 101/76 ([1976] OJ L20/19).
891 Basic principles for a common policy in the fisheries sector 1966 ([1967] JO 862), E.I.1; and the proposal of 6 June 1968 ([1968] JO C91/1) for a regulation establishing a common structural policy for the fisheries sector; and the fishery management proposals of September 1976, COM(76)500, 18.
892 Art 5(2) of Reg 25/62 ([1962] JO 991).
893 Art 15(1) of Reg 17/64 ([1964] JO 586). See, regarding the regional significance of such action, the First EC General Report (1968), 233.
894 Reg 130/66 ([1966] JO 2965) on the financing of the CAP, Arts 4 and 13.
895 Reg 2517/69 ([1969] JO L318/15) laying down certain measures for reorganizing Community fruit production.
896 Reg 541/70 ([1970] JO L68/3).
897 Art 14(1) of Reg 17/64 ([1964] JO 586).
898 Proposal of 19 June 1967 ([1967] JO 254/53) for a regulation on the implementation of a Community programme for the development of agricultural regions in difficulty or backward regions.

Similarly, in the case of fishing, assistance related to sectoral development efforts,[899] though the assistance might not necessarily succeed in promoting such development. For example, assistance was granted for the construction and modernization of vessels for herring fishing. However, the Community sought to restrict herring fishing for conservation reasons.[900] As a result, many of the vessels in respect of which such assistance was granted had very limited use.[901]

Assistance was to be granted to projects,[902] which were supposed to come within the framework of a Community programme.[903] The programmes were to be adopted by the Council,[904] taking into account the Council Decision of 4 December 1962 on the coordination of agricultural structures.[905] Each programme was to specify the objective to be achieved and the nature of the projects to be undertaken; the regions in which assistance should be concentrated; the percentages of assistance for each category of projects; and the total cost and estimated duration of the programme.[906] Projects would have priority for support, when they formed part of a comprehensive system of measures to encourage the harmonious development of the overall economy of the region concerned. They would have priority, because such projects had greater chances of effectiveness.[907] In practice, however, the tendency was for piecemeal financing of individual projects favoured by Member States.[908]

Continued failure so to programme the operations led to the Commission admission in the *Memorandum on the Reform of Agriculture in the European Economic Community*[909] that the social goals of the common agricultural policy were not being met. In particular, the holdings of the majority of farmers remained uneconomically small and inadequately equipped.[910]

---

899 Cf Reg 2722/72 ([1972] JO L291/30) on the financing by the EAGGF, Guidance Section, of conversion projects in the salt cod-fishing industry.

900 See, eg, Reg 2115/77 ([1977] OJ L247/2) prohibiting the direct fishing and landing of herring for industrial purposes other than human consumption.

901 COA annual report for 1979 ([1980] OJ C342/1), para 5.17.

902 See, eg, Grant of aid from the Guidance Section of the EAGGF for 1966 ([1967] JO 181/9).

903 Art 14(1)(a) of Reg 17/64 ([1964] JO 586). See also the proposal of 19 June 1967 ([1967] JO 254/18) for a regulation laying down general provisions concerning Community programmes for actions of the Guidance Section.

904 Art 16(1) of Reg 17/64 ([1964] JO 586).

905 [1962] JO 2892. See also R Priebe, para [388], n 4 above, 5.

906 Art 16(2) of Reg 17/64 ([1964] JO 586).

907 Ibid, Art 15(1).

908 Cf Reg 2511/69 ([1969] JO L318/1) laying down special measures for improving the production and marketing of Community citrus fruits, which provided for Guidance Section assistance to be granted within the framework of plans drawn up by Member States and approved by the Commission (ibid, Art 2).

909 Bull EC, Supp 1/69.

910 Ibid, 11.

Therefore, an 'autonomous' Community structural policy was considered necessary.[911]

C. DEVELOPMENT OF THE COMMON ORGANIZATIONS

As the common organizations developed, interdependence between market policy and structural policy became increasingly apparent.[912] Thus Regulation 729/70[913] provided for assistance from the Guidance Section to facilitate the structural changes necessary for the proper working of the common market.[914] Such assistance was to take account of the Council Decision of 4 December 1962.[915] According to a Resolution of the Council and Representatives of the Governments of Member States of 21 March 1972,[916] it could be directed towards regional development.[917]

The idea emerged that the Guidance Section acted 'in the higher interest of the proper functioning of ... market organizations'.[918] According to this idea, assistance from the Guidance Section was to relate to 'the structural modifications required' for the proper functioning of these organizations.[919] The emphasis was on implementation of the common agricultural policy.

The importance of such assistance was stressed by the Commission in *Stock-taking of the Common Agricultural Policy.*[920] According to the Commission, price support through the Guarantee Section could not, on its own, solve the income and standard-of-living problems associated with agriculture. On the contrary, disparities in farm incomes might well be increased if the support was not accompanied by a dynamic socio-structural policy and effective regional and social policies. Such policies should entail socially acceptable schemes for the gradual laying-off of workers and the

---

911 R Priebe, para [388], n 4 above, 5.
912 D Gadbin, para [386], n 3 above, 219.
913 On the financing of the CAP ([1970] JO L94/13).
914 Ibid, Art 6(1).
915 [1962] JO 2892. Art 6(3) of Reg 729/70 ([1970] JO L94/13) referred to this Decision.
916 On the application of the Resolution of 22 March concerning the realization, in stages, of EMU ([1972] JO C38/3), para 2.
917 Council Resolution of 25 May 1971 ([1971] JO C52/1) on new guidelines for the CAP, para VII. Assistance for cessation, modernization, training, and marketing improvements was envisaged (ibid, para II).
918 Case 97/76 Merkur Aussenhandel GmbH & Co KG v EC Commission [1977] ECR 1063, 1078.
919 Art 2(2)(c) of Reg 25/62 ([1962] JO 991).
920 Bull EC, Supp 2/75, 36.

establishment of a general economic infrastructure by means of a resolute regional development policy.[921]

1. Objectives of assistance

According to Article 1(3) of Regulation 729/70,[922] the Guidance Section was to finance common measures adopted to achieve the objectives in Article 39(1)(a) EEC, including structural adaptation necessary for the proper working of the common market. The adaptation of agricultural structures sought through these measures was considered a 'basic factor' in the development of the common agricultural policy.[923] At the same time, the Commission considered that regional policy should 'underpin policy on agricultural structures in the less developed rural areas'.[924]

The objectives of such assistance were refined by Regulation 797/85.[925] This Regulation was concerned with reforming the common agricultural policy,[926] tackling problems of surplus production,[927] and taking account of the environment.[928] According to Article 1(1) of the Regulation, Community assistance was to encourage the continuous development of agriculture. In particular, the assistance was to help to improve the efficiency of holdings and to develop their structures, while at the same time ensuring the permanent conservation of the natural resources of agriculture.

According to the preamble to the Regulation, such assistance was to contribute to the overall economic and social development of each region concerned.[929] It was asserted that only through assistance to improve the efficiency of agricultural structures, especially in regions suffering very serious problems, could the objectives in Article 39(1)(a) and (b) EEC be met.[930]

---

921 Moreover, according to the Commission, all assistance to the forestry sector should seek, inter alia, to reduce regional disparities. See para 6 in Annex I to the draft Council Resolution concerning objectives and lines of action for Community regional policy regarding forestry and forest-based industries, COM(83)222, 53–9.

922 [1970] JO L94/13.

923 Case 152/79 Kevin Lee v Minister for Agriculture [1980] ECR 1495, 1505. Thus, eg, the assistance could not apply to the provision of a water supply with a view to the construction of dwelling-houses (ibid, 1506).

924 Report and proposals on ways of increasing the effectiveness of the Community's Structural Funds, COM(83)501, Annex, 3.

925 On improving the efficiency of agricultural structures ([1985] OJ L93/1).

926 R Priebe, para [388], n 4 above, 4 and 6.

927 Note, in particular, the restrictions on assistance to products in surplus (Art 3(2), (3), (4) and (5) of Reg 797/85, [1985] OJ L93/1). This consideration was given increased emphasis in Reg 1760/87 ([1987] OJ L167/1) amending Regs 797/85, 270/79, 1360/78, and 355/77 as regards agricultural structures, the adjustment of agriculture to the new market situation, and the preservation of the countryside.

928 Art 1 of Reg 797/85 ([1985] OJ L93/1). See also the 12th recital in the preamble to Reg 1760/87 ([1987] OJ L167/1); and P Godin, 'Environment and the CAP' (1987) 219 Green Europe.

929 [1985] OJ L93/1, 8th recital in the preamble.

930 Ibid, 5th recital in the preamble.

Accordingly, the results of such assistance were to be evaluated by reference to their effect on the structural changes necessitated by the common agricultural policy and on the harmonious development of Community regions.[931]

Thus the emphasis in the new legislation was on facilitating reform of the common agricultural policy. According to *Perspectives for the Common Agricultural Policy*,[932] price and market rules should regulate supply and demand more efficiently. If they were to do so, unacceptable social consequences for the agricultural population had to be avoided. Indeed, avoidance measures might be seen as a condition of the legality of agricultural reforms.[933] Accordingly, assistance would, as far as possible, be linked with social, regional and environmental factors, rather than production.[934]

2. Eligibility for assistance

Initially, assistance under Regulation 729/70[935] might be limited to farmers capable of reaching at the end of a development programme an income level comparable to that of average non-agricultural workers.[936] This limitation reflected concern that the modernization of holdings could be jeopardized if, on the basis of social or regional considerations, assistance was granted to farmers with few development possibilities. If they were assisted, those with better possibilities would not be given enough incentive to undertake structural improvements. Hence, assistance should be limited to farms from which 'the best results [were] to be expected from the point of view of structural policy'.[937] A consequence was that assistance tended to be more readily available in developed regions than in regions where agricultural structures were backward and overall economic imbalance existed.[938]

Recognition of this problem led to removal of this limitation to eligibility in later measures, such as Directive 75/268.[939]

---

931 Ibid, Art 29.

932 COM(85)333, 49. See also 'Un Avenir pour l'agriculture européenne: les orientations de la Commission' (1985) 34 Europe Verte (notes rapides).

933 Case C-353/92 Greece v EU Council: aid to producers of cereals [1994] ECR I-3411, I-3448.

934 E Guth, 'European Agricultural Policy: Is There Really No Alternative?' (1985) Intereconomics 3–9, 7. However, some reforms, such as stabilizers, might penalize those who had failed to catch up in the past. See M Cuddy, 'Community Policy and the Periphery' (1984) 32 Administration 147–62, 157.

935 [1970] JO L94/13.

936 Art 4(2) of Dir 72/159 ([1972] JO L96/1) on the modernization of farms.

937 AG Reischl in Case 121/78 Giuseppe Bardi v Azienda Agricola Paradiso [1979] ECR 221, 243.

938 Report of the Committee on Regional Policy, Regional Planning, and Transport on aspects of the Community's regional policy to be developed in the future, EP Doc 35/77, 49.

939 See paras [409] ff below.

3. Allocation of assistance

The Commission drew up a draft regulation listing agricultural regions having priority for assistance pursuant to Regulation 729/70.[940] However, the draft was not adopted by the Council. As a result, Community legislation failed to ensure that regions with underdeveloped agricultural structures received assistance in proportion to the gravity of their structural problems.[941]

The Commission did publish criteria for the selection of projects[942] for the improvement of processing and marketing to be supported under Regulation 355/77.[943] These criteria were designed to ensure a 'harmonious distribution' of assistance between Member States.[944] The Commission also adopted unpublished 'internal rules' governing rates of assistance.[945] However, even these arrangements failed to ensure that the development of the local processing industry in the less-favoured regions was encouraged.[946]

Besides, the assistance granted by the Guidance Section was only a small proportion of total EAGGF spending. Price-support measures, financed by the Guarantee Section, used as their direct reference the quantity produced and thus tended to favour large, productive farms.[947] Moreover, in general, comparatively developed northern regions of the Community, because of the composition of their agricultural production (cereals, milk and sugar), benefitted from a higher level of support from the Guarantee Section than southern regions. In the latter regions, production of fruit, vegetables and wine was dominant.[948] In 1989, for example, assistance from the Guarantee Section was ECU 3,751 million for the Netherlands, where 4.7 per cent of the working population was engaged in agriculture. Only ECU 174 million was granted to Portugal, where 20.7 per cent of the population were so engaged.[949] Hence, the impact of the Guidance Section was outweighed by the general tendency of the

940 Proposal of 11 October 1973 ([1973] OJ C106/23) for a regulation on the list of priority agricultural regions and areas referred to in the regulation on finance from the Guidance Section of the EAGGF for projects falling within development programmes in priority agricultural regions.
941 Second Report on the ERDF (1977), 46.
942 [1983] OJ C152/2; [1985] OJ C78/7; [1987] OJ C79/3.
943 On common measures to improve the conditions under which agricultural products were processed and marketed ([1977] OJ L51/1).
944 R Priebe, para [388], n 4 above, 24.
945 Case 15/85 Consorzio Cooperative d'Abruzzo v EC Commission [1987] ECR 1005.
946 M Cuddy, para [403], n 3 above.
947 ESC Opinion of 27 November 1991 ([1992] OJ C40/56) on the development and future of the CAP, para 2.7.2.
948 First periodic report on the social and economic situation of the regions of the Community, COM(80)816, 73. See, regarding the failure of the Guarantee Section to promote regional equality, The Regional Impact of Community Policies (Regional Policy and Transport Series No 17, European Parliament, Luxembourg, 1991), 11. See, earlier, the Study on the Regional Effects of the Common Agricultural Policy (Regional Policy Series No 21, EC Commission, Brussels, 1981).
949 ESC Opinion of 25 May 1992 ([1992] OJ C106/20) on the annual report on the implementation of the reform of the Structural Funds.

common agricultural policy to perpetuate, if not exacerbate, regional inequality.[950] At the same time, additionality requirements meant that assistance from the Guidance Section was, in practice, more accessible to Member States with strong economies and administrative organization.[951]

4. Scope of assistance

Assistance was initially provided pursuant to 'horizontal' measures, which were designed to assist agricultural development throughout the Community. However, recognition of the inadequacy of these measures for structural purposes led to the gradual adoption of various measures designed to target assistance more effectively.

Modernization: Directive 72/159[952] provided for assistance to farmers whose incomes were below average non-agricultural earnings to modernize and so increase their income to at least a comparable level. The purpose of this Directive was to initiate reform of agricultural structures.[953] Thus, according to the fifth recital in the preamble, the assistance was to concern the formation and development of farms capable of adjusting to economic developments. Such farms were those where the farmer had adequate occupational skill and competence; where profitability was verified by accounts; and where the adoption of rational methods of production would ensure a fair income and satisfactory working conditions.

Directive 73/440[954] allowed for regional differentiation of such assistance. It provided that a Member State might refrain from applying some or all of the measures envisaged in the above Directive. However, it might do so only in those regions where a major part of the agricultural industry had already attained the objective of comparable income or where land hitherto exploited for agricultural purposes was intended for other uses.[955]

Early retirement: Directive 72/160[956] sought to assist withdrawals from farming. It provided for the grant of an annuity or a lump sum to farmers aged between 55 and 65 years who took early retirement.[957] Special sub-sectoral

---

950 Cf the ESC Opinion of 24 October 1979 ([1980] OJ C53/22) on the proposals on policy with regard to agricultural structures, para 1.3.

951 R Priebe, para [388], n 4 above, 23, n 81.

952 On the modernization of farms ([1972] JO L96/1).

953 Case 107/80 Giacomo Cattaneo Adorno v EC Commission [1981] ECR 1469, 1486.

954 On the general provisions for the regional differentiation of certain measures provided for in the Directives of 17 April 1972 on the reform of agriculture ([1973] OJ L356/85).

955 Similar requirements applied regarding regional differentiation of the application of Dirs 72/160 and 72/161 (see below).

956 Concerning measures to encourage the cessation of farming and the reallocation of utilized agricultural areas for the purposes of structural improvement ([1972] JO L96/9).

957 Ibid, Art 2.

schemes, such as assistance for cessation of milk production, might also be introduced.[958]

Vocational training: Directive 72/161[959] provided for the grant of assistance for socio-economic guidance for the agricultural population;[960] acquisition of occupational skills by persons engaged in agriculture;[961] and, pending implementation of ESF arrangements,[962] vocational retraining of persons engaged in agriculture who wished to take up an occupation outside agriculture.[963] This measure followed the Council Resolution of 25 May 1971[964] on new guidelines for the common agricultural policy. This Resolution called for the Member States and the Commission to assist the creation of new jobs in regions highly dependent on agricultural employment.[965]

However, without systematic efforts to promote the development of the region concerned, assistance under Directive 72/161 might only have a limited impact. Farmers could only move to jobs outside agriculture if new jobs were created. In regions with a surplus of agricultural workers, the most urgent need was for sectoral diversification. This need could not be satisfied adequately through a directive adopted under the agricultural structural policy. At the same time, assistance under the directive might run counter to efforts to maintain farming in difficult natural conditions.[966]

In recognition of the former problem, the Commission proposed a specific allocation of assistance from the Guidance Section over a five-year period to finance the creation of non-farming jobs in predominantly agricultural regions.[967] The aim was to support the creation of jobs outside agriculture which could be taken up by those who ceased agricultural work and their descendants.[968] However, the proposal was not accepted by the Council.[969]

---

958 Reg 1336/86 ([1986] OJ L119/21) fixing compensation for the definitive discontinuation of milk production.

959 Concerning the provision of socio-economic guidance for persons engaged in agriculture and their acquisition of occupational skills ([1972] JO L96/15).

960 Ibid, Arts 1–4.

961 Ibid, Arts 5–6.

962 Before new legislation came into force, the ESF could only assist vocational retraining of persons who were unemployed or whose companies were undergoing conversion. See para [287] above.

963 Art 7 of Dir 72/161 ([1972] JO L96/15).

964 [1971] JO C52/1.

965 Ibid, para VII.

966 COA special report on the application of Dir 75/268 ([1980] OJ C358/1), para 3.1.1.

967 Proposal of 28 May 1971 ([1971] JO C90/19) on the financing by the Guidance Section of the EAGGF of projects included within the framework of regional development operations in priority agricultural regions.

968 Ibid, Art 1.

969 The Council was willing to do no more than adopt Reg 725/75 ([1975] OJ L73/8) on the transfer to the ERDF of ua 150 million out of the appropriations held in reserve by the Guidance Section of the EAGGF.

Preservation of farming under unfavourable natural conditions: Article 42(a) EEC[970] provided that the Council might authorize assistance for farmers handicapped by structural or natural conditions.[971] In accordance with this provision, Directive 75/268[972] was enacted.

The objective of this Directive was to ensure the continuation of farming. A minimum population level or conserving the countryside in three categories of regions was thereby to be maintained.[973]

First, the Directive applied to mountain areas suffering from permanent natural handicaps. These were handicaps mainly associated with very difficult climatic conditions, the slope of the land and a short growing season, which led to high production costs.[974] Secondly, less-favoured areas in danger of depopulation were covered. These were areas where conservation of the countryside was necessary and which suffered from three disadvantages: infertility, a poor economic situation, and a low or declining population dependent on agriculture.[975] Finally, other areas affected by specific handicaps were covered. These included areas in which farming had to be continued to ensure the conservation of the environment; to maintain the countryside; to preserve the tourist potential of the area; or to protect the coastline.[976]

Assistance might take the form of a compensatory allowance.[977] It might also take the form of development assistance,[978] including assistance for the development of a tourist or craft industry,[979] for which farmers would be ineligible under Directive 72/159;[980] assistance for joint investment schemes for fodder production and for improvement and equipment schemes for pasture and hill grazing land which was farmed jointly;[981] and investment assistance for farmers not capable of attaining the level of earned income required under Directive 72/159.[982]

Such assistance might be problematic. For example, the compensatory allowance might lead to the overstocking of mountain areas with sheep and,

---

970 Now Art 36(a) EC.

971 See, more particularly, Reg 3606/86 ([1986] OJ L335/3) establishing a special emergency measure for the less-favoured areas in Ireland; and Reg 1654/86 ([1986] OJ L145/13) introducing a common measure for replanting and converting olive groves damaged by frost in 1985 in certain regions of the Community, which was a common measure 'of an exceptional nature'.

972 On mountain and hill farming and farming in less-favoured areas ([1975] OJ L128/1).

973 Art 1 of Dir 75/268 ([1975] OJ L128/1).

974 Art 3(3) of Dir 75/268 ([1975] OJ L128/1).

975 Ibid, Art 3(4).

976 Ibid, Art 3(5).

977 Arts 5–7 of Dir 75/268 ([1975] OJ L128/1).

978 Ibid, Arts 8–10.

979 Ibid, Art 10(2).

980 [1972] JO L96/1.

981 Art 11 of Dir 75/268 ([1975] OJ L128/1).

982 Ibid, Art 12.

hence, to severe environmental damage.[983] At the same time, it did not necessarily preserve rural populations, since the recipient need not live on the farm.[984]

Moreover, insofar as such assistance simply reduced the costs of farmers, it might tend to reinforce distortions of competition associated with the common agricultural policy generally.[985] More particularly, assistance designed to compensate for permanent natural handicaps had itself to be permanent. It thus amounted to the kind of 'operating aid' to which the Commission in the application of competition policy was opposed.[986]

Improvement of processing and marketing: Regulation 355/77[987] provided for assistance to projects to improve the processing and marketing of agricultural products.[988] Projects had to contribute to improving the situation of the basic agricultural production sector in question[989] and to have a lasting beneficial effect on agriculture.[990] Moreover, they had to guarantee the producers of the basic agricultural product an adequate and lasting share of the resulting economic benefits.[991]

Priority was accorded to projects which would guide production in a direction sought by the common agricultural policy or involve development of new outlets for agricultural production, particularly through the manufacturing of new products; lighten the burden on the intervention mechanisms of the common organization of the markets by meeting a need for structural improvement in the long term; assist regions experiencing particular difficulty in adjusting to the common agricultural policy or benefit such regions;[992] shorten or improve the marketing channels for agricultural products or rationalize the method of processing such products; or contribute to improvement of the quality, presentation and market preparation of products or the better use of by-products, in particular by the recycling of waste.[993]

---

983 COA annual report for 1996 ([1997] OJ C348/1), para 8.46.
984 Though Member States have discretion to impose a residence requirement on the recipient. See Joined Cases C-9 & 118/97 Raija-Liisa Jokela and Laura Pitkäranta [1998] ECR I-6267.
985 COA annual report for 1996 ([1997] OJ C348/1), para 8.46.
986 A Evans, EC Law of State Aid (Oxford Series in EC Law, Clarendon Press, Oxford, 1997).
987 [1977] OJ L51/1.
988 See, eg, Reg 3974/86 ([1986] OJ L370/9) on the rationalization and improvement of health conditions in slaughterhouses in Belgium.
989 Ibid, Art 9(1). Agricultural structures might be indirectly altered. Cf AG Roemer in Joined Cases 10 & 18/68 Società 'Eridania' Zuccherifici Nazionali v EC Commission [1969] ECR 459, 495.
990 8th recital in the preamble to Reg 355/77 ([1977] OJ L51/1).
991 They could be undertaken by the producers themselves. See Case 107/80 Giacomo Cattaneo Adorno v EC Commission [1981] ECR 1469, 1485.
992 Art 17(2)(c) of Reg 355/77 ([1977] OJ L51/1) provided for a higher level of assistance to be granted in the case of such projects.
993 Ibid, Art 11(1).

Development of producer groups: Assistance for producer groups was introduced by Regulation 1360/78.[994] Such assistance was to remedy the structural deficiencies affecting the supply and marketing of agricultural products in certain regions of France, Belgium and Italy. These deficiencies resulted from the absence of sufficient producer groups in the regions concerned. In these regions the market tended to be supplied by many holdings which were uneconomically small.[995]

Special arrangements for assistance of this kind were also made in certain sectors, such as hops,[996] fruit and vegetables,[997] cotton[998] and fisheries.[999]

Infrastructure improvement: Regulation 1760/78[1000] provided for assistance to improve public amenities in rural areas of France and Italy. The areas had to suffer from infrastructural deficiencies. They also had to be covered by Directive 75/268[1001] or be situated in the Mezzogiorno.

The assistance was extended to the West of Ireland by Article 4 of Regulation 1820/80,[1002] to regions of Germany by Article 2 of Regulation 1938/81,[1003] to Northern Ireland by Article 4 of Regulation 1942/81,[1004] and to Greece by Article 4 of Regulation 1975/82.[1005]

Regional development: Assistance might be granted for agricultural improvements in particular regions.[1006] For example, assistance was granted for the restructuring and conversion of winegrowing in certain Mediterranean

994 On producer groups and associations thereof ([1978] OJ L166/1).

995 AG Jacobs in Case 77/88 Stute Nahrungsmittelwerke GmbH & Co KG v Germany [1989] ECR 1755, 1770. It was unclear whether non-producers were excluded from assistance. See ibid, regarding Art 3a of Reg 516/77 ([1977] OJ L73/1) on the common organization of the market in products processed from fruit and vegetables.

996 Reg 1696/71 ([1971] JO L175/1) on the common organization of the market in hops.

997 Reg 1035/72 ([1972] JO L118/1) on the common organization of the market in fruit and vegetables, Arts 14 and 36.

998 Reg 389/82 ([1982] OJ L51/1) on producer groups and associations thereof in the cotton sector. See also Greek requests in the cotton sector, COM(98)10.

999 Arts 6 and 22 of Reg 2142/70 ([1970] JO L236/5); Arts 6 and 24 of Reg 100/76 ([1976] OJ L20/1); Arts 13 and 26 of Reg 3796/81 ([1981] OJ L379/1); and Art 7b of Reg 3759/92 ([1992] OJ L388/1).

1000 On a common measure to improve public amenities in certain rural areas ([1978] OJ L204/1).

1001 [1975] OJ L128/1.

1002 For the stimulation of agricultural development in the less-favoured areas of the west of Ireland ([1980] OJ L180/1).

1003 On a common measure to improve public amenities in certain less-favoured agricultural areas of Germany ([1981] OJ L197/1).

1004 For the stimulation of agricultural development in the less-favoured areas of Northern Ireland ([1981] OJ L197/17).

1005 On the acceleration of agricultural development in certain regions of Greece ([1982] OJ L214/1).

1006 See, generally, Proposals on policy with regard to agricultural structures, COM(79)122.

regions of France;[1007] improving the rearing of beef cattle in certain less-favoured areas of Northern France;[1008] a flood protection programme in the Hérault Valley;[1009] agricultural development in the French overseas departments;[1010] irrigation in Corsica;[1011] collective irrigation operations in the Mezzogiorno;[1012] agricultural development in less-favoured regions of Northern Italy;[1013] the development of agricultural advisory services in Italy;[1014] the adaptation and modernization of the structure of production of beef and veal, sheepmeat and goatmeat in Italy;[1015] a special emergency measure to assist stock farming in Italy;[1016] agricultural development in certain Greek regions;[1017] the seasonal transfer of sheep, goats and cattle for grazing in Greece;[1018] increasing the staff of the departments responsible for quality control of agricultural products in Greece;[1019] improvement of the structures of the wine-making sector in Greece;[1020] irrigation in Greece;[1021] vine-growing in Portugal;[1022] drainage operations in Ireland;[1023] the

1007 Dir 78/627 ([1978] OJ L206/1) on the programme to accelerate the restructuring and conversion of vineyards in certain Mediterranean regions in France.
1008 Reg 1400/86 ([1986] OJ L128/1) introducing a common measure for the encouragement of agriculture by improving the rearing of beef cattle in certain less-favoured areas of France.
1009 Dir 79/174 ([1979] OJ L38/18) concerning the flood protection programme in the Hérault Valley.
1010 Dir 81/527 ([1981] OJ L197/38) on the development of agriculture in the French overseas departments.
1011 Dir 79/173 ([1979] OJ L38/15) on the programme for the acceleration and guidance of collective irrigation works in Corsica.
1012 Reg 1362/78 ([1978] OJ L166/11) on the programme for the acceleration and guidance of collective irrigation works in the Mezzogiorno.
1013 Reg 1401/86 ([1986] OJ L128/5) introducing a common action for the encouragement of agriculture in certain less-favoured areas of Northern Italy.
1014 Reg 270/79 ([1979] OJ L38/6) on the development of agricultural advisory services in Italy.
1015 Reg 1944/81 ([1981] OJ L197/27) establishing a common measure for the adaptation and modernization of the structure of production of beef and veal, sheepmeat, and goatmeat in Italy.
1016 Reg 2969/83 ([1983] OJ L293/7) establishing a special emergency measure to assist stock farming in Italy.
1017 Reg 1975/82 ([1982] OJ L214/1) on the acceleration of agricultural development in certain regions of Greece.
1018 Reg 764/85 ([1985] OJ L86/4) introducing aid for the transhumance of sheep, goats, and cattle in Greece.
1019 Reg 765/85 ([1985] OJ L86/5) on increasing the staff of the departments responsible for quality control of agricultural products in Greece.
1020 Reg 895/85 ([1985] OJ L97/2) on a common measure to improve the structures of the wine-making sector in Greece.
1021 Reg 2968/83 ([1983] OJ L293/5) introducing a common measure for the acceleration of collective irrigation operations in Greece.
1022 Reg 2239/86 ([1986] OJ L196/1) on a specific common measure to improve vine-growing in Portugal
1023 Dir 78/628 ([1978] OJ L206/5) on a programme to accelerate drainage operations in the less-favoured areas of the West of Ireland.

development of sheep farming in Greenland;[1024] agricultural development on Scottish islands;[1025] agricultural development in the less-favoured areas of Northern Ireland;[1026] and improvement of the processing and marketing conditions in the cattlefeed sector in Northern Ireland.[1027]

Sub-sectoral development: Assistance was granted for the development of various 'sub-sectors'. For example, assistance was granted for the restructuring of vineyards;[1028] conversion from wine production to other activities;[1029] abandonment of wine production;[1030] early retirement from wine production;[1031] and conversion from dairy to beef production.[1032]

Measures were also adopted for the fishing industry. In particular, Regulation 1852/78[1033] provided for assistance to the development of inshore fishing in regions where fishing potential made this possible. It also provided for assistance to the development of aquaculture in regions which were particularly suited to this activity.[1034] Regulation 2908/83[1035] went further. It introduced a common measure for restructuring, modernizing and developing the fishing industry and for developing aquaculture. It was designed to meet

1024 Reg 1821/80 ([1980] OJ L180/9) on the development of sheep farming in Greenland.
1025 Reg 1402/86 ([1986] OJ L128/9) introducing a common action for the encouragement of agriculture in the Scottish islands off the northern and western coasts with the exception of the Western Isles (Outer Hebrides).
1026 Reg 1942/81 ([1981] OJ L197/17) for the stimulation of agricultural development in the less-favoured areas of Northern Ireland.
1027 Reg 1943/81 ([1981] OJ L197/23) on a common measure to improve the processing and marketing conditions in the cattlefeed sector in Northern Ireland.
1028 Reg 458/80 ([1980] OJ L57/27) on collective projects for the restructuring of vineyards.
1029 Reg 1163/76 ([1976] OJ L135/34) on the granting of a conversion premium in the wine sector.
1030 Reg 456/80 ([1980] OJ L57/16) on the granting of temporary and permanent abandonment premiums in respect of certain areas under vines and of premiums for the renunciation of replanting; Reg 777/85 ([1985] OJ L88/8) granting for the 1985–86 to 1989–90 wine years of permanent abandonment premiums in respect of certain areas under vines; and Reg 1442/88 ([1988] OJ L132/3) on the granting for the 1988–89 to 1995–96 wine years of permanent abandonment premiums in respect of wine-growing areas, which involved joint financing by both Sections of the EAGGF.
1031 Reg 457/80 ([1980] OJ L57/23) establishing a system of premiums for the cessation of wine-growing in France and Italy.
1032 Reg 1353/73 ([1973] OJ L141/18) introducing a premium system for the conversion of dairy cow herds to meat production and a development premium for the specialized raising of cattle for meat production. See also Reg 1078/77 ([1977] OJ L131/1) introducing a system of premiums for the non-marketing of milk products and for the conversion of dairy herds, and regarding this measure, Case C-181/96 Georg Wilkens v Landwirtschaftskammer Hannover [1999] ECR I-399.
1033 On an interim common measure for restructuring the inshore fishing industry ([1978] OJ L211/30).
1034 Ibid, Art 1(1). Cf the proposal of 28 November 1975 ([1976] OJ C6/2) for a regulation on a programme for restructuring the non-industrial inshore fishing industry; and the amended proposal of 12 June 1978 ([1978] OJ C148/4) for a regulation on a common interim measure for restructuring the inshore fishing industry, Art 7(b).
1035 [1983] OJ L290/1.

the objectives set out in Article 39(1)(a) EEC. Accordingly, the Guidance Section was to finance projects within the framework of multiannual guidance programmes, designed to achieve a satisfactory balance between fishing capacity and fish stocks. In respect of aquaculture, it was to finance projects designed to achieve a substantial and economically profitable volume of production of fish, crustaceans or molluscs.[1036]

Further measures were adopted for forestry development.[1037] For example, Regulation 269/79[1038] provided for assistance to Mediterranean forestry. The assistance was to contribute to 'the conservation and improvement of the soil, the fauna, the flora, and the surface and groundwater balance'. It was also to contribute to 'the productivity of agricultural land by forming windbreaks and shelter belts and by affecting local water and weather conditions'.[1039]

The linking of forestry development and regional development might, in the light of a Council Resolution of 1971,[1040] be sought in measures relating to particular regions. For example, assistance to forestry development was provided for in Regulation 1820/80,[1041] which was concerned with agricultural development in the less-favoured areas of the West of Ireland.

However, assistance directed specifically towards forestry might entail a potential misuse of land, which might not benefit the overall efficiency of the industry. The assistance permitted marketing of timber below cost and increased supply, thus reducing profitability and willingness to invest. Such willingness was in any case already affected by inadequate information in the market. Even if the assistance did promote efficiency, it would do little to sustain rural communities. Hence, it was argued that intervention in forestry should be primarily directed towards the protection of non-marketed benefits, such as environmental protection, the diversity of plant and animal species, and recreational services. However, in some cases, such as in the case of forest wetlands or where the introduction of fast-growing species was assisted, there might be a conflict between environmental protection and forestry development.[1042]

1036 Ibid, Art 3.
1037 Forestry Policy in the EC, Bull EC, Supp 3/79; and Community action programme regarding forestry and forest-based industries, COM(83)222, 48 and 51.
1038 Establishing a common measure for forestry in certain Mediterranean zones of the Community ([1979] OJ L38/1).
1039 Ibid, 9th recital in the preamble.
1040 Resolution of 25 May 1971 ([1971] JO C52/1) on the new guidelines for the CAP, Part III.
1041 For the stimulation of agricultural development in the less-favoured areas of the West of Ireland ([1980] OJ L180/1), Arts 12 and 13.
1042 S Wibe, 'Policy Failures in Managing Forests' in Market and Government Failures in Environmental Management: Wetlands and Forests (OECD, Paris, 1992), 45–82, 78.
1043 [1985] OJ L93/1.

Agricultural structures: Under Regulation 797/85[1043] assistance might be granted to investments in agricultural holdings;[1044] the installation of young farmers;[1045] other measures to assist agricultural holdings, such as the introduction of the keeping of accounts[1046] and the establishment and operation of groups, services and other facilities for the benefit of several undertakings;[1047] specific measures to assist mountain and hill farming and farming in certain less-favoured areas;[1048] specific regional measures;[1049] forestry measures on agricultural holdings;[1050] adjustment of vocational training to the requirements of modern agriculture;[1051] set-aside of arable land;[1052] extensification;[1053] conversion to production of non-surplus products;[1054] and assistance to environmentally friendly farming in environmentally sensitive areas.[1055]

5. Forms of assistance

The forms of assistance evolved along with changes in the scope of assistance.

Common measures: According to Article 6(1) of Regulation 729/70,[1056] assistance was to be provided in the form of 'common measures', adopted by the Council. When adopting such a measure, the Council was to determine the objective to be attained and the nature of the projects to be assisted; the contribution of the Fund to the common measure; the estimated total cost of the common measure and the estimated time for its execution; the economic and financial conditions; and the necessary provisions concerning procedure.[1057]

1043 [1985] OJ L93/1.
1044 Ibid, Arts 2–6 and 8.
1045 Ibid, Art 7.
1046 Ibid, Art 9.
1047 Ibid, Arts 1012.
1048 Ibid, Arts 13–17.
1049 Ibid, Art 18.
1050 Ibid, Art 20. See also Art 15(3) (ibid), in connection with continuation of compensatory allowances after afforestation in regions covered by Dir 75/268 ([1975] OJ L128/1).
1051 Arts 21–22 of Reg 797/85 ([1985] OJ L93/1).
1052 Ibid, Art 1a, as introduced by Reg 1094/88 ([1988] OJ L106/28) amending Regs 797/85 and 1760/87 as regards the set-aside of arable land and the extensification and conversion of production.
1053 Art 1b of Reg 797/85 ([1985] OJ L93/1), as introduced by Reg 1760/87 ([1987] OJ L167/1) and amended by Reg 104/88 ([1988] OJ L106/28). Extensification consisted in the reduction of the normal output of a holding. See Case C-255/95 S Agri SNC and Agricola Veneta Sas v Regione Veneto [1997] ECR I-25, I-53.
1054 Art 1c of Reg 797/85 ([1985] OJ L93/1), as introduced by Reg 1094/88 ([1988] OJ L106/28).
1055 Art 19 of Reg 797/85 ([1985] OJ L93/1), as amended by Reg 1760/87 ([1987] OJ L167/1).
1056 [1970] JO L94/13.
1057 Ibid, Art 6(2).

For example, Regulation 1820/80[1058] introduced a common measure to stimulate the development of agriculture in the West of Ireland. According to the preamble to this Regulation, achievement of the objectives set out in Article 39(1)(a) and (b) EEC required the provision of assistance appropriate to the production conditions of less-favoured areas.[1059] The measure was to bring about a significant improvement in agricultural structures and in agricultural production possibilities in the areas concerned.[1060] To this end, assistance was to be provided for the improvement of public amenities in rural areas; land improvement; the introduction of specific development action aimed at the orientation of farm production; the improvement of processing and marketing facilities; forestry development; and the provision of training facilities and specialized support services. All assistance granted was to fall within the framework of the regional development programme for Ireland.[1061]

Specific programmes: Regulation 355/77[1062] provided for common measures to take the form of 'specific programmes'. The programmes had to ensure a coherent improvement in the processing and marketing of agricultural products. They also had to contain a detailed analysis of the situation in the sector and of the improvements proposed.[1063] In particular, the programmes had to provide information about the relationship of the programme to any other measures to encourage the harmonious development of the region in question.[1064]

Specific common measures: Article 18 of Regulation 797/85[1065] provided for common measures to take the form of 'specific common measures'. Such measures might be adopted to help remove the structural or infrastructural handicaps suffered by agriculture in certain regions. They were to encourage agriculture in the regions concerned. At the same time, they were to 'harmonize' with any development schemes simultaneously undertaken in non-agricultural sectors and with the needs of the environment.[1066] By doing

1058 For the stimulation of agricultural development in the less-favoured areas of the West of Ireland ([1980] OJ L180/1).
1059 Ibid, 6th recital in the preamble.
1060 Ibid, Art 1(1).
1061 Reg 1030/88 ([1988] OJ L102/1) amending Reg 1820/80 extended this measure to all the less-favoured areas of Ireland for the purposes of Dir 75/268.
1062 [1977] OJ L51/1.
1063 Ibid, 7th recital in the preamble.
1064 Ibid, Art 3(1).
1065 [1985] OJ L93/1.
1066 See also the explanatory memorandum to the proposals for regulations establishing a common measure for the acceleration of agricultural development in certain less-favoured areas of France where beef cattle were reared; a common action for the promotion of agriculture in certain less-favoured areas of Northern Italy; and a common action for the promotion of agriculture in the Scottish Islands off the northern and western coasts with the exception of the Western Isles, COM(85)759, 1–3.

so, they were expected to improve the efficiency of agricultural structures in the regions concerned.[1067]

For example, Regulation 1118/88[1068] introduced a specific common measure to encourage the development of agriculture in certain regions of Spain. It aimed to bring about a significant improvement in agricultural structures. It sought to so through reducing production costs and maintaining agriculture in the regions concerned, which all faced major socio-structural handicaps, without favouring surplus production.[1069] It was to cover the less-favoured areas of Spain within the meaning of Directive 75/268.[1070] Assistance concerned the improvement of the agricultural infrastructure; irrigation works; the reparcelling of agricultural land; improvement of privately owned farmland as part of an overall scheme; forestry; and the improvement of farm housing.[1071]

Integrated development programmes: Since agricultural development depended on the integration of farming into the economy as a whole,[1072] such development could not be achieved through assistance to agriculture alone. The implication was that assistance from the Guidance Section had to be complemented by the operations of other Structural Funds. This implication was recognized by the adoption of integrated development programmes. Such programmes were seen by the European Parliament as a means of countering the tendency of expenditure by the Guarantee Section to favour the richer, more productive regions at the centre of the Community.[1073] They were adopted for the Western Isles of Scotland,[1074] Lozère,[1075] and the less-favoured regions of Belgium.[1076]

For example, according to Article 2 of Regulation 1939/81,[1077] the integrated development programme for the Western Isles was to cover not only measures to improve agriculture, including the afforestation of marginal land, operations to improve the marketing and processing of agricultural products, and measures to develop fisheries. It was also to cover measures relating to tourist amenities, crafts, industrial and other complementary activities essential to the improvement of the general socio-economic situation

---

1067 23rd recital in the preamble to Reg 797/85 ([1985] OJ L93/1).

1068 [1988] OJ L107/3.

1069 Ibid, Art 1(1).

1070 Ibid, Art 1(2).

1071 Ibid, Art 2.

1072 Adjustment of the CAP, Bull EC, Supp 4/83, 6.

1073 Resolution of 17 November 1983 ([1983] OJ C342/88) on ways of increasing the effectiveness of the Community's structural funds, especially that of the EAGGF, Guidance Section, para 6.

1074 Reg 1939/81 ([1981] OJ L197/6) establishing an IDP for the Western Isles of Scotland (Outer Hebrides).

1075 Reg 1940/81 ([1981] OJ L197/9) on an IDP for the Department of Lozère.

1076 Reg 1941/81 ([1981] OJ L197/13) on an IDP for the less-favoured areas of Belgium.

1077 [1981] OJ L197/6.

of the Isles. Article 3(2) stipulated that all such measures had to fall within the framework of a regional development programme formulated according to Article 6 of Regulation 724/75,[1078] as amended by Regulation 214/79.[1079] The Guidance Section was to assist measures forming part of the programme and concerning: the improvement of the structure of agricultural production, excluding premiums granted on a unit of production basis; the planting of windbreaks for the protection of agriculture; operations for improving the marketing and processing of agricultural products; the improvement of the agricultural infrastructure; investments in landing-stages and other shore facilities for the inshore fisheries industry; and the development of aquaculture.[1080] By assisting such measures, the Guidance Section would supplement measures supported by the ERDF and the ESF.

These programmes aimed to ensure that agricultural structural measures and assistance from other Structural Funds were mutually supportive.[1081] However, achievement of this aim implied the need for redefinition of the tasks of the three Structural Funds. This need could not be met solely by adoption of an integrated programme.[1082]

D. COHESION

The tasks of the Guidance Section were, according to Article 3(3) of Regulation 2081/93,[1083] strengthening and reorganizing agricultural and forestry structures, including those for the marketing and processing of agricultural and forestry products; helping to offset the effects of natural handicaps on agriculture; ensuring the conversion of agricultural production and fostering the development of supplementary activities for farmers; helping to ensure a fair standard of living for farmers; and helping to develop the social fabric of rural areas, to safeguard the environment and to preserve the countryside,

---

1078 Establishing an ERDF ([1975] OJ L73/1).

1079 [1979] OJ L35/1.

1080 Art 5 of Reg 1939/81 ([1981] OJ L197/6).

1081 See, regarding difficulties of coordination, the Report of the Committee on Agriculture on aspects of the Community's regional policy to be developed in the future, EP Doc 35/77, Annex, 48-50.

1082 COA special report 2/88 ([1988] OJ C188/1) on the integrated approach to Community financing of structural measures.

1083 Amending Reg 2052/88 on the tasks of the Structural Funds and their effectiveness and on the coordination of their activities between themselves and with the operations of the EIB and the other existing financial instruments ([1993] OJ L193/5).

inter alia, by securing the conservation of natural agricultural resources.[1084] These tasks were to be performed in pursuit of Objective 5a as well as Objectives 1 and 5b. Actions under Objective 5a and Objective 5b were intended to be complementary.[1085]

1. Original Objective 5a

Objective 5a was promoting rural development by speeding up the adjustment of agricultural structures in the framework of the reform of the common agricultural policy. It was the responsibility of the Guidance Section, though the Financial Instrument for Fisheries Guidance now became responsible for fisheries.[1086] In practice, this Objective was said to have been designed to compensate farmers for reduced price support from the Guarantee Section.[1087]

Eligibility for assistance: Where the Guidance Section provided assistance in pursuit of Objective 5a, eligibility depended on the functional requirements of the 'common measures' concerned.[1088]

Allocation of assistance: Indicative allocations of assistance were made. They were based on the need for continuity[1089] regarding the use of resources in the previous programming period and the specific structural needs of agriculture.[1090]

Scope of assistance: In pursuit of Objective 5a, assistance might be provided for market-policy accompanying measures contributing to re-establishing a balance between production and market capacity; measures to support farm incomes and to maintain viable agricultural communities in mountain, hill or less-favoured areas, such as compensation for natural

1084 The European Parliament had proposed the creation of Objective 5c, which would have been concerned with conservation of the environment and continuation of farming in certain mountain and less-favoured regions. See the Report of the Committee on Regional Policy and Regional Planning on the amended proposal for a regulation on the tasks of the structural funds and their effectiveness and on coordination of their activities between themselves and with the operations of the EIB and the other existing financial instruments, EP Doc A2-58/88, 6.

1085 Fourth periodic report on the social and economic situation and the development of the regions of the Community, COM(90)609, 55. See also Report on the EAGGF Guidance Section 1992, COM(94)261.

1086 Art 2(1) of Reg 2080/93 ([1993] OJ L193/1) laying down provisions for implementing Reg 2052/88, as regards the FIFG.

1087 P Cheshire, R Camagni, J-P de Gaudemaar and JR Cuadrado Roura, '1957 to 1992: Moving Toward a Europe of Regions and Regional Policy' in L Rodwin and H Sazanami (eds), Industrial Change and Regional Economic Transformation: The Experience of Western Europe (Harper Collins Academic, London, 1991), 268–300, 292.

1088 Art 2 of Reg 2085/93 ([1993] OJ L193/44) amending Reg 4256/88 laying down provisions for implementing Reg 2052/88 as regards the EAGGF, Guidance Section.

1089 Dec 94/279 ([1994] OJ L120/50) establishing the indicative allocation by Member State of the commitment appropriations from the Structural Funds for the agricultural part of Objective 5a except for those fields covered by Objective 1 for 1994–99, as amended by Dec 98/524 ([1998] OJ L233/32); and Objective 5a: indicative breakdown by Member States of commitment appropriations from the Structural Funds, COM(94)268, 4.

1090 Art 12(4) of Reg 2081/93 ([1993] OJ L193/5).

handicaps; and measures to encourage the installation of young farmers. Provision for assistance to such measures confirmed the rejection of the market mechanism as a resource-allocation device implicit in traditional arrangements for the grant of assistance by the Guidance Section. Other measures were aimed in part at assisting adjustment in a declining sector. They included equally traditional measures to improve the efficiency of the structures of holdings; to improve the marketing and processing of agricultural products; and to encourage the establishment of producer groups.[1091]

Accordingly, Regulation 950/97[1092] provided for assistance for investments in agricultural holdings;[1093] setting-up assistance for young farmers;[1094] assistance for the introduction of accounting practices;[1095] setting-up assistance for farmers' groups;[1096] setting-up assistance for farm relief services;[1097] assistance for farm-management services;[1098] assistance to farmers in less-favoured agricultural areas;[1099] and assistance for adjustment of vocational training to the requirements of modern agriculture.[1100]

Moreover, Regulation 951/97[1101] concerned the improvement and rationalization of the treatment, processing and marketing of agricultural products. Assistance might be granted for investments helping to guide production in keeping with foreseeable market trends or encouraging the development of new outlets for agricultural products; investments relieving the intervention mechanisms of the market organizations by furthering long-term structural improvement, where this was needed; investments in regions faced with special problems in adapting to the economic consequences of developments on the agricultural markets and investments of benefit to such regions; investments helping to improve or rationalize marketing channels or processing procedures for agricultural products; investments helping to improve the quality, presentation and preparation of products or encouraging a better use of by-products, particularly by the recycling of waste; investments contributing to the adjustment of sectors facing new situations as a result of reform of the common agricultural policy; investments helping to

---

1091 Art 2 of Reg 2085/93 ([1993] OJ L193/44); and Reg 952/97 ([1997] OJ L142/30) on producer groups and associations thereof. The latter measure applies to Austria, Belgium, Finland, parts of France, Greece, Ireland, Italy, Portugal and Spain (ibid, Art 2).
1092 On improving the efficiency of agricultural structures ([1997] OJ L142/1).
1093 Ibid, Arts 4–9.
1094 Ibid, Arts 10–11.
1095 Ibid, Art 13.
1096 Ibid, Art 14.
1097 Ibid, Art 15.
1098 Ibid, Art 16.
1099 Ibid, Arts 17–25. These provisions replace Dir 75/268 ([1975] OJ L128/1).
1100 Reg 950/97 ([1997] OJ L142/1), Arts 26–28.
1101 On improving the processing and marketing conditions for agricultural products ([1997] OJ L142/22).

facilitate the adoption of new technologies relating to environmental protection; and investments encouraging the improvement and monitoring of quality and of health conditions.[1102] More detailed criteria for the grant of such assistance were provided by Decision 94/173.[1103]

In the fisheries sector, assistance to the formation and (for three years) the operation of producers' organizations might be provided under legislation on the common organization of the market in fishery products.[1104] Moreover, under Regulation 4042/89[1105] assistance could be granted for improving the situation of the production sectors of fishery and aquaculture basic products; directing production and processing towards the objectives pursued by the common fisheries policy; improving the processing and marketing structures for fisheries and aquaculture products; improving the marketing and distribution networks for fisheries and aquaculture products; improving the hygiene, quality, preservation or packaging of products or the use of by-products; promoting technical innovation; adapting processed products to consumer demand at reasonable prices; stabilizing the market for fishery and aquaculture products; and ensuring the regular and adequate supply of raw materials to the fishery and aquaculture product processing sector. Assistance could also be granted to take account of the Community deficit in fishery products and the need for a balanced exploitation of the internal resources of the Community; cohesion requirements;[1106] and the needs of Objective 1 regions.[1107]

In the case of forestry, Regulation 867/90[1108] provided that measures instituted by Regulation 866/90,[1109] substituted by Regulation 951/97,[1110] might be applied to this sector. Assistance was to be directed preferably to small and medium-sized enterprises, where their restructuring and rationalization might contribute to the improvement and economic development of agriculture and rural areas.[1111]

1102 Ibid, Art 1(2).
1103 On the selection criteria to be adopted for investments for improving the processing and marketing conditions for agriculture and forestry products ([1994] OJ L79/29).
1104 Arts 7 and 25 of Reg 3759/92 ([1992] OJ L388/1) on the common organization of the market in fishery and aquaculture products.
1105 On the improvement of the conditions under which fishery and aquaculture products were processed and marketed ([1989] OJ L388/1).
1106 Ibid, Art 1(1)(a).
1107 Ibid, Art 1(1)(b).
1108 On improving the processing and marketing conditions for forestry products ([1990] OJ L91/7).
1109 On improving the processing and marketing conditions for agricultural products ([1990] OJ L91/1).
1110 [1997] OJ L142/22.
1111 Art 1(2) of Reg 867/90 ([1990] OJ L91/7).
1112 [1997] OJ L142/1.

Forms of assistance: Under Regulation 950/97[1112] the Guidance Section part-financed national aid schemes by reimbursing expenditure incurred by Member States.[1113] Under Regulation 951/97[1114] it provided assistance through operational programmes[1115] and global grants.[1116] It might also contribute to technical assistance and information operations, and support studies or pilot schemes concerning the adjustment of agricultural structures and the promotion of rural development at Union level.[1117]

2. Original Objectives 1 and 5b

In pursuit of Objectives 1 and 5b, assistance might go beyond improving farm structures and the processing and marketing of agricultural products, as required under Objective 5a. Assistance under Objectives 1 and 5b might be provided to measures for the sustainable development of the rural environment. These measures might not only concern developing and strengthening agricultural and forestry structures. They might also concern maintaining, enhancing and restoring the landscape.[1118] Assistance under Objective 1 should tackle the backwardness of agricultural structures.[1119]

Eligibility for assistance: Where the Guidance Section provided assistance in pursuit of Objective 1 or 5b, regional criteria for eligibility were applicable.

Allocation of assistance: Indicative allocations of assistance were made. They were based on the need for continuity regarding the use of resources in the previous programming period and the specific structural needs of agriculture. They might entail higher levels of assistance in Objective 1 regions than in Objective 5b regions.[1120]

Scope of assistance: In pursuit of Objectives 1 and 5b, the Fund might support the conversion, diversification, reorientation and adjustment of production potential, including the production of non-food agricultural products; promotion of local agricultural and forestry products; development of rural infrastructures; encouragement of diversification; renovation and development of villages and the protection and conservation of the rural heritage, to the extent that financing was not provided by the ERDF under

1112 [1997] OJ L142/1.
1113 Ibid, Art 2.
1114 [1997] OJ L142/22.
1115 Reg 860/94 ([1994] OJ L99/7) on plans and applications, in the form of operational programmes, for aid from the Guidance Section of the EAGGF for investments for improving the processing and marketing conditions for agricultural and forestry products.
1116 [1997] OJ L142/22, Art 9.
1117 Art 8 of Reg 2085/93 ([1993] OJ L193/44).
1118 Art 3(1) of Reg 2085/93 ([1993] OJ L193/44).
1119 Ibid, Art 3(2).
1120 Reg 223/90 ([1990] OJ L22/62) fixing the rates of Community part financing for the measures referred to in Regs 797/85, 1096/88, 1360/78, 389/82, and 1696/71.

Regulation 2083/93;[1121] reparcelling and associated work; individual or collective land or pasture improvement; irrigation; encouragement for tourist and craft investments; restoration of agricultural and forestry production potential after natural disasters and the introduction of appropriate prevention measures in ultra-peripheral areas particularly at risk from such disasters;[1122] development and exploitation of woodlands and protection of the environment; maintenance of the countryside and restoration of landscapes, to the extent that financing was not provided for under measures accompanying reform of the common agricultural policy; development of agricultural and forestry advisory services and the improvement of facilities for agricultural and forestry vocational training; measures in the area of forestry technological research and development; and financial engineering measures for agricultural and agri-food businesses.[1123]

Forms of assistance: Assistance pursuant to Objectives 1 and 5b was in the main to take the form of operational programmes, including those using integrated approaches, and global grants.[1124] In addition, the Guidance Section could contribute up to 1 per cent of its resources to pilot projects concerning development of rural areas, including forestry development; technical assistance and preparatory studies; evaluation studies; demonstration projects for farmers; and measures necessary for diffusion of results of work and experience regarding improvement of agricultural structures.[1125]

3. New Objective 1

Objectives 5a and 5b have been abolished, and assistance from the Guidance Section limited to pursuit of Objective 1.[1126] A greater contribution from agricultural spending to 'territorial development' and nature protection is sought.[1127]

1121 Amending Reg 4254/88 laying down provisions for implementing Reg 2052/88 as regards the ERDF ([1993] OJ L193/34).

1122 Cf, earlier, Reg 206/66 ([1966] JO 3869) on the contribution of the EAGGF towards the repair of damage caused by catastrophic floods in certain regions of Italy during the autumn of 1966; and Reg 3222/88 ([1988] OJ L288/1) introducing a common measure for the re-establishment of olive groves damaged by frost in certain regions of Greece. The use of such assistance may be problematic. See, eg, the European Parliament Decision regarding the discharge to the Commission in respect of the implementation of the General Budget for 1994 ([1996] OJ L148/44), para 56.

1123 Arts 5 and 6 of Reg 2085/93 ([1993] OJ L193/44).

1124 Arts 4 and 6 of Reg 2085/93 ([1993] OJ L193/44).

1125 Ibid, Art 8.

1126 Art 2(2) of Reg 1260/1999 ([1999] OJ L161/1).

1127 Explanatory memorandum to the Proposal of 19 March 1998 for a regulation laying down provisions on the Structural Funds, COM(98)131, 32.

Eligibility for assistance: The Guidance Section assists rural development measures in areas eligible under Objective 1.[1128]

Allocation of assistance: Initial allocations of assistance are made. They are broken down on an annual basis and use objective criteria which take into account particular situations and needs, and efforts to be undertaken especially for the environment, job creation and maintenance of the landscape.[1129]

Scope of assistance: Assistance may be granted for investments in agricultural holdings;[1130] start-up assistance for young farmers;[1131] professional training;[1132] and for improving processing and marketing of agricultural products. The assistance is designed to guide production in keeping with foreseeable market trends or to encourage the development of new outlets for agricultural products; to improve or to rationalize marketing channels or processing procedures for agricultural products; to improve the presentation and preparation of products or encourage the better use or elimination of by-products or waste; to apply new technologies; to favour innovative investments; to improve and to monitor quality; to improve and to monitor health conditions; and to protect the environment.[1133]

The Guidance Section may also assist the adaptation and development of rural areas. Such assistance may cover land improvement; reparcelling; setting-up of farm relief and farm management services; marketing of quality agricultural products; basic services for the rural economy and population; renovation and development of villages and protection and conservation of the countryside and conservation of the rural heritage; diversification of agricultural activities; agricultural water resources management; and development and improvement of agricultural infrastructure; encouragement for tourist and craft activities; environmental protection and improvement of animal welfare; restoration of agricultural production potential after natural disasters and the introduction of appropriate prevention instruments; and measures in ultra-peripheral areas particularly at risk from such disasters; and financial engineering.[1134]

1128 Art 35(2) of Reg 1257/1999 ([1999] OJ L160/80) on support for regional development from the EAGGF and Art 1(3) of Reg 1258/1999 ([1999] OJ L160/103) on the financing of the common agricultural policy. Reg 1750/1999 ([1999] OJ L214/31) lays down detailed rules for the application of Reg 1257/1999.
1129 Art 46(2) of Reg 1257/1999 ([1999] OJ L160/80).
1130 Arts 4–7 of Reg 1257/1999 ([1999] OJ L160/80).
1131 Ibid, Art 8.
1132 Ibid, Art 9.
1133 Ibid, Arts 25–28
1134 Art 33 of Reg 1257/1999 ([1999] OJ L160/80).

Forms of assistance: Assistance should form part of integrated development programmes for Objective 1 regions.[1135]

E. CONCLUSION

Union assistance to agriculture may have a *national* impact outweighing that of the ERDF. For example, between 1973, when Ireland joined the Union, and 1991, the disparity of average income in Ireland relative to other Member States narrowed by three or four percentage points. This narrowing is regarded as more likely to have been the result of the common agricultural policy than of operations by the ERDF.[1136] Generally, however, comparatively developed northern regions of the Union have benefitted from a higher level of support from the Guarantee Section of the EAGGF than southern regions.[1137] In other words, the Guarantee Section tends to work against the *regional* equality sought by cohesion. This tendency may be reinforced rather than countered by the operations of the Guidance Section of the same Fund. These operations give more emphasis to restructuring demanded by the common agricultural policy than to cohesion.

Some arrangements for assistance from the Guidance Section, notably those for assistance to farming under unfavourable natural conditions, do acknowledge that, in the case of some farmers, such restructuring may be impossible. At the same time, they implicitly recognize that agriculture and, more particularly, food production[1138] are not the only output of rural resources.[1139] Rather, 'public goods' may be involved.

The inference may be drawn that a balance should be sought between assisting agriculture and assisting alternative rural activities. On the one hand, rural development assistance must, it is said, be rooted in agricultural policy, since rural resources are irrevocably integrated with the dominant rural land use, agriculture.[1140] On the other hand, assistance should be designed to reallocate some rural resources at the margin away from agricultural

1135 11th recital in the preamble to Reg 1257/1999 ([1999] OJ L160/80). See also Commission Reg 445/2002 ([2002] OJ L74/1) laying down detailed rules for the application of Reg 1257/1999 on support for rural development from the EAGGF.
1136 EEC regional development policy, House of Lords Select Committee on the European Communities, HL(1991–92)20, 20.
1137 This tendency was reduced following the 1992 reforms of the CAP. See First cohesion report, COM(97)542, 8.
1138 Guidance Section assistance to Objective 2 regions was criticized for its concentration on the food industry rather than on the restructuring of agricultural production and development of the rural infrastructure. See M Quévit, J Houard, S Bodson and A Dangoisse, Impact régional 1992: les régions de tradition industrielle (De Boeck, Brussels, 1991), 350.
1139 J McInerney, 'Agricultural Policy at the Crossroads' (1986) Countryside Planning Yearbook 44–75, 51.
1140 J McInerney, para [466], n 2 above, 57.

products.[1141] However, such reallocation may be inhibited by price support from the Guarantee Section.[1142] For this reason, the scope of the common agricultural policy is said to be operationally too limited, and its stated objectives are said to be too broad.[1143] The Commission considers that the solution is to design assistance to generate prospects for the future which will allow sufficient farmers to stay on the land; diversify employment in rural areas; contribute to better planning; favour local development; and protect the countryside.[1144]

Accordingly, in the context of reforms to the common agricultural policy, the social and regional role of assistance from the Guidance Section in facilitating adjustment by farmers is stressed.[1145] In practice, however, the assistance is generally designed to restructure the agricultural sector in such a way that it becomes less dependent on price support.[1146] Thus, for example, assistance is not to be granted where it may lead to an overall increase in production capacity in sectors where there are surpluses.[1147]

As a result, criticism of the work of the Guidance Section continues. In particular, it is said that assistance from this Section may still favour sectors in a more advantageous structural, organizational, regional and macroeconomic position. At the same time, 'the international context' demands the ever-increasing liberalization of markets and reductions in assistance. As a result, the weakest agricultural sectors may be permanently forced out of the market under the pressure of greater competition on the Union and international markets.[1148]

1141 Ibid, 58.
1142 Ibid, 64.
1143 Ibid, 69.
1144 From the Single Act to Maastricht and beyond: the means to match our ambitions, COM(92)2000.
1145 Cf the ESC Opinion of 23 March 1994 ([1994] OJ C148/12) on possible developments in the policy of arable land set-aside, para 8.3.
1146 J Rosenblatt, T Mayer, K Bartholdy, D Demekas, S Gupta, and L Lipschitz, The Common Agricultural Policy of the European Community: Principles and Consequences (IMF, Washington, 1988), 24.
1147 10th recital in the preamble to Reg 2843/94 ([1994] OJ L302/1) amending Regs 2328/91 and 866/90 with a view to expediting the adjustment of production, processing, and marketing structures within the framework of the reform of the CAP.
1148 It has been urged that Union preference should be set at a level that will not increase the disadvantages faced by peripheral regions in competing with other areas of the Union. See the Report of the Committee on Agriculture, Fisheries, and Rural Development on the development and future of the CAP, EP Doc A3-0342/91/Part C, 31.

5
FINANCIAL INSTRUMENT FOR FISHERIES GUIDANCE

A. INTRODUCTION

Assistance to the fishing industry was originally provided by the Guidance Section of the EAGGF. However, specific features of this industry required increasing resort to 'other Budgetary resources' and, ultimately, led to the creation of the Financial Instrument for Fisheries Guidance.

B. ESTABLISHMENT OF THE COMMON ORGANIZATION

It was recognized that structural adjustment of the fishing industry might be associated with establishment of the common organization for fisheries. However, it was apparently considered that the adjustment could satisfactorily be assisted by the Guidance Section of the EAGGF.[1149]

C. DEVELOPMENT OF THE COMMON ORGANIZATION

The inadequacy of the Guidance Section of the EAGGF for addressing the structural problems of the fishing industry became clear, as the common organization and structural policy for this sector developed. For example, Directive 83/515[1150] provided for assistance to facilitate adjustment of the production capacity of fishing fleets to reduced catch possibilities.[1151] This measure was described as a 'measure of a specific character [which could] not therefore be treated as a common measure' of the kind supported by the Guidance Section.[1152] Hence, specific provision for assistance from the General Budget was made.[1153] At the same time, Regulation 2909/83[1154] sought to encourage redeployment of capacity. It introduced assistance for exploratory fishing and cooperation through joint fishing ventures involving partners in a

1149 See paras [386] ff above.
1150 Concerning certain measures to adjust capacity in the fisheries sector ([1983] OJ L290/15).
1151 Ibid, Art 1(1).
1152 Ibid, final recital in the preamble.
1153 Art 450 of the Budget for 1984 ([1984] OJ L12/5).
1154 On measures to encourage exploratory fishing and cooperation through joint ventures in the fishing sector ([1983] OJ L290/9).

third country on the Mediterranean or West African coast. Again, specific provision for assistance from the General Budget was made.[1155]

Regulation 4028/86[1156] envisaged a more comprehensive approach to the restructuring of the fishing industry. Assistance granted pursuant to this measure was financed under Chapter 47 of the General Budget for 1988,[1157] which was entitled 'New Structural Measures for Fisheries and the Sea'.

1. Objectives of assistance

According to the preamble to Regulation 4028/86,[1158] the objective of assistance was the balanced exploitation of internal resources in Community waters. Broad account was to be taken of the economic and social environment of the industry. More particularly, account was to be taken of the diversity and seriousness of structural problems at regional level.[1159]

2. Eligibility for assistance

Eligibility for assistance depended on the functional requirements of operations to be financed under Regulation 4028/86.[1160]

3. Allocation of assistance

The allocation of the assistance granted under Regulation 4028/86[1161] was controversial. In particular, there were objections to the concentration of such assistance in regions where the problem of excess fishing capacity was most severe.[1162] It was argued that regional and social considerations should have been given closer attention. According to this argument, regions most heavily dependent on fishing should have received more assistance.[1163]

4. Scope of assistance

The Commission favoured assistance to redeployment and reduction of capacity;[1164] early retirement from the fishing industry generally;[1165] the payment of unemployment benefits for fishermen made redundant as a result

---

1155 Art 451 of the Budget for 1984 ([1984] OJ L12/5).
1156 On Community measures to improve and adapt structures in the fisheries and aquaculture sector ([1986] OJ L376/7).
1157 [1987] OJ L226/3.
1158 [1986] OJ L376/7.
1159 Ibid, 8th recital in the preamble.
1160 Regulation 4028/86 ([1986] OJ L376/7).
1161 Regulation 4028/86 ([1986] OJ L376/7).
1162 COA Special report 3/91 ([1994] OJ C2/1) concerning the implementation of the measures for the restructuring, modernization, and adaptation of the capacities of fishing fleets in the Community, para 3.36.
1163 European Parliament Resolution of 15 May 1992 ([1992] OJ C150/317) on the CFP and the adjustments to be made, para 28. See also the Resolution of 28 October 1992 ([1992] OJ C305/56) on the MGPs 1993–96, para 3.
1164 Proposal of 21 October 1977 ([1977] OJ C278/15) for a regulation on certain immediate measures to adjust capacity in the fisheries sector, Art 3.
1165 Ibid, Art 18(1).

of restructuring sponsored by Community assistance;[1166] vocational training;[1167] and the maintenance or creation of jobs for fishermen in disadvantaged regions.[1168]

Regulation 4028/86[1169] turned out to be less socially oriented. It provided for assistance to the restructuring and renewal of the fishing fleet through the purchase or construction of new ships;[1170] the modernization of the fishing fleet;[1171] the development of aquaculture and structural works in coastal waters;[1172] exploratory fishing;[1173] joint ventures;[1174] adjustment of capacities;[1175] provision of facilities at fishing ports;[1176] and the search for new markets.[1177] Article 28 of the Commission draft for this measure[1178] also envisaged a retirement incentive scheme and a lay-off allowance for fishermen on vessels for which laying-up or final cessation premiums had been granted. However no provision for such assistance was included in the Regulation.

In addition, assistance for improvement of the processing and marketing of fishery and aquaculture products was provided under Regulation 4042/89.[1179]

Regulation 4028/86[1180] was amended by Regulation 3944/90,[1181] which stressed the importance of assistance to small-scale fisheries. Such assistance, it was argued, helped to speed up development in the less-favoured regions which were heavily dependent on fisheries.[1182] Hence, assistance for restructuring and renewal of the fishing fleet, modernization of the fishing

---

1166 Ibid, Art 18(2).
1167 An appropriation for 'Actions leading towards the development of a Common Fisheries Training Policy' was included in the Budget for 1984 ([1984] OJ L27/5), Items 4300 and 4301.
1168 See, generally, Social aspects in the Community sea fishing sector, COM(80)725.
1169 [1986] OJ L376/7.
1170 Ibid, Arts 6–8. Having regard to the global overcapacity in the Community fishing fleet, the Commission decided not to grant assistance for the construction of fishing vessels. See Granting of Community assistance to the fisheries and aquaculture sector within the framework of Reg 4028/86 ([1992] OJ L182/4).
1171 Arts 9–10 of Reg 4028/86 ([1986] OJ L376/7).
1172 Ibid, Arts 11–12.
1173 Ibid, Arts 13–17; and Reg 1871/87 ([1987] OJ L180/1) laying down detailed rules for implementing Reg 4028/86 as regards schemes to encourage exploratory fishing.
1174 Arts 18-21 of Reg 4028/86 ([1986] OJ L376/7); and Reg 1955/88 ([1988] OJ L171/1) laying down detailed rules for implementing Reg 4028/86 as regards joint ventures in the fisheries sector.
1175 Arts 22–26 of Reg 4028/86 ([1986] OJ L376/7).
1176 Ibid, Arts 27–28; and Reg 3856/91 ([1991] OJ L362/61) laying down detailed rules for the application of Reg 4028/86 as regards measures for the provision of facilities at fishing ports.
1177 Arts 29–31 of Reg 4028/86 ([1986] OJ L376/7).
1178 Proposal of 18 September 1986 ([1986] OJ C279/3) for a regulation on Community measures to improve and adapt structures in the fisheries and aquaculture sectors.
1179 On the improvement of the conditions under which fishery and aquaculture products were processed and marketed ([1989] OJ L388/1).
1180 [1986] OJ L376/7.
1181 Amending Reg 4028/86 ([1990] OJ L380/1).
1182 Ibid,11th recital in the preamble.

fleet[1183] and adjustment of capacities[1184] was limited by Article 1(4) of the new Regulation to small-scale fishing fleets.[1185] At the same time, assistance was made available for the creation of joint enterprises,[1186] rather than joint ventures, and for redeployment operations.[1187]

The preamble to the new Regulation also stressed that no structural policy measures in the fisheries sector could be successful if, concomitantly, attention was not given to the socio-economic consequences of such measures, particularly as regards employment and the development of regions heavily dependent on fishing.[1188] Indeed, the lack of social support measures was said to have impeded implementation of the multiannual guidance programmes.[1189] Therefore, it was considered necessary to identify those regions which were socially and economically dependent on fishing and related activities and which were likely to be the most seriously affected by the common fisheries policy. It was also considered necessary to define for those regions appropriate socio-economic flanking measures in order to improve cohesion. However, the operative part of the Regulation merely provided for assistance to small-scale pilot schemes to deal with representative cases of socio-economic problems of Community importance.[1190]

5. Forms of assistance

Assistance was to be granted within the framework of multiannual guidance programmes,[1191] which were to be adopted under Regulation 4028/86.[1192] These programmes had to be designed, *inter alia*, to establish a viable fishing fleet in line with the economic and social needs of the regions concerned and

1183 See, eg, Dec 92/30 ([1992] OJ L11/39) on the small-scale fisheries zonal plan (1991–92) submitted by Greece in accordance with Reg 4028/86.
1184 See, for details of the assistance granted, the Commission Reply by Mrs Bonino to WQ E-0411/96 ([1996] OJ C280/25) by Raphael Chanterie. In practice, however, where such assistance was granted, 'the bulk of the capacity in question [was] effectively ... relocated'. See COA special report 3/91 ([1994] OJ C2/1) concerning the implementation of the measures for the restructuring, modernization, and adaptation of the capacities of fishing fleets in the Community, paras 4.8 and 4.9.
1185 Such fleets were defined in Art 1(5) of Reg 3944/90 ([1990] OJ L380/1).
1186 Ibid, Arts 21a–21d; and Reg 1956/91 ([1991] OJ L181/1) laying down detailed rules for implementing Reg 4028/86 as regards measures to encourage the creation of joint enterprises.
1187 Arts 17a–17d of Reg 3944/90 ([1990] OJ L380/1) and Reg 1859/91 ([1991] OJ L181/83) laying down detailed rules for implementing Reg 4028/86 as regards Community financial assistance for redeployment operations.
1188 2nd recital in the preamble to Reg 3944/90 ([1990] OJ L380/1).
1189 ESC Opinion of 27 May 1992 ([1992] OJ C223/30) on the 1991 report on the CFP, para 2.6.3.
1190 3rd indent of Art 32(1) of Reg 4028/86 ([1986] OJ L376/7), as amended. See, eg, Dec 91/566 ([1991] OJ L307/37) on a concerted measure for the implementation of a socio-economic pilot scheme in the fisheries and aquaculture sector in France; and Dec 92/50 ([1992] OJ L20/14) on a concerted measure for the implementation of a socio-economic pilot scheme in the fisheries and aquaculture sector in Denmark.
1191 [1986] OJ L376/7, Art 1(2).
1192 Ibid, Art 2(1).

the foreseeable catch potential in the medium term. They also had to take account of the socio-economic consequences and the regional impact of sectoral developments.[1193]

In addition, specific measures might be adopted to deal with certain regional or sectoral situations.[1194] Such measures might assist the removal of structural handicaps which affected fishing activities in certain regions; the implementation of a structural project covering all the problems related to fishing activities in a particular region; or the implementation of concerted measures to alleviate difficulties affecting a specific aspect of fishing activities.[1195] Assistance for research might also be provided in the form of Community programmes.[1196]

D. COHESION

Assistance came to be provided under Regulation 3699/93[1197] and funded by the Financial Instrument for Fisheries Guidance (FIFG).[1198] Such funding sought to ensure that specific problems of the fishing industry were taken into account more effectively than was previously possible.[1199]

1. Original Objectives 1, 2, 5a and 5b

The Commission favoured the creation of Objective 6 of the Structural Funds,[1200] which would have covered structural measures in the fishing industry.[1201] However, the Member States apparently proved unenthusiastic about creating a new Objective for this sector, and the idea was dropped by the

1193 Ibid, Art 2(2).
1194 18th recital in the preamble to Reg 4028/86 ([1986] OJ L376/7).
1195 Ibid, Art 32(1). See, eg, Dec 91/258 ([1991] OJ L126/17) on a specific measure to alleviate difficulties affecting whiting fishing in the North Sea.
1196 Reg 3252/87 ([1987] OJ L314/17) on the coordination and promotion of research in the fisheries sector; and Dec 87/534 ([1987] OJ L314/20) adopting Community research and coordination programmes in the fisheries sector for 1988–92. The assistance was to be provided under Art 440 of the Budget for 1988 ([1988] OJ L226/3).
1197 Laying down the criteria and arrangements regarding Community structural assistance in the fisheries and aquaculture sector and the processing and marketing of its products ([1993] OJ L346/1).
1198 The European Parliament had called for the establishment of a European Guidance and Guarantee Fund for Fisheries in its Resolution of 17 November 1983 ([1983] OJ C342/88) on ways of increasing the effectiveness of the Community's structural funds, especially that of the EAGGF, Guidance Section, para 22. In 1989 Chapter 47 of the Budget ([1989] OJ L26/3) had been entitled 'European Fisheries Guidance Fund'.
1199 Reg 3699/93 was repealed by Reg 2468/98 ([1998] OJ L312/19) laying down the criteria and arrangements regarding Community structural assistance in the fisheries and aquaculture sector and the processing and marketing of its products.
1200 According to the European Parliament, it should have been Objective 5c. See the Resolution of 10 December 1991 ([1992] OJ C13/37) on the CFP and the adjustments to be made, para 16.
1201 Community finances between now and 1997, COM(92)2001, 25.

Commission. Instead, the Commission took note[1202] of the conclusion of the Edinburgh European Council that 'appropriate attention should be given to the needs of areas dependent on fishing within the relevant Objectives'.[1203] Hence, Objective 5a was redefined to refer to fishing, with a view to integration of fisheries policy and 'the Union's cohesion effort'.[1204]

In accordance with the redefinition of this Objective, the FIFG was to contribute to achieving a sustainable balance between fishery resources and their management; to strengthen the competitiveness of structures and the development of economically viable businesses in the fisheries sector; and to improve market supply and the value added to fishery and aquaculture products.[1205]

This redefinition was criticized for its failure to ensure that sufficient account was taken of cohesion requirements. For example, the Economic and Social Committee considered that the Objective should have been redefined more broadly to include social measures for the workforce.[1206] The European Parliament favoured more radical reform. According to the Parliament, assistance should be designed to guarantee the preservation of economic activities in coastal areas and to promote the appropriate exploitation of their resources.[1207]

Eligibility for assistance: Eligibility for assistance depended not only on the requirements of Objective 5a, particularly the requirements of the common fisheries policy and multiannual guidance programmes.[1208] Most regions suffering from a decline in fishing and fish processing activities were also likely to be covered by Objective 1, 2 or 5b. Restructuring problems in this sector were, therefore, taken into account in the overall assessment of the infrastructure, training and job-creation needs in these regions. Such regions which were not already covered by these Objectives were brought within their scope.[1209] Their selection was based on 'simple socio-economic parameters such as the relative and absolute number of jobs in the fisheries sector and the contribution to the local economy'.[1210] The question whether they were included under Objective 2 or 5b depended essentially on whether industrial and urban development or rural development was required.[1211]

1202 Community Structural Fund operations 1994–99, COM(93)67, 11.
1203 Conclusions of the Presidency (Bull EC 12-1992, I.55).
1204 Community Structural Fund operations 1994–99, COM(93)67, 11.
1205 Art 1(2) of Reg 2080/93 ([1993] OJ L193/1) laying down provisions for implementing Reg 2081/93 as regards the FIFG.
1206 Opinion of 26 May 1993 ([1993] OJ C201/52) on the amendment of the Structural Fund regulations, para 2.5.6.2.
1207 Resolution of 6 November 1997 ([1997] OJ C358/43) on the CFP after 2002.
1208 Art 4(3) of Reg 3699/93 ([1993] OJ L346/1).
1209 See paras [161] and [174] above.
1210 Community Structural Fund operations 1994–99, COM(93)67, 12.
1211 Ibid.

Allocation of assistance: Indicative allocations of assistance for Objective 5a (fisheries) were made to Member States.[1212] For Objective 1 regions allocations were part of the general assistance arrangements under this Objective. Elsewhere, allocations were based on the relative importance of the fishing industry in the Member State concerned in comparison with all the regions outside Objective 1 and the exact structural situation of the sector in each Member State.[1213]

Scope of assistance: Assistance might be granted for the implementation of measures directly contributing towards ensuring compliance with the requirements of the common fisheries policy. In particular, assistance might be granted to redeployment operations; temporary joint enterprises; joint ventures; and adjustment of capacities.[1214] Assistance might also be granted for restructuring and renewal of the fishing fleet; modernization of the fishing fleet;[1215] improvement of the conditions under which fishery and agricultural products were processed and marketed;[1216] development of aquaculture and structural works in coastal waters; exploratory fishing; facilities at fishing ports; search for new markets; and 'specific measures'.[1217]

The specific measures might apparently include assistance to short-term operations of collective interest undertaken by 'members of the trade'[1218] and assistance for the temporary cessation of activities.[1219] However, the latter kind of assistance might only be granted where the temporary cessation entailed a loss of income and was caused by unforeseen and non-repetitive events, particularly those resulting from biological phenomena.

1212 Dec 94/447 ([1994] OJ L183/50) establishing the indicative allocation by Member State of the commitment appropriations from the Structural Funds for Objective 5a (fisheries structures) 1994–99.

1213 Structural Funds, adaptation of fisheries structures (Objective 5a): allocation of financial resources between Member States, COM(94)421, 2.

1214 Art 2(1) of Reg 2080/93 ([1993] OJ L193/1) laying down provisions for implementing Reg 2081/93 as regards the FIFG. It was proposed that assistance to permanent withdrawal from fishing activities should only cover the scrapping of vessels. See the Explanatory memorandum to the Proposal of 8 October 1993 for a regulation laying down detailed rules for implementing Reg 2080/93, COM(93)481, 5. However, this limitation was only partly acceptable to the Council. See Reg 3699/93 ([1993] OJ L346/1), Art 8(2).

1215 It was proposed that assistance for the building of fishing vessels should only be provided in particular circumstances and where it was compatible with MGP objectives. See the explanatory memorandum to the Proposal of 8 October 1993 for a regulation laying down detailed rules for implementing Reg 2080/93, COM(93)481, 5. The legislation is less restrictive. See Art 10 of Reg 3699/93 ([1993] OJ L346/1).

1216 See also Reg 2636/95 ([1995] OJ L271/8) laying down conditions for the grant of specific recognition and financial aid to producers' organizations in the fisheries sector in order to improve the quality of their products.

1217 Art 3(1) of Reg 2080/93 ([1993] OJ L193/1). See also the Proposal of 4 September 1998 for a decision on a specific measure to encourage diversification out of certain fishing activities and amending Dec 97/292, COM(1998)515.

1218 Art 13 of Reg 3699/93 ([1993] OJ L346/1).

1219 Ibid, Art 14.

At the same time, 'socio-economic' assistance might be granted. In particular, such assistance might be granted to early retirement schemes for fishermen; individual compensatory payments to fishermen whose vessel was permanently withdrawn from fishing or transferred to a third country; and establishment of bad-weather unemployment funds and mechanisms for the financial compensation of fishermen, when the market value of products landed fluctuated sharply.[1220]

Form of assistance: Assistance was to be provided within the framework of Community programmes.[1221] The latter were to be drawn up in accordance with the objectives of the common fisheries policy and provisions of multiannual guidance programmes.[1222] Assistance might take the form of the part-financing of operational programmes; part-financing of national aid schemes; provision of global grants; part-financing of projects; or support for technical assistance.[1223] In addition, specific operations might be adopted in favour of small-scale fisheries and small-scale coastal fishing.[1224] Finally, socio-economic studies might be financed.[1225]

2. New Objective 1 and structural actions

Structural assistance to fisheries and aquaculture is now provided for in Regulation 1263/1999.[1226] The Regulation seeks to ensure that specific problems of the fishing industry are taken into account more effectively than was previously possible. Particular importance will be attached to the economic diversification of regions affected by a reduction in fishing activity and to fleet renewal, without involving an increase in fishing efforts.[1227] The Instrument is now to be limited to providing assistance in pursuit of Objective 1 and to other structural actions outside Objective 1 regions.[1228]

The FIFG is to contribute to achieving a sustainable balance between fishery resources and their exploitation; to strengthen the competitiveness of structures and the development of economically viable enterprises in the sector; to improve market supply and the value added to fishery and

---

1220 Art 14a of Reg 3699/93 ([1993] OJ L346/1), as introduced by Reg 2719/95 ([1995] OJ L283/3). See also Crisis in the Community's fishing industry, COM(94)335, 22-3.
1221 Art 4(2) of Reg 3699/93 ([1993] OJ L346/1).
1222 Ibid, Art 4(3).
1223 Ibid, Art 3(2).
1224 Art B2-910 of the 1998 Budget ([1998] OJ L44/3). See, eg, Call for proposals concerning pilot projects to assist small-scale coastal fishing ([1997] OJ C216/30); and Call for proposals for pilot projects to assist women family members in small-scale coastal fishing communities ([1997] OJ C216/31).
1225 In accordance with Art 4(1) of Reg 3760/92 ([1992] OJ L389/1), CFP measures were to be drawn up in the light of the available biological, socio-economic, and technical analyses. See, eg, 1997 Call for proposals for socio-economic study projects in the context of the CFP ([1997] OJ C232/21).
1226 On the FIFG ([1999] OJ L161/54).
1227 Item B2-101 of the General Budget for 2003 ([2003] OJ L54/1).
1228 Reg 1260/1999 ([1999] OJ L161/1), Art 2(2) and 3.

aquaculture products; and to contribute to revitalizing areas dependent on fisheries and aquaculture.[1229] Assistance outside Objective 1 regions will attach particular importance to the economic diversification of regions affected by a reduction in fishing activity and to fleet renewal, without involving an increase in fishing efforts.[1230]

Eligibility for assistance: The Instrument may provide assistance in regions covered by Objective 1 or to structural actions covered by Regulation 1263/1999.[1231]

Allocation of assistance: For Objective 1 regions, allocations are part of the general assistance arrangements under this Objective.[1232] The Commission shall make indicative breakdowns by Member State of the commitment appropriations available for the structural actions in the fisheries sector outside Objective 1 regions by the FIFG.[1233] Allocations are based on the relative importance of the fishing industry in the Member State concerned in comparison with all the regions outside Objective 1 and the exact structural situation of the sector in each Member State.

Scope of assistance: Assistance may be granted for fleet renewal and modernization of fishing vessels; adjustment of fishing effort; joint enterprises; small-scale coastal fishing; socio-economic measures; protection of marine resources in coastal waters; aquaculture; fishing port facilities; processing and marketing of fishery and aquaculture products; measures to find and promote new market outlets; operations by members of the trade; and temporary cessation of activities and other financial compensation.[1234]

Forms of assistance: Measures implemented with assistance from the FIFG in Objective 1 regions shall form part of the programming of this Objective. Other measures shall be subject to a Single Programming Document in each Member State concerned.[1235] In addition, the FIFG may contribute to innovative actions, including transnational operations and the establishment of networks for those operating in the sector and areas dependent on fisheries and aquaculture, and technical assistance measures.[1236]

1229 Art 1(2) of Reg 1263/1999 ([1999] OJ L161/54).
1230 Item B2-130 of the General Budget for 2003 ([2003] OJ L54/1).
1231 Art 2(2) of Reg 1260/1999 ([1999] OJ L161/1). See also Reg 2792/1999 ([1999] OJ L337/10) laying down the detailed rules and arrangements regarding Community structural assistance in the fisheries sector; and Reg 366/2001 ([2001] OJ L55/3) laying down detailed rules for implementing the measures provided for in Reg 2792/1999.
1232 Art 2(2) of Reg 1263/1999 ([1999] OJ L161/54).
1233 Art 7(3) of Reg 1260/1999 ([1999] OJ L161/1).
1234 Art 2(3) of Reg 1263/1999 ([1999] OJ L161/54).
1235 Art 2(2) of Reg 1263/1999 ([1999] OJ L161/54).
1236 Ibid, Art 2(5).

E. CONCLUSION

Union assistance to fishing has been criticized for its failure[1237] to reduce capacity[1238] and for doing nothing to tackle the growing capability of the fleet which results from technological advances.[1239] Such criticism suggests that the main concern of assistance should be to encourage more effective efforts to reduce capacity. In connection with such efforts, Article 11 of Regulation 3760/92[1240] required the Council to set the objectives and detailed rules for restructuring the sector. The Council was to do so with a view to achieving a sustainable balance between resources and their exploitation. Such restructuring was to take account on a case-by-case basis of possible economic and social consequences for fishing regions. However, in Decision 94/15[1241] the Council simply set the same requirements as to reduction in fishing capacity for each Member State.[1242]

At the same time, criticism has been levied against the failure of the legislation to ensure that adequate account is taken of regional and social considerations. Accordingly, it has been argued that a more efficient social policy, particularly in the least-favoured maritime regions, is needed to alleviate the impact of the restructuring of the Union fleet.[1243]

1237 Eg, in the case of France, compare Dec 88/121 ([1988] OJ L62/21) on the MGP for the fishery fleet forwarded by France with Dec 90/229 ([1990] OJ L124/48) amending Dec 86/121 concerning the MGP for the fishing fleet (1987–91) forwarded by France.

1238 Report on the CFP, SEC(91)2288. Results remained mixed. See, eg, Annual report on the results of the MGPs for the fishing fleets at the end of 1996, COM(97)352. But cf the view that aid to joint enterprises was effective in reducing capacity in the COA annual report 1997 ([1998] OJ C349/1), 57 (Commission reply).

1239 Review of the CFP, House of Lords Select Committee on the European Communities, HL(1992–93)9, 11. See also the European Parliament Resolution of 15 May 1992 ([1992] OJ C150/317) on the CFP and the adjustments to be made, para 2.

1240 Establishing a Community system for fisheries and aquaculture ([1992] OJ L389/1).

1241 Relating to the objectives and detailed rules for restructuring the Community fisheries sector over the period 1 January 1994 to 31 December 1996 with a view to achieving a lasting balance between the resources and their exploitation ([1994] OJ L10/20).

1242 Cf, regarding the account taken of special regional needs in the allocation of fishing quotas, Case C-4/96 Northern Ireland Fish Producers' Organization Ltd and Northern Ireland Fishermen's Federation v Dept of Agriculture for Northern Ireland [1998] ECR I-681.

1243 European Parliament Resolution of 15 May 1992 ([1992] OJ C150/317) on the CFP and the adjustments to be made, para 28. See also Resolution of 28 October 1992 ([1992] OJ C305/56) on the MGPs 1993–96, para 3.

6
OTHER FINANCIAL INSTRUMENTS

A. INTRODUCTION

Other financial instruments include the Cohesion Fund; European Investment Bank (EIB) loans and guarantees;[1244] New Community Instrument (NCI) loans and guarantees; Euratom loans and guarantees; structural measures financed by the Guarantee Section of the EAGGF; Framework Programmes for research and technological development; trans-European networks; Phare; and other Budgetary resources, particularly those allocated to other structural measures.[1245] In addition, there are the Financial Instrument for the Environment (LIFE) and the EEA Financial Mechanism.

These instruments may contribute, each according to the specific provisions governing its operations, to attaining the Structural Fund Objectives.[1246]

B. COHESION FUND

The Cohesion Fund was established in accordance with the Protocol on Economic and Social Cohesion and Article 130d EEC.[1247] In effect, the Fund was designed to assist Ireland, Portugal, Spain and Greece in meeting the economic convergence requirements for participation in the third stage of monetary union (ie, replacement of their national currencies with the Euro).

1. Objectives of assistance
The Cohesion Fund shall contribute to the strengthening of economic and social cohesion in the Union.[1248] In this context the Fund shall assist achieving Treaty objectives in the fields of environmental protection and trans-European transport infrastructure.[1249] The Commission has adopted guidelines to help national and regional authorities to prepare their programming strategies for Objectives 1, 2 and 3 of the Structural Funds and their links with the Cohesion Fund.[1250]

1244 According to Art 2(6) of Reg 1260/1999 ([1999] OJ L161/1), the EIB shall contribute to achieving the Objectives of the Structural Funds.

1245 Ibid, Art 2(5).

1246 Art 2(6) of Reg 1260/1999 ([1999] OJ L161/1).

1247 Now Art 161 EC.

1248 Art 1(2) of Reg 1164/94 ([1994] OJ L130/1).

1249 Ibid, Art 2(1).

1250 Commission Communication concerning the Structural Funds and their Coordination with the Cohesion Fund: Guidelines for programmes in the period 2000–06 ([1999] OJ C267/2), 1.

2. Eligibility for assistance

Unlike the Structural Funds, in the context of Objectives 1 and 2, eligibility for assistance from the Cohesion Fund is not to be determined on a regional basis. Rather, the Fund is to provide financial assistance to eligible projects in Member States with a *per capita* GNP, measured in purchasing power parities, of less than 90 per cent of the Union average and which have a programme leading to the fulfilment of the conditions of economic convergence referred to in Article 104 and a programme provided for in Articles 3 and 7 of Regulation 1466/97.[1251] At present four Member States are eligible, namely Greece, Spain, Portugal and Ireland. Their eligibility will be reconsidered at the end of 2003 in the light of their GDP levels.[1252]

Assistance from the Fund will principally accrue to two categories of projects.[1253] Environmental projects must contribute to the objectives of Union environmental policy laid down in Article 174 EC, namely: preserving, protecting and improving the quality of the environment; protecting human health; the prudent and rational utilization of natural resources; and promoting measures at international level to deal with regional or worldwide environmental problems. These shall include projects resulting from measures adopted pursuant to Article 175 (action to be taken by the Union in order to achieve the above objectives) and in particular projects in line with the priorities identified in the Programme of Policy and Action in relation to the Environment and Sustainable Development.

The transport infrastructure projects must be identified within the framework of the guidelines adopted by Decision 1692/96[1254] on the development of the trans-European transport network.[1255] Article 155(1) EC provides that the Union 'shall establish a series of guidelines covering the objectives, priorities and broad lines of measures envisaged in the sphere of trans-European networks which shall identify projects of common interest'.

A suitable balance shall be struck between projects in the field of the environment and those relating to transport infrastructure. This balance shall take account of the principle, contained in Article 175(5) EC, that the polluter should pay, other than in cases where the costs involved are deemed to be disproportionate for the public authorities of a Member State.[1256]

The Cohesion Fund may also grant financial assistance (up to 0.5 per cent of the total allocation of the Fund)[1257] in respect of the following:

1251 On the strengthening of the surveillance of budgetary positions and the surveillance and coordination of economic policies ([1997] OJ L209/2).
1252 Art 2(4) of Reg 1164/94, as amended by Reg 1264/1999 ([1999] OJ L161/57).
1253 Art 3(1) of Reg 1164/94, as amended by Reg 1264/1999 ([1999] OJ L161/57)..
1254 [1996] OJ L228/1.
1255 Art 3(1) of Reg 1164/94, as amended by Reg 1264/1999 ([1999] OJ L161/57).
1256 Art 10(2) of Reg 1164/94, as amended by Reg 1264/1999 ([1999] OJ L161/57).
1257 Art 7(4) of Reg 1164/94, as amended by Reg 1264/1999 ([1999] OJ L161/57).

(a) preliminary studies related to eligible projects including those necessary for their implementation;

(b) technical support measures, including publicity and information campaigns, particularly:

(i) horizontal measures such as comparative studies to assess the impact of Union assistance;

(ii) measures and studies which contribute to the appraisal, monitoring, supervision or evaluation of projects and to strengthening and ensuring the coordination and consistency of projects, particularly their consistency with other Union policies; and

(iii) measures and studies helping to make the necessary adjustments to the implementation of projects.[1258]

3. Allocation of assistance

An indicative allocation by Member State of the total resources of the Fund is to be made on the basis of precise and objective criteria, principally population, *per capita* GNP, taking account of the improvement in national prosperity attained over the previous period, and surface area. It shall also take account of other socio-economic factors, such as deficiencies in transport infrastructure.[1259] The indicative allocation is laid down in Annex I to Regulation 1164/94.[1260] This provides that Spain is to receive between 61 and 63.5 per cent, Greece and Portugal between 16 and 20 per cent each, and Ireland between 2 and 6 per cent[1261]

The decision to allocate funding on a national rather than a regional basis has led to the exclusion of two of the poorest regions of the Union, namely the Mezzogiorno in Italy and the East German *Länder*. The establishment of the Fund should be viewed as a significant political victory for Spain, which, while it encompasses just 7 per cent of the population of Objective 1 regions, encompasses 60 per cent of the population of the cohesion countries.

The rate of Union assistance granted by the Fund shall be between 80 and 85 per cent of expenditure by public or equivalent bodies.[1262] The actual rate of assistance is to be fixed according to the type of operation to be carried out. Where assistance is granted for a project which generates revenue, the amount of assistance shall be established by the Commission, taking account of revenue where this constitutes substantial net revenue for the promoters. In so doing, it shall work in close collaboration with the beneficiary Member

1258 Ibid, Art 3(2).
1259 Art 5 of Reg 1164/94, as amended by Reg 1264/1999 ([1999] OJ L161/57).
1260 Ibid.
1261 Annex I to Reg 1164/94, as replaced by Reg 1264/1999 ([1999] OJ L161/57).
1262 Art 7(1) of Reg 1164/94, as amended by Reg 1264/1999 ([1999] OJ L161/57).

State.[1263] Preliminary studies and technical support measures, including those undertaken at the Commission's initiative, may exceptionally be financed at a rate of 100 per cent.[1264]

No item of expenditure may benefit both from the Cohesion Fund and any one of the Structural Funds.[1265] The combined assistance of the Fund and other Union aid for a project shall not exceed 90 per cent of total expenditure relating to that project.[1266]

4. Scope of assistance

According to Regulation 16/2003,[1267] the Fund may part-finance planning and design; land purchase; site preparation; construction; equipment; project management; and expenditure on publicity and information measures undertaken pursuant to Commission Decision 96/455.[1268] Other categories of expenditure may be eligible, provided that they are specified in the Commission decision.

5. Forms of assistance

The Cohesion Fund may contribute to the financing of projects, or stages of a project which are technically and financially independent, or groups of projects linked to a visible strategy which form a coherent whole.[1269] It may also contribute to preliminary studies related to eligible projects and to technical support measures.[1270]

6. Conditionality

Article 104(6) EC provides that the Council may decide, after an overall assessment, whether an excessive deficit exists within the meaning of Article 104(1) EC and the Protocol on the Excessive Deficit Procedure. In so doing, it may act by a qualified majority on a recommendation from the Commission, after considering any observations put by the Member State concerned. Where the Council determines that an excessive deficit does exist within a given Member State, it shall make recommendations to it with a view to bringing that situation to an end within a given (specified) period.[1271] The Council shall

---

1263 Ibid, Art 7(2).

1264 Ibid, Art 7(4).

1265 Art 9(1) of Reg 1164/94, as amended by Reg 1264/1999 ([1999] OJ L161/57).

1266 Ibid, Art 9(2).

1267 Laying down special detailed rules for implementing Reg 1164/94 as regards eligibility of expenditure in the context of measures part-financed by the Cohesion Fund ([2003] OJ L2/7), Arts 9 and 10.

1268 Concerning information and publicity measures to be carried out by the Member States and the Commission concerning the activities of the Cohesion Fund ([1996] OJ L188/47).

1269 Art 1(3) of Reg 1164/94, as amended by Reg 1264/1999 ([1999] OJ L161/57).

1270 Ibid, Art 3(2).

1271 Art 104(7) EC.

abrogate its decision determining the existence of such a deficit to the extent that this, in its view, has been corrected by the Member State concerned.[1272]

Where the Council finds that a Member State has not implemented a programme in such a way as to avoid an excessive government deficit, no new projects (or in the case of multi-stage projects, no new stages of a project) shall receive assistance from the Fund in the Member State concerned.[1273] Suspension of funding will cease when the Council finds that measures to implement the programme have been taken.[1274] Exceptionally, in the case of projects directly affecting more than one Member State, the Council may, by a qualified majority, on a Commission recommendation, decide to defer suspension.[1275]

In practice, conditionality meant that government deficits were examined by reference to targets set annually by the Council. If the deficit was 'significantly off the mark for reasons other than exceptional circumstances outside the control of the Member State', assistance would be suspended.[1276] Beneficiary Member States must now implement a programme as provided for in Council Regulation 1466/97[1277] in such a way as to avoid an excessive government deficit[1278] and comply with the Stability and Growth Pact [1279]

7. Procedures relating to the grant of assistance

Applications for assistance: Applications for assistance for projects are to be submitted by the cohesion Member States.[1280] These should contain the following information:

(a) the body responsible for implementation;

(b) the nature of the investment and a description thereof, its costs and location, including, where applicable, an indication of projects of common interest situated on the same transport axis;

(c) the timetable for implementation;

(d) a cost–benefit analysis including the direct and indirect effects on employment;

(e) information enabling the impact on the environment to be assessed;

(f) information on public contracts;

1272 Art 104(12) EC.
1273 Cf Art 1 of Reg 792/93 ([1993] OJ L79/74) establishing a cohesion financial instrument, adopted under Art 235 EEC.
1274 Art 6(1) of Reg 1164/94, as amended by Reg 1264/1999 ([1999] OJ L161/57).
1275 Ibid, Art 6(2).
1276 Annual report on the Cohesion Fund 1996, COM(97)302, 8.
1277 On the strengthening of the surveillance of budgetary positions and the surveillance and coordination of economic policies ([1997] OJ L209/2), Arts 3 and 7.
1278 Arts 2(4) and 6(1) of Reg 1164/94, as amended by Reg 1264/1999 ([1999] OJ L161/57).
1279 [1997] OJ C236/1.
1280 Art 10(3) of Reg 1164/94, as amended by Reg 1264/1999 ([1999] OJ L161/57).

(g) the financing plan including, where possible, information on the economic viability of the project and the total financing which the Member State is seeking from the fund and any other Union source; and

(h) information providing the required proof that the projects comply with Regulation 1164/94[1281] and that there are medium-term economic and social benefits commensurate with the resources deployed.[1282]

Preliminary studies and technical support measures[1283] may be undertaken on the initiative of the Commission.

Approval of applications for assistance: The projects to receive assistance from the Cohesion Fund shall be adopted by the Commission in agreement with the beneficiary cohesion Member State.[1284] On receipt of a request for assistance, before approving the application, the Commission shall carry out a thorough appraisal in order to assess the proposed project's consistency with the following criteria:

(a) their medium-term economic and social benefits, which shall be commensurate with the resources deployed (in the light of a cost–benefit analysis);

(b) the priorities established by the beneficiary Member States;

(c) the contribution which projects can make to the implementation of Union policies on the environment, including the polluter pays principle, and trans-European networks;

(d) the compatibility of projects with Union policies and their consistency with other Union structural measures;[1285] and

(e) the establishment of an appropriate balance between the fields of the environment and transport infrastructure.[1286]

The Commission may invite the EIB to contribute to the assessment of projects as necessary.[1287] The Commission shall appraise the projects to determine their anticipated impact in terms of the objectives of the Fund, quantified using appropriate indicators.[1288] The Commission shall examine applications with a view to verifying in particular that the administrative and financial mechanisms are adequate for the effective implementation of the project.[1289] The Commission may, in agreement with the beneficiary cohesion State, group projects together and designate technically and financially

1281 Ibid.
1282 Ibid, Art 10(4)
1283 Referred to in Art 3(2) of Reg 1164/94, as amended by Reg 1264/1999 ([1999] OJ L161/57).
1284 Art 10(1) of Reg 1164/94, as amended by Reg 1264/1999 ([1999] OJ L161/57).
1285 See also Art 8 (ibid) on coordination and compatibility.
1286 Ibid, Art 10(5).
1287 Art 10(3) of Reg 1164/94, as amended by Reg 1264/1999 ([1999] OJ L161/57).
1288 Ibid, Annex II, Art B(2).
1289 Ibid, Annex II, Art B(1).

separate stages of a project for the purpose of granting assistance.[1290] Such a stage may cover preliminary, feasibility and technical studies needed for carrying out a project.[1291]

In addition, the Commission, in vetting applications for assistance, shall take into account the findings of appraisal and evaluation.[1292]

Subject to the concept of conditionality, and compliance with the relevant criteria, the Commission shall decide, as a general rule, on the grant of assistance within three months of the receipt of an application. Commission decisions approving projects (or stages of projects or groups of related projects) shall determine the amount of financial assistance and lay down a financial plan together with such provisions and conditions necessary for the implementation of the project.[1293] The 'key details' of these decisions are to be published in the Official Journal of the European Communities.[1294]

Financial control: Without prejudice to the Commission's responsibility for implementing the Union budget, Member States shall take responsibility in the first instance for the financial control of projects. To that end, the measures they take shall include:

(a) verifying that management and control arrangements have been set up and are being implemented in such a way as to ensure that Union funds are being used efficiently and correctly;

(b) providing the Commission with a description of these arrangements;

(c) ensuring that projects are managed in accordance with all the applicable Union rules and that the funds placed at their disposal are used in accordance with the principles of sound financial management;

(d) certifying that the declarations of expenditure presented to the Commission are accurate and guaranteeing that they result from accounting systems based on verifiable supporting documents;

(e) preventing and detecting irregularities, notifying these to the Commission, in accordance with the rules, and keeping the Commission informed of the progress of administrative and legal proceedings. In that context, the Member States and the Commission shall take the necessary steps to ensure that the information exchanged remains confidential;

(f) presenting to the Commission, when each project, step of project or group of projects is wound up, a declaration drawn up by a person or department having a function independent of the designated authority. This declaration shall summarize the conclusions of the checks carried out during previous years and shall assess the validity of the application

1290 Ibid, Annex II, Art A(1).
1291 Ibid, Annex II, Art A(3).
1292 Art 13(5) of Reg 1164/94, as amended by Reg 1264/1999 ([1999] OJ L161/57).
1293 Art 10(6) of Reg 1164/94, as amended by Reg 1264/1999 ([1999] OJ L161/57).
1294 Ibid, Art 10(7).

for payment of the final balance and the legality and regularity of the expenditure covered by the final certificate. The Member States may attach their own opinion to this declaration if they consider it necessary;

(g) cooperating with the Commission to ensure that Union funds are used in accordance with the principles of sound financial management; and

(h) recovering any amounts lost as a result of an irregularity detected and, where appropriate, charging interest on late payments.[1295]

The Commission in its responsibility for the implementation of the Union budget shall ensure that Member States have smoothly functioning management and control systems so that Union funds are efficiently and correctly used.[1296]

To that end, without prejudice to checks carried out by the Member States in accordance with national laws, regulations and administrative provisions, Commission officials or servants may, in accordance with arrangements agreed with the Member State in the framework of cooperation,[1297] carry out on-the-spot checks, including sample checks, on the projects financed by the Fund and on management and control systems with a minimum of one working day's notice. The Commission shall give notice to the Member State concerned with a view to obtaining all the assistance necessary. Officials or servants of the Member State concerned may take part in such checks.

The Commission may require the Member State concerned to carry out an on-the-spot check to verify the correctness of one or more transactions. Commission officials or servants may take part in such checks.

The Commission shall ensure that any checks that it carries out are performed in a coordinated manner so as to avoid repeating checks in respect of the same subject matter during the same period. The Member State concerned and the Commission shall immediately exchange any relevant information concerning the results of the checks carried out.

Detailed rules for the application of these requirements are to be adopted by the Commission.[1298]

Monitoring, appraisal and evaluation: *Monitoring:* The Member States and the Commission shall ensure that implementation of Cohesion Fund projects is effectively monitored and projects must be adjusted on the basis of the results of monitoring.[1299] Monitoring shall be carried out by way of jointly

---

1295 Art 12(1) of Reg 1164/94, as amended by Reg 1264/1999 ([1999] OJ L161/57).
1296 Art 12(2) of Reg 1164/94, as amended by Reg 1264/1999 ([1999] OJ L161/57).
1297 Annex II, Art G(1) of Reg 1164/94, as amended by Reg 1264/1999 ([1999] OJ L161/57).
1298 Art 12(4) of Reg 1164/94, as amended by Reg 1264/1999 ([1999] OJ L161/57); Commission Reg 1386/2002 ([2002] OJ L201/5) laying down detailed rules for the implementation of Reg 1164/94 as regards the management and control systems for assistance granted from the Cohesion Fund and the procedure for making financial corrections.
1299 Art 13(1) of Reg 1164/94 ([1994] OJ L130/1).

agreed reporting procedures, sample checks and the establishment of *ad hoc* committees[1300] (set up by arrangement between the Member State concerned and the Commission),[1301] with reference to physical and financial indicators relating to the specific character of the project and its objective. These indicators shall aim to show the stage reached in relation to the plan and objectives originally laid down and the progress achieved on the management side and any related problems.[1302] More generally, the detailed rules on monitoring and monitoring arrangements are to be laid down in the relevant Commission decisions approving projects.[1303]

The body designated for the purpose at national level by the Member State shall submit progress reports to the Commission within three months of the end of each full year of implementation and submit a final report to the Commission within six months of completion of the project (or stage of project).[1304]

On the basis of the results of the monitoring process and taking into account the comments of the monitoring committee, the Commission shall adjust the amounts and conditions for granting assistance as initially approved, as well as the financial plan envisaged, if necessary, on a proposal from the Member State concerned.[1305]

Appraisal: In order to ensure the effectiveness of Union assistance, the Commission and the relevant Member State shall, in cooperation with the EIB, where appropriate, carry out a systematic appraisal of projects.[1306] Similarly, on receipt of a request for assistance, and before approving a project, the Commission shall carry out a thorough appraisal in order to assess the consistency of the project with the criteria laid down in Article 10(5). The EIB shall be invited by the Commission to take part in the appraisal, as necessary.[1307]

Evaluation: The Member States shall ensure that the implementation of Cohesion Fund projects is effectively monitored and projects must be adjusted on the basis of the results of evaluation.[1308] In addition, in order to ensure the effectiveness of Union assistance, the Commission and the Member States (in cooperation with the EIB where appropriate) are to carry out a systematic

---

1300 Ibid, Annex II, Art F(1).
1301 Ibid, Annex II, Art F(3). The entities designated by the Member State, the Commission and, where appropriate, the EIB are to be represented on these monitoring committees, as are representatives of regional and local authorities, where these bodies are competent for the execution of a project and, where appropriate, they are directly concerned by it (ibid).
1302 Ibid, Annex II, Art F(2).
1303 Ibid, Art 13(6) and Annex II, Art F(7).
1304 Annex II, Art F(4) of Reg 1164/94 ([1994] OJ L130/1).
1305 Annex II, F(5) of Reg 1164/94 ([1994] OJ L130/1).
1306 Art 13(2) of Reg 1164/94 ([1994] OJ L130/1).
1307 Ibid, Art 13(3).
1308 Art 13(1) of Reg 1164/94 ([1994] OJ L130/1).

evaluation of projects.[1309] During the course of implementing projects and following their completion, the Commission and the Member State concerned are to evaluate the manner in which they have been carried out and the potential and actual impact of their implementation. This is designed to assess whether their original objectives can be, or have been, achieved. This evaluation is to address, *inter alia*, the environmental impact of the project, in compliance with existing Community rules.[1310] The Commission is to take into account such evaluations in vetting individual applications for assistance.[1311]

Reports: The Commission shall present, on an annual basis, a report on the activities of the Cohesion Fund to the European Parliament, the Council, the Economic and Social Committee and the Committee of the Regions.[1312] This report is to contain the following information:

1. financial assistance committed and paid by the Fund, with an annual breakdown by Member State and the type of project (environment or transport);

2. the economic and social impact of the Fund in the Member States and on economic and social cohesion in the Union, including the impact on employment;

3. a summary of information on the programs implemented in the beneficiary Member States to fulfil the conditions of economic convergence and on the application of conditionality;

4. information on the conclusions drawn by the Commission, with regard to the suspension of financing, from decisions taken by the Commission, such as those concerning conditionality.

5. the contribution which the Fund has made to the efforts of the beneficiary Member States to implement Union environmental policy and to strengthen trans-European transport infrastructure networks; the balance between projects in the field of the environment and projects relating to transport infrastructure;

6. assessment of the compatibility of operations of the Fund with Union policies, including those concerning environmental protection, transport, competition, and the award of public contracts;

7. the measures taken to ensure coordination and consistency between projects financed by the Fund and measures financed with contribution from the Union budget, the EIB, and other financial instruments of the Union;

1309 Ibid, Art 13(2).
1310 Ibid, Art 13(4). See also Art 8(1) (ibid) which, as in the case of the Structural Funds, introduces the principle of compatibility, including environmental compatibility.
1311 Ibid, Art 13(5).
1312 Art 14(1) of Reg 1164/94 ([1994] OJ L130/1).

8. the investment efforts of the beneficiary Member States in the fields of environmental protection and transport infrastructure;

9. the preparatory studies and technical support measures financed, including a specification of the types of such studies and measures;

10. the results of appraisal, monitoring and evaluation of projects, including information on any adjustment of projects to accord with the results of these;

11. the contributions of the EIB to the task of evaluation; and

12. a summary of information on the results of checks carried out, irregularities found and administrative and judicial proceedings in progress.[1313]

This report is presented for the purposes of examination and with a view to receiving the opinion of the above bodies. The European Parliament shall deliver its opinion as soon as possible, and the Commission shall in turn report on how it has applied the observations contained in this Parliamentary opinion.[1314]

However, the principle of conditional assistance[1315] raises the possibility that assistance may be stopped at an 'inopportune moment' for the purposes of regional development.[1316] In essence, therefore, the Cohesion Fund appears more an instrument of convergence than cohesion.[1317] As a result, cohesion efforts which are not favoured by 'liberal market economics' may be starved of resources.[1318]

C. LOANS AND GUARANTEES FROM THE EUROPEAN INVESTMENT BANK

The European Investment Bank (EIB) is independent in the management of its financial affairs, though it is intended to contribute to attainment of Treaty objectives.[1319] It may thus be described as an 'instrument' of the Union.[1320]

1313 Ibid, Annex to Annex II.
1314 Art 14(1) of Reg 1164/94 ([1994] OJ L130/1).
1315 Art 6 of Reg 1164/94 ([1994] OJ L130/1). Cf Art 1 of Reg 792/93 ([1993] OJ L79/74) establishing a cohesion financial instrument, adopted under Art 235 EEC.
1316 ESC Opinion of 23 February 1993 ([1993] OJ C108/53) on the proposal for a regulation establishing a cohesion financial instrument and the revised draft proposal for a regulation establishing a Cohesion Fund, para 2.3.1.
1317 See also the European Parliament Resolution of 19 April 1996 ([1996] OJ C141/265) on the complement to the Commission's annual report on the Cohesion Fund (1994), paras 25-9.
1318 Cf A Cutler, C Haslam, J Williams, and K Williams, 1992 – the Struggle for Europe (Berg, New York, 1989), 102.
1319 Case 85/86 EC Commission v Board of Governors of the EIB [1988] ECR 1281, 1320.
1320 AG Roemer in Joined Cases 27 & 39/59 Alberto Campolongo v ECSC High Authority [1960] ECR 391, 418. .

1. Establishment of the common market

The Spaak Report[1321] envisaged the creation of an investment fund for financing 'global aids' to Member States to support conversion efforts and the creation of new activities. During negotiation of the EEC Treaty, however, the preference emerged for a financial institution with the characteristics of a bank,[1322] which was created as the EIB.

The Bank apparently owed its creation to a concern that undertakings should not be denied opportunities to participate in the common market by their lack of access to investment capital.[1323] Hence, Article 130(b) EEC gave the Bank the task of financially supporting 'projects for modernizing or converting undertakings or for developing fresh activities called for by the progressive establishment of the common market'. Such support was expected to be consistent with the free competition sought through establishment of the common market, because the Bank only provided finance through interest-bearing loans.[1324]

According to Article 3(j) EEC, the Bank was intended to facilitate the economic expansion of the Community by opening up fresh resources. This provision implied that the Bank should contribute to achievement of Article 2 objectives.[1325] This implication was confirmed by Article 130. This provision required the Bank to contribute to the balanced establishment of the common market.

Accordingly, its Statute provided that the Bank was to 'promote the attainment of the common market'.[1326] Further details were provided in the General Directives for the Credit Policy of the Bank.[1327] According to these Directives, the Bank was to participate in financing projects aimed at the modernization or conversion of enterprises or the creation of new activities furthering the progressive establishment of the common market. It was to do so as soon as the repercussions of this market on given enterprises could be seen with sufficient accuracy.[1328]

1321 Comité Intergouvernemental Crée par la Conference de Messine, Rapport des Chefs de Délégation aux Ministres des Affaires Etrangères (Secretariat of the Committee, Brussels, 1956).
1322 R Quadri, R Monaco, and A Trabucchi, Trattato istitutivo della Comunità economica europea: commentario (Giuffré, Milan, 1965), ii, 992.
1323 M Keating, 'Europeanism and Regionalism' in B Jones and M Keating (eds), The European Union and the Regions (Clarendon Press, Oxford, 1995), 1–22, 17.
1324 DA Pinder, 'Small Firms, Regional Development, and the European Investment Bank' (1986) 24 JCMS 171–86, 172.
1325 AG Mancini in Case 85/86 EC Commission v Board of Governors of the EIB [1988] ECR 1281, 1305. See, regarding Art 2 EEC, paras [54] ff above.
1326 Art 20(1)(b) of the Statute of the EIB.
1327 EIB, Luxembourg, 1981, 32–3.
1328 Ibid, Section II.

In practice, assistance to the less developed regions was expected to be the 'principal task' of the Bank.[1329] This expectation reflected recognition that 'mechanical integration' of the Member States could harm such regions.[1330] The inference drawn was that assistance from the Bank was necessary to counter the tendency of the common market to increase the differences between developed and less developed regions.[1331]

Originally, assistance was allocated to infrastructure projects[1332] and large industrial projects. However, in 1968, global loans, passed on through sub-loans to small and medium-sized enterprises, were introduced.[1333] The bulk of the assistance went to the poorer regions, especially in Italy.[1334] For example, loans were made for irrigation and other rural projects in the Mezzogiorno, and numerous transport and industrial rehabilitation schemes benefitted. These loans apparently had only a marginal impact on employment in such regions.[1335]

Much assistance from the Bank concerned projects to develop less developed regions.[1336] The regions had to be less developed by Community rather than national standards.[1337] During negotiation of the Treaty, Germany had favoured an express statement that the assistance should be designed to adjust the economic level of the less developed regions to that of other regions. However, no such statement was included in the Treaty.

The Bank also assisted projects concerned with the modernization[1338] or conversion of undertakings or the development of fresh activities called for by the progressive establishment of the common market. Such projects had to be of such a size or nature[1339] that they could not be entirely financed by the various means available in the individual Member States.[1340] The expression 'progressive' was seen as implying that assistance from the Bank should be

---

1329 Second EEC General Report (1959), 54.

1330 R Quadri, R Monaco, and A Trabucchi, para [541], n 2 above, ii, 962.

1331 Ibid, ii, 1008.

1332 H Clout, Regional Variations in the European Community (Cambridge University Press, 1986), 39.

1333 Annual Report of the EIB 1968 (EIB, Luxembourg, 1969), 79–80.

1334 Between 1958 and 1973 46% of total EIB lending related to projects in Italy.

1335 DA Pinder, 'Small Firms, Regional Development and the European Investment Bank' (1986) 24 JCMS 171–86.

1336 Art 130(a) EEC.

1337 R Quadri, R Monaco, and A Trabucchi, para [541], n 2 above, ii, 1009.

1338 Germany had argued that modernization should not be covered, because it was a normal and permanent task of undertakings (R Quadri, R Monaco, and A Trabucchi, para [541], n 2 above, 327).

1339 Ie, they must not be purely local or particular (ibid, ii, 1009).

1340 Art 130(b) EEC. France had proposed a stipulation in the Treaty that the projects must be viable (S Neri and H Sperl, para [283], n 2 above, 326). This stipulation was included, instead, in para 3 of the General Directives of the Bank (see para [544], n 2 above, 3–4).

limited to the transitional period for establishment of the common market.[1341] However, it was recognized that operations could not be confined to problems shown to be caused by the establishment of the common market.[1342]

Finally, the Bank assisted projects of common interest to several Member States. These projects also had to be of such a size or nature that they could not be entirely financed by the various means available in the individual Member States.[1343] Such projects included, in particular, those which would contribute to the integration of the economies of the Member States.[1344] The German Government inferred that 'supraregional' projects could be assisted.[1345]

The Bank granted assistance in the form of loans and guarantees.[1346]

2. Development of the common market

The New Community Instrument (NCI)[1347] was established by Decision 78/870.[1348] It assisted investment projects to strengthen the link between the EIB and the implementation of policies demanded by the development of the common market.[1349] Its administration and the selection of projects to be assisted were responsibilities of the Bank, though the Commission was responsible for determining the eligibility of projects.[1350]

Projects assisted by the Instrument were to contribute to greater convergence and integration of the economic policies of the Member States. More particularly, the projects were to help attain Community objectives for energy, industry and infrastructure. Account was to be taken, *inter alia*, of the regional impact of the projects and the need to combat unemployment.[1351]

1341 S Neri and H Sperl, para [283], n 2 above, 327.
1342 Ibid.
1343 Art 130(c) EEC.
1344 Second EEC General Report, para [545], n 1 above, 54.
1345 S Neri and H Sperl, para [283], n 2 above, 325.
1346 Art 20(2) of its Statute prohibits the Bank, in principle, from participating in risk capital.
1347 C André, 'Le Nouvel instrument communautaire d'emprunts et de prêts (NIC)' (1980) RMC 66–71; and L Battistotti, 'I Finanziamenti concessi della banca europea per gli invetimenti ed il nuovo strumento communitario' (1985) Cronache Economiche 63–8.
1348 Empowering the Commission to contract loans for the purpose of promoting investment within the Community ([1978] OJ L298/9); and Dec 83/200 ([1983] OJ L112/26) empowering the Commission to contract loans under the NCI for the purpose of promoting investment within the Community.
1349 Recession and UK entry implied the need for increased attention to declining industries. See H Clout, para [546], n 1 above, 39.
1350 Art 5 of Dec 78/870 ([1978] OJ L298/9).
1351 Art 1 Dec 78/870 ([1978] OJ L298/9). However, where government policies aimed to bring down inflation through control of public borrowing, the NCI facility merely added to public spending and might, therefore, not be available in practice. See the ESC Opinion of 28 October 1981 ([1981] OJ C343/53) on the new regional policy guidelines and priorities, para II.5.2.

The allocation of assistance from the Instrument was to take account of three priorities.[1352] The first priority concerned investment projects, mainly those of small and medium-sized enterprises, in industry and directly allied services. They were to promote, in particular, the dissemination of innovation and new technology and job creation. The second priority concerned projects for the rational of energy, replacement of oil by other sources of energy, and infrastructure projects facilitating such replacement. The third priority concerned infrastructure projects associated with the development of productive activities. They had to contribute to regional development or to be of Community interest, as in the case of telecommunications, including information technology, and transport, including the transmission of energy.

Assistance from the Instrument was provided for investment projects of small and medium-sized enterprises, especially innovatory projects. Infrastructure and energy projects were also assisted.[1353] Such assistance was to be directed, in particular, to the application of new technologies and innovation and to improving the rational use of energy. At the same time, account was to be taken of the need to reduce regional disparities.[1354]

Loans were provided by the New Community Instrument. Guarantees on the loans might be financed from the General Budget.[1355]

3. Cohesion

Article 130 EEC has now been replaced by Article 267 EC. The new provision contains the same wording as its predecessor. It thus maintains the original tasks of the EIB. However, a final paragraph is added. According to this paragraph, in carrying out its tasks, the Bank is to facilitate the financing of investment programmes in conjunction with assistance from the Structural Funds and other financial instruments. Moreover, according to the Protocol on Economic and Social Cohesion, the Bank should continue to devote the majority of its resources to the promotion of cohesion.[1356] Article 267 EC and the Protocol are said to have established the Bank as a 'real regional development bank'.[1357]

Objectives of assistance: The EIB shall cooperate in attaining the Objectives of the Structural Funds, in accordance with the procedures laid

1352 Art 3 of Dec 84/383 ([1984] OJ L208/53) implementing Dec 83/200.
1353 Art 3 of Dec 87/182 ([1987] OJ L71/34) empowering the Commission to borrow under the NCI for the purpose of promoting investment within the Community.
1354 Ibid, 8th recital in the preamble. See, regarding assistance to rural regions through the NCI, the explanatory memorandum to the amended proposal for a decision empowering the Commission to borrow under the NCI for the purpose of promoting investment within the Community, COM(89)440, 4–5.
1355 See, eg, Art B0-202 of the Budget for 1998 ([1998] OJ L44/3). See, generally, Guarantees covered by the General Budget, COM(97)464.
1356 Para 13 of the Protocol.
1357 C Mestre and Y Petit, 'La Cohesion économique et sociale après le Traité sur l'union européenne' (1995) RTDE 207–43, 231.

down in its Statute.[1358] To this end, coordination and consistency between EIB assistance and assistance from the Structural Funds and other financial instruments is sought.[1359]

Eligibility for assistance: Member States or private or public undertakings may be eligible for EIB loans.[1360] Funds must be unavailable from other sources on reasonable terms, though, as far as possible, loans shall be granted only on condition that other sources of finance are also used.[1361] When a loan is granted to an undertaking or body other than a Member State, the loan is conditional either on a guarantee from the Member State in whose territory the project is to be carried out or on the basis of other adequate guarantees.[1362]

In addition, public or private undertakings with loans from other sources may be eligible for an EIB guarantee.[1363]

In the case of projects carried out by undertakings in the production sector, loans and guarantees may only be granted where interest and amortization payments are covered out of operating profits or, in other cases, either by a commitment entered into by the State in which the project is carried out or by some other means. Moreover, the execution of the projects must contribute to an increase in economic productivity in general and promote the attainment of the common market.[1364]

Allocation of assistance: The allocation of assistance has now been affected by the creation of the European Investment Fund, the Temporary Lending Facility, and the Special Action Programme.

European Investment Fund: The European Investment Fund[1365] is to contribute to the strengthening of the internal market, the promotion of economic recovery in Europe, and the furthering of cohesion.[1366]

The Fund provides loans for large infrastructural projects, particularly those related to trans-European networks in the areas of transport, telecommunications and energy. It also provides loans for the development of small and medium-sized enterprises,[1367] particularly in Union-assisted

---

1358 Art 2(6) of Reg 1260/1999 ([1999] OJ L161/1).

1359 Ibid, Art 10(2).

1360 Art 18(1) of the Protocol on the Statute of the EIB.

1361 Ibid, Art 18(2). EIB loans are generally limited to 50% (and often substantially less) of the capital cost of the project except in respect of projects relating to environmental protection where a higher rate is applied.

1362 Art 18(3) of the Protocol on the Statute of the EIB.

1363 Art 18(4) of the Protocol on the Statute of the EIB.

1364 Art 20(1) of the Protocol on the Statute of the EIB.

1365 Act amending the Protocol on the Statute of the EIB empowering the Board of Governors to establish an EIF ([1994] OJ L173/14).

1366 5th recital in the preamble to Dir 94/7 ([1994] OJ L89/17) adapting Dir 89/647 ([1989] OJ L386/14) on a solvency ratio for credit institutions as regards the technical definition of 'multilateral development banks'; and Dec 94/375 ([1994] OJ L173/12) on Community membership of the EIF.

1367 Art 2 of the Statute of the Fund ([1994] OJ L173/1).

regions.[1368] In addition, the Fund may provide guarantees for loans in whatever form is permitted by the rules of law applicable. In practice, such guarantees are provided in respect of investments by small and medium-sized enterprises resulting in significant environmental benefits.[1369] Finally, the Fund may acquire, hold and manage equity participations in any enterprise.[1370]

Temporary Lending Facility: The Temporary Lending Facility[1371] provides loans designed to accelerate the financing of infrastructure projects, notably those connected with trans-European networks. Small and medium-sized enterprises which obtain such loans receive interest subsidies from the Union Budget.[1372]

Special Action Programme: The Special Action Programme[1373] extends assistance in the areas of education, health, urban environment, and environmental protection. It will also step up its interventions in relation to large infrastructure projects and small and medium-sized enterprises.

Scope of assistance: Loans may be granted for investment projects to be carried out in the Union.[1374] In addition, loans contracted by public or private undertakings for the purpose of carrying out projects provided for in Article 267 EC may be guaranteed by the EIB.[1375] The financing of investment programmes in conjunction with assistance from the Structural Funds and other Union financial instruments,[1376] particularly the Cohesion Fund,[1377] may thereby be facilitated.

Forms of assistance: Assistance may take the form of loans or guarantees.

Procedures for granting loans or guarantees: According to the Statute of the EIB, applications for loans or guarantees may be made to the Bank either through the Commission, the Member State concerned or directly by the undertaking seeking finance. In practice, the direct route tends to be preferred.[1378]

1368 European Investment Fund, COM(93)3, 2.
1369 Coordination of activities to assist SMEs and the craft sector 1997, COM(97)610.
1370 Art 3(1) of the Statute of the Fund.
1371 EIB Annual Report 1993 (EIB, Luxembourg, 1994), 12–13. See also Notice of implementation of the ETF start-up facility and the SME guarantee facility under the growth and employment initiative ([1998] OJ C302/8).
1372 Dec 94/217 ([1994] OJ L107/57) on the provision of Community interest subsidies on loans for SMEs extended by the EIB under its temporary lending facility.
1373 Board of Governors: Endorsement of the Bank's Amsterdam special action programme ([1998] OJ C10/10).
1374 Art 18(1) of the Protocol on the Statute of the EIB.
1375 Ibid, Art 18(4).
1376 Art 267(2) EC.
1377 Art 8(2) of Reg 1164/1994 ([1994] OJ L130/1).
1378 Art 21 of the Statute of the EIB. Acting unanimously, the Board of Governors, on a proposal from the Board of Directors, may grant loans for investment projects outside of the territory of the Union.

Applications submitted through the Commission shall be sent to the Member State in whose territory the project is to be carried out. Applications made through a Member State shall be submitted to the Commission for an opinion. Direct applications shall be submitted to both the Member State concerned and the Commission. The relevant Member State and the Commission shall deliver their opinions within two months and, if within this period no reply is received, the EIB may assume that neither the Commission nor the Member State has any objection to the project in question.[1379]

The application will first be examined by the Bank's Management Committee. The Management Committee shall examine whether applications for loans and guarantees submitted comply with the provisions of the Statute of the EIB. Where this Committee is in favour of granting a loan or guarantee, it shall submit a draft contract to the Board of Directors. Its favourable opinion may be conditional. Where the Management Committee does not favour the granting of a loan or guarantee, it shall submit its opinion, together with the relevant documentation, to the Board of Directors. Where either the Commission or the Management Committee delivers an unfavourable opinion, the Board of Directors may grant the loan or guarantee only if its decision is unanimous. Where both the Commission and the Management Committee deliver unfavourable opinions, the Board of Directors is precluded from granting the loan or guarantee.[1380]

The Board of Directors shall have sole power to take decisions in respect of the granting of loans and guarantees. It shall fix the interest rates on loans granted and the commission on guarantees.[1381]

However, the contribution of the work of the Bank to cohesion is disputed. Its security and credit-worthiness requirements are no less than for loans from the national banking systems. Moreover, loans are subject to other conditions, such as very high minimum qualifying conditions, which make them still less attractive to small and medium-sized enterprises. At the same time, its interest rates must respect market conditions,[1382] and any interest subsidies from the Member State concerned must comply with Article 87 EC,[1383] concerning State aid. In addition, its lending is related to specific projects. Hence, its time

---

1379 Art 21(2) of the Statute of the EIB.

1380 Art 21(4)–(7) of the Statute of the EIB.

1381 Art 11(1) of the Statute of the EIB. The Board of Governors has power to lay down general directives for the credit policy of the Bank, with particular reference to the objectives to be pursued as progress is made in the attainment of the common market (ibid, Art 9(2)). It must, for example, satisfy itself that the applicant undertaking is financially sound as to the security of the interest and repayment schedule, and that the proposed project is technically feasible and of general economic interest and (in the case of projects in the production sector) sufficiently profitable.

1382 According to Art 19(1) of the Statute of the EIB, interest rates on EIB loans and commissions on guarantees shall be adjusted to capital market conditions and enable the Bank to meet its obligations, cover its expenses, and build up a reserve fund.

1383 Ibid, Art 19(2).

perspective will necessarily be shorter than that adopted by the Commission in the multiannual programming used for the Structural Funds. For these reasons, comprehensive integration between the work of the Funds and that of the Bank[1384] is difficult to achieve.[1385]

D. EURATOM LOANS AND GUARANTEES

Under the Euratom Treaty the development of nuclear energy may be assisted.[1386]

The objectives of Euratom assistance include promoting research, facilitating investment and ensuring the establishment of the basic installations necessary for the development of nuclear energy.[1387]

The bulk of Euratom assistance is allocated to nuclear power stations and industrial installations involved in the fuel cycle within Member States.[1388] Only the criteria for allocation of assistance to research expressly refer to the contribution to the strengthening of cohesion. Even in the case of such assistance, consistency with the pursuit of scientific and technical quality is required.[1389]

According to the European Parliament, however, nuclear energy policy should be treated as an essential element of cohesion. The Parliament has demanded that, to this end, the allocation of Euratom assistance for construction of nuclear plants should have regard to regional development

1384 Cf the formal requirement of Art 21(1) (ibid) that applications for EIB assistance should be forwarded to the Commission for its opinion.

1385 In any event, the EIB is subject to little scrutiny. The European Parliament considers that the Court of Auditors (COA) should have full audit access to the operations of this Fund, so that it can report to the Budget authority on matters relating to the Budget. See the Resolution on giving discharge to the Commission in respect of the implementation of the General Budget for 1994 ([1996] OJ L148/44), para 53. According to Art 248(3) EC, the COA is only to have 'access to information necessary for the audit of Community expenditure and revenue managed by the Bank'.

1386 The proposal for the Euratom Treaty was apparently seen by Germany as an attempt by France to gain subsidies for the development of its nuclear industry. See S Weber and H Wiesmith, 'Issue Linkage in the European Community' (1991) 29 JCMS 255–67, 256.

1387 Art 2 Euratom; and Dec 77/270 ([1977] OJ L88/9) empowering the Commission to issue Euratom loans for the purpose of contributing to the financing of nuclear power stations, as amended by Dec 94/179 ([1994] OJ L84/41).

1388 Commission Reply by Mr de Silguy to WQ E-2878/94 ([1995] OJ C103/47) by Undine-Uta Block von Blottnitz.

1389 Annex II to Dec 94/268 ([1994] OJ L115/31) concerning a framework programme of Community activities in the field of research and training for Euratom (1994–98). Cf, now, Dec 2002/668 ([2002] OJ L232/34) concerning the sixth framework programme of Euratom for nuclear research and training activity also contributing to the creation of the European Research Area (2002–2006).

considerations.[1390] In practice, despite Parliamentary demands, such assistance apparently remains primarily concerned with reduction of Union dependence on imported energy.[1391] Consequently, its allocation may be ill adapted to promotion of cohesion.

Assistance may be provided for research,[1392] training and investment,[1393] particularly in the case of joint undertakings.[1394]

Assistance may take the form of loans[1395] and loan guarantees.[1396] There is also a Framework Programme of Community activities in the field of research and training for Euratom.[1397] It provides assistance to research, technological development, international cooperation, dissemination and exploitation activities, and training in the fields of nuclear energy and safety.[1398] It is implemented by two specific programmes. One concerns the Joint Research Centre.[1399] The other concerns research and training in the field of nuclear energy.[1400]

E. EAGGF, GUARANTEE SECTION

The Guarantee Section of the EAGGF assists structural measures under Regulation 1257/1999[1401] on support for regional development from the EAGGF. This assistance is designed to make available resources additional to those of the Structural Funds for agricultural restructuring.[1402]

1390 Resolution of 27 June 1966 (JO 1966 2427) on regional policy in the EEC.

1391 M Quévit, J Houard, S Bodson, and A Dangoisse, Impact régional 1992: les régions de tradition industrielle (De Boeck, Brussels, 1991), 351.

1392 Arts 6(a) and 7 Euratom.

1393 Art 172(4) Euratom.

1394 Art 47(a) Euratom.

1395 See, eg, Annex II to Part B of the Budget for 1998 ([1998] OJ L44/3).

1396 See, eg, Art B0-201 (ibid). See, generally, Guarantees covered by the General Budget, COM(97)464.

1397 Dec 2002/668 ([2002] OJ L232/34) concerning the sixth framework programme of Euratom for nuclear research and training activity also contributing to the creation of the European Research Area (2002–2006).

1398 Ibid, Art 1(2).

1399 Dec 2002/838 ([2002] OJ L294/86) adopting a specific programme for research and training to be carried out by the JRC by means of direct actions for Euratom (2002–2006); and Dec 2004/185 ([2004] OJ L57/25) concerning the adoption of a supplementary research programme to be implemented by the JRC for Euratom.

1400 Dec 2002/837 ([2002] OJ L294/74) adopting a specific programme (Euratom) for research and training in nuclear energy (2002–2006).

1401 [1999] OJ L160/80.

1402 Cf the 12th recital in the preamble to Reg 2079/92 ([1992] OJ L215/91) instituting a Community assistance scheme for early retirement from farming.

---

1. Objectives of assistance

The Guarantee Section is to assist attainment of Objective 2.[1403] It is also to assist rural development in areas outside Objective 1.[1404]

2. Eligibility for assistance

Measures accompanying reform of the common agricultural policy are eligible for assistance from the Guarantee Section throughout the Union. Other rural development measures in areas outside Objective 1 are eligible for assistance from the same section.[1405]

3. Allocation of assistance

Initial allocations of assistance from the Guarantee Section are made. They are broken down on an annual basis and use objective criteria which take into account particular situations and needs, and efforts to be undertaken especially for the environment, job creation, and maintenance of the landscape.[1406]

4. Scope of assistance

The Guarantee Section provides support for early retirement,[1407] less-favoured areas and areas with environmental restrictions,[1408] agri-environment,[1409] and afforestation[1410] throughout the Union.

Outside Objective 1 areas, the Guarantee Section may also assist 'other regional development measures'. They include investments in agricultural holdings;[1411] start-up assistance for young farmers;[1412] professional training;[1413] and improving processing and marketing of agricultural products. The assistance is designed to guide production in keeping with foreseeable market trends or encourage the development of new outlets for agricultural products; to improve or rationalize marketing channels or processing procedures for agricultural products; to improve the presentation and preparation of products or encourage the better use or elimination of by-products or waste; to apply new technologies; to favour innovative investments; to improve and monitor quality; to improve and monitor health

---

1403 Art 2(3) of Reg 1260/1999 ([1999] OJ L161/1).
1404 Art 40 of Reg 1257/1999 ([1999] OJ L160/80).
1405 Art 35 of Reg 1257/1999 ([1999] OJ L160/80).
1406 Art 46(2) of Reg 1257/1999 ([1999] OJ L160/80).
1407 Arts 10–12 of Reg 1257/1999 ([1999] OJ L160/80).
1408 Ibid, Arts 13–21.
1409 Ibid, Arts 22–24.
1410 Ibid, Art 31.
1411 Arts 4–7 of Reg 1257/1999 ([1999] OJ L160/80).
1412 Ibid, Art 8.
1413 Ibid, Art 9.
1414 Ibid, Arts 25–28

conditions; and to protect the environment.[1414] The Guarantee Section may also assist the adaptation and development of rural areas.[1415]

5. Forms of assistance

'Other regional development measures' assisted by the Guarantee Section may form part of the programming for Objective 2 regions.[1416] Outside such regions, they shall form part of rural development plans.[1417]

Compensatory allowances may be granted in naturally less-favoured areas and areas with environmental restrictions. In the former areas, the assistance is designed to ensure continued agricultural land use and thereby contribute to the maintenance of a viable rural community; to maintain the countryside; and to maintain and promote sustainable farming systems which in particular take account of environmental protection requirements. Assistance in the latter areas is designed to ensure implementation of environmental requirements and to safeguard farming in areas with environmental restrictions.[1418]

The Guarantee Section may also, on the initiative of the Commission, finance studies related to rural development programming.[1419]

F. FRAMEWORK PROGRAMMES FOR RESEARCH AND TECHNOLOGICAL DEVELOPMENT

The EEC Treaty originally made no provision for research and development. However, the need for Community assistance to such development became clear, as the common market itself developed.

The research and development policy of the Community[1420] had its origins in concerns for particular sectors,[1421] such as nuclear energy, data

---

1414 Ibid, Arts 25–28
1415 Ibid, Art 33.
1416 Art 40(2) of Reg 1257/1999 ([1999] OJ L160/80).
1417 Ibid, Arts 40(3) and 41–44.
1418 Arts 13 and 14 of Reg 1257/1999 ([1999] OJ L160/80).
1419 Art 45(2) of Reg 1257/1999 ([1999] OJ L160/80).
1420 See, generally, J Elizade, 'Legal Aspects of Community Policy on Research and Technological Development (RTD)' (1992) 29 CMLRev 309–46.
1421 See, eg, the Memorandum on industrial policy in the EEC, COM(70)100.

processing,[1422] aerospace,[1423] agriculture[1424] and ceramics.[1425] Various instruments, such as the Esprit programme for research and development in information technologies[1426] and the Joint European Torus for nuclear research,[1427] were employed in implementation of this policy.[1428]

The first Framework Programme for assistance to research and development was adopted in 1983,[1429] and the second in 1987.[1430] The second Programme was intended, along with other financial instruments, to contribute to strengthening scientific and technological infrastructures and potential throughout the Community. Assisted activities concerned quality of life; development of an information and communications society; modernization of industrial sectors; exploitation and optimum use of biological resources; energy; science and technology for development; exploitation of the seabed and use of marine resources; and improvement of European cooperation in science and technology.[1431]

More particularly, the strategic programme for innovation and technology transfer (Sprint) was established by Decision 83/624.[1432] Assistance was envisaged for development of an innovation infrastructure to enable Member

---

1422 Council Resolution of 15 July 1974 ([1974] OJ C86/1) on a Community policy on data processing, para 3.

1423 Action programme for the European aeronautical sector, COM(75)475.

1424 Reg 1728/74 ([1974] OJ L182/1) on the coordination of agricultural research; and Dec 83/641 ([1983] OJ L358/36) adopting joint research programmes and programmes for coordinating agricultural research.

1425 Proposal of 5 June 1979 ([1979] OJ C155/4) for a decision on the adoption of a programme of technological research in the field of clay minerals and technical ceramics.

1426 Dec 84/130 ([1984] OJ L67/54) concerning a European programme for R & D in information technologies.

1427 Dec 78/471 ([1978] OJ L151/10) on the establishment of the JET Joint Undertaking.

1428 Eureka (see Eureka and the European technology community, COM(86)664) was not integrated into Community programmes. See CA Colliard, 'Eureka ou une coopération technologique européenne' (1988) RTDE 5–22. Indeed, the Commission apparently used Eureka to fund collaborative R & D which was not clearly precompetitive and could not be conducted easily under the Framework Programme because of conflicts with competition law. See J Peterson, 'Technology Policy in Europe: Explaining the Framework Programme and Eureka in Theory and Practice' (1991) 29 JCMS 269–90.

1429 Council Resolution of 25 July 1983 ([1983] OJ C208/1) on framework programmes for Community research, development, and demonstration activities and a first Framework Programme 1984–87. It was adopted under Art 235 EEC and Art 7 Euratom.

1430 Dec 87/516 ([1987] OJ L302/1) concerning the Framework Programme for Community activities in the field of RTD (1987–91). It was adopted under Art 130q EEC, but prepared under Art 235 EEC.

1431 [1987] OJ L302/1, Art 1. Further details of the activities envisaged were given in Annex II (ibid).

1432 Concerning a plan for the transnational development of the supporting infrastructure for innovation and technology transfer (1983–85) ([1983] OJ L353/15).

States with weaker infrastructures to participate fully in transnational projects.[1433]

The impact of such assistance on regional disparities might be 'only an indirect one',[1434] and there was a risk that such disparities might be increased.[1435] In practice, recipients tended to be located in regions which were already well developed.[1436] For example, the share of Esprit assistance allocated to the less developed Member States was substantially lower than their share of Community gross domestic product and population. Even the Esprit assistance which was allocated to these Member States was 'highly concentrated' in capital cities and more developed regions.[1437] A solution might be sought through orienting assistance towards the less prosperous regions,[1438] though such orientation might not apparently mean that the assisted activities had to take place in such regions.[1439]

An express basis for the grant of assistance to research and development was introduced into the Treaty by Articles 130f to 130q EEC, as amended by the Single European Act.[1440] These provisions have now been replaced by Articles 163 to 173 EC.

1. Objectives of assistance

Article 163(1) EC lays down the objectives of assistance for research and development. According to this provision, they are 'strengthening the scientific and technological bases of European industry and encouraging it to become more competitive at international level,[1441] while promoting all the research activities deemed necessary by virtue of other chapters of this Treaty'. To this end, Article 163(2) requires that 'the Community shall, throughout the Community, encourage undertakings, including small and medium-sized

---

1433 Ibid, Art 3.

1434 Common policy for science and technology: impact of Community R & D on horizontal policies, COM(81)66, 5–6.

1435 A Community strategy to develop Europe's industry, COM(81)639, 14.

1436 ESC Opinion of 29 January 1986 ([1986] OJ C75/12) on national regional development aid, para 4.3.

1437 COA special report 6/93 ([1994] OJ C45/1) concerning the Esprit programme, paras 2.19–2.20.

1438 Common policy for science and technology: impact of Community R & D on horizontal policies, COM(81)66, 7.

1439 Ibid, 3–4. The changes proposed to the Union's regional policy in 1981 (ERDF _ revision of the regulation, COM(81)589) were said fully to accommodate this objective. See A Community strategy to develop Europe's industry, COM(81)639, 13.

1440 [1987] OJ L169/1.

1441 Art 157(1) EC also provides that the Union and the Member States shall foster better exploitation of the industrial potential of policies of innovation, research and technological development.

undertakings, research centres and universities in their research and technological development activities of high quality'.[1442]

According to Article 130f(3) EEC, pursuit of such objectives had to take account of 'the establishment of the internal market and the implementation of common policies, particularly as regards competition and trade'.[1443] This requirement was removed in the EC Treaty.

2. Eligibility for assistance

According to Article 163(2) EC, undertakings, research centres and universities are eligible for assistance.

3. Allocation of assistance

According to Article 163(2) EC, assistance is to be allocated throughout the Union to 'research and technological development activities of high quality'.

In practice, assistance may seek to reconcile the promotion of the competitiveness of Union industry with the strengthening of cohesion. In particular, the Framework Programme for 1990 to 1994 was adopted by Decision 90/221.[1444] It emphasized the importance of rendering Union industry more competitive. According to the Commission, assistance was to be directed towards the needs of business and boosting the competitiveness of the Union economy.[1445] Thus industry-relevant, 'high tech' research topics were to be assisted. A possible implication is that the Programme was designed primarily as a response to the needs of larger corporations and stronger Member States.[1446]

At the same time, references were made to cohesion. For example, according to Annex II, paragraph III.6 of Decision 90/221,[1447] the creation of research networks was envisaged. These networks were to extend to all Union regions. Particular attention was to be paid to the needs of peripheral regions

---

1442 See also Growth, Competitiveness, and Employment (Bull EC, Supp 6/93).

1443 See, regarding the kind of reconciliation problems involved, M van Empel, 'Technology and Common Market Law' in Asser Institute Colloquium on European Law, Technological Development and Cooperation in Europe – Legal Aspects (TMC Asser Institute, The Hague, 1986), 57–71. See also B Hawk, 'La Recherche et le développement en droit communautaire et en droit antitrust americain' (1987) Revue Internationale de Droit Economique 211–69.

1444 Concerning the Framework Programme of Community activities in the field of RTD (1990–94) ([1990] OJ L117/28).

1445 Community's finances between now and 1997, COM(92)2001, 26. See, more particularly, The European motor vehicle industry: situation, issues at stake, and proposals for action, COM(92)166, 10.

1446 Evaluation of the Effects of the EC Framework Programme for Research and Technological Development on Economic and Social Cohesion in the Community (EC Commission, Brussels, 1991), 35.

1447 [1990] OJ L117/28.

and regions that were currently lagging behind. Highly qualified scientific and technical potential was thus to be built up in these regions.[1448]

Somewhat greater significance was attached to cohesion requirements in the Fourth Framework Programme, which covered the period 1994 to 1998 and was adopted by Decision 1110/94.[1449] The Preamble to this Decision referred to the obligation to take account of cohesion requirements. It also maintained that the programme should play its part, along with other Union funds, in contributing to strengthening scientific and technological capacity and potential throughout the Union.[1450] Accordingly, criteria for the provision of assistance included the contribution of the research to the strengthening of cohesion and the promotion of the overall harmonious development of the Union, though there must be consistency with the pursuit of scientific and technical quality.[1451] Moreover, the research priorities set for the 'first activity' by Article 164 EC[1452] must take account of the interests and capacities of all Member States, including the less advanced ones.[1453]

According to the Sixth Framework Programme, the participation of the outermost regions in Union research and technological development actions through appropriate mechanisms adapted to their particular situation should be facilitated.[1454]

As regards 'citizens and governance in a knowledge-based society', Union action will focus, *inter alia*, on the theme of knowledge-based society and social cohesion. This will involve research into improving the quality of life, social, employment and labour market policies, lifelong learning, and

---

1448 See also the 11th recital in the preamble (ibid). See, more particularly, the 9th recital in the preamble to Dec 88/279 ([1988] OJ L118/32) concerning the European strategic programme for R & D in information technologies (Esprit) and the 5th recital in the preamble to Dec 91/394 ([1991] OJ L218/22) adopting a specific RTD programme in the field of information technologies (1990–94). See also Call for the specific programme for RTD, including demonstration, in the field of information technologies (Esprit) ([1997] OJ C280/15).

1449 Concerning the Fourth Framework Programme of the EC activities in the field of RTDD ([1994] OJ L126/4). See also Dec 182/1999 ([1999] OJ L26/1) concerning the Fifth EC Framework Programme for RTDD activities (1998–2002).

1450 16th recital in the preamble to Dec 1110/94 ([1994] OJ L126/4).

1451 Ibid, Annex II.

1452 See para [610] below.

1453 Annex III to Dec 1110/94 ([1994] OJ L126/4). Research activities which might also be of interest to the coal and steel industries would be incorporated into the relevant themes under the first activity, on condition that they complied with the eligibility criteria of the Framework Programme, in particular as regards their precompetitive and multisectoral nature.

1454 14th recital in the preamble to Dec 1513/2002 ([2002] OJ L232/1) concerning the Sixth Framework Programme for research, technological development and demonstration activities, contributing to the creation of the European Research Area and to innovation (2002 to 2006). There is a separate programme for the coal and steel sectors (Dec 2002/234 ([2002] OJ L79/42) on the financial consequences of the expiry of the ECSC Treaty and on the research fund for coal and steel).

---

strengthening social cohesion and sustainable development with due consideration for the various social models in Europe.[1455]

Assistance is also envisaged for research related to underpinning the economic potential and cohesion of a larger and more integrated European Union. Research under this heading will include improved means to assess economic development and cohesion.[1456]

It is questionable whether the needs of research and development and those of cohesion can be easily reconciled. Rather, there may be conflict between regional development needs and the 'excellence' criterion for allocation of assistance.

This criterion does not necessarily discriminate against the less-favoured regions. For example, the Race programme concerned research and development in relation to advanced telecommunications.[1457] Over the period 1988 to 1992, 53 assisted projects (60 per cent of the total) 'involved organizations from the less-favoured regions of the Community'.[1458]

Indeed, according to the Commission, the criterion has played a part in promoting cohesion. The criterion has done so because it constitutes an attainable standard of reference for such regions.[1459] It stimulates them continuously to upgrade their scientific performance and to reach common technical, managerial and cultural standards for further collaborative transnational research and development.[1460]

In practice, however, application of the excellence criterion may favour regions with large firms already enjoying a relative technological advantage[1461] and links with similar regions.[1462] For example, the participation rate of small and medium-sized enterprises in specific programmes under the Second Framework Programme varied from 2 per cent to 18 per cent. This participation rate was much lower in relative terms than the contribution of such enterprises to GDP.[1463] Again, the participation rate of Objective 1 regions

---

1455 Dec 1513/2002 ([2002] OJ L232/1), Annex I, para 1.1.7.

1456 Ibid, para 1.2.1.A.3.

1457 Dec 88/28 ([1988] OJ L16/35) on a Community programme in the field of telecommunications technologies _ R & D in advanced communications technologies in Europe.

1458 Final report on phase I (1988–92) of the 10-year Race programme, COM(93)118, 18.

1459 Evaluation of the Effects of the EC Framework Programme for Research and Technological Development on Economic and Social Cohesion in the Community (EC Commission, Brussels, 1991), 29.

1460 Ibid, 45.

1461 Cf, earlier, Common policy for science and technology: impact of Community R & D on horizontal policies, COM(81)66, 3.

1462 European Parliament Resolution of 15 July 1993 ([1993] OJ C255/195) on the Community response to the problem of restructuring in East Germany and the economic and social crisis, para 17.

1463 Evaluation of the Effects of the EC Framework Programme for Research and Technological Development on Economic and Social Cohesion in the Community (EC Commission, Brussels, 1991), 31.

under the Fourth Framework Programme as a whole was 12.6 per cent.[1464] Hence, it is argued that new efforts are necessary to help small and medium-sized enterprises from such regions to participate. Indeed, in certain sectors, barriers to market entry, which include research and development costs, may render entry by such enterprises effectively dependent on public assistance.[1465]

At the same time, insofar as research and development assistance is granted to less-favoured regions, there may be detrimental effects. It commits scarce science and technology resources in the region concerned, particularly personnel, to projects which often have little direct relevance or spin-offs to the region.[1466] Indeed, since such resources are inelastic in the short and medium term, assisted projects may simply 'crowd out' unassisted ones.[1467] The possibility cannot be excluded that the latter projects would, if implemented, be of greater benefit to regional development than the former.

Therefore, influencing the sectoral and spatial distribution of technological advantage through technology transfer[1468] and promotion of 'human capital mobility'[1469] may be favoured.[1470] However, the need for planning and the allocation of substantial resources to technology transfer in parallel with the scientific effort is said not to be reflected in the Framework Programmes.[1471]

4. Scope of assistance

The Union is required by Article 164 EC to carry out four 'activities'. First, it is to implement research, technological development and demonstration programmes by promoting cooperation with and between undertakings, research centres and universities. Secondly, it is to promote cooperation in this field with third countries and international organizations. Thirdly, it is to

---

1464 R & TD activities of the EU 1998, COM(1998)439, 11.

1465 Evaluation of Economic Effects: Relevance and Impacts of EC Programmes promoting Industrial R & D with Special Emphasis on Small and Medium-Sized Enterprises (EC Commission, Brussels, 1992), 112–13.

1466 J Howells and D Charles, 'Research and Technological Development in the "Less-Favoured" Regions of the European Community: a UK Dimension' in K Dyson (ed), Local Authorities and New Technologies: the European Dimension (Croom Helm, London, 1988), 24–58, 45.

1467 J Gilchrist and D Deacon, 'Curbing Subsidies' in P Montagnon (ed), European Competition Policy (Pinter, London, 1990), 31–51.

1468 Dec 89/412 ([1989] OJ L200/23) adopting a specific programme for the dissemination and utilization of scientific and technological research results (Value) 1989–92; and Dec 92/272 ([1992] OJ L141/1) on the dissemination and exploitation of knowledge resulting from the specific RTD programmes of the Community.

1469 Cohesion and RTD policy, COM(93)203, 12.

1470 ESC Opinion of 28 March 1990 ([1990] OJ C124/22) on the declining industrial areas, para 2.5.

1471 Evaluation of the Effects of the EC Framework Programme for Research and Technological Development on Economic and Social Cohesion in the Community (EC Commission, Brussels, 1991), 30.

---

disseminate and optimize the results of the activities. Finally, it is to stimulate the training and mobility of researchers in the Union.

This provision may be seen as confirming the importance of assistance for technology transfer, which had already been sought under the EEC Treaty. In particular, the Sprint programme was revised in 1989.[1472] The programme was now to concern strengthening the innovative capacity of European producers of goods and services; enhancing the effectiveness and coherence of existing instruments and policies, whether at regional, national or Community level, in the field of innovation and technology transfer; and promoting the rapid penetration by new technologies and the dissemination of innovation throughout the economic fabric of the Community, thus strengthening cohesion in the field of innovation and technology transfer.[1473] Accordingly, science parks[1474] and networks[1475] might be assisted.

More particularly, assistance was to extend to projects having a transnational character, emphasizing industrial cooperation, and involving the application of generic technologies to targeted industrial sectors in regions of lagging development or of industrial decline.[1476] Higher rates of assistance might be available to such regions.[1477]

Moreover, the Community action programme in education and training for technology (Comett)[1478] concerned, *inter alia*, facilitating the balanced economic and social development of the Community[1479] and promoting cohesion.[1480] Hence, particular efforts were to be made in regions where cooperation between universities and industry was 'not very highly developed'.[1481] Special attention in the selection of projects was to be paid to association in their execution of universities and industrial partners from less-developed regions.[1482] Support was extended to preparatory activities, particularly in the case of such regions.[1483]

1472 Dec 89/286 ([1989] OJ L112/12) on the implementation at Community level of the main phase of the strategic programme for innovation and technology transfer (1989–93).
1473 Ibid, Art 2(2).
1474 Call for proposals to take part in the science park consultancy scheme launched within the Sprint programme ([1992] OJ C185/18).
1475 Communication regarding calls for proposals concerning the implementation of network support measures under the Sprint programme ([1992] OJ C205/8).
1476 Para B of the Annex to Dec 89/286 ([1989] OJ L353/15).
1477 Ibid, Art 6(4).
1478 Dec 89/27 ([1989] OJ L13/28) adopting the second phase of the programme on cooperation between universities and industry regarding training in the field of technology (Comett II) (1990–94).
1479 Ibid, Art 3.
1480 Ibid, Annex, para 1.
1481 Ibid, Annex, para 2.
1482 Ibid, Annex, para 2.C(e)(iv).
1483 Ibid, Annex, para 2.D(a)(i).

Such programmes may have favoured technology transfer. It is uncertain, however, whether they could compensate for the apparent failure of the Framework Programme to reconcile research and development efforts with cohesion objectives.

5. Forms of assistance

All Union activities in support of research and technological development are now to be set out in a multiannual Framework Programme. This Programme shall establish the scientific and technological objectives to be achieved by the activities, fix the relevant priorities and indicate the broad lines of such activities. It shall also fix the maximum overall amount of, and the detailed rules for, Union financial participation in the Programme and the respective shares in each of the supported activities.[1484]

Implementation of the Framework Programmes is to be based on specific programmes developed within each activity. A specific programme shall define the detailed rules for implementing it, fix its duration and provide for the financial resources deemed necessary. The sum of the amounts deemed necessary shall not exceed the overall maximum amount fixed for the Framework Programme and each activity.[1485]

Accordingly, the Sprint programme has been replaced by a specific programme for the dissemination and optimization of the results of activities in the field of research and technological development, including demonstration, for 1994 to 1998.[1486] This programme was seen as benefitting, in particular, small and medium-sized enterprises in the Member States and regions least involved in research and technological development. It was thus viewed as contributing to improved cohesion.[1487] However, even programmes of this kind may not necessarily be adequate to compensate for the failure of the Framework Programme generally to reconcile assistance to research and development with cohesion requirements.

G. TRANS-EUROPEAN NETWORKS

In the transport sector Community assistance was originally seen as addressing transport policy problems associated with the development of the

---

1484 Art 166(1) EC.
1485 Art 166(3) EC.
1486 Dec 94/917 ([1994] OJ L361/101). See, now, Reg 2321/2002 ([2002] OJ L355/23) concerning the rules for the participation of undertakings, research centres and universities in, and for the dissemination of research results for, the implementation of the EC Sixth Framework Programme (2002–2006).
1487 Ibid, 18th recital in the preamble. See, eg, the Call for proposals for the implementation of regional innovation and technology transfer strategies and regional technology transfer projects ([1995] OJ C240/15).

common market. Such assistance now has the function of promoting trans-European networks.

Early arrangements for consultation regarding transport infrastructure of Community interest were said to have proved inadequate to the needs of developing the common market[1488] and were revised by Decision 78/174.[1489] Article 1(2) of the Decision provided that a transport infrastructure project was of Community interest where it: was a major project designed to create new transport links, remove a bottleneck, or appreciably increase the capacity of transport links, and concerned cross-frontier routes; had a significant effect on traffic between Member States or with third countries; affected a Community policy, particularly regional policy; or made use of new transport technologies relevant to long-distance inter-urban transport.

A Commission proposal of July 1976 for a regulation providing for Community assistance to such projects[1490] was not accepted by the Council. However, from 1982 the Council annually adopted regulations to make use of amounts entered in the General Budget for supporting projects of this kind. These regulations were originally based simply on 'the EEC Treaty'[1491] and subsequently on Article 75 EEC, concerning transport policy.[1492]

Regulation 3359/90,[1493] adopted under Article 75 EEC, established a triennial plan for an action programme in the field of transport infrastructure with a view to the completion of an integrated transport market in 1992. The plan was to promote the harmonious development of transport infrastructure in the Community.[1494] Assistance for transport infrastructure projects was envisaged from appropriations designated for the purpose in the General Budget, the Structural Funds, the European Investment Bank and other financial instruments.[1495] In particular, projects might be assisted where they

1488 Development of the Common Transport Policy, Bull EC, Supp 8/71, 5.

1489 Instituting a consultation procedure and setting up a committee in the field of transport infrastructure ([1978] OJ L54/16). See, regarding the work of the committee, the Triannual report (1984–87), COM(88)289.

1490 Proposal of 5 July 1976 ([1976] OJ C207/9) for a regulation on support for projects of Community interest in transport infrastructure.

1491 Reg 3600/82 ([1982] OJ L376/10) on the granting of limited support in the field of transport infrastructure. See also Art 781 of the Budget for 1982 ([1982] OJ L31/3). See, later, Reg 3620/84 ([1984] OJ L333/58) on a specific measure in the field of transport infrastructure (see, eg, Dec 85/66 ([1985] OJ L30/19) granting financial support to implement the modernization of the Mulhouse-Nord railway junction project).

1492 Reg 4059/86 ([1986] OJ L378/24) on the granting of financial support to transport infrastructure projects (1985); Reg 4070/87 ([1987] OJ L380/33) (1986 and 1987); and Reg 4048/88 ([1988] OJ L356/5) (1988 and 1989).

1493 [1990] OJ L326/1.

1494 Ibid, 5th recital in the preamble.

1495 Ibid, Art 2.

contributed to the integration of areas which were either landlocked or situated on the periphery of the Community.[1496]

The Commission maintained that integration of the peripheral regions into the Community's transport network should be a priority for assistance. Accordingly, criteria for the grant of assistance should include the degree to which the isolation of such regions was reduced. The criteria should also include the coherence of the project with other Community actions in the field of transport or with other Community policies.[1497]

In practice, however, the possibility may not be excluded that regional disparities were increased by the assistance granted, in that the main inter-regional links were strengthened and peripheral regions marginalized.[1498] Certainly, the triennial plan emphasized establishment of a European high-speed rail network and promotion of combined transport. The plan thus gave the impression that assistance was basically designed to meet the operational needs of trans-European transport systems, rather than to promote regional development. Hence, the European Parliament criticised the lack of attention to connecting lines and extensions necessary to provide services to the peripheral and inaccessible regions of the Community.[1499]

Essentially, the same issues now arise in connection with assistance to trans-European networks.

1. Objectives of assistance

Article 154(1) EC now requires that, to achieve cohesion 'and to enable citizens of the Union, economic operators and regional and local communities to derive full benefit from the setting up of an area without internal frontiers, the Union shall contribute to the establishment and development of trans-European networks in the areas of transport, telecommunications and energy infrastructures'. More particularly, Article 154(2) EC requires that, within the framework of a system of open and competitive markets, assistance shall aim at promoting the interconnection and interoperability of national networks as well as access to such networks. It shall take particular account of the need to link island, landlocked and peripheral regions with the central regions of the Union.

1496 Ibid, Art 1. See, later, Art 2 of Reg 1738/93 ([1993] OJ L161/4) for an action programme in the field of transport infrastructure with a view to the completion of an integrated transport market in 1992.

1497 Community action programme, COM(90)585, 16.

1498 Report of the Committee on Transport and Tourism on transport and regional development, EP Doc A3-255/92, 12–13.

1499 Resolution of 13 December 1990 ([1991] OJ C19/267) on the Commission proposal for a Council decision concerning the establishment of a network of high speed trains.

As regards transport networks, the objective is to integrate land, sea and air transport infrastructure throughout the Union.[1500] According to the Commission, this objective does not simply entail the equalization of endowments. Geographically remote and sparsely populated regions are likely to need greater provision in terms of road or rail track length per head of population than other regions.[1501]

As regards telecommunications networks, the objectives are: the interconnection of networks in the sphere of telecommunications infrastructure; the establishment and development of interoperable services and applications; and improvement of access to them. Transition to an information society, increased competitiveness, cohesion, and job-creation are to be facilitated thereby.[1502]

As regards energy networks, the objective is to help to reduce energy supply costs. To this end, the interconnection, interoperability and development of such networks are envisaged.[1503] A higher rate of economic growth, more employment and enhanced competitiveness of the European economy are to be sought thereby.[1504]

2. Eligibility for assistance

According to Regulation 2236/95,[1505] projects are eligible for assistance if they are covered by guidelines[1506] adopted by the Council and Parliament under Article 155(1) EEC. Account is to be taken of the contribution of the project to the smooth running of the internal market and to cohesion. Particular account is to be taken of the contribution to the connection of island, landlocked and peripheral regions to the central regions of the Union; the importance to development of trade at European level; the contribution to increasing the competitiveness of the European economy; compliance with environmental considerations; and consistency with Union regional planning.

3. Allocation of assistance

The European Parliament proposed that priority in the allocation of assistance should be given to regions eligible under the Structural Funds. However, this

---

1500 Art 2(1) of Reg 1692/96 ([1996] OJ L228/1) on Community guidelines for the development of the trans-European transport network.
1501 Fifth periodic report on the situation and socio-economic development of the regions of the Community, COM(94)322, 67.
1502 Art 2 of Dec 1336/97 ([1997] OJ L183/12) on a series of guidelines for trans-European telecommunications networks.
1503 Dec 1229/2003 ([2003] OJ L176/1) laying down a series of guidelines for trans-European energy networks and repealing Dec 1254/96, Art 3.
1504 See also Dec 96/391 ([1996] OJ L161/154) laying down a series of measures aimed at creating a more favourable context for the development of TENs in the energy sector, Art 3.
1505 Laying down general rules for the granting of Community financial assistance in the field of TENs ([1995] OJ L228/1), Art 2(1).
1506 Dec 1229/2003 ([2003] OJ L176/1); Dec 1692/96 ([1996] OJ L228/1); and Dec 1336/97 ([1997] OJ L183/12).

proposal did not win the approval of the Council. The latter felt that the proposal disregarded 'the balance apparent in Article 154(1) EC, which [referred] to a multiplicity of objectives'.[1507] As a result, priority in the allocation of assistance depends on the contribution to the establishment of trans-European networks; harmonization of technical standards; interconnection and interoperability of national networks; integration of the various networks; and the reliability and safety of networks.[1508]

4. Scope of assistance

The Union may not only assist trans-European transport networks. It may also assist telecommunications networks and energy networks.

5. Forms of assistance

Assistance may, according to Article 155 EC, take the form of project financing. It may also take the form of assistance to studies related to projects; interest subsidies; contributions to fees for loan guarantees; direct grants to investments; or any combination of these forms.[1509] In addition, innovative actions concerning combined transport may be assisted[1510] and risk capital may be provided.[1511]

Closer coordination of such assistance with operations of the ERDF is sought. In particular, since both this Fund and assistance to trans-European networks seek to improve the accessibility of disadvantaged regions, clearer organizational links between the two are demanded.[1512]

However, coordination may be more than a matter of organizational links. It may require a broader view of transport policy, including recognition of the desirability of assistance to the maintenance of loss-making routes. For example, the Committee on Regional Policy and Regional Planning of the European Parliament favours 'a system of specific subsidies for transport costs linked to the additional costs imposed on Irish traders [in trade with the rest of the Union] by distance and the sea-crossing'.[1513] The Court of Auditors favours similar assistance for the outermost regions.[1514]

1507 Common Position 3/95 ([1995] OJ C130/1).
1508 Art 6(1) of Reg 2236/95 ([1995] OJ L228/1).
1509 Art 4(1) of Reg 2236/95 ([1995] OJ L228/1).
1510 Reg 2196/98 ([1998] OJ L277/1) concerning the granting of Community financial assistance for actions of an innovative nature to promote combined transport.
1511 Art 4 of Reg 1655/1999 amending Reg 2236/95 ([1999] OJ L197/1).
1512 COA annual report for 1988 ([1989] OJ C312/1), para 10.7. See, more particularly, regarding inadequate coordination of transport assistance and ERDF assistance, COA special report 1/93 ([1993] OJ C69/1) on the financing of transport infrastructure, paras 5.3–12.
1513 Report on the Community's regional development activities in Ireland, EP Doc A3-0275/90, 18.
1514 COA special report 5/97 ([1997] OJ C159/1) on management of the Community cereals trade involving export refunds, special import arrangements, and regional aid schemes.

More fundamental issues are raised by the literature. According to the literature, modern transport and communications technology means that geographically peripheral regions need not necessarily be economically peripheral. Peripheral regions are those lacking in mutual interactions between natural and built-up environments and social and economic actors within the region. In such a region, economic actors belong to networks which have few contact points within the region.[1515] Creation of networks favouring the integration of such regions into the Union economy may depend on more than simply physical transport infrastructure; it may also depend on the relationship between assistance for trans-European networks and more general cohesion efforts.

H. PHARE

The Phare programme has been primarily concerned with economic restructuring in Central and East European countries, pending their accession to the Union. However, cooperation between border regions in these countries and border regions within the Union has also been assisted.[1516] Such cooperation has received complementary assistance from this programme, the Structural Funds,[1517] and a special heading in the General Budget.[1518]

In particular, coordination of activities of the ERDF, notably Interreg,[1519] and Phare activities may take place.[1520] In addition, network support might be provided under the Ecos-Ouverture programme.[1521]

1515 F Snickars, 'Structural Change in Peripheral and Rural Areas – An Introduction' in U Wiberg and F Snickars (eds), Structural Change in Peripheral and Rural Areas (Swedish Council for Building Research, Stockholm, 1987), 7–14, 7.
1516 Reg 2760/98 ([1998] OJ L345/49) concerning the implementation of a programme for cross-border cooperation in the framework of the Phare programme.
1517 7th recital in the preamble to Reg 2082/93 ([1993] OJ L193/20) amending Reg 4253/88 laying down provisions for implementing Reg 2052/88 as regards coordination of the activities of the different Structural Funds between themselves and with the operations of the EIB and the other existing financial instruments.
1518 Art B7-502, 'Transfrontier cooperation in the field of structural operations', in the Budget for 1996 ([1996] OJ L22/3).
1519 Commission Communication laying down guidelines for a Community initiative concerning trans-European cooperation intended to encourage harmonious and balanced development of the European territory – Interreg III ([2000] OJ C143/6).
1520 Art 20(2) of Reg 1260/1999 ([1999] OJ L161/1). See also, regarding coordination with other Union financial instruments, Reg 1266/1999 ([1999] OJ L161/68) on coordinating aid to the applicant countries in the framework of the accession strategy and amending Reg 3906/89, cl 8 in the preamble and Art 10.
1521 See paras [145] ff above.

I. 'OTHER BUDGETARY RESOURCES'

Use of 'other Budgetary resources' has been advocated in the case of various industries, such as shipbuilding. Their use has been particularly prominent in relation to development of, or conversion from, textiles, energy and armaments production. At the same time, they may be used 'horizontally' to support small and medium-sized enterprises, to tackle balance-of-payments problems, and to assist reconstruction after natural disasters.

1. Proposed instruments for shipbuilding

Various kinds of assistance have been proposed for the shipbuilding sector. In particular, provision of assistance for the restructuring of shipbuilding and development of alternative industries in the regions concerned by such restructuring was proposed by the Commission in 1979.[1522] Introduction of a scheme to assist the scrapping and building of ships was also proposed in the same year.[1523] According to the proposed scheme, the building of new ships would be assisted by the Community,[1524] provided that the owner scrapped twice the tonnage represented by the new ships. However, the proposals were not accepted by the Council.

Provision of assistance for research and development in the shipbuilding sector has also been advocated by the Commission,[1525] with the support of the Economic and Social Committee[1526] and the European Parliament.[1527] However, no specific provision for such assistance in this sector has been made in Council legislation.[1528]

Increasingly, the concern of the Commission has been not so much with development of the industry as that reduction of shipbuilding capacity should not be impeded by fear of consequential social problems.[1529] Thus in 1987 the Commission proposed the grant of assistance to workers in the shipbuilding

---

1522 Proposal of 11 January 1979 (COM(78)769) for a decision on Community assistance for restructuring or conversion investments in the shipbuilding industry.

1523 Shipbuilding: State of the Industry and Crisis Measures, Bull EC, Supp 7/79.

1524 In its Resolution of 13 June 1974 ([1974] OJ C76/41) on the proposal for a directive on aid to the shipbuilding industry and on the memorandum on procedures for action in the shipbuilding industry, para 2, the European Parliament had maintained that, if necessary, the Commission should help to provide credit for shipbuilding investments generally.

1525 Proposals on the shipbuilding industry, COM(73)1788, 5. Such assistance was considered to be necessitated, inter alia, by the deficiencies of small and medium-scale shipyards. See the Third Report on Competition Policy (1974), 83.

1526 Opinion of 28 March 1974 ([1974] OJ C97/40) on the proposals on the shipbuilding industry, para III.

1527 Resolution of 12 December 1986 ([1987] OJ C7/325) on the proposal for a sixth directive on aid to shipbuilding, para 14(v).

1528 Though various Community R & D programmes might be available to assist shipbuilders. See Shipbuilding: industrial, social, and regional aspects, COM(87)275, 18.

1529 See, eg, State of the shipbuilding industry in the Community (situation as at 1 January 1982), COM(82)564, 21.

---

industry who were made redundant or threatened with redundancy.[1530] Assistance going beyond that available from the ESF and the ERDF was envisaged. The former Fund concentrated on job creation for young people under 25 and vocational training for workers over 25 affected by restructuring.[1531] Operations of the latter Fund were, in turn, limited to certain regions. The proposed new assistance would have covered measures to encourage absorption into economic life and socio-occupational integration; measures to promote geographical mobility; and measures to ease the transition to permanent retirement from working life. However, the Council failed to adopt the proposal. This failure is said to have exacerbated the social problems associated with the reduction of shipbuilding capacity.[1532]

2. Textiles

Restructuring of the textiles industry has been considered necessary, particularly in less developed regions.[1533] To mitigate the social impact, assistance has been advocated for modernization of this sector, vocational training, and redeployment of workers.[1534]

Assistance to synthetic fibres was provided for in Regulation 2914/79.[1535] Such assistance could be granted to investments to help create new jobs intended primarily for workers made redundant by the reduction of production capacity or by the total or partial closure of undertakings in this sector. Assistance could also be provided for conversion by undertakings in this sector to activities other than the production of synthetic fibres for textile purposes. At the same time, assistance could be provided for restructuring which led to a significant reduction in production capacity of the recipients.[1536]

1530 Proposal of 31 July 1987 ([1987] OJ C291/11) for a regulation instituting a specific Community programme of accompanying social measures to assist workers in the shipbuilding industry who were made redundant or threatened with redundancy; and the amended proposal of 12 September 1988 ([1988] OJ C249/5). See also Shipbuilding – industrial, social, and regional aspects, COM(87)275. See, regarding assistance for retraining, the proposed amendment of the European Parliament to the proposal for a directive on aid to shipbuilding ([1990] OJ C324/343).

1531 Reg 2950/83 ([1983] OJ L289/1) on the implementation of Dec 83/516 on the tasks of the ESF.

1532 ESC Opinion of 19 September 1990 ([1990] OJ C332/131) on the proposal for a directive on aid to shipbuilding, para 1.3.

1533 Report of the Committee on Economic and Monetary Affairs and Industrial Policy on restructuring the textile and clothing industry in the Community, EP Doc A3-0257/91, 8–9.

1534 European Parliament Resolution of 22 October 1991 ([1991] OJ C305/19) on restructuring the textile and clothing industry in the Community, paras 30-8.

1535 On Community assistance for industrial restructuring and conversion operations in the man-made fibres sector ([1979] OJ L326/36).

1536 Ibid, Art 1.

Moreover, research and development assistance for the footwear industry[1537] was introduced by Decision 75/266[1538] and Decision 77/188.[1539] Such assistance was extended to textiles more generally by Decision 81/1014.[1540] However, a more 'horizontal' approach to research and development assistance came to be preferred. Accordingly, in 1983 the Commission proposed adoption of a programme relating to the application of new technologies, which was to apply to textiles as a first experiment.[1541] Since this proposal was not accepted by the Council, research and development assistance to this sector was left to depend on the Brite programme.[1542]

3. Portuguese textiles

A specific programme for the modernization of the Portuguese textile and clothing industry was established by Regulation 852/95,[1543] according to the last paragraph of Article 159 EC. This paragraph provides for the grant of assistance outside the operations of the Structural Funds.[1544] The programme was seen as promoting cohesion[1545] and as assisting this industry to face increased competition resulting from World Trade Organization agreements.[1546] However, paragraph 1 of the Annex to the Regulation stipulated that there should be no overall increase in Portuguese production capacity in this industry. This stipulation was controversial, particularly from the perspective of cohesion. According to the Committee of the Regions, it

---

1537 See, eg, Item 3.7.2.1 of the Budget for 1980 ([1980] OJ L242/3).

1538 Establishing a programme of technological research in the textile sector ([1975] OJ L111/34).

1539 Adopting a technological research programme for the footwear industry ([1977] OJ L61/29).

1540 Adopting a second research and development programme in the field of textiles and clothing (indirect action 1981–83) ([1981] OJ L367/29).

1541 Proposal of 24 June 1983 ([1983] OJ C230/6) for a decision adopting a multiannual R & D programme in the field of the application of new technologies.

1542 Dec 85/196 ([1985] OJ L83/8) concerning a multiannual R & D programme in the fields of basic technological research and the application of new technologies (1985–88). It has now been brought within the scope of Framework Programmes for RTDD.

1543 On the grant of financial assistance to Portugal for a specific programme for the modernization of the Portuguese textile and clothing industry ([1995] OJ L86/10). Item B5-3201 of the Budget for 1991 ([1991] OJ L30/3) had envisaged assistance for restructuring the textile and clothing industry in Greece, Portugal, Spain and the former GDR.

1544 It was originally proposed as a Community initiative. See Notice laying down guidelines for the initiative concerning the modernization of the Portuguese textile and clothing industry ([1994] OJ C180/15). However, the European Parliament opposed financing of the programme under the Structural Funds, because Community initiatives should not be used in favour of one sector in one Member State. See the Resolution of 3 May 1994 ([1994] OJ C205/121) on this notice, paras 6–12.

1545 1st recital in the preamble to Reg 852/95 ([1995] OJ L86/10).

1546 Ibid, 2nd recital.

---

should be reviewed, given that this industry had 'been identified as a strategic element in the Portuguese economy'.[1547]

4. Energy

Various kinds of assistance to non-nuclear energy have been granted.[1548] In particular, assistance is granted to regional energy planning studies, priority being given to studies relating to frontier regions, outlying regions, and industrial and agricultural regions in economic difficulties.[1549] As a rule, however, such assistance takes little specific account of cohesion.[1550] Therefore, according to the European Parliament, existing arrangements must be reformed, so that the assistance may encourage development of the energy industry in line with the requirements of cohesion and environmental protection.[1551]

5. Armaments

Various regions might face major structural problems both because of arms industry conversion to civil production and because of cuts in military installations.[1552] Accordingly, in Article B2-610 of the General Budget for 1991,[1553] ECU 40 million was committed for the Perifra programme. The Community territory as a whole was eligible for assistance, but preference was given to regions covered by Objective 1, 2 or 5b. However, the limited sums available[1554] meant that assisted actions were of small scale and generally of a demonstration nature.

1547 Opinion of 17 May 1994 ([1994] OJ C217/14) on the Community initiative on the modernization of the textile and clothing industry of Portugal.

1548 See, eg, Dec 1999/21 ([1999] OJ L7/16) adopting a multiannual framework programme for actions in the energy sector (1998–2002) and connected measures.

1549 Regional and urban planning: Commission invitation to submit proposals ([1991] OJ C12/12; [1994] OJ C163/29). See, now, Dec 1230/2003 ([2003] OJ L176/29) adopting a multiannual programme for action in the field of energy 'Intelligent Energy – Europe programme (2003 to 2006)' ([2002] OJ C203/47).

1550 Increased attention to cohesion issues was envisaged in the Proposal of 15 April 1994 ([1994] OJ C158/6) for a regulation concerning a Community programme providing financial support for the promotion of European energy technology 1995–98 (Thermie-II); and Item B4-1000 of the Budget for 1998 ([1998] OJ L44/3). See also Arts 6(3)(c) and 11 of the resulting Reg 2008/90 ([1990] OJ L185/1) concerning the promotion of energy technology in Europe (Thermie programme). More recent measures may refer to cohesion in their preambles. See, eg, Dir 2001/77 ([2001] OJ L283/35) on the promotion of electricity produced from renewable energy sources in the internal electricity market.

1551 Resolution of 12 March 1992 ([1992] OJ C94/279) on a common energy policy, para 11.

1552 Resolution of the European Parliament of 22 November 1991 ([1991] OJ C326/267) on the Perifra programme.

1553 [1991] OJ L30/3.

1554 Though some increase in expenditure was envisaged for 1992 and 1993. See the Budget for 1992 ([1992] OJ L26/3), Art B2-61.

Perifra was replaced by the Konver programme.[1555] Assistance could be provided to training, innovation and 'environmental rehabilitation'. However, arrangements for the grant of such assistance remained problematic. For example, many of the regions affected by cuts in military expenditure, including a large part of Aquitaine and Provence-Alpes-Côte d'Azur in France, were not eligible for assistance. The programme subsequently became a Community initiative,[1556] but it has been discontinued.

6. Small and medium-sized enterprises

Business and Innovation Centres (BICs) have been supported by the Commission since 1983.[1557] The development of a network of these bodies, the European Business and Innovation Centre Network (EBN), has also been assisted by the Commission.[1558] They operate in regions assisted by the ERDF and other regions adversely affected by major industrial decline.[1559] They are designed to create innovative activities with growth potential through detecting and selecting entrepreneurs; finding, assessing and developing technologies; management training; rigorous business planning; and the supply of common premises. In other words, they seek to assist regions in developing their indigenous potential.[1560] They concentrate their work on new or existing firms which put forward innovative development projects adding value to the economy of the region.[1561]

However, the performance of the Business and Innovation Centres has been criticised, partly because 'innovation' has been interpreted as any activity, product or process that is new to the industrial environment of the area concerned.[1562]

Article 157(1) EC provides that the Union and the Member States shall encourage an environment favourable to initiative and to the development of undertakings throughout the Union, particularly small and medium-sized enterprises. This provision reflects a long-standing recognition of the desirability of assistance for such enterprises.[1563] This recognition is based on the view that financial structures are ill suited to the launching of new developments by small and medium-sized enterprises, even though such enterprises have an important role to play in the Union economy. In

1555 It was launched at the request of the European Parliament on 'an ad hoc basis' (Bull EC 4-1993, 1.2.100); Budget for 1993 ([1993] OJ L31/3), Items B2-142 (ERDF) and B2-143 (ESF).
1556 See paras [145] ff above.
1557 Explanatory memorandum to the proposal for a decision concerning a Community programme to create and develop BICs and their network, COM(86)785, 3.
1558 Bull EC 11-1984, 2.1.82.
1559 Art B2-601 of the Budget for 1996 ([1996] OJ L22/3).
1560 Explanatory memorandum to the proposal for a decision concerning a Community programme to create and develop BICs and their network, COM(86)785, 1.
1561 Commission Reply by Mr Millan to WQ 1939/91 ([1992] OJ C126/16) by Mr François Musso.
1562 Special report 5/93 ([1994] OJ C13/1) concerning BICs, para 13.
1563 Cf N Moussis, 'Small and Medium Enterprises in the Internal Market' (1992) ELR 483–98.

particular, assistance may be necessary because they may be too small to benefit from the economies of scale expected to result for their larger competitors from integration.[1564]

Assistance was provided for in Decision 91/319.[1565] This measure was designed to revise existing arrangements[1566] so as to take account of the impact of completion of the internal market. The preamble referred to the importance of such enterprises for economic activity in general and regional development in particular.[1567] Their importance was said to derive from their dynamism, productivity, adaptability and innovation.[1568] Accordingly, a multiannual programme for assistance to such enterprises was instituted under Decision 93/379.[1569] At the same time, to facilitate coordination between the various measures in their favour, an integrated programme was established.[1570]

Assistance to such enterprises is expected to favour cohesion.[1571] Accordingly, there is to be coordination between such assistance and the operations of the Structural Funds. Thus the Structural Funds may assist small and medium-sized enterprises and the encouragement of services supplied to them, such as management advice and market surveys.[1572]

Moreover, in accordance with a pilot scheme launched in 1989,[1573] the Commission has provided financial assistance for the creation and development of seed-capital funds to acquire equity holdings in new or

1564 Cf Public procurement: regional and social aspects, COM(89)400 and, more particularly, Promoting SME participation in public procurement in the Community, COM(90) 66.

1565 Revising the programme on the improvement of the business environment and the promotion of the development of enterprises, in particular SMEs in the Community ([1991] OJ L175/32).

1566 Dec 89/490 ([1989] OJ L239/33) on the improvement of the business environment and the promotion of the development of enterprises, and in particular SMEs, in the Community. See, now, Dec 2000/819 ([2000] OJ L333/84) on a multiannual programme for enterprise and entrepreneurship, and in particular for small and medium-sized enterprises (2001–2005).

1567 See, eg, Assistance in the field of transnational cooperation between small enterprises and the craft sector _ call for proposals ([1996] OJ C232/47).

1568 See also Assistance for craft enterprises and small enterprises: call for proposals ([1997] OJ C117/43).

1569 Dec 93/379 ([1993] OJ L161/68) on a multiannual programme of Community measures to intensify the priority areas and to ensure the continuity and consolidation of policy for enterprise, in particular SMEs, in the Community. See, now, Dec 2000/819 ([2000] OJ L333/84).

1570 Integrated programme in favour of SMEs and the craft sector, COM(94)207.

1571 8th recital in the preamble to Dec 89/490 ([1989] OJ L239/33). Art 777 of the Budget for 1987 ([1987] OJ L86/3) had envisaged financing for analysis of problems specific to SMEs in peripheral regions and of their solutions.

1572 Art 2(1)(c) of Reg 1783/1999 ([1999] OJ L213/1) on the ERDF. See also Reg 1784/1999 ([1999] OJ L213/5) on the ESF, cl 9 in the preamble.

1573 Pilot action to create and develop seed-capital funds ([1988] OJ C306/12).

embryonic companies.[1574] Risk capital may also be available to small and medium-sized enterprises generally through Union-supported arrangements such as 'Venture consort' and 'Eurotech capital'.[1575] In relation to such schemes, the importance of 'integrating the outlying regions' is recognized, but is not apparently treated as a priority.[1576]

7. Balance-of-payment loans

Balance-of-payment loans were introduced by Regulation 397/75,[1577] and are now provided for in Regulation 332/2002.[1578] They were originally designed to assist Member States in tackling balance-of-payment difficulties attributable to the increase in oil prices without disruption of the common market. However, the original arrangements were reformed by Regulation 682/81,[1579] and such loans now seek more generally to assist Member States with monetary problems that may hamper investment and growth.[1580] For example, loans to Greece have been concerned with more fundamental structural problems.[1581] They have been designed to assist the strengthening and modernization of productive structures, and use of the latest loan is to have regard to the Community Support Framework for Greece.[1582] Guarantees on these loans are financed from the General Budget.[1583]

8. Reconstruction after natural disasters

Budgetary resources may be used to assist reconstruction after natural disasters. For example, grants and interest subsidies were provided following

1574 Twenty-Fifth EC General Report (1992), 93; and Call for proposal on the launching of a 'seed capital' action ([1998] OJ C363/30). See, now, Rule 8 in the Annex to Reg 1685/2000 ([2000] OJ L193/39) laying down detailed rules for the implementation of Reg 1260/1999 as regards eligibility of expenditure of operations co-financed by the Structural Funds.

1575 Twenty-Sixth EC General Report (1993), 25; and Improvement of the fiscal environment of SMEs, COM(94)206. See, now, Rule 8 in the Annex to Reg 1685/2000 ([2000] OJ L193/39).

1576 Financial engineering, COM(86)723, 3; and Chapter B5-33 of the Budget for 1996 ([1996] OJ L33/2).

1577 Concerning Community loans ([1975] OJ L46/1). Cf, earlier, Dec 71/143 ([1971] JO L73/15) setting up machinery for medium-term financial assistance.

1578 Establishing a facility providing medium-term financial assistance for Member States' balances of payments ([2002] OJ L53/1).

1579 Adjusting the Community loan mechanism designed to support the balance of payments of Member States ([1981] OJ L73/1).

1580 The EIB, the other financial instruments and strengthening economic and social cohesion, COM(88)244, 2. See, eg, Dec 93/67 ([1993] OJ L22/121) concerning a Community loan in favour of Italy.

1581 Dec 85/543 ([1985] OJ L341/17) concerning a Community loan in favour of Greece.

1582 8th recital in, and para 4 of, the preamble to Dec 91/136 ([1991] OJ L66/22) concerning a Community loan in favour of Greece.

1583 See, eg, Art B0-200 of the Budget for 1998 ([1998] OJ L44/3). See, generally, Guarantees covered by the General Budget, COM(97)464. See, now, Rule 9 in the Annex to Reg 1685/2000 ([2000] OJ L193/39) laying down detailed rules for the implementation of Reg 1260/1999 as regards eligibility of expenditure of operations co-financed by the Structural Funds.

an earthquake in Italy in 1976.[1584] Again, following earthquakes in Greece in 1986, the Budget was used to fund interest rate subsidies on loans granted by the European Investment Bank in the regions stricken.[1585] Similar assistance was provided following earthquakes in Italy in 1980[1586] and in Greece in 1981[1587] and 1999,[1588] and following a cyclone in Madeira in 1993.[1589] In such circumstances, direct grants may now be made from the EU Solidarity Fund.[1590]

J. FINANCIAL INSTRUMENT FOR THE ENVIRONMENT

The EEC Treaty originally made no provision for environmental policy. However, the need for Community assistance to environmental protection became clear, as the common market developed.

Assistance for environmental protection was first envisaged in the General Budget for 1975.[1591] More particularly, in 1980 assistance to develop 'clean' technologies was envisaged.[1592] Moreover, in 1982 assistance for pilot projects for such technologies was envisaged.[1593] The possibility was also foreseen of Community contributions to the investment needed for implementation of certain Community obligations, particularly those concerning water quality, air quality, and the management of toxic waste.[1594]

1584 Reg 1505/76 ([1976] OJ L168/9) on the Community contribution towards repairing the damage caused to agriculture by the earthquake in May 1976 in the region of Friuli/Venezia Giulia; Reg 1506/76 ([1976] OJ L168/11) on the Community contribution towards repairing the infrastructural damage caused by the earthquake in May 1976 in the region of Friuli/Venezia Giulia.
1585 Dec 88/561 ([1988] OJ L309/32) relating to exceptional Community aid for the reconstruction of the areas stricken by earthquakes which took place in Greece in September 1986.
1586 Dec 81/19 ([1981] OJ L37/21) on Community aid granted by way of exception for the reconstruction of the regions affected by the Italian earthquake in November 1980.
1587 Dec 81/1013 ([1981] OJ L367/27) on Community aid granted by way of exception for the reconstruction of the regions affected by the Greek earthquakes in February and March 1981.
1588 Dec 2000/786 ([2000] OJ L313/25) on the grant of funds to Greece in order to compensate partially for the interest paid on EIB loans for the reconstruction of the region which was devastated by the earthquake of September 1999.
1589 Dec 95/250 ([1995] OJ L159/16) relating to exceptional Community aid for the reconstruction of the areas stricken by the cyclone that hit Madeira in October 1993.
1590 Reg 2012/2002 ([2002] OJ L311/3) establishing the EU Solidarity Fund.
1591 [1975] OJ L54/2, Art 357, on 'environmental projects'. See also Dec 73/126 ([1973] OJ L153/11) adopting a research programme for the EEC on the protection of the environment.
1592 Item 3.5.1.1 of the Budget for 1980 ([1980] OJ L378/3).
1593 Item 6610 of the Budget for 1982 ([1982] OJ L31/3).
1594 Ibid, Item 6612.

Such plans led to establishment of the Ace (Action by the Community relating to the environment) programme. According to Regulation 1872/84,[1595] this programme was originally to run for three years. Regulation 2247/87[1596] extended the range of activities concerned, their geographical scope, and the resources available.[1597] ECU 24 million was provided for a further four years.

Article 1(1) of the latter Regulation stated that the Community might grant financial assistance for demonstration projects aimed at developing new clean technologies, which caused little or no pollution and which might also be more economical in the use of natural resources; demonstration projects aimed at developing techniques for recycling and reusing waste, including waste water; demonstration projects aimed at developing techniques for locating and restoring sites contaminated by hazardous wastes or substances; demonstration projects aimed at developing techniques and methods for measuring and monitoring the quality of the natural environment; projects favouring the maintenance or re-establishment of seriously threatened biotopes which were the habitat of endangered species and were of particular importance to the Community under Directive 79/409;[1598] and projects favouring the protection or re-establishment of land threatened or damaged by fire, erosion or desertification.

Article 175(4) EC now provides that, 'without prejudice to certain measures of a Community nature, the Member States shall finance and implement the environmental policy measures'. The implication is that the Union may provide certain environmental assistance.

In the case of the Cohesion Fund,[1599] the implication is confirmed by Article 175(5) EC. According to this provision, 'without prejudice to the principle that the polluter should pay, if a measure ... involves costs deemed disproportionate for the public authorities of a Member State, the Council shall, in the act adopting that measure, lay down appropriate provisions [for] financial support from the Cohesion Fund'.[1600]

At the same time, Medspa was established by Regulation 563/91.[1601] It provided for the grant of assistance for environmental protection in the

---

1595 On action by the Community relating to the environment ([1984] OJ L176/1).

1596 On action by the Community relating to the environment ([1987] OJ L207/8).

1597 However, the proposal of 11 March 1987 ([1987] OJ C141/3) for a decision establishing a 5-year Community programme of projects to demonstrate how environmental measures could help to create jobs was not accepted by the Council.

1598 On the conservation of wild birds ([1979] OJ L103/1).

1599 Reg 1164/94 ([1994] OJ L130/1) establishing a Cohesion Fund, as amended by Reg 1264/1999 ([1999] OJ L161/57).

1600 Art 130r(4) EEC previously required that, in the application of the 'polluter pays' principle, particular account should be taken of the economic and social development of the Community as a whole.

1601 On action by the Community for the protection of the environment in the Mediterranean region ([1991] OJ L63/1).

Mediterranean, to complement the Integrated Mediterranean Programmes.[1602] Similarly, Regulation 3908/91[1603] established Norspa. It provided for the grant of assistance to protect the environment in the coastal areas and coastal waters of the Irish Sea, North Sea, English Channel, Baltic Sea and North-East Atlantic Ocean. Regulation 1973/92,[1604] which has now been replaced by Regulation 1655/2000,[1605] established a Financial Instrument for the Environment (Life).

1. Objectives of assistance

The objectives of the Financial Instrument for the Environment are to contribute to the implementation, updating and development of Union environmental policy and of environmental legislation, in particular as regards the integration of the environment into other policies and to sustainable development in the Union.[1606]

2. Eligibility for assistance

The projects financed by LIFE shall meet the following general criteria: be of Union interest by making a significant contribution to the above objectives; be carried out by technically and financially sound participants; and be feasible in terms of technical proposals, timetable, budget and value for money.[1607]

3. Allocation of assistance

Priority may be given to projects based on a multinational approach when this is likely to have more effective results in terms of achievement of objectives taking into account feasibility and costs.[1608] The need to help the less prosperous Member States to honour their environmental commitments has been stressed by the European Parliament.[1609]

4. Scope of assistance

LIFE shall consist of the three thematic components: 'LIFE-nature', 'LIFE-environment' and 'LIFE-third countries'.[1610]

'LIFE-nature' concerns the implementation of Union rules on the conservation of wild birds and the conservation of natural habitats and of wild

---

1602 Annex II(a) of Reg 2088/85 ([1985] OJ L197/1) concerning the IMPs provided that in the agricultural sector such programmes might provide for operations aimed, inter alia, at operations to protect the environment.
1603 On Community action to protect the environment in the coastal areas and coastal waters of the Irish Sea, North Sea, English Channel, Baltic Sea, and North-East Atlantic Ocean ([1991] OJ L370/28).
1604 Establishing a Financial Instrument for the Environment ([1992] OJ L206/1).
1605 Concerning the Financial Instrument for the Environment ([2000] OJ L192/1).
1606 Art 1 of Reg 1655/2000 ([2000] OJ L192/1).
1607 Art 2 of Reg 1655/2000 ([2000] OJ L192/1).
1608 Art 2 of Reg 1655/2000 ([2000] OJ L192/1).
1609 Resolution of 8 April 1992 ([1992] OJ C125/122) on the implementation of EC environmental legislation, paras 12-13.
1610 Art 2 of Reg 1655/2000 ([2000] OJ L192/1).

fauna and flora.[1611] 'LIFE-environment' concerns the development of innovative and integrated techniques and methods and to the further development of Union environment policy.[1612] 'LIFE-third countries' concerns the establishment of capacities and administrative structures needed in the environmental sector and in the development of environmental policy and action programmes in third countries bordering on the Mediterranean and the Baltic Sea other than the countries of central and eastern Europe which have concluded Association Agreements with the Union.[1613]

The Commission is to secure coordination and coherence as between such assistance and operations of the other Union funds.[1614] The problems facing such coordination[1615] were impliedly recognized by the Envireg initiative.[1616] However, this initiative was too limited to overcome problems of reconciling environmental assistance and Union spending generally[1617] and, in any case, has been discontinued.

5. Forms of assistance

LIFE assistance may take the form of nature conservation projects,[1618] demonstration projects,[1619] preparatory projects,[1620] or technical assistance projects.[1621] It may also take the form of accompanying measures,[1622] to which a maximum of 5 per cent of available appropriations may be devoted.[1623]

K. EEA FINANCIAL MECHANISM

When the European Economic Area (EEA) Agreement[1624] was concluded with EFTA States,[1625] Member States demanded compensation for trade liberalization with the comparatively developed EFTA States. According to the preamble to the Agreement, the Contracting Parties aim to promote a harmonious development of the European Economic Area. They are convinced

---

1611 Art 3(1) of Reg 1655/2000 ([2000] OJ L192/1).

1612 Ibid, Art 4(1).

1613 Ibid, Art 5(1).

1614 Art 7(2) of Reg 1655/2000 ([2000] OJ L192/1).

1615 J Scott, Development Dilemmas in European Community Law (Open University Press, Buckingham, 1995).

1616 See paras [144] ff above.

1617 See, eg, COA annual report for 1994 ([1995] OJ C303/1), para 6.42.

1618 Art 3(2)(a) of Reg 1655/2000 ([2000] OJ L192/1).

1619 Ibid, Art 4(2)(a).

1620 Ibid, Art 4(2)(b).

1621 Ibid, Art 5(2)(a).

1622 Ibid, Arts 3(2)(b), 4(2)(c) and 5(2)(b).

1623 Ibid, Art 8(3).

1624 [1994] OJ L1/3. See, generally, A Evans, European Community Law, including the EEA Agreement (Kluwer, Deventer, 1994).

1625 Iceland, Liechtenstein and Norway.

of the need to contribute through the application of this Agreement to the reduction of economic and social regional disparities.[1626] Article 115 of the Agreement confirms the concern of the Parties to reduce such disparities. To this end, Article 116 provided for the establishment by the EFTA States of a Financial Mechanism, details of which were set out in Protocol 38 to the Agreement.[1627]

The Protocol provided for assistance in the form of grants and interest rebates.[1628] Decisions regarding such assistance were subject to approval by the EFTA States and to a Commission opinion.[1629] For the period 1999 to 2003, EFTA States would provide €119.6 million in assistance.[1630]

Assistance was limited to projects in Greece, the island of Ireland, Portugal, and the regions of Spain listed in the Annex to the Agreement.[1631] The shares allocated to each beneficiary region were to be determined in the light of the region's relative level of economic development, population size and 'other relevant factors'.[1632] Priority was to be given to projects emphasizing the environment (including urban development), transport (including transport infrastructure), or education and training. Among projects submitted by the private sector, special consideration was to be given to small and medium-sized enterprises. The maximum grant element for any project supported by the Financial Mechanism should be fixed at a level which was not inconsistent with Union policies in this regard.[1633]

It has now been replaced by an EEA Financial Mechanism in accordance with Protocol 38a to the EEA Agreement, which was introduced by the EEA Enlargement Agreement.[1634] It makes available a total of €600 million over five years. The assistance is provided to Greece, Portugal, Spain and the 10 new Member States. Projects must concern: environmental protection, promotion of sustainable development, conservation of European cultural heritage, human resources development, and health and childcare.

1626 6th recital in the preamble to the EEA Agreement.
1627 Art 117 EEA.
1628 Art 1(2) of Protocol 38. It was limited by EEA Joint Committee Dec 47/2000 ([2000] OJ L159/74) to providing assistance in the form of grants.
1629 Report of the Committee on External Economic Relations on economic and trade relations between the EC and the EFTA countries in the EEA, EP Doc. A3-306/92.
1630 Art 1 of EEA Joint Committee Dec 47/2000 ([2000] OJ L174/59).
1631 Art 4(1) of Protocol 38.
1632 Art 8(1) of Reg 2894/94 ([1994] OJ L305/6) concerning arrangements for implementing the EEA Agreement.
1633 Art 4(2) of Protocol 38.
1634 It is accompanied by the Norwegian Financial Mechanism.

L. CONCLUSION

In practice, Member States and their representatives in the Council seem more willing to approve measures to reduce the costs of implementing agreed sectoral policies than they are to design such measures according to cohesion requirements. As a result, the operation of sectoral instruments may be ill adapted to pursuit of such requirements. Indeed, the very focus of such assistance on particular industries may mean that it is also ill adapted to the promotion of cohesion.[1635]

The assistance provided through horizontal instruments may not necessarily be effective in strengthening cohesion. These instruments do little to direct assistance to less developed regions and may be ill adapted to the specific problems of such regions.

Some horizontal instruments, such as loans and guarantees from the EIB, may by their nature be ill adapted to the promotion of cohesion. More usually, the operations of horizontal instruments tend to be determined primarily by the perceived requirements of the particular policy pursued. The legal rules embodying these requirements may not necessarily attach the same importance to questions of profitability as does Commission practice controlling the grant of State aid under Article 87 EC.[1636] Hence, Union assistance may not necessarily promote efficient use of resources. Even insofar as the assistance is capable of doing so, its effect may be to increase rather than decrease regional disparities. It may have this effect, because the more developed regions may be best qualified to obtain and to use the assistance efficiently.[1637] Hence, the possibility cannot be excluded that the work of horizontal instruments may sometimes be positively harmful to cohesion.

The inference may be drawn that the more assistance is provided by such instruments, the less effective assistance from the ERDF will be. Indeed, the latter assistance may be alleged merely to offset the additional geographical distortions of competition resulting from the operations of horizontal instruments.[1638] An efficient approach to promotion of cohesion would, it is said, be either to eliminate such operations, so as to reduce the overall level of assistance, or to adapt them to cohesion requirements and channel them to less developed regions.[1639]

1635 ESC Opinion of 29 April 1981 ([1981] OJ C185/20) on the revision of the ERDF Regulation, para 4.
1636 A Evans, EC Law of State Aid (Oxford EC Law Series, Clarendon Press, Oxford, 1997).
1637 D O'Hearn, 'Global Competition, Europe and Irish Peripherality' (1993) The Economic and Social Review 169–97.
1638 Cf, regarding disputes in the Commission whether assistance to car companies for training would drain Union funds away from regional and social objectives with no guarantee that competitiveness would be improved, The Financial Times, 29 April 1992.
1639 ESC Opinion of 29 January 1986 ([1986] OJ C75/12) on national regional development aid.

7
PROCESSES

A. INTRODUCTION

The practice of the Union funds depends on various processes. They include processes associated with legislation, budgetary provision, 'soft law', administrative decisions, contracts, committees, partnership and judicial review. Such processes may interact with those of the intergovernmental kind. Indeed, both kinds of processes may focus on and seek to elaborate the same legal rules. However, the differences between their respective legal contexts imply the possibility that their substantial results may diverge.

B. LEGISLATION

Union legislation has to be adopted, or at least authorized, by representatives of Member States in the Council of the Union. Hence, such legislation may offer a means of implementing intergovernmental bargains such as those embodied in the Treaties.

However, attitudes to the role of such legislation may vary between Member States. For example, net recipients may see Council legislation[1640] as ensuring that they receive their share of resources from the Union funds, as allocated by such bargains. Net payers, for their part, may see such legislation as ensuring that the resources are genuinely devoted to promotion of cohesion or, at least, that distortion of competition is minimized.[1641] Indeed, the latter Member States may regard the effective operation of Union processes as a precondition for progress in intergovernmental bargaining. In 1982, for example, the House of Lords Select Committee warned that Member States which had little direct return from the ERDF were becoming more determined to ensure that the Fund should not be simply a mechanism for transferring resources to the less-developed Member States. Therefore, 'a genuine Community dimension to regional development had to be guaranteed' by Union processes if the net payers were to continue to support the Fund.[1642]

1640 Such as Reg 1164/94 ([1994] OJ L130/1) establishing a Cohesion Fund.
1641 Cf, regarding the concern of net payers to secure 'value for money' from the Union funds without prejudicing their own freedom to pursue their regional policies, S George, Politics and Policy in the European Union (Oxford University Press, 3rd edn, 1996), 240.
1642 Revision of the ERDF, House of Lords Select Committee on the European Communities, HL(1981–82)126, xix-xx. See, later, EEC regional development policy, House of Lords Select Committee on the European Communities, HL(1991–92)20, 37. Cf, regarding Danish attitudes, L Lyck, 'Regional Policy' in L Lyck (ed), Denmark and EC Membership Evaluated (Pinter, London, 1992), 158–64.

Such divergence of attitudes within the Council may reduce the matters on which the Council can agree and, hence, may limit the role played by Council legislation in regulating the operations of the Union funds.

The same divergence of attitudes may also limit the readiness of the Council to authorize the Commission to adopt implementing legislation.[1643] Even where such authorization is granted, it tends to relate to 'technical' matters, such as calculation of the amount of assistance payable from the Union funds and procedures for applications for such assistance. For example, in connection with the ESF, the Commission was each year to determine the amounts of assistance to be granted per person and per unit of time for each Member State.[1644] More generally, Regulation 1260/1999[1645] empowers the Commission to draw up detailed legislation on technical financial matters and on information and publicity concerning assistance from the Union funds and as necessary in unforeseen circumstances. In such cases, concern to secure efficiency gains may militate in favour of the grant of some legislative powers to the Commission.[1646] In other cases, the Council may be reluctant to grant such powers.

Such features of Council practice may lead to conflict between the Council and other Union institutions. The latter institutions may perceive legislation as having a function other than that of giving effect to intergovernmental bargains. In fact, they may perceive it as a means of establishing and developing the Union's own policies for cohesion. For example, according to the European Parliament, it is necessary to impress on Member States that operations of the Union funds are intended to reduce regional disparities and not to overcome financing difficulties in national treasuries.[1647] Such conflict may add to controversy surrounding legislative activity in this area.

1. Unanimity issues

Particular controversy may attach to the question whether the Council should be required to act unanimously or by a qualified majority.[1648] For example, in the case of specific Community regional development measures, Article 13(3)

1643 R Priebe, 'Le Droit communautaire des structures agricoles' (1988) CDE 3–38, 15. See, generally, regarding such legislation, A Evans, A Textbook on EU Law (Hart Publishing, Oxford, 1998), Section 2.3.1.
1644 Art 2(2) of Reg 2950/83 ([1983] OJ L289/1) on the implementation of Dec 83/516 on the tasks of the ESF. See, eg, Dec 83/621 ([1983] OJ L350/25) on the rates of assistance from the ESF towards expenditure on recruitment and employment premiums.
1645 Laying down general provisions on the Structural Funds ([1999] OJ L161/1), Art 53.
1646 R Priebe, n 1 above, 16. See, eg, Reg 2064/97 ([1997] OJ L290/1) establishing detailed arrangements for the implementation of Reg 4253/88 as regards the financial control by Member States of operations co-financed by the Structural Funds.
1647 Resolution of 15 July 1993 ([1993] OJ C255/171) on the annual report on the implementation of the reform of the Structural Funds in 1991, para 9.
1648 See, regarding such a majority, Art 205(2) EC.

of Regulation 214/79[1649] provided that the Council, acting unanimously on a Commission proposal, was to adopt a special programme for each measure. The programme was to determine the nature of the operations to which the ERDF might contribute; the regions which the Fund might assist;[1650] the national aid taken into consideration in granting Fund assistance; the contribution of the Fund; the categories of beneficiaries of Fund assistance; and the detailed rules for financing. The European Parliament objected that the requirement of Council unanimity entailed a right of veto which was contrary to the rules governing the Fund since its creation.[1651] Possibly in response to such objections, Article 7(4) of Regulation 1787/84[1652] subsequently provided that frameworks for Community programmes were to be established by a Council decision adopted by qualified majority.

Article 161 EC now provides that basic principles concerning the Structural Funds are to be established by the Council acting unanimously with the assent of the European Parliament. However, 'implementing decisions'[1653] regarding the ERDF are to be adopted by the Council according to the 'co-decision' procedure under Article 162 EC. This procedure means that such decisions may usually be adopted by a qualified majority. Their adoption only requires unanimity where the Council wishes to overrule the European Parliament or to amend a Commission proposal.[1654]

2. Regulatory failure

Whether Council unanimity or merely a qualified majority is required for legislative enactments, or whether legislative powers are delegated to the Commission, the role of legislation in regulating the operations of the Union funds may be criticised as too limited. According to the European Parliament, the resulting regulatory shortcomings may lead to confusion and abuses in the grant of assistance.[1655] They may also restrict the scope of internal controls and prevent applicants for assistance from bringing proceedings before the

1649 Amending Reg 724/75 ([1979] OJ L35/1).
1650 The Commission proposal (Art 13 of the Proposal of 3 June 1977 ([1977] OJ C161/11) for a regulation amending Reg 724/75) that the eligible regions should be decided by a qualified majority vote in the Council was rejected by the latter.
1651 Resolution of 19 June 1981 ([1981] OJ C172/117) on the fifth annual report on the ERDF, para 10.
1652 On the ERDF ([1984] OJ L169/1).
1653 See, regarding the meaning of this expression, Art 3(4) of Reg 2081/93 ([1993] OJ L193/5) amending Reg 2052/88 on the tasks of the Structural Funds and their effectiveness and on coordination of their activities between themselves and with the operations of the EIB and the other existing financial instruments. See, now, Art 53 of Reg 1260/1999 ([1999] OJ L161/1).
1654 Art 251 EC.
1655 Cf, regarding doubts whether the legislation on the Structural Funds is 'properly applied', the COA annual report 1997 ([1998] OJ C349/1), para 8.6.3.

European Courts to uphold their legitimate interests.[1656] Hence, the Parliament considers that more detailed rules should be established by future legislation.[1657]

C. BUDGETARY PROVISION

The General Budget may be used simply to give effect to the financial implications of legislation. Provision may also be made in the Budget for the financing of preparatory actions[1658] or pilot schemes,[1659] pending adoption of the necessary legislation. More problematic is the use of the Budget as a long-term substitute for the enactment of legislation.[1660]

1. Integrated Mediterranean Programmes

In the case of Integrated Mediterranean Programmes, the General Budget offered an instrument for ensuring the availability of finance to implement legislative requirements.[1661] Thus legislation governing these Programmes provided for resources under Article 551 of the Budget[1662] to be devoted to measures which were ineligible for assistance from the Structural Funds.[1663]

2. Integrated Development Operations

A pilot project for an Integrated Development Operation was established for Naples in 1979,[1664] and another was planned for Belfast.[1665] The Naples operation was considered to have been successful in making it possible to detect a significant number of bottlenecks for a number of investments planned for that region. At the same time, the operation made it possible to exert some pressure on national authorities to take decisions which had been delayed.[1666]

1656 Resolution giving discharge to the Commission in respect of the General Budget for 1994 ([1996] OJ L148/44), para 44.
1657 Ibid, para 48.
1658 Case C-106/96 UK v EC Commission: social assistance [1998] ECR I-2729.
1659 Interinstitutional Agreement of the Commission, Parliament, and Council ([1998] OJ C344/1) on legal bases and implementation of the budget, para 2(a).
1660 Joined Cases C-239 & 240/96R UK v EC Commission: social assistance [1996] ECR I-4475, I-4489-91.
1661 From 1983 the Commission had been using the General Budget to support preparatory pilot actions for IMPs (Art 550 of the Budget for 1983, [1983] OJ L19/3). See, eg, Dec 84/70 ([1984] OJ L44/1) instituting in the area of Ogliastra (Italy) a pilot action in preparation for the IMPs.
1662 See, eg, for 1986, [1986] OJ L358/3.
1663 Art 3 of Reg 2088/85 ([1985] OJ L197/1) concerning the IMPs.
1664 Commission Reply by Mr Schmidhuber to WQ 1033/87 ([1988] OJ C46/17) by Mr Francesco Compasso.
1665 Fifth Annual Report on the ERDF (1980), 27–8.
1666 Report of the Committee on Regional Policy and Regional Development on the fifth annual report on the ERDF, EP Doc 1-181/81, 15–16.

Accordingly, in the Budget for 1982, ECU 2 million was assigned under Item 5410 to 'Preparatory studies for integrated operations'. Moreover, under Item 5411, ECU 16 million was assigned to 'Community measures in the framework of integrated operations'.[1667] These sums enabled the Commission to contribute to financing the preliminary studies needed to prepare integrated operations.[1668] They also enabled the Commission to finance measures which were not eligible for assistance from the Structural Funds.

However, the perceived need for legislative intervention might affect such use of the Budget. For example, the Commission proposed to the Council in November 1981 a Regulation instituting a specific action on behalf of housing in Northern Ireland within the framework of the integrated operation for Belfast.[1669] This proposal sought to make finance available for housing projects. It was a response to a Resolution of the European Parliament,[1670] which stressed the worsening social and economic problems of Northern Ireland, particularly Belfast, and requested remedial measures. The Commission had hoped to use funds from Item 5411 of the Budget to finance the proposed action. However, the Council was unable to agree on the proposal. Instead, the Council adopted a new Commission proposal for a regulation introducing an exceptional Community measure to promote urban renewal in Northern Ireland (Belfast).[1671]

3. International Fund for Ireland

A contribution to the International Fund for Ireland was first made from the General Budget in 1989.[1672] For several years the Budget apparently continued to be used to substitute legislative action. However, in 1994 the Commission sought through the enactment of a Council regulation 'a more formal legal basis',[1673] which would constitute 'a framework for continued Community support'.[1674] Accordingly, Regulation 2687/94, on Community financial contributions to the International Fund for Ireland,[1675] was enacted.

1667 [1982] OJ L31/1.
1668 See also the Commission Reply by Mr Varfis to WQ 1877/87 ([1989] OJ C202/2) by José Garcia Raya.
1669 Proposal of 23 November 1981 ([1981] OJ C346/1).
1670 Of 19 June 1981 ([1981] OJ C172/122) on Community regional policy and Northern Ireland.
1671 Reg 1739/83 ([1983] OJ L171/1). According to Art 2 (ibid), infrastructure projects contributing to urban renewal in the Belfast area would be assisted.
1672 [1989] OJ L26/3, Art 547.
1673 Proposal of 2 March 1994 for a regulation on Community financial contributions to the International Fund for Ireland, COM(94)60, explanatory memorandum, 2.
1674 Ibid, 15th recital in the preamble.
1675 [1994] OJ L286/5. See, now, Reg 2236/2002 ([2002] OJ L341/6) concerning Community contributions to the International Fund for Ireland (2003-2004).

4. Business and Innovation Centres

The Commission submitted proposals for the creation of Business and Innovation Centres (BICs) to the Council on 23 January 1987[1676] and 7 July 1988,[1677] but these proposals were not adopted. Hence, Union funding of these Centres has been based on Budget headings alone.[1678] The Court of Auditors considers that, if this funding is to continue, it should be placed within a more formal framework, in order to define its objectives and improve transparency.[1679] The Commission view, however, is that these ends can satisfactorily be achieved through the Community Support Frameworks.[1680] In other words, the Commission apparently considers that 'soft law'[1681] can satisfactorily combine with Budgetary provision to substitute legislation.[1682]

However, according to a Joint Declaration by the European Parliament, the Council and the Commission,[1683] the implementation of Budgetary appropriations for significant new Union action requires a 'basic regulation'.[1684] This requirement is confirmed in the Financial Regulation.[1685] According to the case law, the requirement applies, unless it is demonstrated that action is 'non-significant'.[1686] In the absence of such a demonstration, there may be a breach of the Regulation and of Article 7(1) EC,[1687] according to which Union institutions must act within the limits conferred on them by the

---

1676 [1987] OJ C33/5.

1677 [1988] OJ C214/65.

1678 See, eg, Art B2-601 in the Budget for 1996 ([1996] OJ L22/3).

1679 Special report 5/93 ([1994] OJ C13/1) concerning BICs, para 23.

1680 Ibid, para 23 (reply of the Commission).

1681 CSFs may be regarded as an example of 'soft law'. See paras [712] ff below.

1682 Cf the implicit Commission view that a call for proposals may be an adequate substitute for legislation in COA special report 4/94 ([1994] OJ C383/1) on the urban environment, para 3.5 (Commission reply), regarding studies on the conservation of European cities (Item B2-6023 of the Budget for 1992, [1992] OJ L26/1).

1683 On various measures to improve the budgetary procedure ([1982] OJ C194/1).

1684 Ibid, para IV.3(c). See, regarding the actions which may be financed without a regulation, directive, or decision, the Interinstitutional Agreement of the Commission, Parliament, and Council ([1998] OJ C344/1) on legal bases and implementation of the budget, para 2.

1685 Art 22(1) of the Financial Regulation of 21 December 1977 ([1977] OJ L356/1), as amended by Reg 610/90 ([1990] OJ L70/1). See also the Report on the implementation of the inter-institutional agreement on budgetary discipline and improvement of the budgetary procedure, COM(98)165, 10.

1686 Case C-106/96 UK v EC Commission: social assistance [1998] ECR I-2729.

1687 Ibid.

Treaty. Whether such breaches really can be avoided through resort to soft law is uncertain.[1688]

D. 'SOFT LAW'

'Soft law'[1689] may be defined as 'rules of conduct which, in principle, have no legally binding force but which nevertheless may have practical effect'.[1690] A possible problem with this definition is that rules having practical effect may not always be readily distinguishable from those having binding legal force.

Indeed, such law usually 'elaborates' rules contained in Union legislation. In doing so, it may create legitimate expectations about the maintenance of established Commission practice.[1691] For example, the Commission must not depart from an 'internal directive' without giving the reasons which lead it to do so. Otherwise, the principles of legitimate expectation and equality of treatment may be infringed.[1692] The inference may be drawn that soft law constitutes 'rules of law which the Community judicature must enforce'.[1693] However, in compliance with 'the order of preference of legal rules', soft law must be interpreted in the light of the purpose of the legislation, which it elaborates.[1694]

The forms taken by soft law may be various. Its effects on the operations of the Union funds may also be various.

1688 Eg, because of a Council failure to adopt the necessary legislation the Commission may cancel a call for proposals. See Financial support for cooperatives, mutual societies, associations, and foundations: cancellation of the call for proposals ([1997] OJ C233/81). However, the Commission still took a 'specific decision' to finance 12 of the projects which had been submitted. See the Commission Reply by Mr Papoutsis to WQ E-3169/97 ([1998] OJ C196/2) by Raymonde Dury.

1689 See, generally, KC Wellens and GM Borchardt, 'Soft Law in European Community Law' (1989) ELR 267–321. Cf, regarding the use of such law by national administrations, G Ganz, Quasi-Legislation (Sweet and Maxwell, London, 1987).

1690 F Snyder, 'The Effectiveness of European Community Law: Institutions, Processes, Tools, and Techniques' (1993) 56 MLR 19–54, 32.

1691 See, regarding a form attached to a Commission decision and a Commission working document submitted to the Permanent Representatives of the Member States, Case 84/85 UK v EC Commission: assistance for part-time employment [1987] ECR 3765, 3796.

1692 See, regarding internal Commission rules for determining the maximum contribution available from the Guidance Section of the EAGGF under Reg 355/77 ([1977] OJ L51/1) on common measures to improve the conditions under which agricultural products were processed and marketed, which were based on the power of the Commission to organize its own departments, AG Mischo in Case 15/85 Consorzio Cooperative d'Abruzzo v EC Commission [1987] ECR 1005, 1015.

1693 Joined Cases T-369/94 & 85/95 DIR International Film Srl v EC Commission [1998] ECR II-357. This is so even when the 'rules' are drawn up by a private body and approved and applied by the Commission (ibid, II-386).

1694 Ibid.

1. Regional development plans

A development plan means the analysis of the situation prepared by a Member State in the light of Structural Fund Objectives and the priority needs for attaining those Objectives, together with the strategy, the planned action priorities, their specific goals and the related indicative financial resources.[1695]

Content: The plans submitted under Objectives 1, 2 and 3 shall be based on appropriate national and regional priorities and shall take account of the indicative guidelines to be adopted by the Commission. They shall include a description, quantified where it lends itself to quantification, of the current situation with regard to disparities, gaps, and potential for development in the regions covered by Objective 1, in terms of conversion in the areas covered by Objective 2, and in terms of developing human resources and employment policy in the Member State and the areas covered by Objective 3.[1696]

There must also be a description of an appropriate strategy to attain Structural Fund Objectives and the priorities selected for the sustainable development and conversion of regions, including rural areas, and the related development of human resources and the adaptation and modernisation of policies and systems for education, training and employment. In addition, Member States shall demonstrate in each Objective 3 plan that the priorities planned are consistent with the prevailing national employment plan, by reference to a description of the main aims of the strategy and the main means of attaining them. Similarly, Member States shall demonstrate that the activities provided for in each Objective 2 plan on human resources and employment to be assisted by the ESF are integrated into the conversion strategy, coordinated with the other Funds and consistent with the *ex-ante* evaluation relating to human resources and employment. If these needs do not amount to a significant sum, they shall be covered by Objective 3.

There must be an indication of the planned use and form of the financial contribution from the Structural Funds and, where appropriate, the EIB and the other financial instruments, including, for information, the total amount from the EAGGF Guarantee Section for assistance to the adaptation and development of rural areas; the expected requirement for technical assistance; and an indication as regards additionality.[1697] For Objective 1, this should take the form of an indicative overall financing table summarising the public or equivalent and, where appropriate, estimated private resources and the Union structural resources allocated corresponding to each priority proposed in the plan. In any case, the plans shall distinguish between the financial envelopes

---

1695 Art 9(b) of Reg 1260/1999 ([1999] OJ L161/1). Apart from arrangements for transitional assistance and the Peace Programme, plans, CSFs, SPDs and operational programmes shall cover a period of 7 years (ibid, Art 14(1)).
1696 There must also be a description of the financial resources deployed and the main results of operations undertaken in the previous programming period with regard to the evaluation results available.
1697 In accordance with Art 11(2) of Reg 1260/1999 ([1999] OJ L161/1).

allocated to areas receiving transitional support and those allocated to other areas covered by Objective 1 or 2. In the case of ESF assistance under Objective 2 or 3, the percentage contribution may be higher in Objective 2 areas than in others. In the case of Objective 3, the concentration of appropriations planned for the areas facing structural problems of economic and social conversion must be shown. Finally, an account of arrangements made to consult partners must be included.[1698]

Member States shall indicate the particulars relating to each Structural Fund, including the amount of the financial contribution requested and an outline of the operational programmes planned with particular regard to their specific aims and the main types of actions planned.[1699]

For regions covered by Objective 1, the plans shall include all relevant measures for economic and social conversion, the development of human resources, having regard to the frame of reference, and rural development and fisheries structures. Where a Member State is covered in its entirety by Objective 1, the plan shall demonstrate compatibility with the national employment plan.[1700]

Plans submitted under Objective 1 shall be drawn up at the geographical level deemed by the Member State concerned to be most appropriate but shall, as a general rule, cover a single region at NUTS Level II. However, Member States may submit a general development plan covering some or all of their regions included in the list of Objective 1 regions or benefitting from transitional support under this Objective, the Peace Programme, or the Special Programme for Swedish Regions.[1701]

Plans submitted under Objective 2 shall be drawn up at the geographical level deemed by the Member State concerned to be most appropriate but shall, as a general rule, comprise all the areas covered by a single NUTS Level II region included in the list of Objective 2 regions or benefitting from transitional support under this Objective. However, the Member States may submit a plan covering certain or all of their eligible regions. Where plans cover regions other than those eligible under Objective 2, they shall distinguish between operations in regions or areas covered by Objective 2 and operations elsewhere.[1702]

Plans submitted under Objective 3 shall cover the territory of a Member State in respect of assistance outside the regions covered by Objective 1. Taking into account the general needs of areas facing structural problems of

1698 Ibid, Art 16(1).
1699 Art 16(3) of Reg 1260/1999 ([1999] OJ L161/1).
1700 Art 16(2) of Reg 1260/1999 ([1999] OJ L161/1).
1701 Art 13(1) of Reg 1260/1999 ([1999] OJ L161/1).
1702 Art 13(2) of Reg 1260/1999 ([1999] OJ L161/1).

socio-economic conversion, they shall provide, for the whole of the national territory, a framework of reference for developing human resources.[1703]

Preparation and approval: In respect of Objectives 1, 2 and 3, Member States shall submit a plan to the Commission. That plan shall be drawn up by the competent authorities designated by the Member State at national, regional, and other level. In cases where assistance is to take the form of a Single Programming Document, the plan shall be dealt with as a draft Single Programming Document. In respect of Objective 1, Community Support Frameworks shall be employed for all regions covered by Objective 1. However, where the Union allocation is less than or does not substantially exceed €1 billion, the Member States shall, as a general rule, submit a draft Single Programming Document. In respect of Objectives 2 and 3, Single Programming Documents shall as a general rule be employed, though Member States may elect to have a Community Support Framework drawn up.[1704]

The plans shall be submitted by the Member State to the Commission after consultation with the partners, who shall express their views within a period of time consistent with the applicable deadline. Unless otherwise agreed with the Member State concerned, plans shall be submitted not later than four months after the lists of eligible regions have been drawn up.[1705]

The Commission shall appraise these plans to determine whether they are consistent with the aims of Regulation 1260/1999,[1706] taking account of the policy frame of reference, other Union policies, and *ex-ante* evaluation requirements. The Commission shall also appraise each Objective 3 plan in the light of the consistency of the measures envisaged with the national plan for implementing the European employment strategy[1707] and having regard to the manner in which and the degree to which the general needs of areas facing structural problems of socio-economic conversion are taken into account.[1708]

Where applicable, the Commission shall draw up the Community Support Frameworks in agreement with the Member State concerned. The EIB may be involved in the preparation of the Frameworks. The Commission shall take a decision on the contribution from the Structural Funds not later than five months after receiving the relevant plan or plans, provided they contain all the requisite features. In order to expedite the examination of applications for assistance and the implementation of programmes, the Member States may submit, at the same time as their plans, draft operational programmes. The Commission shall appraise the programmes, to determine whether they are consistent with the aims of the corresponding Community Support

1703 Art 13(3) of Reg 1260/1999 ([1999] OJ L161/1).
1704 Art 15(1) of Reg 1260/1999 ([1999] OJ L161/1).
1705 Art 15(2) of Reg 1260/1999 ([1999] OJ L161/1).
1706 Reg 1260/1999 ([1999] OJ L161/1).
1707 In accordance with Art 16(1)(b) (ibid). See also the European Council Resolution of June 1997 on growth and employment ([1997] OJ C236/3).
1708 Ibid, Art 15(3).

Framework and compatible with other Union policies. It shall adopt a decision on the contribution of the Funds and in agreement with the Member State concerned, provided that the proposals contain all the requisite features.[1709]

For the purposes of consultation, Member States shall ensure that publicity is given to the plans.[1710] The managing authority is responsible for ensuring that publicity is given to the package and particularly for informing potential final beneficiaries, trade and professional bodies, the economic and social partners, bodies promoting equality between men and women, and the relevant non-governmental organizations about the opportunities afforded by the assistance. The managing authority is also responsible for informing the general public about the role played by the Union in the assistance concerned and its results.[1711] The Member States shall consult the Commission and inform it each year of the initiatives taken for these purposes.[1712]

2. Community Support Frameworks

A Community Support Framework (CSF) is defined as the document approved by the Commission, in agreement with the Member State concerned, following appraisal of the development plan submitted by a Member State and containing the strategy and priorities for action of the Funds and the Member State, their specific objectives, and the contribution of the ERDF and other financial resources. It shall be divided into priorities and implemented by means of one or more operational programmes.[1713] It shall provide for coordination of all Union structural assistance in the regions concerned, including assistance for the development of human resources.[1714] The EIB may be involved in the preparation of the CSF.[1715]

Each CSF shall include a statement of the strategy and priorities for joint Union and national action; their specific objectives, quantified where they lend themselves to quantification; evaluation of the expected impact; an indication of how this strategy and these priorities have taken account of Commission guidelines, the economic policies, the strategy for developing employment through improving the adaptability and skills of people and, where appropriate, the regional policies of the Member State concerned; and an indication of the nature and the duration of the operational programmes not decided at the same time as the CSF, including their specific aims and the priorities selected.

1709 Art 15(4) of Reg 1260/1999 ([1999] OJ L161/1).
1710 Art 46(1) of Reg 1260/1999 ([1999] OJ L161/1).
1711 Ibid, Art 46(2).
1712 Ibid, Art 46(3). See also Commission Reg 1159/2000 ([2000] OJ L130/30) on information and publicity measures to be carried out by the Member States concerning assistance from the Structural Funds.
1713 Art 9(d) of Reg 1260/1999 ([1999] OJ L161/1).
1714 Ibid, Art 17(1).
1715 Ibid, Art 15(4).

There must also be an indicative financing plan specifying, for each priority and each year, the financial allocation envisaged for the contribution of each Union fund, where they contribute directly to the financing plan concerned, and the total amount of eligible public and estimated private funding relating to the contribution of each Structural Fund. In the case of Objective 3, the financing plan shall show the concentration of appropriations planned for the areas facing structural problems of economic and social conversion. The financing plan shall distinguish the funding planned for the regions receiving transitional support. The total contribution of the Funds planned for each year for each CSF shall be compatible with the relevant financial perspective, taking account of degressivity requirements.

The provisions for implementing a CSF must also be indicated. They concern designation by the Member State of a managing authority responsible for managing the CSF and arrangements for involving the partners in the monitoring committees and, where appropriate, for providing information on the appropriations required for preparing, monitoring and evaluating assistance. The CSFs shall also include the *ex-ante* verification of additionality and the appropriate information concerning the transparency of financial flows, in particular from the Member State concerned to the beneficiary regions.[1716]

When adopting its decision on a CSF, the Commission shall also approve the operational programmes submitted at the same time as the development plans, provided they include all the requisite features.[1717]

The Frameworks are said to constitute 'programme contracts', which bind the Commission and the national authorities.[1718] However, according to the Commission, the legislation provides a consistent and precise definition of the content of the Frameworks. Hence, the legislation makes it possible for the latter to take account of the problems peculiar to individual regions and of possible solutions.[1719] The implication is that the relationship between soft law and legislation may be so complicated that the latter may be seen as an integral element of the former.

In practice, however, while the Frameworks adopted may incorporate the outline legislative requirements, their content is left to depend largely on negotiations between the Commission and the Member States. Legislation merely authorizes and structures such negotiation. The results of the latter may be controversial.

Indeed, it is said that the CSFs lack an assessment of strengths and assets on which a development strategy can rely and to which both specific and

---

1716 Art 17(2) of Reg 1260/1999 ([1999] OJ L161/1).
1717 Art 15(4) of Reg 1260/1999 ([1999] OJ L161/1).
1718 F Celimene, 'La Reforme de l'action des fonds structurels européens' (1991) AJDA 251–66, 259.
1719 Annual report on the implementation of the reform of the Structural Funds 1989, COM(90)516, 301.

general interventions can be targeted.[1720] Thus they do not generally constitute strategic documents in the strict sense.

Commission decisions on CSFs are to be published in the Official Journal. At the request of the European Parliament, the CSF itself is to be transmitted to the Parliament.[1721]

3. Single Programming Documents

A Single Programming Document (SPD) is a single document approved by the Commission and containing the same information as a CSF and operational programme.[1722] Assistance under Objectives 2 and 3 and assistance under Objective 1 which does not substantially exceed €1 billion shall, as a general rule, take the form of SPDs.

On the basis of the plans, the Commission shall take a decision on the SPDs in agreement with the Member State concerned, consulting the relevant committee. The EIB may be involved in the preparation of the SPDs.[1723]

Their use, instead of CSFs, highlights the favourable attitude of the Union legislature towards linking formulation of regional policy by Member States and operations of the Union funds. In practice, however, 'red tape' may lessen the attractiveness of SPDs.[1724] Their adoption requires just as much data and preparatory work as does separate presentation of plans and applications for assistance.[1725] Hence, their negotiation may be lengthy.[1726]

An Objective 1 SPD shall include all relevant measures for economic and social conversion and the development of employment through improving adaptability and skills of people, having regard to the frame of reference and rural development and fisheries structures. An Objective 2 SPD shall provide for coordination of all Union structural assistance, including the coordination of rural development measures assisted by the Guarantee Section of the EAGGF but excluding assistance for developing human resources granted under Objective 3, in all the areas covered by Objective 2. An Objective 3 SPD shall provide for coordination of all Union structural assistance for the

---

1720 RP Camagni, 'Development Scenarios and Policy Guidelines for the Lagging Regions in the 1990s' (1992) Regional Studies 361–74.
1721 Art 15(7) of Reg 1260/1999 ([1999] OJ L161/1).
1722 Art 9(g) of Reg 1260/1999 ([1999] OJ L161/1).
1723 Art 15(5) of Reg 1260/1999 ([1999] OJ L161/1).
1724 It is recognized that, in the case of Objectives 1, 3 and 4 at least, Member States may not always be able to provide the information necessary for the Commission to adopt operational programmes at the same time as it adopts the SPD. See Community Structural Funds 1994–99, COM(93)67, 18.
1725 COR Opinion of 21 March 1996 ([1996] OJ C182/7) on the new regional programmes under Objectives 1 and 2, para 16.
1726 See, eg, the Commission Reply by Mrs Wulf-Mathies to WQ E-0472/98 ([1998] OJ C310/78) by Richard Howitt.

development of human resources in the areas eligible for Objective 3 assistance, excluding aid granted under Objective 2.[1727]

Each SPD shall contain a statement of the strategy and priorities for joint Union and national action; their specific objectives, quantified where they lend themselves to quantification; an evaluation of the expected impact, including the environmental impact; an indication of how this strategy and these priorities have taken account of Commission guidelines, the economic policies, the strategy for developing employment through improving the adaptability and skills of people and, where appropriate, the regional policies of the Member State concerned; a summary description of the measures planned to implement the priorities, including the information needed to check the compliance with aid schemes pursuant to Article 87 EC; and, where appropriate, the nature of the measures required to prepare, monitor and evaluate the SPD.

There must also be an indicative financing plan specifying for each priority and each year the financial allocation envisaged for the contribution of each Union fund as well as the total amount of eligible public or equivalent and estimated private funding relating to the contribution of each Structural Fund. This financing plan shall distinguish the funding planned for the regions receiving transitional support. The total contribution of the Funds planned for each year shall be compatible with the relevant financial perspective, taking account of degressivity requirements. In the case of Objective 3, the financing plan shall indicate the concentration of appropriations planned for the areas facing structural, economic and social reconversion problems.

The provisions for implementing an SPD shall include the designation by the Member State of a managing authority responsible for managing the SPD; a description of the arrangements for managing the SPD; a description of the systems for monitoring and evaluation, including the role of the monitoring committee; a definition of the procedures concerning the mobilization and circulation of funding to ensure that flows are transparent; a description of the specific arrangements and procedures for checking on the SPD; and, where appropriate, information on the resources required for preparing, monitoring and evaluating assistance. The SPD shall include the *ex-ante* verification of additionality for the relevant objective or objectives agreed between the Member State and the Commission and appropriate information concerning the transparency of financial flows, in particular from the Member State concerned to the beneficiary regions.[1728]

Each SPD shall be supplemented by a programme complement.[1729] A programme complement is the document implementing the assistance strategy and priorities and containing detailed elements at measure level,

1727 Art 19(2) of Reg 1260/1999 ([1999] OJ L161/1).
1728 Art 19(3) of Reg 1260/1999 ([1999] OJ L161/1).
1729 Art 19(4) of Reg 1260/1999 ([1999] OJ L161/1).

drawn up by the Member State or managing authority and revised as necessary.[1730]

The Member State or the managing authority shall adopt the programme complement after the agreement of the monitoring committee if the programme complement is drawn up after the Commission decision on the contribution of the Structural Funds, or after consulting the relevant partners if it is drawn up before the decision on the contribution of the Funds. In the latter case, the monitoring committee shall either confirm the programme complement or request an adjustment. Within three months of the Commission decision approving an operational programme or SPD, the Member State shall send the programme complement to the Commission in a single document for information.[1731]

The programme complement shall contain the measures implementing the corresponding priorities in the operational programme; an *ex-ante* evaluation of quantified measures, where they lend themselves to quantification, and the relevant monitoring indicators; the definition of the types of final beneficiary of measures; the financing plan specifying for each measure the financial allocation envisaged for the contribution of the Union fund concerned and the amount of eligible public or equivalent funding and estimated private funding relating to the contribution of the Structural Funds; the percentage contribution of a Fund to a measure and the total amount of Union funds allocated to the priority concerned. This financing plan shall distinguish the funding planned for the regions receiving transitional support. The financing plan shall be accompanied by a description of the arrangements for providing the co-financing for measures, taking account of the institutional, legal and financial systems of the Member State concerned. Measures intended to publicise the operational programme must also be indicated, and arrangements agreed between the Commission and the Member State concerned for the computerised exchange, where possible, of the data required to fulfil management, monitoring and evaluation requirements must be described.[1732]

Commission decisions on SPDs are to be published in the Official Journal. At the request of the European Parliament, the SPD itself is to be transmitted to the Parliament.[1733]

4. Evaluation

In order to gauge its effectiveness, Union assistance shall be the subject of *ex-ante*, mid-term and *ex-post* evaluation designed to appraise its impact with respect to the Objectives and to analyse its effects on specific structural

1730 Ibid, Art 9(m).
1731 Art 15(6) of Reg 1260/1999 ([1999] OJ L161/1).
1732 Art 18(3) of Reg 1260/1999 ([1999] OJ L161/1).
1733 Art 15(7) of Reg 1260/1999 ([1999] OJ L161/1).

problems.[1734] The effectiveness of the operations of the funds shall be measured by their overall impact on the goals set out in Article 158 EC, and in particular the strengthening of cohesion, and the impact of the priorities proposed in the development plans and of the priorities incorporated in each CSF and in each case of assistance.[1735]

The competent authorities of the Member States and the Commission shall assemble the appropriate resources and collect the data required to ensure that evaluation can be carried out in the most effective manner. In this connection, evaluation shall make use of the various particulars that the monitoring arrangements may yield, supplemented where necessary by the gathering of information to improve its relevance. On the initiative of the Member States or the Commission, after informing the Member State concerned, supplementary evaluations, if appropriate on a specific topic, may be launched with a view to identifying transferable experience.[1736]

The results of the evaluation shall be made available to the public, on request. As regards the results of the mid-term evaluation, the monitoring committee's agreement shall be required according to the institutional arrangements of each Member State.[1737] The evaluation procedures shall be laid down in the CSFs and forms of assistance.[1738]

***Ex-ante* evaluation:** The purpose of *ex-ante* evaluation shall be to provide a basis for preparing the development plans, assistance, and programme complement of which it shall form part. The evaluation shall be the responsibility of the authorities responsible for their preparation.[1739]

It shall involve an analysis of the strengths, weaknesses and potential of the Member State, region or sector concerned. In the light of the specified criteria, it shall assess the consistency of the strategy and targets selected with the specific features of the regions or areas concerned, including demographic trends, and the expected impact of the planned priorities for action, quantifying their specific targets in relation to the starting situation, where they lend themselves thereto. The evaluation shall take into account, amongst other things, the situation in terms of competitiveness and innovation, small and medium-sized enterprises, employment and the labour market having regard to the European employment strategy, the environment, and equality between men and women.[1740]

Mid-term evaluation: Mid-term evaluation shall examine, in the light of the *ex-ante* evaluation, the initial results of the assistance, their relevance, and

---

1734 Art 40(1) of Reg 1260/1999 ([1999] OJ L161/1).
1735 Ibid, Art 40(2). 'Assistance' means: SPDs, operational programmes, Community initiatives, and support for technical assistance and innovative measures (ibid, Art 9(e)).
1736 Art 40(3) of Reg 1260/1999 ([1999] OJ L161/1).
1737 Art 40(4) of Reg 1260/1999 ([1999] OJ L161/1).
1738 Ibid, Art 40(5).
1739 Art 41(1) of Reg 1260/1999 ([1999] OJ L161/1).
1740 Art 41(3) of Reg 1260/1999 ([1999] OJ L161/1).

the extent to which the targets have been attained. It shall also assess the use made of financial resources and the operation of monitoring and implementation.[1741] Mid-term evaluation shall be carried out under the responsibility of the managing authority, in cooperation with the Commission and the Member State. It shall cover each CSF and each assistance. It shall be carried out by an independent assessor, be submitted to the monitoring committee for the CSF or assistance concerned, and then be sent to the Commission, as a general rule three years after adoption of the CSF or assistance, with a view to revision.[1742] The Commission shall examine the relevance and quality of the evaluation on the basis of criteria defined beforehand by the Commission and the Member State in partnership, with a view to reviewing the assistance and allocating the reserve.[1743] It shall be updated for each CSF and assistance and completed no later than 31 December 2005 in order to prepare for subsequent assistance operations.[1744]

Ex-post evaluation: On the basis of the evaluation results already available, *ex-post* evaluation shall cover the utilization of resources, the effectiveness and efficiency of the assistance and its impact, and shall draw conclusions regarding cohesion policy. It shall cover the factors contributing to the success or failure of implementation and the achievements and results, including their sustainability.[1745] *Ex-post* evaluation shall be the responsibility of the Commission, in collaboration with the Member State and the managing authority. It shall be carried out by independent assessors. It shall be completed not later than three years after the end of the programming period.[1746]

5. Periodic reports

Article 159 EC requires the Commission to submit a report to the European Parliament, the Council, the Economic and Social Committee, and the Committee of the Regions every three years on the progress made towards achieving cohesion. The report must detail the manner in which the Union funds have contributed to this progress. The report may, if necessary, be accompanied by appropriate proposals. It is to include an analysis of the regions and their economic and social development.[1747] The first such 'cohesion report' was published in 1996.[1748]

This report shall review in particular: progress in achieving economic and social cohesion, including the socio-economic situation of the regions and any

---

1741 Art 42(1) of Reg 1260/1999 ([1999] OJ L161/1).
1742 Ibid, Art 42(2).
1743 Ibid, Art 42(3).
1744 Ibid, Art 42(4).
1745 Art 43(1) of Reg 1260/1999 ([1999] OJ L161/1).
1746 Ibid, Art 43(2).
1747 56th recital in the preamble to Reg 1260/1999 ([1999] OJ L161/1).
1748 First cohesion report, COM(96)542.

changes observed, and an analysis of direct investment flows and their impact on the Union employment situation; the role of the Structural Funds, the Cohesion Fund, the EIB and other financial instruments, as well as the impact of other Union and national policies in accomplishing this process; and any proposals concerning Union measures and policies which may need to be adopted in order to strengthen economic and social cohesion.[1749]

In addition, before 1 November of each year, the Commission shall forward to the European Parliament, the Council, the Economic and Social Committee and the Committee of the Regions a report on the implementation of Regulation 1260/1999[1750] during the preceding year. This report shall review in particular: the activities of each Structural Fund, the utilization of their resources and the concentration of assistance, and the deployment of the other financial instruments for which the Commission has responsibility, and the concentration of their resources;[1751] the coordination of assistance from the Structural Funds among themselves and with the assistance granted by the EIB and the other existing financial instruments; as soon as they are available, the results of the evaluations, indicating any adjustments to the assistance, and an evaluation of the consistency of measures taken by the Structural Funds with Union policies; a list of the major projects to which the Structural Funds have contributed; the results of checks carried out by the Commission and the lessons to be drawn from them, including an indication of the number of recorded irregularities, the amounts in question and the financial corrections made;[1752] and information on the opinions of committees delivered.[1753]

6. Guidelines

Guidelines produced by the Commission have the explicit function of 'regulating' the operations of the Union funds.[1754] Guidelines were to be adopted by the Commission, after consulting all Member States, no later than one month from the entry into force of Regulation 1260/1999.[1755] Further guidelines are to be adopted with the same consultation before the mid-term review. They are designed to help the competent national and regional

1749 Art 45(1) of Reg 1260/1999 ([1999] OJ L161/1).
1750 [1999] OJ L161/1.
1751 This review shall include: an annual breakdown by Member State of appropriations committed and paid in respect of each fund, including Community initiatives; an annual evaluation of innovative actions and technical assistance.
1752 Reg 1260/1999 ([1999] OJ L161/1), Art 30(4). See also Reg 448/2001 ([2001] OJ L64/13) laying down detailed rules for the implementation of Reg 1260/1999 as regards the procedure for making financial corrections to assistance granted under the Structural Funds.
1753 Reg 1260/1999 ([1999] OJ L161/1), Art 45(2).
1754 However, 'in no cases should these guidelines mean that the Commission has the right unilaterally to interpret regulations adopted by the Council'. See the COR Opinion of 17 September 1998 ([1998] OJ C373/1) on the proposal for a regulation laying down provisions on the Structural Funds, para 2.1.3.4.
1755 [1999] OJ L161/1.

authorities to draw up development plans,[1756] CSFs[1757] and SPDs[1758] and to carry out any revision of Union assistance. They also concern coordination of the work of the Structural Funds with that of the other financial instruments,[1759] particularly the Cohesion Fund.[1760] This guidance shall be published in the Official Journal of the European Communities.[1761]

Such procedural requirements reflect the idea that, to be 'effective', soft law must concern matters within the competence of the Commission, be published in the Official Journal, and be clearly written and informative.[1762] More fundamentally, they not only demonstrate the importance which legislation may attach to soft law. They also demonstrate the extent to which procedures for adoption of soft law may approximate to those for adoption of implementing legislation by the Commission.[1763]

7. Commission notices

Commission notices may, in contrast to the (bilateral) CSFs and SPDs, unilaterally lay down conditions for the grant of Union assistance. Such notices may determine the scope of the procedure for approval of applications for various kinds of assistance, including that provided pursuant to Community initiatives, pilot and demonstration projects, and environmental measures. In doing so, they have legal consequences.[1764]

Community initiatives: Community initiatives are adopted by the Commission on the basis of notices. The notices lay down guidelines for operational programmes or global grants, which Member States are invited to establish with financial assistance from the Structural Funds.[1765] Such notices apparently constitute 'acts' for the purposes of judicial review of their legality by the European Courts.[1766]

The guidelines are adopted by the Commission in accordance with the management committee procedure, and after their notification for information to the European Parliament they are published in the Official Journal. They

---

1756 Ibid, Art 16(1).
1757 Ibid, Art 17(2).
1758 Ibid, Art 19(3).
1759 Ibid, Art 10(1).
1760 Commission Communication concerning the Structural Funds and their coordination with the Cohesion Fund: Guidelines for programmes in the period 2000 to 2006 ([1999] OJ C267/2), Introduction.
1761 Art 10(3) of Reg 1260/1999 ([1999] OJ L161/1).
1762 A Mattera, Le Marché unique européen: ses règles, son fonctionnement (2nd edn, Jupiter, Paris, 1990), 45. See, generally, M Melchior, 'Les Communications de la Commission' in Mélanges en honneur de Fernand Dehousse (Labor, Brussels, 1979), ii, 243–58.
1763 A Evans, A Textbook on EU Law (Hart Publishing, Oxford, 1998), Section 2.3.1.
1764 Joined Cases C-239 & 240/96R UK v EC Commission: social assistance [1996] ECR I-4475, I-4486.
1765 Art 21(1) of Reg 1260/1999 ([1999] OJ L161/1).
1766 Joined Cases C-239 & 240/96R UK v EC Commission: social assistance [1996] ECR I-4475, I-4486. See, regarding judicial review, paras [794] ff below.

describe the aims, scope and appropriate implementation method for each initiative.[1767]

Innovative actions and technical assistance: Calls for proposals for innovative actions[1768] and technical assistance[1769] may be made by Commission notices embodying applicable guidelines. According to the notices, applications for assistance may be submitted by public or private bodies. Where they are submitted by the latter, they must be accompanied by proof that the local, regional and national authorities have been consulted and have consented to the implementation of the project and, where applicable, that they will provide financial and/or practical support.[1770]

Environmental measures: Legislation regarding applications for assistance from the Financial Instrument for the Environment is comparatively elaborate. According to this legislation, the Commission may ask any legal or natural person established in the Union to submit applications for assistance in respect of measures of particular interest to the Union. The Commission may do so by means of a notice published in the Official Journal.[1771] Where assistance is to be granted, 'a contract or agreement governing the rights and obligations of the parties' is concluded with the person concerned.[1772]

E. ADMINISTRATIVE DECISIONS

Legislation may confer on the Commission powers to take decisions concerning the grant of Union assistance. Article 249(4) EC states that decisions are binding in their entirety upon those to whom they are addressed. In principle, such decisions merely entail application of pre-existing rules. In practice, they may modify such rules or even generate new ones. Certainly, insofar as actors can induce 'general principles' from such decisions, they may 'spontaneously' modify their conduct accordingly.[1773] Much may depend, however, on whether the decisions are published and in what detail they are published.

1767 Art 21(1) of Reg 1260/1999 ([1999] OJ L161/1).
1768 Art 22(1) of Reg 1260/1999 ([1999] OJ L161/1).
1769 Ibid, Art 23(1).
1770 See, eg, Call for proposals for pilot projects and demonstration projects relating to the adjustment of agricultural structures and the promotion of rural development ([1994] OJ C303/17), para 1.
1771 Art 9(2) of Reg 1404/96 ([1996] OJ L181/1) amending Reg 1973/92 establishing a financial instrument for the environment. See, eg, Life 1997: call for proposals ([1996] OJ C363/11). See, similarly, in the RTD field, second call for proposals for RTD actions for the specific programme for RTDD in the field of advanced communications technologies and services (1994–98) ([1995] OJ C240/7).
1772 Art 9(5) of Reg 1404/96 ([1996] OJ L181/1).
1773 M Melchior, para [743], n 1 above, 246.

Such decisions were required in the case of intervention programmes within a Community programme,[1774] as well as decisions determining eligible regions in each Member State;[1775] national programmes of Community interest;[1776] integrated development programmes;[1777] Integrated Mediterranean Programmes[1778] and pilot actions to prepare such programmes;[1779] and programmes under Regulation 355/77.[1780] Alternatively, the Commission might, as under Regulation 950/97,[1781] be required to take decisions approving national implementing measures.[1782]

Commission decisions are now required for determination of regions covered by Objectives 1 and 2[1783] and regarding indicative allocations of assistance by Member State.[1784] Equally, the Commission takes decisions on CSFs[1785] and SPDs.[1786]

Moreover, provided that all the requirements of Regulation 1260/1999[1787] are fulfilled, the Commission shall adopt in a single decision the contributions of all the Structural Funds within five months of receipt of the application for assistance. A maximum contribution from the Funds shall be set for each priority in the assistance.[1788]

The contribution of the Funds shall be differentiated in the light of the gravity of the specific problems, in particular of a regional or social nature, to

---

1774 Arts 7(5), 13 and 40 of Reg 1787/84 ([1984] OJ L169/1). See, eg, Dec 88/48 ([1988] OJ L30/25) approving the intervention programme for Greece implementing the Valoren programme.

1775 See, eg, regarding Spain, Dec 91/91 ([1991] OJ L50/24) on the areas referred to in Art 3(2) of Reg 2506/88 instituting a Community programme to assist the conversion of shipbuilding areas.

1776 Arts 11(5), 13 and 40 of Reg 1787/84 ([1984] OJ L169/1). See, eg, Dec 89/523 ([1989] OJ L272/16) on the granting of a contribution from the ERDF for measures under a national programme of Community interest (Azores).

1777 See, eg, Dec 87/227 ([1987] OJ L94/27) approving an integrated approach for the area Oost-Groningen/Oost-Drenthe, Netherlands.

1778 Art 7 of Reg 2088/85 ([1985] OJ L197/1). See, eg, Dec 88/259 ([1988] OJ L107/41) approving an IMP for the Abruzzo region.

1779 See, eg, Dec 84/70 (JO 1984 L44/1) instituting in the area of Agliastra, Nuoro Province, Sardinia, a pilot action in preparation for the IMP.

1780 [1977] OJ L51/1. See, eg, Dec 87/384 ([1987] OJ L203/49) approving an Italian programme on the treatment and marketing of feed grains and green fodder. Cf Dec 85/597 ([1985] OJ L373/44) withholding approval from the Bavarian market structure programme for Franconian wine.

1781 On improving the efficiency of agricultural structures ([1997] OJ L142/1), Arts 29–30.

1782 See, eg, Dec 89/79 ([1989] OJ L30/78) on improving the efficiency of agricultural structures in Italy (Calabria).

1783 Arts 3 and 4 of Reg 1260/1999 ([1999] OJ L161/1).

1784 Ibid, Art 7(3).

1785 Ibid, Art 15(4).

1786 Ibid, Art 15(5).

1787 [1999] OJ L161/1.

1788 Priority: means one of the priorities of the strategy adopted in a Community support framework or assistance; to it is assigned a contribution from the Funds and other financial instruments and the relevant financial resources of the Member State and a set of specified targets (ibid, Art 9(h)).

---

be tackled by the assistance; the financial capacity of the Member State concerned, taking into account in particular its relative prosperity and the need to avoid excessive increases in budgetary expenditure; within the framework of the Objectives of the Structural Funds, the importance attaching to the assistance and the priorities from the Union viewpoint, where appropriate, for the elimination of inequalities and the promotion of equality between men and women and for the protection and improvement of the environment, principally through the application of the precautionary principle, the principle of preventive action, and the polluter pays principle; the importance attaching to the assistance and priorities from the regional and national viewpoint; the particular characteristics of the type of assistance and priority concerned, to take account of the needs identified by the *ex-ante* evaluation, in particular with regard to human resources and employment; and the optimum utilization of financial resources in the financing plans, including the combination of public and private resources, the use made of appropriate financial instruments, and the choice of forms of financing. Where the contribution of the ESF is differentiated, this shall be done taking account of the needs identified by the *ex-ante* evaluation, notably in the field of human resources and employment.[1789]

The contribution from the Structural Funds shall be calculated in relation to either the total eligible cost or the total public or similar eligible expenditure (national, regional or local, and Union) under each assistance.[1790] The contribution of the Funds shall be subject to a maximum of 75 per cent of the total eligible cost and, as a general rule, at least 50 per cent of eligible public expenditure in the case of measures carried out in the regions covered by Objective 1. Where the regions are located in a Member State covered by the Cohesion Fund, the Union contribution may rise, in exceptional and duly justified cases, to a maximum of 80 per cent of the total eligible cost and to a maximum of 85 per cent of the total eligible cost for the outermost regions and for the outlying Greek islands which are under a handicap due to their distant location; and a maximum of 50 per cent of the total eligible cost and, as a general rule, at least 25 per cent of eligible public expenditure in the case of measures carried out in areas covered by Objective 2 or 3.

In the case of investment in firms, the contribution of the Structural Funds shall comply with the ceilings on the rate of aid and on combinations of aid set in the field of State aid.[1791] Where the assistance concerned entails the financing of revenue-generating investments, the contribution from the Funds to these investments shall be determined in the light of their intrinsic characteristics, including the size of the gross self-financing margin which would normally be expected for the class of investments concerned in the light

---

1789 Art 29(1) of Reg 1260/1999 ([1999] OJ L161/1).
1790 Art 29(2) of Reg 1260/1999 ([1999] OJ L161/1).
1791 Art 29(3) of Reg 1260/1999 ([1999] OJ L161/1).

of the macro-economic circumstances in which the investments are to be implemented, and without there being any increase in the national budgetary effort as a result of the contribution by the Funds.

Expenditure in respect of operations shall be eligible for a contribution from the Funds only if these operations form part of the assistance concerned.[1792] Expenditure may not be considered eligible for a contribution from the Funds if it has actually been paid by the final beneficiary before the date on which the application for assistance reaches the Commission. That date shall constitute the starting point for the eligibility of expenditure. The final date for the eligibility of expenditure shall be laid down in the decision to grant a contribution from the Funds. It shall relate to payments made by the final beneficiaries. It may be extended by the Commission at the duly justified request of the Member State.[1793] The relevant national rules shall apply to eligible expenditure except where, as necessary, the Commission lays down common rules on the eligibility of expenditure.[1794]

The Member States shall ensure that an operation retains the contribution from the Structural Funds only if that operation does not, within five years of the date of the decision of the competent national authorities or the managing authority on the contribution of the Funds, undergo a substantial modification. Such a modification is one which either affects the nature of the operation or its implementation conditions or gives to a firm or a public body an undue advantage and results either from a change in the nature of ownership in an item of infrastructure or a cessation or change of location in a productive activity. The Member States shall inform the Commission of any such modification. Where such a modification occurs, the rules on financial corrections apply.

However, the Commission may wish to avoid 'seriously burdening' the Official Journal by publishing in full all its decisions in this field.[1795] The difficulties caused by the resulting lack of transparency in decision making have not passed entirely unnoticed by the Union legislature. Thus Article 10 of Regulation 4253/88[1796] provided for the publication in the Official Journal of decisions approving CSFs as 'declarations of intent'.[1797] The legislation now simply requires publication of the decisions. It is also provided that, at the

---

1792 Art 30(1) of Reg 1260/1999 ([1999] OJ L161/1).
1793 Ibid, Art 30(2).
1794 Ibid, Art 30(3).
1795 Commission submission in Joined Cases 10 & 18/60 Società 'Eridania' Zuccherifici Nazionali v EC Commission [1969] ECR 459, 464.
1796 Laying down provisions for implementing Reg 2052/88 as regards coordination of the activities of the different Structural Funds between themselves and with the operations of the other existing financial instruments ([1988] OJ L374/1).
1797 Cf AG Darmon in Case C-157/90 Infortec Projectos & Consultadoria, Lda v EC Commission [1992] ECR I-3525, I-3547, who apparently interpreted the requirement as applying to assistance decisions more generally.

request of the European Parliament, the Commission must transmit to the Parliament the decision together with the relevant CSF.[1798] However, other decisions concerning assistance from the Union funds may remain unpublished. Thus, for example, regional operational programmes are adopted as decisions,[1799] but the decisions are not published.

In the case of the Cohesion Fund, the legislation requires that the 'key details' of Commission decisions granting assistance be published in the Official Journal.[1800] In the case of agricultural structure decisions, the Commission itself had decided in 1989 to amend its practice along similar lines. This category of decisions, which took effect on notification to the respective Member States, would no longer be published in full, 'except in exceptional cases'.[1801]

F. CONTRACTS

Contracts may be seen as a suitable legal form for giving content to administrative decisions.[1802] Such contracts may have as parties regions and individuals as well as the Commission and Member States. However, their enforcement through proceedings under Article 288(1) EC[1803] may be precluded, insofar as operations of the Union funds are characterized as 'unilateral acts falling within the province of public law'.[1804] On the other hand, conditions annexed to a decision granting assistance may have binding force for the purposes of other proceedings.[1805]

In particular, a Community programme or national programme of Community interest had to be adopted by the Commission after consultation of the Committee for the ERDF. It then became the subject of agreement between the Commission and the Member State or Member States concerned

---

1798 Art 15(7) of Reg 1260/1999 ([1999] OJ L161/1).

1799 See, regarding operational programmes under Community initiatives, the Commission Reply by Mr Millan to WQ E-1735/93 ([1994] OJ C255/9) by Alexandros Alavanos.

1800 Art 10(7) of Reg 1164/94 ([1994] OJ L130/1), Art 10(7). See, eg, Publication of main points of decisions to grant financial assistance under Reg 1164/94 ([1996] OJ C325/1).

1801 Communication of agricultural structure decisions ([1989] OJ L174/31).

1802 The European Parliament had called for the implementation of regional development programmes in the agricultural sector to be founded on a contractual relationship between the Community, the Member State and, whenever possible, the region concerned. See the Resolution of 17 November 1983 ([1983] OJ C342/98) on new guidelines for the Community's structural policy in the agricultural sector, para 41(c). Cf Art 3 of the proposal for a regulation instituting a specific Community programme of accompanying social measures to assist workers in the shipbuilding industry who were made redundant or threatened with redundancy, COM(87)275.

1803 It provides that the contractual liability of the EC shall be governed by the law applicable to the contract in question.

1804 AG Verloren van Themaat in Case 44/81 Germany v EC Commission: deadline for claiming payment of ESF assistance [1982] ECR 1855, 1881.

1805 Case T-331/94 IPK-München GmbH v EC Commission [1997] ECR II-1665, II-1682.

---

and constituted a 'programme agreement' for the purposes of Regulation 1787/84.[1806] Moreover, implementation of Integrated Mediterranean Programmes was, according to Article 9 of Regulation 2088/85,[1807] to be regulated by programme contracts. These contracts were to be concluded between the parties concerned (the Commission, Member States, regional authority, or any other authority designated by the Member States) and were to set out their respective commitments. The standard contents of the contracts were specified[1808] in Annex IV to the Regulation.[1809]

In practice, implementation of such contracts proved more effective in some Member States than in others. For example, in 1989, the Integrated Mediterranean Programmes for France and Greece had recorded outturn rates (that is, commitments and payments in relation to estimates) of 97 per cent and 93 per cent, respectively. In the case of the Italian programmes, the outturn rate was just 47 per cent. According to the Commission, the greatest difficulties in Italy arose from 'demarcation disputes' between national and regional authorities and within the latter authorities.[1810]

Apparently, the limits to the capacity of contracts to resolve such problems are recognized. Thus current legislation seeks to rely, instead, on CSFs and SPDs. Their operational content is apparently to depend not simply on their terms but also on committee work and partnership.

G. COMMITTEES

In implementing Regulation 1260/1999,[1811] the Commission shall be assisted by four committees: the Committee on the Development and Conversion of Regions; the Committee on Agricultural Structures and Rural Development; the Committee on Structures for Fisheries and Aquaculture; and the ESF Committee.[1812]

Where the first three committees are acting as consultative committees, the following procedure applies. The Commission representative shall submit to the committee a draft of the measure to be taken. The committee shall deliver its opinion on this draft within a time limit which the chairman may lay down according to the urgency of the matter; the matter may be put to a vote where appropriate. The opinions of the committee shall be entered in the minutes; each Member State shall in addition have the right to ask for its position to be

---

1806 [1984] OJ L169/1, Art 13(1).
1807 [1985] OJ L197/1.
1808 The relevant clauses may have 'mandatory status'. Cf Case C-324/96 Odette Nikon Petridi Anonymos Kapnemporiki v Athanasia Simou [1998] ECR I-1333, I-1370.
1809 See, eg, Dec 88/62 ([1988] OJ L32/23) approving an IMP for Corsica.
1810 IMP _ progress report for 1989, SEC(91)553.
1811 [1999] OJ L161/1.
1812 Ibid, Art 47(1).

included in the minutes. The Commission shall take the utmost account of the opinions delivered by the committee. It shall inform the committee of the manner in which it takes account of its opinions.[1813]

Where the same three committees are acting as management committees, the following procedure applies. The Commission representative shall submit to the committee a draft of the measure to be taken. The committee shall deliver its opinion on this draft within a time limit which the chairman may lay down according to the urgency of the matter under consideration. The opinion shall be delivered by the majority stipulated in Article 205(2) EC in the case of decisions which the Council is requested to adopt on a proposal from the Commission. When a matter is put to the vote within the committee, the votes of the Member States' representatives shall be weighted as provided for in Article 205(2) EC. The chairman shall not vote. The Commission shall adopt measures which shall apply immediately. However, if they are not in accordance with the opinion delivered by the committee, they shall be communicated forthwith by the Commission to the Council. In that event, the Commission may defer application of the measure which it has decided for a period of not more than one month from the date of such communication. The Council, acting by a qualified majority, may take a different decision within the time limit.[1814]

The Commission shall refer the reports to the committees. It may seek the opinion of a committee on any matter concerning assistance under the Structural Funds, including matters primarily dealt with by other committees.[1815] Each committee's opinions shall be brought to the attention of the other committees.[1816] Each committee shall draw up its rules of procedure.[1817] The European Parliament shall be regularly informed of the work of the committees.[1818]

More particular rules apply to the work of each committee.

1. Committee on the Development and Conversion of Regions

The Advisory Committee on the Development and Conversion of Regions[1819] is composed of Member States' representatives and is chaired by a

---

1813 Art 47(2) of Reg 1260/1999 ([1999] OJ L161/1).
1814 Art 47(3) of Reg 1260/1999 ([1999] OJ L161/1).
1815 Art 47(4) of Reg 1260/1999 ([1999] OJ L161/1).
1816 Ibid, Art 47(5).
1817 Ibid, Art 47(6).
1818 Ibid, Art 47(7).
1819 Local and regional authorities – as part of their national delegations – should be guaranteed a place on the advisory and management committees. See COR Opinion of 17 September 1998 ([1998] OJ C373/1) on the proposal for a regulation laying down provisions on the Structural Funds, para 2.5.1.

Commission representative. The EIB shall appoint a non-voting representative.[1820]

The Committee shall act as a management committee when it deals with the implementing rules adopted by the Commission;[1821] the guidelines relating to the Community initiatives 'Interreg' and 'URBAN'; and the guidelines for the different types of innovative measures, in the case of support from the ERDF.[1822]

The Committee acts as a consultative committee when it discusses establishment and revision of the list of areas eligible under Objective 2; the CSFs and the corresponding information contained in the SPDs, under Objectives 1 and 2; the types of technical-assistance measure in the case of support from the ERDF; and any other questions concerning Community initiatives and innovative actions.[1823]

2. Committee on Agricultural Structures and Rural Development

The Committee on Agricultural Structures and Rural Development is composed of representatives of the Member States and chaired by the Commission. The EIB shall appoint a non-voting representative.[1824]

The Committee acts as a management committee when it deals with the implementing rules and transitional rules for the EAGGF and the guidelines relating to the Community initiative 'Leader'.[1825]

The Committee acts as a consultative committee when it discusses the establishment and revision of the list of areas eligible under Objective 2; the parts of the intervention concerning agricultural structures and rural development included in the draft Commission decisions relating to the CSFs and corresponding information contained in the SPDs, for the regions under Objectives 1 and 2; the implementing rules adopted by the Commission under Article 53(2) of Regulation 1260/1999;[1826] the types of technical assistance measures in the case of support from the EAGGF; and any other questions concerning Community initiatives and innovative actions.[1827]

1820 Art 48(1) of Reg 1260/1999 ([1999] OJ L161/1).
1821 Other committees shall be consulted under their consultative competence on these rules, in so far as they are concerned. See also, regarding the rules which may be adopted, Art 53(2) of Reg 1260/1999 ([1999] OJ L161/1).
1822 Ibid, Art 48(2).
1823 Art 48(3) of Reg 1260/1999 ([1999] OJ L161/1).
1824 Art 50(1) of Reg 1260/1999 ([1999] OJ L161/1).
1825 Art 50(2) of Reg 1260/1999 ([1999] OJ L161/1).
1826 [1999] OJ L161/1.
1827 Ibid, Art 50(3).

3. Committee on Structures for Fisheries and Aquaculture

The Committee on Structures for Fisheries and Aquaculture is composed of Member States' representatives and chaired by a Commission representative. The EIB shall appoint a non-voting representative.[1828]

The Committee shall act as a management committee when it deals with the implementing rules for the FIFG and the guidelines for the different types of innovative measures, in the case of support from the FIFG.[1829]

The Committee acts as a consultative committee when it discusses the establishment and revision of the list of areas eligible under Objective 2; the parts of the intervention concerning fisheries structures included in the draft Commission decision relating to the CSFs and corresponding information contained in the SPDs under Objective 1; the implementing rules adopted by the Commission under Article 5(2) of Regulation 1260/1999;[1830] the types of technical assistance measures in the case of support from the FIFG; and any other questions concerning innovative actions.[1831]

4. ESF Committee

The ESF Committee is composed of two government representatives, two representatives of the workers' organisations and two representatives of the employers' organisations from each Member State. The Member of the Commission responsible for chairing the Committee may delegate that responsibility to a senior Commission official. For each Member State, an alternate shall be appointed for each category of representative. In the absence of one or both members, the alternate shall be automatically entitled to take part in the proceedings. The members and alternates shall be appointed by the Council, acting on a proposal from the Commission, for a period of three years. They may be reappointed. The Council shall, as regards the composition of the Committee, endeavour to ensure fair representation of the different groups concerned. For the items on the agenda affecting it, the EIB shall appoint a non-voting representative.[1832]

The Committee shall deliver opinions on the draft Commission decisions relating to SPDs and to CSFs under Objective 3, as well as on the CSFs and corresponding information contained in the SPDs, under Objectives 1 and 2, in the case of support from the ESF; deliver its opinion on the implementing rules to be adopted by the Commission under Article 53(2) of Regulation 1260/1999;[1833] be consulted on the implementing rules for the ESF; deliver opinions on draft Commission guidelines relating to the Community initiative 'EQUAL' and for the various types of innovative measure in the case of

1828 Art 51(1) of Reg 1260/1999 ([1999] OJ L161/1).
1829 Art 51(2) of Reg 1260/1999 ([1999] OJ L161/1).
1830 [1999] OJ L161/1.
1831 Ibid, Art 51(3).
1832 Art 49(1) of Reg 1260/1999 ([1999] OJ L161/1)..
1833 Reg 1260/1999 ([1999] OJ L161/1).

support from the ESF;[1834] and be consulted on the types of technical assistance measures in the case of support from the ESF.[1835]

For their adoption, the opinions of the Committee shall require an absolute majority of the votes validly cast. The Commission shall inform the Committee of the manner in which it has taken account of its opinions.[1836]

Similar procedures may apply to use of other funds.[1837] The relevant committees may be mainly intended to provide the means of establishing a link between the representatives of the Member States and the Commission. Their work may, however, be criticized on the ground that they do not aim specifically to ensure that the price of the operations financed is a fair one.[1838]

5. Monitoring committees

Monitoring committees are established for Structural Fund operations generally. A representative of the Commission and, where appropriate, of the EIB, shall participate in the work of the monitoring committee in an advisory capacity. The monitoring committee shall draw up its own rules of procedure within the institutional, legal and financial framework of the Member State concerned and agree them with the managing authority. In principle, the monitoring committee shall be chaired by a representative of the Member State or the managing authority.[1839]

The Commission had also proposed that representation of local and environmental authorities and economic and social partners would be obligatory.[1840] The representatives of all the partners which contributed to the financing of the assistance should have the right to vote, when the committee adopted its decisions. Moreover, in the case of decisions concerning human resources, the representatives of the other partners should have the same right. Generally, however, the representatives of partners who did not contribute to the financing of the assistance only serve in an advisory capacity.[1841] The rationale for this limitation to voting rights was, according to the Commission, to ensure that 'procedures [were] not slowed down'.[1842]

1834 The Commission may also refer further questions to it concerning Community initiatives and innovative actions.
1835 Art 49(2) of Reg 1260/1999 ([1999] OJ L161/1).
1836 Art 49(3) of Reg 1260/1999 ([1999] OJ L161/1).
1837 See, eg, in the case of Thermie, Reg 2008/90 ([1990] OJ L185/1) concerning the promotion of energy technology in Europe, Art 29(1) and (2).
1838 COA special report 3/92 ([1992] OJ C245/1), para 2.8.
1839 Art 35(2) of Reg 1260/1999 ([1999] OJ L161/1).
1840 Explanatory memorandum to the Proposal of 19 March 1998 for a regulation laying down provisions on the Structural Funds, COM(98)131, 22.
1841 Ibid.
1842 Ibid, 10.

These arrangements were not accepted by the Council. Regulation 1260/1999[1843] merely provides that monitoring committees shall be set up by the Member State, in agreement with the managing authority[1844] after consultation with the partners. The partners shall promote the balanced participation of women and men. The monitoring committees shall be set up no more than three months after the decision on the contribution of the Structural Funds. The monitoring committees shall act under the authority and within the legal jurisdiction of the Member State.[1845]

Each CSF or SPD and each operational programme shall be supervised by a monitoring committee. The monitoring committee shall satisfy itself as to the effectiveness and quality of the implementation of assistance. To that end, it shall confirm or adjust the programme complement, including the physical and financial indicators to be used to monitor the assistance. Its approval must be obtained before any further adjustment is made; it shall consider and approve the criteria for selecting the operations financed under each measure within six months of approval of the assistance; it shall periodically review progress made towards achieving the specific objectives of the assistance; it shall examine the results of implementation, particularly achievement of the targets set for the different measures and the mid-term evaluation; it shall consider and approve the annual and final implementation reports before they are sent to the Commission; it shall consider and approve any proposal to amend the contents of the Commission decision on the contribution of the Funds; and it may in any event propose to the managing authority any adjustment or review of the assistance likely to make possible the attainment of the Objectives or to improve the management of assistance, including in respect of financial management.[1846]

H. 'PARTNERSHIP'

Union actions shall complement or contribute to corresponding national operations. They shall be drawn up in close consultation, ie, the 'partnership', between the Commission and the Member State, together with the authorities and bodies designated by the Member State within the framework of its national rules and current practices, namely: the regional and local authorities and other competent public authorities, the economic and social partners, and any other relevant competent bodies within this framework. The partnership shall be conducted in full compliance with the respective institutional, legal and financial powers of each of the partners. In designating the most

---

1843 [1999] OJ L161/1.
1844 Ie, the authority authorized by the Member State to manage Union assistance (ibid, Art 9(n)).
1845 Ibid, Art 35(1).
1846 Art 35(3) of Reg 1260/1999 ([1999] OJ L161/1).

representative partnership at national, regional, local or other level, the Member State shall create a wide and effective association of all the relevant bodies,[1847] according to national rules and practice, taking account of the need to promote equality between men and women and sustainable development through the integration of environmental protection and improvement requirements. All the designated parties shall be partners pursuing a common goal.[1848]

Partnership shall cover the preparation, financing, monitoring and evaluation of assistance. Member States shall ensure the association of the relevant partners at the different stages of programming, taking account of the time limit for each stage.[1849] Thus partners are to be consulted on development plans before they are submitted to the Commission.[1850] Moreover, the plans must include and account of arrangements made to consult partners.[1851] The Commission itself must also consult annually the European-level organizations representing the social partners about Union structural policy.[1852]

However, in application of the principle of subsidiarity, the implementation of assistance shall be the responsibility of the Member States, at the appropriate territorial level according to the arrangements specific to each Member State, and without prejudice to the powers vested in the Commission, notably for implementing the General Budget of the European Communities.[1853] Thus Member States 'will maintain a central role and will ensure that national administrative rules are fully respected'.[1854]

This role revolves around the managing authority. A managing authority is any public or private authority or body at national, regional or local level designated by the Member State to manage assistance for the purposes of Regulation 1260/1999.[1855] If the Member State designates a managing authority other than itself, it shall determine all the modalities of its relationship with the managing authority and of the latter's relationship with the Commission. If the Member State so decides, the managing authority may

1847 It is now proposed that Member States 'shall ensure broad and effective involvement of all appropriate bodies'. See Art 10(1) of the Proposal of 14 July 2004 for a regulation laying down general provisions on the ERDF, the ESF, and the Cohesion Fund, COM(2004)492.
1848 Art 8(1) of Reg 1260/1999 ([1999] OJ L161/1).
1849 Art 8(2) of Reg 1260/1999 ([1999] OJ L161/1). The 'relevant partners shall be associated in the preparation, monitoring and evaluation of assistance' (ibid, cl 27 in the preamble).
1850 Ibid, Art 14(2).
1851 Ibid, Art 16(1)(d).
1852 Ibid, Art 8(5).
1853 Art 8(3) of Reg 1260/1999 ([1999] OJ L161/1).
1854 Explanatory memorandum to the Proposal of 19 March 1998 for a regulation laying down provisions on the Structural Funds, COM(98)131, 19.
1855 [1999] OJ L161/1.

be the same body as the paying authority[1856] for the assistance concerned.[1857] The managing authority shall be responsible for the efficiency and correctness of management and implementation.[1858]

Accordingly, every year, when the annual implementation report is submitted, the Commission and the managing authority shall review the main outcomes of the previous year, in accordance with arrangements to be defined by agreement with the Member State and the managing authority concerned. After this review, the Commission may make comments to the Member State and the managing authority. The Member State shall inform the Commission of the action taken on these comments. Where in duly substantiated cases the Commission considers that the measures taken are inadequate, it may make recommendations to the Member State and the managing authority for adjustments aimed at improving the effectiveness of the monitoring or management arrangements for the assistance. If it receives any such recommendations, the managing authority shall subsequently demonstrate the steps taken to improve the monitoring or management arrangements or it shall explain why it has not taken any.[1859]

Moreover, the managing authority shall, at the request of the monitoring committee or on its own initiative, adjust the programme complement, without changing the total amount of the contribution from the Structural Funds granted to the priority concerned or its specific targets. After approval by the monitoring committee, it shall inform the Commission of the adjustment within one month. Any amendments to the elements contained in the decision on the contribution of the Funds shall be decided by the Commission, in agreement with the Member State concerned, within four months of delivery of the monitoring committee's approval.[1860]

The managing authority and the monitoring committee shall carry out their monitoring by reference to physical and financial indicators specified in the operational programme, SPD, or programme complement. In drawing up their indicators, they should take into account the indicative methodology and list of examples of indicators published by the Commission, as well as a categorization of fields of intervention to be proposed by the Commission upon entry into force of Regulation 1260/1999.[1861] The indicators shall relate to the specific character of the assistance concerned, its objectives and the

---

1856 The paying authority is one or more national, regional or local authorities or bodies designated by the Member States for the purposes of drawing up and submitting payment applications and receiving payments from the Commission. The Member State shall determine all the modalities of its relationship with the paying authority and of the latter's relationship with the Commission (ibid, Art 9(o)).
1857 Ibid, Art 9(n).
1858 Ibid, Art 34(1).
1859 Art 34(2) of Reg 1260/1999 ([1999] OJ L161/1).
1860 Art 34(3) of Reg 1260/1999 ([1999] OJ L161/1).
1861 [1999] OJ 161/1.

socio-economic, structural and environmental situation of the Member State concerned and its regions, as appropriate. These indicators shall include, in particular, those used for allocating the performance reserve.[1862]

For multiannual assistance, the managing authority shall, within six months of the end of each full calendar year of implementation, submit to the Commission an annual implementation report. A final report shall be submitted to the Commission at the latest six months after the final date of eligibility of the expenditure. The report shall be examined and approved by the monitoring committee before it is sent to the Commission. Once the Commission has received an annual report, it shall indicate within a period of two months if the report is considered unsatisfactory; otherwise, the report shall be deemed to be accepted. In the case of a final report, the Commission shall respond within a period of five months from its receipt of the report.[1863]

I. JUDICIAL REVIEW

Judicial review implies possibilities for the European Courts and national courts to contribute to processes concerning regional policy. The European Courts have plenary jurisdiction to hear claims that a Member State is in breach of Union law, to review the legality of Union acts or inaction, and to hear claims for compensation against the Union. The Court of Justice also has jurisdiction to deliver preliminary rulings on questions of the meaning and validity of Union law referred to it by national courts. The latter are to apply directly effective provisions of Union law. They are also to provide remedies for violations of Union law.

1. *Locus standi*

If a Member State does not fulfil its obligations under Union law rules governing the Union funds, the Commission has standing to bring proceedings before the Court of Justice under Article 226 EC.[1864] A Member State may also challenge the grant or non-grant of Union assistance before the Court under Article 230 or 232 EC, respectively.[1865] Interim measures suspending the relevant Union decisions may be sought under Article 242.[1866]

In particular, at least in the context of operations under the ESF, 'legitimate expectations' regarding the grant of assistance may arise for a Member State.

1862 Ibid, Art 36(1).

1863 Art 37(1) of Reg 1260/1999 ([1999] OJ L161/1).

1864 See, eg, Case 272/83 EC Commission v Italy: producer groups [1985] ECR 1057; and Case 309/84 EC Commission v Italy: abandonment of vine-growing [1986] ECR 599. Another Member State may bring proceedings under Art 227 EC.

1865 See, regarding the extent to which Commission practice may be classified as a reviewable act, Case C-107/99 Italy v EC Commission: Community initiatives [2002] ECR I-1091.

1866 Case T-84/96R Cipeke – Comércio e Indústria de Papel Lda v EC Commission [1996] ECR II-1313.

The Court may enforce these expectations against the Commission.[1867] Moreover, a Member State participates in the exercise of legislative and budgetary powers and contributes to the General Budget. Therefore, in proceedings before the Court, it can rely on the damage which would arise from expenditure being incurred contrary to the rules governing the powers of the Union and its institutions.[1868]

Such proceedings must be brought within the period of two months laid down by Articles 230 and 232. This requirement does not apply, however, where the alleged defect in the decision is so serious that, if substantiated, the decision 'would lack any legal foundation in the context of the Community'.[1869] Moreover, where the decision in dispute is not published or notified, the period within which proceedings must be instituted cannot start to run until the challenger has precise knowledge of the content and grounds of the act in question.[1870] In the absence of publication or notification, the party which learns of a decision concerning it is expected to request the whole text thereof within a reasonable period.[1871]

A natural or legal person may also challenge before the Court of First Instance (with the possibility of an appeal on points of law to the Court of Justice)[1872] the legality of a decision addressed to him under Article 230 or of a failure to address a decision to him under Article 232. In the latter case there must have been an obligation on the relevant Union institution to act.[1873]

He may also challenge a decision which, although in the form of a regulation or decision addressed to another person, is of direct and individual concern to him.[1874] However, a decision addressed to a Member State may leave the national authorities such a margin of discretion with regard to the manner of its implementation that he cannot be considered directly concerned.[1875] Moreover, according to the traditional case law of the European Courts, he has not been considered individually concerned unless the decision affected him by reason of certain attributes peculiar to him or by reason of

---

1867 Case 84/85 UK v EC Commission: assistance for part-time employment [1987] ECR 3765, 3798.

1868 Case C-239 & 240/96R UK v EC Commission: social assistance [1996] ECR I-4475, I-4492.

1869 Joined Cases 6 & 11/69 EC Commission v France: export aid [1969] ECR 523, 539.

1870 Case T-109/94 Windpark Groothusen GmbH & Co Betriebs KG v EC Commission [1995] ECR II-3007, II-3017.

1871 Case C-48/96P Windpark Groothusen GmbH & Co Betriebs KG v EC Commission [1998] ECR I-2873.

1872 Art 49 of the Statute of the ECJ.

1873 AG Roemer in Joined Cases 10 & 18/68 Società 'Eridania' Zuccherifici Nazionali v EC Commission [1969] ECR 459, 494.

1874 'The EC Treaty does not grant individuals the same capacity to act as national law' (AG Roemer, ibid, 493).

1875 Case C-181/90 Consorgan – Gestaõ de Empresas, Lda v EC Commission [1992] ECR I-3557, I-3568.

circumstances differentiating him from all other persons and distinguishing him individually just as in the case of the person addressed.[1876]

Recipients of assistance: Persons whom the Commission has agreed to assist or even persons making an initial application for assistance,[1877] at least where they have participated in protracted procedures for evaluation of their application,[1878] may have standing to bring proceedings under Articles 230 and 232. Where the Commission refuses payment of assistance which it has previously undertaken to grant, it disputes a prior commitment or denies the existence of the commitment. Thus it adopts an act which has legal effects and may be challenged under Article 230.[1879] If the action leads to a declaration that the refusal to make payment is void, the Commission will be obliged, pursuant to Article 233 EC,[1880] to ensure that the payment which has been unlawfully refused is made. If the Commission fails to reply to a request for payment, the same result may be obtained by means of proceedings under Article 232.[1881]

For example, a decision reducing assistance from the ESF, though addressed to a Member State, is of direct and individual concern to the recipient. This is because it deprives the recipient of part of the assistance originally granted, the Member State having no discretion in the matter.[1882] Hence, the recipient has standing to challenge the legality of the decision under Article 230.

Competitors: A competitor of the recipient of assistance may challenge the legality of a decision to grant the assistance where his market position has been 'significantly affected' by the assistance.[1883] However, the mere fact that a decision may affect competition in the market in question cannot suffice to allow any trader in any competitive relationship whatever with the recipient to

---

1876 Case 25/62 Plaumann & Co v EEC Commission [1963] ECR 95, 107.

1877 Case 107/80 Giacomo Cattaneo Adorno v EC Commission [1981] ECR 1469; and Case T-478/93 Wafer Zoo Srl v EC Commission [1995] ECR II-1479.

1878 Case T-465/93 Consorzio Gruppo di Azione Locale 'Murgia Messapica' v EC Commission [1994] ECR II-361, II-373.

1879 Cf the argument of the Commission in Case T-585/93 Stichting Greenpeace Council (Greenpeace International) v EC Commission [1995] ECR II-2205, II-2217-18 that the payment of assistance was not an act for the purposes of this provision. The CFI did not find it necessary to address this argument (ibid, II-2232).

1880 According to this provision, the institution whose act has been declared void or whose failure to act has been declared contrary to the Treaty shall be required to take the necessary measures to comply with the judgment.

1881 Case 44/81 Germany v EC Commission: deadline for claiming payment of ESF assistance [1982] ECR 1855, 1874. However, the Commission may lawfully set a deadline for claims for payment of approved assistance to be made (ibid, 1877).

1882 Case T-85/94 EC Commission v Eugénio Branco Lda [1995] ECR II-45, II-55.

1883 Cf Case 169/84 Cie Française de l'Azote (COFAZ) SA v EC Commission [1986] ECR 391, 415; and Joined Cases T-447-449/93 Associazione Italiana Tecnico Economica del Cemento, British Cement Association, Titan Cement Company SA v EC Commission [1995] ECR II-1971, II-1994-6 and II-2002.

be regarded as directly and individually concerned by that decision. Only the existence of specific circumstances gives standing under Article 230.[1884] Thus a competitor must be concerned in a particular manner,[1885] as for example where he is in the same region as the recipient.[1886] Account may be taken of whether the competitor has participated in the procedures leading to the adoption of the contested decision.[1887]

Interest groups: The 'administration of justice' may imply that trade associations should be entitled to bring proceedings, given the 'valuable role' they may play in administrative procedures. In particular, they are in a better position than their individual members to put their sector's case to the Commission.[1888] However, trade associations must have a 'personal' interest in bringing proceedings.[1889] This condition is not met unless the association is shown to have an interest which is distinct from the interests of the industrial policy of the Member State concerned.[1890] Nor is the condition met in the case of an act that has consequences affecting the general interests of the category of persons the association represents.[1891] Hence, an association may only bring an action for annulment where its members may also do so individually.[1892] Such thinking may be appropriate in the case of trade associations representing the market interests of their members. If the latter interests are not affected, it may be argued that the association itself is not affected.[1893]

The same thinking may be more problematic in the case of interest groups other than trade associations. An example is provided by *Stichting Greenpeace Council (Greenpeace International) v EC Commission*.[1894] Here assistance from the ERDF for the building of two power stations in the Canary Islands was

1884 Joined Cases 10 & 18/68 Società 'Eridania' Zuccherifici Nazionali v EC Commission [1969] ECR 459, 481.

1885 AG Roemer (ibid, 491).

1886 Ibid, 492.

1887 Submission of the Commission (ibid, 473).

1888 Cf AG Slynn in Joined Cases 67, 68 & 70/85 Kwekereij Gebroeders van der Kooy [1988] ECR 219, 246. Cf also the view of the EFTA Court in Case E-2/94 Scottish Salmon Growers Association Ltd v ESA [1995] 1 CMLR 851, 862.

1889 AG Roemer in Joined Cases 10 & 18/68 Società 'Eridania' Zuccherifici Nazionali v EC Commission [1969] ECR 459, 493.

1890 Case 282/85 Comité de Développement et de Promotion du Textile et de l'Habillement v EC Commission [1986] ECR 2469, 2481.

1891 Joined Cases 16 & 17/62 Confédération Nationale des Producteurs de Fruits et Legumes v EEC Council [1962] ECR 471, 479-80; and Case T-117/94 Associazione Agricoltori della Provincia di Rovigo v EC Commission [1995] ECR II-455, II-466.

1892 Case T-585/93 Stichting Greenpeace Council (Greenpeace International) v EC Commission [1995] ECR II-2205, II-2230-1; and Case T-197/95 Sveriges Betodlares Centralförening and Sven Åke Henrikson v EC Commission [1996] ECR II-1283, II-1296-7.

1893 Cf Joined Cases 67, 68 & 70/85 Kwekereij Gebroeders van der Kooy [1988] ECR 219, 268-9; and the EFTA Court in Case E-4/97 Norwegian Bankers' Association v ESA [1998] 3 CMLR 281, 290.

1894 Case T-585/93 [1995] ECR II-2205.

challenged on environmental grounds by local residents and economic operators and by the environmental group, Greenpeace. The Court of First Instance was urged to go beyond consideration of 'purely economic interests' in determining whether the challengers had standing.[1895] According to the Court, however, *locus standi* had to be limited to those whose competitive position was significantly affected by a contested decision. This limitation was necessary, in accordance with Article 230, to ensure that only those who were individually concerned by a decision had standing to challenge it.[1896] Thus, to have standing, it was not enough to be a resident, fisherman, farmer or tourist in a region where the Union was to assist the construction of a power station.[1897]

However, cohesion implies that the relationship between individuals is to be based on more than simply the market. The implication is that individuals should have standing to challenge decisions regarding the grant of assistance which may significantly affect their cohesion prospects. Assistance for building a power station in a coastal region may affect such prospects through, for example, damaging tourism and fishing.[1898]

In essence, such damage may result from environmental degradation. Whereas the environment provides assets in the form of natural resources, environmental degradation constitutes a restraint on development.[1899] Thus, as the European Parliament has argued, cohesion efforts should be *founded* on the principle of environmentally sustainable development.[1900] The inference may be drawn that environmental protection is such an integral element of cohesion that any Union assistance to environmentally harmful investments will damage cohesion prospects for residents.

In accordance with such thinking, it may be argued that groups representing such persons should have standing to challenge decisions regarding operations of the funds before the European Courts. However, Greenpeace was found to have no standing because the interests of its members were not individually affected. The possibility that the credibility and campaigning capacity of Greenpeace might be adversely affected by the denial of standing was apparently disregarded. Certainly, an earlier Opinion of

---

1895 Ibid, II-2220.
1896 Ibid, II-2227.
1897 Ibid, II-2229.
1898 Cf the argument of AG Cosmas in Case C-321/95P Stichting Greenpeace Council (Greenpeace International) v EC Commission [1998] ECR I-1651, I-1694 that standing could derive from particular damage to non-market interests suffered by certain individuals.
1899 Industrial competitiveness and protection of the environment, SEC(92)1986, 11. Note also the link made between environmental policy and cohesion in Art 174(3) EC.
1900 Report of the Committee on Regional Policy, Regional Planning, and Relations with Regional and Local Authorities on the impact of Community regional policy on the environment, EP Doc. A3-0170/92.

Advocate General Lenz arguing that an interest group might have standing, even if its members were not individually affected,[1901] was disregarded.

Nor was it enough for Greenpeace to have complained to the Commission about the grant of assistance.[1902] This was because the legislation governing the Structural Funds did not provide specific procedures for associating such bodies with decisions implementing the ERDF.[1903] Apparently, then, limitations to judicial intervention were thought to be justified by perceived limitations to the legislation. However, it is questionable whether the latter limitations were correctly perceived. Certainly, the importance attached by the Commission to involvement of the social partners in the 'partnership' required by the legislation suggests that a range of actors, including environmental groups, is to be associated with decisions concerning assistance from the Union funds.[1904]

More fundamentally, the ruling conflicts with the view of the European Courts that questions of *locus standi* are to be resolved in the light of the Treaty system and the structure of the Union legal order.[1905] The systemic or structural significance of cohesion for *locus standi* questions seems to be neglected by these Courts, when they decide such questions in cases relevant to promotion of cohesion.

This neglect not only means that the range of cohesion requirements likely to be invoked and, hence, activated and developed in proceedings before the European Courts is narrowed down. The incentive is also reduced for other Union institutions, notably the Commission, to devise procedures consistent with promoting cohesion requirements and learning what the requirements mean for the operations of the Union funds. Even the apparent willingness of these Courts to consider arguments about the effectiveness of Union assistance[1906] has reduced significance.

The underlying thinking of the Courts is illustrated by the case law concerning State aid. According to this case law, a distinction may be made between a decision declaring State aid compatible with the common market and a decision declaring it incompatible. Persons who consider themselves adversely affected by a decision of the former type are fully entitled to judicial protection, because the Treaty guarantees them protection against aid which distorts competition. It is not so with persons complaining of a decision of the second type, because the Treaty does not guarantee, but at most tolerates, State

1901 Case 297/86 Confederazione Italiana Dirigenti di Azienda (CIDA) v EC Council [1988] ECR 3531, 3543.
1902 Cf Case T-465/93 Consorzio Gruppo di Azione Locale 'Murgia Messapica' v EC Commission [1994] ECR II-361, II-373.
1903 [1995] ECR II-2205, II-2229
1904 See paras [786] ff above.
1905 AG Roemer in Case 25/62 Plaumann & Co v EEC Commission [1963] ECR 95, 114–15.
1906 Joined Cases C-248 & 249/95 SAM Schiffahrt GmbH and Heinz Stapf v Germany [1997] ECR I-4475, I-4505.

aid. In other words, the aid has its source not in the Treaty but in the will of the Member State concerned. Where the Commission considers the aid unlawful, the Member State may or may not challenge the Commission's decision. If it brings a challenge, the interests of the aid recipients are indirectly protected by this challenge. If the Member State does not bring a challenge, either because it considers the decision well founded or because its policy has changed, no one can remedy its lack of will.[1907]

Such thinking concentrates on the right to free competition. It does not allow for recognition of the possibility that a right to aid, or at least to assistance from the Union,[1908] may derive from the establishment of cohesion as a Union objective. Rather, in the absence of an express basis in Union legislation, the Courts seem reluctant to conceptualize individual rights other than by reference to the competition sought through the common market.[1909] Hence, unless market interests are at stake,[1910] rights may only arise for individuals from their embodiment in legislation approved by representatives of Member States in the Council. This narrow definition of individual rights apparently may preclude the Courts from recognizing the standing of representatives of cohesion interests.

The approach of the Courts may appear to be a reasonable reflection of Commission concern that there should not be a proliferation of judicial challenges to its decision making.[1911] The approach appears more problematic if regard is had to the 'constitutionalization' of cohesion and to the 'establishment' of Union Citizenship by Article 17 EC.[1912] The apparent implication is that Union Citizens should be recognized as having rights to cohesion.[1913] The further implication is that these rights should be judicially enforceable[1914] and fully taken into account in the operations of Union funds.

Regional authorities: The Court of Justice has not ruled out the possibility that a decision addressed to a Member State may leave the latter with so little discretion that it may be of direct concern to regional authorities affected by

1907 AG Mancini Case 282/85 Comité de Développement et de Promotion du Textile et de l'Habillement (DEFI) v EC Commission [1986] ECR 2469, 2474.
1908 Case T-465/93 Consorzio Gruppo di Azione Locale 'Murgia Messapica' v EC Commission [1994] ECR II-361, II-373.
1909 Cf A Evans, 'Union Citizenship and the Constitutionalization of Equality in European Union Law' in M La Torre, European Citizenship: an Institutional Challenge (Kluwer, Deventer, 1997).
1910 Cf AG Lenz in Case C-309/89 Cordoniu SA v EU Council [1994] ECR I-1853, I-1868, regarding the criterion of 'economic repercussions'.
1911 Case C-312/90 Spain v EC Commission: Cenemesa [1992] ECR I-4117, I-4122.
1912 Cf Case T-330/94 Syndical des Producteurs de Viande Bovine de la Coordination Rurale v EC Commission [1996] ECR II-1579, II-1589, where the ECJ rejected a claim under Art 288(2) EC based on harm suffered by the applicant 'like any citizen of a member country'.
1913 Cf, regarding a right to development as a fundamental right, J Scott, para [669], n 1 above, 71.
1914 Cf, regarding Union Citizenship and equality before the law, AG Lenz in Case C-91/92 Paola Faccini Dori v Recreb Srl [1994] ECR I-3325, I-3340.

it.[1915] However, a wide circle of persons in the region, including employers, customers, suppliers and businessmen, may also be affected. Hence, the decision may not easily be regarded as of individual concern to a regional authority.[1916]

It has also been argued that a regional authority would have standing to challenge a measure affecting its own prerogatives.[1917] However, the Court of Justice apparently recognizes no link between such prerogatives and cohesion requirements. Certainly, the Court infers from cohesion requirements no need to discourage centralization within Member States. For example, according to the Court, 'the Member State is the sole interlocutor of the [European Social] Fund'[1918] or at least has a 'central role' in the operations of this Fund.[1919] Therefore, while regional authorities may have a vital role to play in the articulation of cohesion requirements, the Court is uncertain about securing such a role for them in judicial proceedings.

The importance of reforms regarding standing is not without recognition in the European Court of Justice. In *Unión de Pequeños Agricultores v EU Council*[1920] an association of small Spanish agricultural businesses appealed to the European Court of Justice against a Court of First Instance judgment that the association lacked standing to challenge a Council regulation substantially amending the common organization of the market in olive oil. Advocate General Jacobs argued for reform of the approach to determining whether a 'non-privileged' applicant was individually concerned by a Union act. According to the Advocate General, an applicant should have standing to challenge a Union act 'where the measure has, or is liable to have, a substantial adverse effect on his interests'.[1921] The Court itself avoided addressing this argument, considering that it was not directly related to the grounds on which

---

1915 Cf, regarding Commission authorization of State aid, Case 222/83 Municipality of Differdange v EC Commission [1984] ECR 2889.

1916 AG Lenz (ibid, 2905). But cf, in an application for interim measures, Case T-37/04R Autonomous Region of the Azores v EU Council, 7 July 2004.

1917 M Vellano, 'Coesione economica e sociale e ripartizione di competenze: Le nuove iniziative comunitarie' (1995) Rivista di Diritto Europeo 193–208, 194.

1918 Case C-291/89 Interhotel v EC Commission [1991] ECR I-2257, I-2280. Cf, earlier, Case 310/81 Ente Italiano di Servizio Sociale v EC Commission [1984] ECR 1341, 1353. Such case law reflected Commission practice. See, eg, Communication concerning the procedures laid down by the Member States for the submission of applications for assistance from the ESF and their transmission ([1982] OJ C6/4).

1919 Case C-304/89 Establecimentos Isodoro M Oliveira SA v EC Commission [1991] ECR I-2283, I-2313.

1920 Case C-50/00P [2002] ECR I-6677.

1921 Ibid, I-6715. Note that the qualifying clause 'by reason of his particular circumstances' (I-6698) was omitted from the concluding paragraphs of the Opinion.

1922 ECJ, ibid, I-6732.

the appeal was based.[1922] According to the Court, if standing were to be broadened, amendment of Article 230 EC would be necessary.[1923]

The Court has now 'reconsidered' its position. According to *EC Commission v Jégo Quéré*,[1924] a 'non-privileged' applicant is directly concerned where a measure 'affects his legal position, in a manner which is both definite and immediate, by restricting his rights or by imposing obligations on him'.[1925]

At the same time, the draft Constitution of the EU envisages Treaty amendment. According to Article III-270(4) of the draft, any natural or legal person may institute proceedings against an act addressed to that person or which is of direct and individual concern to him or her, and against a regulatory act which is of direct concern to him or her and does not entail implementing measures. In other words, in relation to regulatory acts (which means that European laws and Framework laws are not included[1926]), there is no requirement of *individual* concern.[1927]

The inference may be drawn that adoption of the draft Constitution is a necessary condition for rendering the 'constitutionalization' of cohesion effective. However, the case law suggests that Article III-270(4) alone may be an inadequate condition. According to the case law, a Union act which prejudices the cohesion interests of a region may not be treated as concerning the relevant regional institution at all.[1928] Hence, the removal of the requirement of individualization of a regulatory act does in itself mean that a regional institution will have standing under Article III-270(4) to challenge an act affecting its cohesion interests. Therefore, the implications of Article III-270(4) for the meaning of provisions on the Structural Funds may depend on how the framework provided by the Constitution changes judicial thinking about cohesion issues. In the absence of changed thinking, standing for advocates of cohesion interests may still be denied, and the European Courts, may, in the language of AG Jacobs, remain 'blind'[1929] to problems in the meaning of provisions governing the Structural Funds, and articulation of the meaning of these provisions may remain impaired.

A person who lacks standing under Article 230 or 232 may still claim compensation for unlawful action or inaction under Article 288(2) EC.[1930] Strictly speaking, no claim for payment of Union assistance may be

1922 ECJ, ibid, I-6732.
1923 Ibid, I-6736.
1924 Case C-263/02P, 1 April 2004.
1925 Ibid, para 51.
1926 Art I-26 of the draft EU Constitution.
1927 CERCLE I WD 08, 10/3/03.
1928 Case T-238/97 Comunidad Autónoma de Cantabria v EC Commission [1998] ECR II-2271, II-2285.
1929 Case C-50/00 Unión de Pequeños Agricultores v EU Council [2002] ECR I-6677, I-6700.
1930 Case T-185/94 Geotronics SA v EC Commission [1995] ECR II-2795, II-2809. Conversely, the annulment of a measure does not necessarily mean that compensation is payable. See Case T-478/93 Wafer Zoo Srl v EC Commission [1995] ECR II-1479, II-1500.

brought.[1931] Indeed, the Commission once maintained that claims for compensation under Article 288(2) had to be distinguished from 'actions for the provision of benefits' and that the latter were not admissible under this provision.[1932] However, the Court of Justice accepts that compensation may be claimed for damage resulting from non-payment of Union assistance.[1933] For such compensation to be awarded, there need only be illegality, damage, and a causal link between the two.[1934]

Even so, the utility of such proceedings for representatives of cohesion may be limited. The concern of such representatives may be more with the content of decisions regarding the grant of Union assistance than with compensation for the effects of such decisions. However, proceedings for compensation constitute an abuse of procedure, if their real purpose is to secure the withdrawal of a decision which has become definitive.[1935]

Opportunities to *intervene* in proceedings before the European Courts may be more generally available to consumer groups,[1936] trades unions,[1937] regional authorities[1938] and, presumably, environmental groups. However, an intervener must accept the case as he finds it at the time of his intervention.[1939] Hence, he may be precluded from raising arguments of specific relevance to his interests.

2. Substantive illegality

According to Article 230, Union decisions may be annulled on three substantive grounds. First, they may be annulled on grounds of lack of competence. For example, Commission departments are only competent to exercise delegated powers, in the name of the Commission, and, subject to its control, to take clearly defined measures of management or administration. If they adopt a decision concerning the grant of assistance which goes beyond such limits, the decision may be annulled for lack of competence.[1940]

Secondly, Union decisions may be annulled for infringement of the Treaty or of any rule of law relating to its application. For example, they may be

---

1931 Case 44/81 Germany v EC Commission: deadline for claiming payment of ESF assistance [1982] ECR 1855, 1874-5.
1932 Joined Cases 261 & 262/78 Interquell Starke GmbH & Co KG and Diamalt AG v EC Council and EC Commission [1979] ECR 3045, 3050.
1933 Ibid, 3062.
1934 Case C-200/89 Funoc v EC Commission [1990] ECR I-3669, I-3695.
1935 Case T-514/93 Cobrecaf SA v EC Commission [1995] ECR II-621, II-641.
1936 Joined Cases 41, 43-48, 50, 111, 113 & 114/73 Société Anonyme Générale Sucrerie v EC Commission [1973] ECR 1465.
1937 Case 22/74 Union Syndicale v EC Council [1975] ECR 401, 410.
1938 Case T-194/95Intv I Area Cova SA [1996] ECR II-591.
1939 Art 93(4) of the Rules of Procedure of the ECJ ([1991] OJ L176/7).
1940 Case T-450/93 Lisrestal _ Organizacaõ Gestaõ de Restaurantes Colectivos Lda v EC Commission [1994] ECR II-1177, II-1191-2. See also Case T-218/95 Azienda Agricola 'Le Canne' Srl v EC Commission [1997] ECR II-2055.

annulled for breach of the principles of legitimate expectations and legal certainty.[1941] The rationale is that foreseeability as to the payment of assistance is necessary to enable the recipients to commit themselves to expenditure free of the risk of ultimately having themselves to bear the burden of it.[1942] Consistently with this rationale, the principles may be more demanding where expenditure has been incurred than when only an application for assistance has been made.[1943] By the same token, acquired rights, which must usually be respected by the Commission, do not arise from unapproved expenditure or expenditure above the amount approved.[1944]

However, in the case of withdrawal of unlawfully granted assistance, there may be conflict between the requirements of the principle of legality and the requirements of the principle of legal certainty.[1945] In particular, the former principle may have priority over the latter, where the equality principle would otherwise be violated.[1946] In other words, there may be conflict between the 'public interest in legality and the sound management of public funds' and 'the private interest' of the recipient of assistance.[1947]

At the same time, decisions must also comply with the principle of equality of treatment.[1948] Thus, distinctions in the grant of assistance must be based on 'objective' criteria.[1949]

However, judicial review must be circumspect where the Commission is judging economic circumstances of fact which involve elements of economic and structural policy;[1950] where the Commission is assessing 'complex facts and accounts';[1951] or where several Union objectives are relevant and the

1941 Case 15/85 Consorzio Cooperative d'Abruzzo v EC Commission [1987] ECR 1005, 1037; and Case T-478/93 Wafer Zoo Srl v EC Commission [1995] ECR II-1479.
1942 AG Darmon in Case C-157/90 Infortec Projectos & Consultadoria, Lda v EC Commission [1992] ECR I-3525, I-3354 and in Case C-291/89 Interhotel v EC Commission [1991] ECR I-2257, I-2267.
1943 Case 44/81 Germany v EC Commission: deadline for claiming payment of ESF assistance [1982] ECR 1855, 1877.
1944 AG Darmon in Case C-304/89 Establicementos Isodoro M Oliveira SA v EC Commission [1991] ECR I-2283, I-2298.
1945 AG Mischo in Case 15/85 Consorzio Cooperative d'Abruzzo v EC Commission [1987] ECR 1005, 1025.
1946 Joined Cases T-551/93 & 231-234/94 Industrias Pesqueras Campos SA, Transacciones Maritimas SA, Recursos Marinos SA, Makuspesa SA v EC Commission [1996] ECR II-247, II-278.
1947 Submission of the Commission in Case C-200/89 Funoc v EC Commission [1990] ECR I-3669, I-3679.
1948 AG Capotorti in Case 107/80 Giacomo Cattaneo Adorno v EC Commission [1981] ECR 1469, 1497-8, where a breach of Reg 355/77 ([1977] OJ L51/1) was also involved. See also Case T-85/94 EC Commission v Eugénio Branco Lda [1995] ECR II-45.
1949 Case 8/57 Groupement des Hauts Fourneaux et Aciéries Belges v ECSC High Authority [1957-8] ECR 245, 257
1950 Joined Cases 10 & 18/68 Società 'Eridania' Zuccherifici Nazionali v EC Commission [1969] ECR 459, 502.
1951 Case T-142/97 Eugénio Branco Lda v EC Commission [1998] ECR II-3567.

Commission must make the necessary reconciliation as best it can between the interests entrusted to it. In such circumstances, 'considerable, although not unlimited, discretion' is available to the Commission.[1952]

For example, the Commission enjoys such discretion in assessing the existence of conditions justifying the grant of assistance and the 'overriding requirements of the proper administration of Community finances'.[1953] It also enjoys such discretion in determining whether expenditure has been properly incurred by the recipient.[1954] Hence, the Court of First Instance cannot undertake a detailed re-examination of an application for assistance during proceedings before it.[1955] Even less is it the function of the Court to undertake investigations into the use of assistance of the kind performed by the Court of Auditors.[1956]

Nevertheless, a Commission assessment may be overturned where there is found to have been an *erreur manifeste d'appréciation* (clear error of assessment). For example, where it is clear from the description of a project proposed in an application for assistance that the project fits in with the policies adopted to meet Union priorities laid down by the Council, the Commission may commit such an error in refusing assistance.[1957]

Finally, a Union decision may be annulled for a misuse of power.[1958] A decision may be annulled on this ground where it appears, on the basis of objective, relevant and consistent factors, to have been taken with the purpose of achieving ends other than those stated.[1959] It may also be annulled on the same ground where it represents a departure, without reasons being given, from 'rules of conduct' regarding the grant of assistance, by which the Commission considers itself to be bound.[1960]

1952 AG Lagrange in Case 13/57 Wirtschaftsvereinigung Eisen- und Stahlindustrie Carl Bönnhoff, Gußstahlwerk Witten, Ruhrstahl, and Eisenwerk Annahütte Alfred Zeller v ECSC High Authority [1957-8] ECR 265, 301.

1953 AG Da Cruz Vilaça in Case 84/85 UK v EC Commission: assistance for part-time employment [1987] ECR 3765, 3781.

1954 Ibid, 3797.

1955 Case T-109/94 Windpark Groothusen GmbH & Co Betriebs KG v EC Commission [1995] ECR II-3007, II-3026; and Case T-465/93 Consorzio Gruppo di Azione Locale 'Murgia Messapica' v EC Commission [1994] ECR II-361, II-379.

1956 Joined Cases T-551/93 & 231-234/94 Industrias Pesqueras Campos SA, Transacciones Maritimas SA, Recursos Marinos SA, Makuspesa SA v EC Commission [1996] ECR II-247, II-307. See, regarding such investigations, A Evans, A Textbook on EU Law (Hart Publishing, Oxford, 1998), Section 6.3.1.

1957 Case C-213/87 Gemeente Amsterdam and Stichting Vrouwenvakschool voor Informatica Amsterdam (VIA) v EC Commission [1990] ECR I-221.

1958 Case T-109/94 Windpark Groothusen GmbH & Co. Betriebs KG v EC Commission [1995] ECR II-3007, II-3026.

1959 AG Mischo in Case 15/85 Consorzio Cooperative d'Abruzzo v EC Commission [1987] ECR 1005, 1024-5.

1960 Ibid, 1016.

---

3. Procedural illegality

The European Courts may, according to Article 230, annul Union decisions on grounds of procedural illegality, that is, infringement of an essential procedural requirement. Such an infringement may, for example, take the form of a failure by the Commission to consult an advisory committee[1961] or a management committee,[1962] to authenticate a decision,[1963] to grant a fair hearing, or to give adequate reasons for its decisions.

Fair hearing: Any person who may be adversely affected by a decision should be placed in a position in which he may effectively make known his views on the evidence against him which the Commission has taken as the basis for the decision at issue.[1964] For example, 'the Member State is the sole interlocutor of the [European Social] Fund'. Hence, the opportunity for it to comment before a definitive decision to reduce assistance is adopted constitutes an essential procedural requirement the disregard of which renders a decision void.[1965]

A private recipient of assistance must also be placed, practical problems notwithstanding,[1966] in a position in which he can effectively make known his views on the evidence relied on against him to justify a decision reducing his assistance.[1967] Insofar as the recipient has not been afforded the opportunity to comment on the evidence, the Commission may not use the evidence in a decision. However, for such an infringement of the right to a fair hearing to result in annulment of the decision concerned, it must be established that, had it not been for that infringement, the decision might have been different.[1968]

In the case of applicants for assistance, where hundreds of applications must be evaluated and the selection procedure is conducted on the basis of the documentation submitted by the applicants, the denial of a hearing may be

1961 AG Da Cruz Vilaça in Case 84/85 UK v EC Commission: assistance for part-time employment [1987] ECR 3765, 3788–9.
1962 AG Mischo in Case 15/85 Consorzio Cooperative d'Abruzzo v EC Commission [1987] ECR 1005, 1019.
1963 Case C-107/99 Italy v EC Commission: Community initiatives [2002] ECR I-1091, regarding a decision adjusting allocations of assistance under Community initiatives.
1964 Case T-450/93 Lisrestal _ Organizaõ Gestaõ de Restaurantes Colectivos Lda v EC Commission [1994] ECR II-1177, II-1194.
1965 Case C-291/89 Interhotel v EC Commission [1991] ECR I-2257, I-2280; see also Case 310/81 Ente Italiano di Servizio Sociale v EC Commission [1984] ECR 1341, 1353. Cf Case C-304/89 Establicementos Isodoro M Oliveira SA v EC Commission [1991] ECR I-2283, I-2313.
1966 Case C-32/95P EC Commission v Lisrestal _ Organizaçaõ Gestaõ de Restaurantes Colectivos Lda [1996] ECR I-5373, I-5399.
1967 Case T-109/94 Windpark Groothusen GmbH & Co Betriebs KG v EC Commission [1995] ECR II-3007, II-3024.
1968 Case C-142/87 Belgium v EC Commission: Tubemeuse [1990] ECR I-959, I-1016. This case was invoked by the Commission in Case T-109/94 Windpark Groothusen GmbH & Co Betriebs KG v EC Commission [1995] ECR II-3007, II-3023.

considered reasonable.[1969] The underlying idea is that a right to a hearing only arises for an individual where the Commission contemplates the imposition of a penalty or the adoption of a measure likely to have an adverse effect on his legal position.[1970] The Commission also considers that notice to those who have an interest contrary to the grant of assistance is not required.[1971]

Reasons: Article 253 EC requires that regulations, directives and decisions 'state the reasons on which they are based'. The European Courts are entitled to review, even of their own motion, the statement of reasons for Union decisions challenged before them.[1972] The statement must be appropriate to the decision at issue and must not be contradictory.[1973] It must disclose in a clear[1974] and unequivocal fashion the reasoning of the Commission in such a way as to enable the persons concerned to ascertain the reasons for the decision and to enable the European Courts to carry out their review.[1975] Moreover, sufficient detail must be given to alert the Member States and the individuals concerned to the elements of the Commission's reasoning.[1976]

The duty of confidentiality imposed on the Commission by Article 287 EC may offer no defence to a failure to meet these requirements. According to this provision, the Commission must not 'disclose information of the kind covered by the obligation of professional secrecy, in particular, information about undertakings, their business relations or their cost components'. However, this provision cannot be interpreted so broadly that the duty to give reasons is 'deprived of its essential content'. In particular, recipients of assistance, their competitors and others may not be denied the information needed to ascertain whether a decision is well founded and whether they have an interest in starting legal proceedings.[1977] In any case, some relevant facts may manifestly be of a non-confidential nature. At the same time, the entry into force of a

1969 Case T-109/94 Windpark Groothusen GmbH & Co Betriebs KG v EC Commission [1995] ECR II-3007, II-3023.
1970 Case C-48/96P Windpark Groothusen GmbH & Co Betriebs KG v EC Commission [1998] ECR I-2873.
1971 Joined Cases 10 & 18/68 Società 'Eridania' Zuccherifici Nazionali v EC Commission [1969] ECR 459, 476.
1972 Case C-304/89 Establicementos Isodoro M. Oliveira SA v EC Commission [1991] ECR I-2283, I-2312.
1973 AG Mischo in Case 15/85 Consorzio Cooperative d'Abruzzo v EC Commission [1987] ECR 1005, 1023.
1974 Case T-85/94 EC Commission v Eugénio Branco Lda [1995] ECR II-45, II-57. See also Case C-181/90 Consorgan – Gestaõ de Empresas, Lda v EC Commission [1992] ECR I-3557, I-3569; and Case T-450/93 Lisrestal _ Organizacaõ Gestaõ de Restaurantes Colectivos Lda v EC Commission [1994] ECR II-1177, II-1197.
1975 AG Darmon in Case C-157/90 Infortec Projectos & Consultadoria, Lda v EC Commission [1992] ECR I-3525, I-3541.
1976 AG Mischo in Case 15/85 Consorzio Cooperative d'Abruzzo v EC Commission [1987] ECR 1005, 1023.
1977 AG Roemer in Joined Cases 10 & 18/68 Società 'Eridania' Zuccherifici Nazionali v EC Commission [1969] ECR 459, 488.

decision is not dependent on its publication in the Official Journal pursuant to Article 254 EC. Hence, information which is confidential can be omitted from the published text.[1978]

On the other hand, the question whether the statement meets the requirements of Article 253 must be assessed with regard not only to its wording. Regard must also be had to the nature of the decision,[1979] to its context, and to all the rules governing the matter in question.[1980] If, for example, the reduction of assistance has been proposed by the national authorities, which have given an explanation to the recipient, it may be sufficient for the Commission to refer with sufficient clarity to the national measure containing that explanation.[1981] Again, reasoning requirements may be less demanding in the case of an unsuccessful applicant for assistance, who has incurred no expenditure on the project for which assistance is sought.[1982] An applicant for assistance is only entitled to an objective examination of the application in the course of the selection procedure. Special features of the procedure, such as publication of the criteria for eligibility and the participation of committees in the selection of projects, may mean that there is no need for an individual, detailed statement of reasons.[1983]

At the same time, the reasoning need not go beyond what is necessary, regard being had to the requirements and constraints inherent in the functioning of the Union institutions.[1984] In the determination of what is necessary, account may be taken of whether the person concerned is able to defend sufficiently his point of view before the European Courts. Account may also be taken of whether the ability of these Courts to review the lawfulness of the decision has been diminished or impaired.[1985] For example, where the addressee of a decision has taken part in the preparation of the decision, a limited statement of reasons may be found to satisfy Article 253. The

1978 Cf Joined Cases 296 & 318/82 Netherlands and Leeuwarder Papierwarenfabriek BV v EC Commission [1985] ECR 809, 826. This judgment was invoked by the applicant in Case T-109/94 Windpark Groothusen GmbH & Co. Betriebs KG v EC Commission [1995] ECR II-3007, II-3020.

1979 Case 181/90 Consorgan – Gestaõ de Empresas, Lda v EC Commission [1992] ECR I-3557, I-3569.

1980 Case C-213/87 Gemeente Amsterdam and Stichting Vrouwenvakschool voor Informatica Amsterdam (VIA) v EC Commission [1990] ECR I-221, I-222.

1981 Case T-85/94 EC Commission v Eugénio Branco Lda [1995] ECR II-45, II-58.

1982 AG Darmon in Case 157/90 Infortec Projectos & Consultadoria, Lda v EC Commission [1992] ECR I-3525, I-3541-2.

1983 Case C-48/96P Windpark Groothusen GmbH & Co. Betriebs KG v EC Commission [1998] ECR I-2873.

1984 AG Darmon in Case C-157/90 Infortec Projectos & Consultadoria, Lda v EC Commission [1992] ECR I-3525, I-3541.

1985 AG Capotorti in Case 107/80 Giacomo Cattaneo Adorno v EC Commission [1981] ECR 1469, 1496.

statement need only contain the indispensable elements which permit the addressee to determine whether the decision is vitiated by a defect.[1986]

More particularly, a summarized statement of the reasons for rejecting an application for assistance may be regarded as 'an inevitable consequence of the computerized handling of several thousands of applications for assistance on which the Commission is required to give a decision rapidly'. In such a situation, a more detailed statement of reasons in support of each decision would be likely to jeopardize the rational and efficient allocation of the Union assistance.[1987]

Such case law may be consistent with the Commission argument that a distinction should be made between the performance of its public service duties (*Leistungsverwaltung*) and the exercise of its prerogatives as a public authority (*Eingriffverwaltung*). According to the Commission, its duty to give reasons should be less demanding in relation to the former than in relation to the latter. This is because only the latter limits the rights of those subject to its administration. The assumption of the Commission is that there is no right to Union assistance, and the inference drawn by the Commission is that its refusal causes no damage to applicants.[1988]

Thinking of this kind may be reflected in the literature. According to the latter, where action is to benefit individuals in the framework of a largely discretionary policy, judicial control has less of a role than where the action takes place through coercive measures.[1989] The underlying idea is that such control is concerned with protecting market interests. The literature thus highlights the difficulty for the market-based thinking which informs the case law to recognize the legal implications of adoption of cohesion as a Union objective.

4. National courts

National legislation and administrative practice must allow individuals to obtain Union assistance without particular difficulties. Thus the relevant procedures must not be different from those for obtaining national aid[1990] and must respect general principles of Union law.[1991] National courts may have a role in securing such respect, particularly in connection with interpretation of Union law, the validity of Union decisions, and enforcement.

1986 AG Darmon in Case C-157/90 Infortec Projectos & Consultadoria, Lda v EC Commission [1992] ECR I-3525, I-3542.
1987 Case C-213/87 Gemeente Amsterdam and Stichting Vrouwenvakschool voor Informatica Amsterdam (VIA) v EC Commission [1990] ECR I-221, I-222.
1988 Cf Case T-109/94 Windpark Groothusen GmbH & Co Betriebs KG v EC Commission [1995] ECR II-3007, II-3024.
1989 R Priebe, para [682], n 2 above, 5.
1990 R Priebe, para [682], n 2 above, 30.
1991 Joined Cases 201 & 202/85 Marthe Klensch v Secrétaire d'Etat à l'Agriculture et à la Viticulture [1986] ECR 3477, 3507.

Interpretation of Union law: Under Article 234(1)(a) EC, national courts may request preliminary rulings on the interpretation of Union law from the Court of Justice. Such rulings may have importance for the interpretation by Member States of Union law governing the funds. For example, the Court stresses the need for the common agricultural policy to be managed in conditions of equality between traders in the Member States. The inference drawn by the Court is that the national authorities of a Member State should not, by the expedient of a wide interpretation of a Union law provision regarding assistance from the EAGGF, favour producers in that Member State to the detriment of those in Member States applying a stricter interpretation.[1992] With the help of preliminary rulings, national courts may prevent such divergent interpretations.

Validity of Union decisions: Individuals may take proceedings before national courts against national measures implementing a Union decision. Such courts may refer questions of the validity of the decision being implemented to the Court of Justice under Article 234(1)(b) EC. There is no requirement in this provision that the decision be of direct and individual concern to the litigant.[1993] In considering the validity of the decision, the Court of Justice may apparently have regard to cohesion requirements in the Treaty.[1994] A ruling that the decision is invalid means that it cannot provide a defence to the challenge to national implementing action. Even in the absence of such action, a ruling on the validity of a Union decision may apparently be obtained.[1995]

However, this procedure only operates where there is a basis in rights deriving from directly effective Union law or in national law for mounting a challenge. In the absence of such rights, the challenge may have to be based on national law,[1996] and so the procedure may merely allow for national law consistent with cohesion requirements to be protected from being undermined by Union decisions. Therefore, where a narrow definition of individual rights underlies lack of standing in plenary proceedings before the European Courts, the preliminary ruling procedure may be unable to compensate for the consequences of lack of standing in plenary proceedings.

1992 Case 11/76 Netherlands v EC Commission: EAGGF [1979] ECR 245, 279.
1993 Case T-271/94 Eugénio Branco Lda v EC Commission [1996] ECR II-749.
1994 Cf, regarding Arts 39 and 40(3) EC and the general principles of proportionality and non-discrimination, Case C-27/97 Woodspring v Nilsea [1997] ECR I-1847.
1995 J Usher, 'Direct and Individual Concern – an Effective Remedy or a Conventional Solution? (2003) ELR 575–600. See, more particularly, J Temple Lang, 'Declarations, Regional Authorities, Subsidiarity, Regional Policy Measures, and the Constitutional Treaty' (2004) ELR 94–105.
1996 According to AG Cosmas in Case C-321/95P Stichting Greenpeace Council (Greenpeace International) v EC Commission [1998] ECR I-1651, I-1681, issues of Union financing cannot per se be raised before national courts. According to the ECJ itself, rights recognized by Union law may only be indirectly affected by such financing (ibid, I-1660).

Enforcement: Where directly effective provisions of Union law are present, national authorities may not grant or deny assistance from the Union funds contrary to such provisions.[1997] For example, in *Banfi*[1998] the Court of Justice ruled that legal persons could not be denied assistance under Directive 72/159[1999] solely because they had assumed a specific legal form. Again, *Omada*[2000] concerned cotton producer groups recognized under Article 2 of Regulation 389/82.[2001] The Court ruled that Article 5 of the Regulation obliged Member States to grant such groups assistance for investments included in national programmes to promote cotton production and marketing approved by the Commission. In both cases, national denial of assistance was found to be contrary not only to the relevant Community legislation but also to the prohibition of discrimination in Article 40(2) EEC. Hence, the national courts concerned had to overrule the denial of assistance by their national authorities.

Again, damages may be awarded by a national court where a Member State, in deciding on the grant of assistance partly financed by the Union funds, has violated a Union law provision intended to confer rights on individuals.[2002] Thus the grant or denial of assistance contrary to such a provision may be challenged before a national court.

However, Treaty provisions governing cohesion and many of the legislative provisions governing the Union funds often lack the precision necessary for them to be directly effective.[2003] Moreover, there is nothing to suggest that the law governing the Union funds is interpreted as being intended to confer rights on individuals other than recipients of assistance and their competitors. Consequently, no Union law provision on which to base a claim for damages may be available to representatives of cohesion interests. As a result, the role of national courts in securing the realization of cohesion requirements may be limited.

J. CONCLUSION

While all Union decision making takes place within the framework of the Treaties, these Treaties embody several 'subframeworks' for such decision making. Formally, the subframeworks may represent legislative (or 'soft

---

1997 D Comijs, 'Individual Legal Protection under the Structural Funds' (1995) Maastrict Journal 187–95.
1998 Case 312/85 SpA Villa Banfi v Regione Toscana [1986] ECR 4039, 4055. See, now, Case C-164/96 Regione Piemonte v Saiagricola SpA [1997] ECR I-6129.
1999 On the modernization of farms ([1972] JO L96/1).
2000 Case 8/87 Omada Paragogon Vamvakiou Andrianou-Gizinou & Co v Greece [1988] ECR 1001, 1014.
2001 On producer groups and associations thereof in the cotton sector ([1982] OJ L51/1).
2002 Cf Case C-66/95 R v Secretary of State for Social Security, ex p Eunice Sutten [1997] ECR I-2163, I-2191.
2003 AG Warner in Case 152/79 Kevin Lee v Minster for Agriculture [1980] ECR 1495, 1514.

legislative'), budgetary, administrative or judicial perceptions of Treaty requirements.

Operation of one subframework rather than another in any given instance may be assumed to be decisive for the effects of the resulting decisions. For example, according to this assumption, soft law may be seen simply as implementing Council legislation. Again, individual administrative decisions may be seen simply as entailing application of the rules embodied in such legislation. Thus the Commission may distinguish between 'the legislative process and ... actual execution',[2004] while an Advocate General may distinguish between 'substantive rules of policy and administrative rules'.[2005]

In reality, the relationship between the different legal processes is more complicated. It may, in fact, be of a horizontal rather than vertical kind, with cohesion requirements established pursuant to one process articulating the requirements established pursuant to another process.[2006] An example is provided by the Communication laying down guidelines for operational programmes or global grants within the framework of the Community initiative on Employment and the Development of Human Resources.[2007] According to paragraph 8 of the Communication, all eligible measures which may be financed under this initiative are listed in the Communication. In other words, they are listed in soft law. However, when preparing their proposals for operational programmes or for global grants, which are to be adopted by individual administrative decisions, Member States are invited to select, in cooperation with the Commission, a more limited list of measures on which to concentrate financial assistance. Thus successive opportunities for negotiation and renegotiation may be entailed by organic Union decision making.

However, the various subframeworks are such that the negotiation and renegotiation may be essentially limited to interests expressed by the Commission and national governments. Thus the resulting law may reflect relations in which regional actors have little opportunity to contribute to the articulation of cohesion requirements.[2008] Even the European Parliament may

---

2004 Explanatory memorandum to the Proposals of 15 October 1979 for regulations instituting specific Community regional development projects under Art 13 of the ERDF Regulation, COM(79)540, 12.

2005 AG Verloren van Themaat in Case 44/81 Germany v EC Commission: deadline for claiming payment of ESF assistance [1982] ECR 1855, 1885.

2006 Cf, regarding the 'recursive interaction' of Commission practice and decision making by the European Courts, F Snyder, 'Soft Law and Institutional Practice in the European Community' in S Martin (ed), The Construction of Europe (Kluwer, Deventer, 1994), 197–225.

2007 [1996] OJ C200/13.

2008 Cf European Parliament Resolution of 5 September 1996 ([1996] OJ C277/29) on the sixth annual report on the Structural Funds in 1994, para 9. See, more particularly, the Resolution of 5 September 1996 ([1996] OJ C277/40) on development problems and structural measures under Objectives 1, 2, and 5b in Spain (1994–99), para 10.

object that its decision-making role in this field is more limited than in other fields.[2009]

It is recognized that this situation is unsatisfactory and that Commission efforts alone may be unable to maximize the potential of the Union funds for strengthening cohesion. In particular, there is felt to be a risk that the Union will fail to secure the full benefits of the funds. It may fail to do so because of lack of care, lack of available resources to provide proper project monitoring, or the absence of a satisfactory administrative process for evaluating results.[2010] The implication is that development of pluralistic, decentralized control of the operations of the funds may be necessary. For example, according to the Parliament, the very nature of regional development is such as to render it dependent on participation in decision making by the public through their elected representatives at all levels.[2011] However, Union law processes are not favourable to such participation.

2009 Cf the Code of conduct on the implementation of structural policies by the Commission ([1993] OJ C255/19), which was designed to improve arrangements for consultation of the Parliament.
2010 COA special report 3/92 ([1992] OJ C245/1) concerning the environment, para 1.21.
2011 Resolution of 12 October 1977 ([1977] OJ C266/35) on the guidelines for Community regional policy, para 10.

8
CONCLUSIONS

Union decision making is ill adapted to the articulation of cohesion requirements in Articles 158 and 159 EC. In other words, it is ill adapted to determining what the reduction of regional disparities demands of the Union funds and thus to giving real meaning to these provisions. Hence, regulation of the operations of these funds may be left to depend partly on the outcomes of intergovernmental bargaining, particularly outcomes concerned with reciprocity between Member States. It may also be left to depend partly on the needs of the common market, particularly needs expressed by competition policy.[2012]

In such bargaining, the operations of the Union funds are seen as means of equalizing the financial capacity of Member States to intervene in their national economies. Such equalization is sought through the transfer of resources from the stronger to the weaker Member States.[2013] In practice, the consequence is that Union assistance concentrates on infrastructure and training measures,[2014] because such measures tend to be favoured by transferee Member States as being in the national economic interest. In other words, assistance is generally granted according to 'essentially Member State-initiated priorities'.[2015]

At the same time, concentration on infrastructure and training measures may be broadly consistent with competition policy requirements.[2016] This is because assistance to measures of this kind may be treated as less likely to distort competition than other kinds of assistance.[2017] Such concentration may thus meet the demands of net transferors that the distorting effects of fund

2012 Cf Communication on the links between regional and competition policy – reinforcing concentration and mutual consistency ([1998] OJ C90/3). More particularly, the grant of Union assistance to a regional aid scheme may be withheld, pending Commission authorization of the scheme under Art 87 EC. See, eg, Art 7 of Dec 98/586 ([1998] OJ L282/20) on the approval of the multiregional SPD for the conversion of the activities of defence in the areas concerned by Objective 2 in France.

2013 RR Barnett and V Borooah, 'The Additionality (or Otherwise) of the European Community Structural Funds' in S Hardy, M Hart, L Albrechts and A Katos (eds), An Enlarged Europe (Jessica Kingsley, London, 1995), 180–91, 189.

2014 Around 30% of the resources of the Structural Funds might go to infrastructure and around 30% to training. See, eg, First cohesion report, COM(96)542, 9.

2015 Future of Community initiatives under the Structural Funds, COM(93)282, 4.

2016 A Cutler, C Haslam, J Williams, and K Williams, 1992 – the Struggle for Europe (Berg, New York, 1989), 80–2.

2017 Cf Annual report of the Cohesion Fund 1997, COM(1998)543, 17. See, generally, A Evans, EC Law of State Aid (Clarendon Press, Oxford, 1997).

operations[2018] should be limited without their own freedom to intervene being substantially affected by legislation governing these operations.[2019] At this point, intergovernmentalism and the needs of the common market may be reconciled. However, the reconciliation is achieved at the expense of regional participation in Union decision making and, consequently, at the expense of the regional equality required by Article 158 EC.

Regional authorities and other actors at the regional level are denied guaranteed opportunities[2020] to contribute to the articulation of cohesion requirements through participation in such decision making.[2021] This denial may mean that threats to the implementation of intergovernmental bargains or to the competition sought through the common market are avoided. On the other hand, it may also explain why the operations of the Union funds 'resonate with the overarching ideology, preferred policy instruments, and institutional interests of the main actors' in the Union.[2022]

In these circumstances, the concentration of Union assistance on infrastructure and training goes largely unchallenged by reference to cohesion requirements. However, such assistance does not necessarily facilitate the development of weaker regions. For example, improvements in infrastructure, particularly transport infrastructure, may render the markets of these regions more open to producers from outside and may do little to assist regional producers. Again, training may lead those acquiring new skills to migrate to more developed regions where these skills are in demand.[2023] As a result, such assistance may tend to support national economic development[2024] and, as the

2018 Cf, regarding concern to ensure that assistance does not lead to 'delocalization' problems, the Explanatory memorandum to the Proposal of 19 March 1998 for a regulation laying down provisions on the Structural Funds, COM(98)131, 26.

2019 Such demands may explain why arrangements for Commission control of fund operations have been most developed in the case of IMPs and the Cohesion Fund, where there has been only a limited number of beneficiary Member States.

2020 See, regarding the role of regional authorities in the different Member States, the Seventh annual report on the Structural Funds, COM(96)502, 229–34.

2021 Cf the view that intergovernmental decision making has a negative impact on Union decision making, in that the bargains struck between Member States limit the room for manoeuvre of the Union institutions in S Padgett, 'The Single European Market: The Politics of Realisation' (1992) 30 JCMS 53–75, 54.

2022 JJ Anderson, 'Structural Funds and the Social Dimension of EU Policy: Springboard or Stumbling Block?' in S Leibfried and P Pierson (eds), European Social Policy (Brookings Institute, Washington, 1995) 123–58, 150.

2023 Cf, regarding 'liberal market tutelage', A Cutler, C Haslam, J Williams, and K Williams, para [856], n 1 above, 80–2.

2024 A Cutler et al, para [856], n 1 above, 79.

2025 First Cohesion Report, COM(96)542, 5–6; Unity, Solidarity, Diversity for Europe, its People and its Territory, Summary of the Cohesion Report, 2002.

Commission recognizes,[2025] may thus reduce disparities between Member States more than between regions.[2026]

At the same time, lack of articulation of cohesion requirements means that operations of the Union funds may depend on the requirements of various, more articulated, Union policies. In other words, cohesion requirements risk 'dilution'.[2027] This risk does not derive from the role of policy as something extraneous from the law. Rather, it illustrates the integral role which policy plays in the operation of the law through demanding selectivity in the activation and development of the various requirements embodied in legal provisions.

Such selectivity may be heavily influenced by the role of various interest groups in Union decision making. For example, sectoral interests, such as agricultural interests,[2028] may be effectively represented in the procedures leading to the adoption of decisions concerning the Union funds. Indeed, the 'deficient rationality' of Union decision making may guarantee the success of such interests.[2029] Thus they may even play a central role in drawing up guidelines applied by the Commission in the allocation of assistance.[2030] The representation of regional interests may be more limited.[2031] In these circumstances, the operations of the funds may tend merely to give effect to 'fair return' bargains[2032] between Member States in sectoral contexts.

More particularly, insofar as sectoral interests are well entrenched in stronger regions, the result may be that more Union assistance is directed to

---

2025 First Cohesion Report, COM(96)542, 5–6; Unity, Solidarity, Diversity for Europe, its People and its Territory, Summary of the Cohesion Report, 2002.

2026 European Governance, COM(2001)428, Report 4C, 23. See, similarly, A Modern Regional Policy for the United Kingdom, 20 (www.hm-treasury.gov.uk/media/E41/19/modregdevcondoc03_1to4.pdf). See, more particularly, regarding the limited impact of Union assistance to the Mezzogiorno, COA special report 15/98 ([1998] OJ C347/1) on the assessment of Structural Fund intervention for the 1989–93 and 1994–99 periods, para 7.2.

2027 Cf A Liberatore, 'The Integration of Sustainable Development Objectives into EU Policy-Making' in S Baker, M Kousis, R Richardson and S Young, The Politics of Sustainable Development (Routledge, London, 1997), 107–26, 119.

2028 The 'political decision-making mechanisms at Community level have particularly favoured the promotion of the specific group interests of agriculture' (E Guth, 'European Agricultural Policy: Is There No Alternative?' (1985) Intereconomics 3–9, 9).

2029 Cf J Habermas, Legitimation Crisis (Polity Press, Cambridge, 1988), 60.

2030 Joined Cases T-369/94 & 85/95 DIR International Film Srl v EC Commission [1998] ECR II-357.

2031 An analogy may be drawn with the problems of taking specific account of consumer interests in the application of competition policy. See A Evans, 'Article 85(3) Exemption: "Allowing Consumers a Fair Share of the Resulting Benefit"' in M Goyens (ed), European Competition Policy and the Consumer Interest (Bruylant, Brussels, 1985), 99–120. Cf, regarding 'latent interests' generally, M Teutemann, Completion of the Internal Market: an Application of Public Choice Theory (Economic Papers No 83, EC Commission, Brussels, 1990), 8.

2032 Cf, regarding the practical problems involved in calculating 'fair returns', the Commission Reply by Mr Liikanen to WQ E-3815/97 ([1998] OJ C174/135) by Caroline Jackson.

such regions than is consistent with promotion of cohesion.[2033] In other cases, insofar as sectoral policy entails denial of assistance, there may also be harmful effects for cohesion. Such effects may arise because assistance which may enable weaker regions to exploit unrealized comparative advantages may be denied. Thus it has been argued that, in 'crisis' sectors, regions with growth potential may be penalized by the denial of Union assistance.[2034] Similarly, criticism may be made of the lack of regional differentiation in application of the common agricultural policy to products in surplus.[2035]

Again, horizontal policies may mean that assistance supporting achievement of various objectives, such as promotion of small and medium-sized enterprises and of research and development, is granted. However, limited account may be taken of cohesion requirements. In practice, such assistance tends to assist stronger regions, particularly those with an established research and development capacity or dynamic small and medium-sized enterprises. As a result, pursuit of such policies may also have harmful effects for cohesion.

The operations of the ERDF itself may be indirectly affected by pursuit of various policies. In practice, this Fund may be viewed as a way of compensating those Member States which benefit little from other Union 'expenditure policies', such as the common agricultural policy. More generally, it may be viewed as a means of securing the consent of weaker Member States to further market integration. Less importance is attached to ensuring that the operations of this Fund effectively promote cohesion. Thus even the contribution of this Fund to the promotion of regional equality may be impaired.[2036]

Therefore, the pursuit of various sectoral and horizontal policies may have the effect of reinforcing the tendency of Union assistance to reduce disparities between Member States rather than between regions. The Committee of the Regions infers the need for increased participation by regional authorities in the pursuit of 'European structural policy'.[2037]

The need for 'democratization' of intergovernmental bargaining is apparently implied. The Treaties may provide a basis for such reform. In particular, regard may be had to the concept of subsidiarity in Article 1 TEU.

2033 DJ Neven and J Vickers, 'Public Policy towards Industrial Restructuring: Some Issues Raised by the Internal Market Programme' in K Cool, DJ Neven and I Walter (eds), European Industrial Restructuring in the 1990s (Macmillan, London, 1992) 162–98, 175.
2034 The Regional Impact of Community Policies (Regional Policy and Transport Series No 17, European Parliament, Luxembourg, 1991), 15 and 83.
2035 ESC Opinion of 30 April 1992 ([1992] OJ C169/41) on the Commission proposals on the prices for agricultural products and on related measures (1992/3), para 1.8.
2036 H Armstrong and J Taylor, Regional Economics and Policy (Harvester Wheatsheaf, London, 2nd edn, 1993), 296.
2037 Opinion of 19 November 1997 ([1998] OJ C64/5) on the views of the regions and local authorities in arrangements for European structural policy after 1999, para 1.3.6.

According to this provision, decisions should be 'taken as closely as possible to the citizen'. Regard may also be had to the constitutional implications of the 'establishment' of Union Citizenship by Article 17 EC. These provisions raise questions whether it is consistent with Union law for the constitutional procedures mentioned in Article 48 TEU to be regarded as permitting national ratification of Treaty amendments agreed between Member States solely on the basis of consent from central institutions of the Member States.[2038] If Article 48 were interpreted as demanding more pluralism in intergovernmental decision making, such decision making might entail increased articulation of cohesion requirements. At least, the articulation might go beyond the minimum considered necessary by national governments to secure a 'fair return' for their participation in market integration.

At the same time, reform of Union decision-making procedures may enable the Union funds more effectively to reduce disparities between regions.[2039] For example, if the legislation governing partnership were appropriately amended, regional representatives might be able to ensure that Union assistance more closely addressed the problems of their regions.[2040] Evolution in the case law may also have a role to play. In particular, recognition by the European Courts of standing for actors other than Member States and Union Institutions to invoke cohesion requirements in plenary proceedings concerning the operations of the Union funds may be critical. Recognition of such standing would enable supposed beneficiaries of cohesion to participate in the articulation of its requirements through judicial proceedings.

In other words, effective pursuit of the regional equality sought through cohesion and promotion of institutional equality – that is, equal opportunities as between regions and other actors and as between regions themselves to participate in Union decision making – may be interdependent processes. Reforms which go beyond the changes to 'economic law' envisaged in Regulation 1260/1999[2041] and more fully recognize this interdependence of economic law and institutional law may not simply be a constitutional imperative.[2042] If cohesion is to be strengthened, such reforms may also be an inherent necessity.

2038 Art 48 TEU provides that Treaty amendments must be 'ratified by all the Member States in accordance with their respective constitutional requirements'. Cf the Belgian statement on the signing of treaties by Belgium as a Member State of the EU ([1998] OJ C351/1).

2039 See, regarding the need to broaden participation at regional and local level and to involve the social partners, First cohesion report, COM(96)542, 11.

2040 Cf, ibid, 114. However, problems of 'departmental specialization' within the Commission may remain, where assistance is granted outside the framework programme.

2041 Reg 1260/1999 ([1999] OJ LL161/1) laying down general provisions on the Structural Funds.

2042 Cf the view that 'state aid control in the EU is of constitutional nature, both with respect to substance and procedure' (C-D Ehlermann, 'State Aid Control in the European Union: Success or Failure?' (1994–95) 18 Fordham International Law Journal 1212–29, 1214).

Obstacles to such reforms may derive from structural features of the Union legal system. The European Courts infer from the structure of the Union legal system that individual rights are essentially market-based in character. The result is to limit opportunities for representatives of cohesion interests to take proceedings before these Courts. In other words, the 'constitutionalization' of cohesion may be contradicted, and reforms of the above kind may be precluded.

Failure to secure such reforms may mean that 'transaction cost' problems, implicit in the increased diversity of regional problems with enlargement of the Union, may be exaggerated. According to Coase, a firm will tend to expand until the costs of organizing an extra transaction within the firm become equal to the costs of carrying out the same transaction by means of an exchange on the open market.[2043] Dynamic analysis would take account of the capacity of the firm internally to reorganize and thereby to reduce the relative costs of expansion. If an analogy between the expansion of a firm and the enlargement of the Union is justified, it seems that Union practice will need to be adapted to cope with future enlargements. The importance of such adaptation may be greater for the Union than for the firm, given that Union enlargement, at least in relation to Central and East European countries, may have the characteristics of a political imperative.

The Commission acknowledges that the accession of such countries renders the Union much more heterogeneous and that the nature of the likely impact on existing 'cohesion countries' is uncertain.[2044] Some impact seems inevitable, given that the need is inferred for greater concentration of Union assistance and strict application of the criteria for determining eligibility.[2045] The Commission further acknowledges that better targeting and a broader range of policies will be needed and that more local (or regional or national) participation in Union decision making may be appropriate.[2046] Nevertheless, the Commission still thinks essentially of transfers from western countries[2047] and of preventing 'discrepancies' between national and Union instruments.[2048] According to such thinking, the reduction of regional disparities is assumed to be a likely consequence of reducing the 'overall gap' between Central and East European countries and the Union average.[2049] The record of the Union funds suggests that this assumption is questionable.

2043 RH Coase, 'The Nature of the Firm' (1937) 4 Economica 386–405.

2044 Agenda 2000, Bull EC, Supp 5/97, 108.

2045 Ibid, 112. See also Agenda 2000: the legislative proposals: overall view, COM(98)182, 4. See, now, the Proposal of 14 July 2004 for a regulation laying down general provisions on the ERDF, the ESF, and the Cohesion Fund, COM(2004)492.

2046 Agenda 2000, Bull EC, Supp 5/97, 109. See, now, the Proposal of 14 July 2004 for a regulation establishing a European grouping of cross-border cooperation, COM(2004)496.

2047 Agenda 2000, Bull EC, Supp 5/97, 108.

2048 Ibid, 110.

2049 Ibid, 111.

More fundamentally, the assumption may be questioned that 'absorption' of new Member States and maintaining the 'momentum of European integration' are liable to conflict.[2050] At least as regards regional disparities, the problems of absorption and of maintaining the momentum of integration are essentially the same. They revolve around the need more effectively to pursue cohesion.[2051] Insofar as this need is recognized in both the broadening and deepening of integration, the two processes may reinforce each other.

2050 According to the European Council meeting of June 1993, 'the Union's capacity to absorb new members, while maintaining the momentum of European integration, is ... an important consideration in the general interest of both the Union and the candidate countries' (Bull EC 6-1993, I.13).
2051 This need is recognized in the preamble (particularly 25th recital) to Reg 1260/1999 ([1999] OJ L161/1). However, its achievement is seen as basically dependent on the closer monitoring and evaluation of fund operations by Member States.

Index

GENERAL REFERENCE